# THE EARLY MORNING LIGHT

EDWARD FORDE HICKEY

D1354053

Matador
9 Priory Business Park
Kibworth Beauchamp
Leicestershire LE8 0RX, UK
Tel: (+44) 116 279 2299
Fax: (+44) 116 279 2277
Email: books@troubador.co.uk
Web: www.troubador.co.uk/matador


ISBN 978 1784622 398

British Library Cataloguing in Publication Data.
A catalogue record for this book is available from the British Library.

Typeset in Aldine by Troubador Publishing Ltd
Printed and bound in the UK by TJ International, Padstow, Cornwall

**Matador** is an imprint of Troubador Publishing Ltd

www.edwardfordehickey.co.uk

# Introduction

The Story of Teddy – a newborn child evacuated from the German Blitz of WW2 and brought up by his grandmother (Dowager) and uncle (Blue-eyed Jack) – took place in a tiny Irish outpost known as Rookery Rally. In years gone by it had been a place for the gentry with their high chandeliers and balls, hunting and steeplechasing, killing the odd fat woodpigeon and long-tailed pheasant – but also a place of menial husbandry and drudgery for the rest of mankind.

Move forward several years and you'd fine it hard to imagine the dark days of World War II when the local country-folk (if they had a bit of land) often felt as though there was no world-war worth talking about, such was their daily lack of any ache or pain resulting from this war's cruelties. Indeed they were seen to be living on their little hillside farms as contented as any rich lord and his lady. Forget about the salmon, forget about the trout and the countless rabbits that they hunted. Hadn't they six or seven shorthorn cows to milk each morning and the creamery cheque each month? Hadn't Teddy and his two guardians their two ploughed fields of spuds (the red for themselves and the white for the pigs) with cabbages and turnips thrown in alongside? Hadn't they money in their fist from the sale of this year's big fat pig (even after bringing home a young pig from the market inside in The Roaring Town) and another pig fattening in the pig-house, ready to be killed and salted? Hadn't they hens and ducks for their eggs? Hadn't they Dowager's black-handled knife to saw the neck of her best goose into oblivion or else make use of her hatchet to chastise a hen's neck when the need arose? Whoever heard of The Famine?

Amongst these farmers this little English boy's story rests, at first within the folds of Dowager's apron and then spreading out on freedom's wings alongside his uncle (Blue-eyed Jack) and around the little farm's nine fields that crept down to The Bog Wood and eased their way into the black waters of River Laughter. The farm was almost five hundred miles away from the bombed-out ruins of London and his true parents (Little Nell and Shy Patsy). It was the safest and most pleasant spot on earth for any child to be developing his young soul, surrounded by tall windy trees atop of which a colony of rooks kept up a perpetual cawing – hence giving the place the name of Rookery Rally. In tune with all this was the sound of merrily babbling waters which went on from September till April when several mountain springs gushed up out of the earth and melodious little streams tore their eager pathways through every farmyard on their downward sweep from The Hills-of-The-Past towards the distant rumblings of River Laughter and from there on into The Roaring Town River and finally tossed their way through The Jackass Falls as they hurried on into The Mighty Shannon River itself.

Into the eyes and soul of this growing toddler were poured images of the men, women and children, who lived alongside him during the first five years of his life. He would forever remember the lively laughter of them all – flourishing from dawn until dusk, like bunches of untamed nettles – and their daily lives would one day seem to him as something akin to a tune played out by Nature's own vibrant orchestra – at least for most of the time he was in their midst.

# ONE

# The Dance

*When Little Nell met Shy Patsy*
*at The Platform Dance*
*in Judy's Meadow*

It was June in the year of 1937. The Hills-of-The-Past had always had its fair share of mischief-makers. But there were times when the mountain slopes saw the other side of the coin and the fields echoed with innocent laughter and pure joy. It was then that you'd notice how the rascally devilment that was in the hearts of the boys was replaced with this other gentler mood, namely the shy little sighs out of the older girls and their shivery longing for a bit of feathery romance during a summer's twilight. You'd never see any of these girls climbing up the back of a thatched roof and tying the potato-sacking round the chimney before throwing a terrified chicken down into the fire to persecute the two poor old souls who were saying their evening rosary inside at the fireside. Unlike their brothers, these girls saw no fun in listening to the old folk cursing like blazes and scraping their hobnail boots around the floor as they ran here and there and (blinded with smoke) tried to catch the chicken and throw her out the door. No – our girls were content to spend their summer afternoons leaning on their elbows at the front table and looking out over the scarlet geraniums on the windowsill underneath the thatch. The little dreamers could imagine a gallant horseman on his shining white steed as he pranced out from the pages of their novel and came racing in across the flagstones and up the cobbled yard to the half-door to carry them off to The

Land of Pleasure. If only… if only… and they gave a little shudder and they shook themselves back into their day-to-day reality.

The days during this month of June (1937) were growing longer and they were getting hotter. The girls' hearts were bursting to be off to one of the platform dances that were held out across the fields. Their tingling feet couldn't stay quiet for another minute. The hillside fairies and the woodland fairies and the river fairies (and we all believed in their existence) were in one agreement: there was no place on this earth as wonderfully charming as The Platform Dance in Judy Rag's Meadow. There'd be a crowd of sixty dancers up there, each one anxious to make the most of these fine hot evenings. When summer came to its end they knew that the only dance they'd ever get away to would be the great winter Wran-Byze-Ball above in The Welcoming Room of Din-Din-Dinny-the-Stammerer. This took place on the day after Christmas (St. Stephen's night). The piles of shiny coppers that the youngsters had collected from their house-to-house singing for the old men and women in the hills would allow them to set their skirts a-swirling and their hobnail boots aflame beneath Dinny's rumbling rafters. And there'd be a fine fat feast thrown in as well.

The day before the dance saw Dowager's young charmers doing more than their usual share of the housework: dusting the four corners of the rooms with the big goose-wings and using the little wings for all the more particular work. Their knees were red-raw from scrubbing The Welcoming Room floor. The cups, saucers and plates on the top of the dresser were as white as a haystack in the snow. It would do no harm (such was their cunning logic) for a young girl to have her mother on her side when planning an evening's escape to the hillside dance, which was nothing less than a trip into Dreamland itself.

Once the housework was completed to Dowager's satisfaction they took their bowls of dripping and their pig-grease down to Abbey Cross and they sold them to the passersby or they traded them in over the counter at Curl 'n' Stripes drinking-shop for the price of four pennies, which would get them a few lemonades and a contribution to the musicians at the dance.

The boys, of course, escaped from all the housework but they showed just as much dedication as the girls and they carried back their six buckets of water from the well and they chopped the logs for the fire. Blue-eyed

Jack (the older brother) looked on approvingly and he helped them to stack up the woodpile at the pig-house wall. He could see his own face reflected in theirs. He knew how much his brothers longed for an evening when they could venture like their sisters into the unreal world of Fairyland and escape from the monotony of the house-fire and the ticking of the old clock on the press cupboard shelf.

Wednesday was the evening for the dance and the girls wore their one-and-only posh frock. Maybe it was a cast-off dress from a much older sister. Maybe it was a dress made by their mother from a fine garment given to them by one of the rich ladies in The Big House. One or two of the girls had rich dresses (blue, lavender and even pink) from kinfolk living in that heavenly spot way out across the sea that was still referred to as The Land of The Silver Dollar. Dressed out to kill, they were sure to catch the nod and the wink of every young lad the minute they made their first few tentative dance-steps round the field's dance-boards.

On the evening before the dance (Tuesday) Dowager's daughters knelt down before the bedtime fire. They raised their pious eyes to the oil-lamp on the tapestry and they offered up their prayers for the souls of one or two of their brothers; for these lads were the proud owners of the shiny bikes that the girls would need for cycling the few miles across the countryside to the dance. They stormed into The Big Cave Room behind the hob. They helped Blue-eyed Jack to repair the tyres with the patches, the powder and glue from the yellow tin. When the tyres were pumped up good and hard they helped him to grease and oil the metal parts. They made sure to test the safety of the brakes for the downward journey home when the moon might be fast asleep in her corner behind the clouds. Most girls travelled three-to-a-bike to the dance, taking it in turns to ride the old 'hackle' (their name for a bicycle) with one of them on the saddle and steering the handlebars and the other two on the crossbar and the carrier respectively.

Blue-eyed Jack could do nothing but cast an envious eye at his young brothers and sisters. He knew he was too old and stiff in the knees to go off and enjoy an evening's dancing. All he had these days were a few faded memories of the rosy-cheeked girls that he once held warmly in his arms above in Judy's Meadow. He stood there, admiring his younger brothers; tomorrow they'd be getting themselves dressed up for the dancing frenzy.

They'd be speeding their boots across the shortcut through the wooded slopes of Lisnagorna to meet up with their cycling sisters. But the big man had another little thought inside in his head: it wasn't just running off to this evening's dance they'd be doing (he thought), for a year or two from now each one of them would be flying away from Dowager's nest and taking the Limerick Junction train to faraway Dublin or even the cattle-boat out across the stormy Irish Sea. And whereas there was nothing to keep them here at home, he was the oldest of them all and he had his family duty to be doing – to stay at home and look after his dear old mother and to tend to the little farm – now that his father (Handsome Johnnie) was lying in his grave below in Abbey Acres after coughing up the last bits of his liver. From that day onwards himself and his mother had been known as The Old Pair.

# *The Day of the Dance*

And now it was Wednesday morning and two or three of Dowager's seven sons were stripped to the waist and they were splashing themselves with a fair share of the water from the freezing yard-stream and the girls were fixing up their hair in front of the looking-glass with their papers and their hot rags and they were getting ready to put on their cotton dresses laid out on top of their mother's bed. Four of the older boys now jumped in over John's Gate. They headed down towards River Laughter. When they were in under the metal bridge they threw off their shirts and their trousers and they mocked and laughed at each other's private manly bits, what they called their private credentials. They threw the carbolic soap from one to the other, now and then hitting an unsuspecting daydreamer on the back of his poll with it and soon they were as clean as any scraped pig.

Their laughter and roars echoed out from under the bridge. It caught the ear of Fanny Adams above near the hayshed of her uncle Mikey. That very minute she had arrived breathlessly after her fifteen-mile bike-ride from beyond The Roaring Town. She was here for the birth of her aunt Nora's baby. It was to be a most unexpected little gift, since her uncle Mikey was old enough to be put out to grass like an old horse and it was a pure miracle how he had possessed the energy to be fathering a child at this stage of his life, the crafty rascal. Fanny stood at the cowshed door, admiring

Mikey as he milked his cows and groaned his homemade songs into the cows' ears, encouraging them to spill their swishing milk into the echoing depths of his bucket. She couldn't help from laughing; for whilst her uncle hadn't a stem of music inside in his head, he was the only soul in Rookery Rally who had brains big enough to memorise the words of every song imaginable: wouldn't he make a fine solicitor, she thought? And now she begged him to let her into the bedroom and make herself useful to her poor aunt Nora who was already sweating like a pig on top of the bed and gripping the sheets for dear life, but Mikey good-naturedly hunted her away from the bedroom scene.

Just then, stepping out into the yard, Fanny saw little Sing-me-a-song, the eight-year-old daughter of Cackles. Cackles was a good kind neighbour and she would be down soon to deliver and wash the new baby. Young Sing-me-a-song hopped out over the wire fence on top of the ditch, eagerly looking for news of how many more hours and minutes it might take for the baby to come crawling out from underneath Nora's skirts. To distract her Fanny took Sing-me-a-song by the hand. 'Coom with me, let ye!' she said and she led the child away through the pine-trees. Their feet slipping gingerly over the pine needles, they made their way down over the second wire fence at the lower end of Mikey's orchard. They tiptoed towards River Laughter where the roars of the boys could still be heard.

What a sight met their eyes when they got there! The big girl and the little girl saw Dowager's sons and their friend (Restless Rody) frolicking around in the tea-coloured river. They were bouncing upstream like a frog on one leg and they were pretending to be a band of skilful swimmers, although none of them could swim a single stroke – no one in Rookery Rally could! Little Sing-me-a-song let a frightening yell out of her throat when she saw the boys' hairy nakedness and she watched them as they bent down and cupped their hands coyly between their thighs. 'Don't bother hiding yeer private credentials from us,' said Fanny Adams, 'we have seen them all now!' And she rudely placed her thumb between her fingers and she shouted out words of admiration (or was it scorn?) for the attributes of each young lad. She was a very fortunate young missy to get herself back home unscathed before the boys had a chance to lay their hands on the hem of her dress. If they had caught a hold of this unseemly madam, they'd have shown her that they weren't a pack of soft foreign gentry-folk in their dealings with the fair sex: they'd have dragged her into the river and introduced her to such mysterious and earth-shaking games as she had never played in all her born days. But that wasn't the end of the matter: what a little heathen this pretty miss and her leering eyes turned out to be; for she did not go back through the pine-trees empty-handed but took home Restless Rody's shirt and his trousers and left him without a stitch of clothing to put on!

Not long afterwards (it was almost two o'clock) Dowager's younger children were playing with their jackstones on the flagstones. One or two of them were trying to draw their mother's face with their coloured pebbles from the river, when they saw the strangest of sights coming on up The Open Road. It was Blue-eyed Jack's four young brothers and half-a-dozen sympathetic men from the drinking-shop. They were marching along in a silent huddle. Unbeknownst to these little ones and hidden away from their prying eyes was the hapless shape of Restless Rody and he was bringing nothing in the world home with him except his own shivery nakedness. The children stopped their play and they scratched their heads and they wondered at the strange spectacle of men marching along like a bunch of soldiers at this unearthly hour of the day. They could see the suspicious eyes of the group peering back into their midst from time to time to see if their prize was safe. What in God's holy name could these men be hiding?

'Is it an escaped calf?' they pondered. It could be.

'Have they brought us back a dead crane?' Maybe.

'Is it a deer that they have just this minute killed with the sickle?'

They were awfully anxious to get a little peep and to know the answer to this mystery of all mysteries. Finally the men reached the stile outside Mikey's grove. Then they reached Dowager's flagstones where they came to a sudden halt. There followed a cute little pause and it seemed to last for as long as eternity itself. Suddenly (and with enough volume to awaken the dead below in the graveyard) the marchers let out a deafening roar and then (the rascally tinkers that they were) they ran off over the singletree and out across Dowager's haggart! Oh me, oh my, oh misery! Oh sheer and dreadful wretchedness! There in the middle of The Open Road stood the misfortunate spectacle of Restless Rody and he pure terrified. He was wearing nothing but his coy little birthday suit and he was holding onto his private credentials for dear life. The laughing children danced around him.

They began poking at him with twigs and they tried to get a little look in under his crossed legs. What tales they'd have for their schoolmaster (Dang-the-skin-of-it) when he asked them for their daily news – the tale of a shy young man and his two fists firmly grasped around his private credentials!

# The Journey

Bless the bit! It would soon be six o'clock and the dancers would be late if they didn't hurry on. Dowager frantically tried to shoo her girls towards the bikes at the hen-house wall. 'Can't ye see how the sun's trembling rays (she was always known for her scholarly words) are already starting to depart from ye – she'll soon be hiding herself out over Galway and the sea.'

Within the hour the mountain pathways would be filled with streams of young dancers pedalling (faster, faster, faster – the girls) and running over ditches (the racing boys) towards Judy's platform. The gaiety of the music was like a ship's siren calling to each of them. Judy herself, however, wouldn't be able to hear a single stem of the fine music for she was as deaf as a post and she was a hundred-and-five years of age according to Dowager (who knew everything).

Dowager stood with her daughters at the half-door, fussing over their hair and admiring the dazzle of her would-be charmers. She turned proudly towards her boys, shaking her head unbelievably at the stamp of them. They were in their best Sunday jackets and the white shirts with the collars out over the jacket and their hair was curved back in a wavy quiff with lashings of soapy water. She thought how lucky were the girls that they would be holding in their arms this evening and, as though she were blessing the crops in her fields, she gave each one of them a good shower of her holywater and she said, 'Be good and mind how ye go and always remember what I have taught ye – God is always looking!'

Then she watched them as they set off. 'Look at them daughters of mine,' said she whimsically to herself. 'They are like a crowd of cackling hens, each one of them on the look-out for a handsome young cockerel,' and she re-entered through the half-door, a wise old smile on her jaw as she remembered her own girlhood days.

Her younger children came running out into the yard. They almost knocked her over as they hurried over the flagstones to give a last wave of goodbye to the bigger girls. There was a mixture of smiles and sadness on their mystified little faces. They would do their own share of praying this evening and get down on their knees and ask God to hold off the rain in the hope that their older sisters would have the merriest of times doing the heel-and-toe above on Judy's wooden boards. In a year or two's time when it was their own turn to reach a certain age of comeliness and maturity they themselves would go off and seek out the heart-rending music and do their own tidy dance steps – steps that'd knock the very strength out of the hills (so they'd be telling you).

With hearts as light as thistledown Dowager's girls and their leggy limbs shot ever onwards, cycling through the green and lush countryside. It was steep at the beginning, up around Mureeny. Then more and more dancers met them beyond the crossroads where once their parents had danced and caroused to the tunes of paper-and-comb and The Shy Scissors Sisters playing their polkas from inside the ditch. And then the hilly lanes suddenly wound upwards and the girls got off and they pushed their bikes. Then they came to the white cross where Little Jack had been crushed to his death by the mistress's unexpecting car on his very first day's outing to the school-house.

Once passed Mureeny the dancers got back on their bikes and they raced on towards the music. Their skirts flapped off of their knees and their heads hung low in the face of the dewy breezes coming down at them through the Lisnagorna pine-trees. They were as determined as a dog with a rusty kettle tied to its tail. From time to time one of the bike's chains came off from the inner cranks and wheels. It was then that a girl's unholy curses could be heard polluting the airy hills: 'Mee feckin chain! Mee feckin chain! – Shit! Will ye look at it!' The other girls ran to the ditches and they brought back fists of sand with which they covered the chain and cranks and away they went again, the sand causing the chain to grip once more. In the distant meadow at the other end of The Black Banks (joy to their ears) they heard the timeless swell of the music, coming from the fiddles and the melodions. Their hearts seemed to be bursting in pounding anticipation and they pedalled faster than ever and they couldn't wait to throw their pennies into the hat at the field gateway.

# And Then They Were There

The meadow was edged with four blackened ditches, heaped high with smoothed-away quarry-stones. There were no coloured lanterns or romantic lamps hanging down to glorify the dance-floor and the only illumination was the big yellow moon and the dreamy stars and the lofty silvery clouds dancing gaily across the purple sky. In less than no time the girls raced out onto the platform, their hearts drunkenly full of the music and the thumping hobnail boots of their partners, those strange mountainy men in the 'round-the-house-and-mind-the-dresser' half-sets. Whether the sky glowed or not didn't seem to be bothering the older girls. Indeed the darker it got, the better for some of these romantic little hussies – the music and excitement gradually making them a good bit bolder than their priest in his confession-box would have wished. And as the evening wore on, some of them were sure to indulge themselves in the odd bit of shy and slobbery kissing in the darkened corners of Judy's field, whispering their words of romance into some poor befuddled lad's ears.

# Little Nell

During this same sunny June (1937) Little Nell, the future mother of Teddy, was spending her days working from dawn till dusk for a cruel farmer (Sallyswitch) in his great big mansion. She was Dowager's oldest daughter. With her father dead, it was her duty (as soon as she reached thirteen and had made The Sacramment of Confirmation) to take on the role of a pure slave and send home the matchbox with the brown ten-shilling note in it, delivered each month by one of the local farmers on his way home from the creamery. By now it was her seventh year of hard labour and at twenty-years-of-age she was heartily sick of it. Indeed there were times when she was beginning to feel as old as her own mother.

This Wednesday evening would prove to be her one and only chance of a night's enjoyment above in Judy's meadow and she grabbed her dancing shoes with eager hands and she tiptoed out the back-window. She felt almost like a thief. Never again would she get so good a chance to escape from her drudgery and from the lustful clutches of her drunken old taskmaster, not to mention the yard-brush with which his cruel hag-of-a-wife (La-dee-dah) belted the back of her legs whenever she needed a little bit of extra amusement. The two old heathens had gone to sell their best racehorses at the sales in Newmarket across The Irish Sea and wouldn't be back till the following evening. Little Nell would remember this night's dancing for as long as she lived; for before the night was over she'd find her heartstrings twisted into a great big muddle at the sight of Shy Patsy and his galloping jig-steps.

Prayerful-Tim was a 'silenced' priest (the penalty for innocently mismanaging the diocesan funds) and he was the sharer of Little Nell's gloomy existence in the rat-and-mouse-infested attic. He planned to give her the loan of his rusty old bike as soon as her two cruel taskmasters were on board the big ship. Only too well did a grateful Little Nell know that her slavery would start again at the crack of dawn when she'd be up once more and pulping the turnips and mangols for the six angry sows. But for this one evening in her life she'd be damned if her platform dance wouldn't give her a sweet taste of glory and her life of slavery could go drown itself to hell in one of the many nearby bog-holes!

Earlier in the morning she had run down behind the hen-house, taking with her the broken bit of looking-glass from her drawer. Prayerful-Tim fixed the looking-glass on the hedgerow for her. He helped her with the papers and the hot rags for twisting her hair into ringlets and curls. He carefully combed out her raven locks. Little Nell put a little of La-dee-dah's Sunday-Mass powder to her cheeks and the rouge (a little) to her lips. Her heart was all of a shiver as she shyly stepped out of her old calicos and belted on her best Sunday-Mass frock. Finally Prayerful-Tim (as though he were Cinderella's very own fairy godmother) helped her smooth out the folds of her lovely dress and he made her do a few quick turns and twists around in the yard: 'Nell, my dearest Nell, you look fit to sit at the table with Queen Maeve of Ireland!' She gazed at her face in the looking-glass and she fervently prayed that her wishes would come true and that she'd meet her handsome young prince at Judy's dance this very evening.

Free! Free! Free! Like a bird flown out the window from its cage Little

Nell raced away from inside the imprisoning thirty-foot-high gates. She pedalled like fury towards the end of The Black Banks. Half-an-hour later she heard the music coming at her from far away behind Judy's little cabin. She arrived breathlessly and she jumped off of Prayerful-Tim's bike and she threw it against the ditch. She scampered across the meadow towards the platform where the scraping and stamping of the hobnail boots was already raking the floor as the boys and girls embroiled themselves in the mysteries of the dance-steps. They were making enough noise to frighten the Devil in hell. For the moment Little Nell stood in a trance and gazed open-mouthed at the strange sight and the sound of the hammering feet attacking the rickety timbers. With her eyes spinning like saucers it was a pure drink of fresh water to her as she took in the sights: the skill and liveliness of the older dancers: the feathery fleetness of the young men as they dashed towards the women and clasped them ('Coom into mee arms!') to their chests for the final swing. She found herself hurried out onto the floor with the rest of the dancers. Her sisters were more surprised than anyone at seeing her here and they waved excitedly to her from across the floor.

She was getting a reel in her head from all the spinning and the skirt-cutting swings of the men and she saw one or two of the mountainy lads swinging their young ladies clean off their feet and out over their heads (round and round and round) before once more dropping them down daintily – softly and gentlemanly – onto their little tippy-toes. With the laughter and the sighs of the women at being so fiercely manhandled you'd think a cow had just calved! 'Why, Badger, by the poker and the bellows, aren't you the wild naygar!' roared Nancy Finn to her partner, laughing the two eyes out of her head.

'Look at Moll-from-Currywhibble!' said a voice behind Little Nell. 'She's got a fire in her eyes and her cheeks are as red as a lobster from battering out her mother's jig-steps.'

'Look at Danny Minogue!' said another. 'The sparks flying from the cleets on his boots like a shower of fire-crackers – it's a wonder he hasn't set fire to the benches of hay where the musicians are playing.'

Little Nell couldn't stop laughing at the sight of Big Red! His resounding toecaps were splintering the floor in several places. And then she saw Fatty-Matty whaling into the Mureeny Polka. He was undoubtedly as long in the tooth as her big brother (Blue-eyed Jack) and he was almost old enough to be the father of some of the young school-leavers enjoying their first outing to the dance. Already he had made a gap in the left corner of the floor with the energy of his heel-and-toe steps and his boot was stuck in a hole where it'd remain a prisoner for the rest of the evening. Once more Little Nell took a hearty fit of laughing. She hadn't felt as happy as this in donkey's years and her sisters ran over to her and they surrounded her with their hugs and their greetings.

## Let the Music Sway

Deep in the corner under the three oak trees sat the scintillating musicians on their benches of hay, flittering and fluttering their jigs and their polkas out into Judy's night sky. In the middle of them sat Fiddler-Joe. His two elbows were flying like an ass's tail in summer's heat. His son (Sweeney) was newly learning his fiddle-trade and with an occasional smack on the head from his father's speedy bow he kept to his work like a merry young Trojan. Bejaizus was the leader of the group. He turned the whites of his eyes up towards the stars as if seeking out a promise of help from The Almighty above. The smile never left his jaw and the horsehair kept flying in shreds from off of his bow and his playing would woo the Devil's own feet. Tom and Tim (the Sandy Boys) had come over from the sandpits around Growl River – themselves and their wimpled melodions. Hammer-the-Smith had brought his own music-box and was sitting in between the two of them. One or two young girls, barely out of their cradle, had joined in with their long blue quarry slates and their spoons, to rattle up the magical rhythms. 'Give us the whole of yeer hearts, byze,' the crowd roared as they encouraged the talents of the musicians to even greater bouts of vim and gusto. So mesmerised were the ears of the dancers that you'd think these fine players had at least ten arms apiece on them.

The second foray of the dancers took to the floor for the Clare batter and the famed Ballycommon five-part half-set. Donie Tenderfoot began the attack in great style. He had the legs of a stork and was as nimble as a young pig. In the advance and retire he repeatedly dug his two heels into the floor as though he were the coulter of his father's plough. A stones-throw away Thundering Timmy made an awkward beeline for young Katie Spanners. The poor fellow had two shovels for feet on him and though he had the steps inside in his head he couldn't seem to get them down into his feet. He gave the floor such a welting that before the half-set was over he had fractured three of poor Katie's toes. 'He looks pretty good with his left leg but he's no good at all with the right leg!' remarked Little Nell with a smile. And her sisters laughed.

The girls' dresses swished sinuously. Their beefy arms and wrists entwined with the men and the hills and their fairies were ablaze from the pace and pitch of the music's cadences and the thrashing of the boots and the yelling of the men. The old-fashioned steps were soon replaced by bits of extemporisation. Thundering Timmy bounced across the floor on his knees in a desperate effort to impress the broken-toed Katie. Sweat was falling off of his brow like rain from a thatched reck. The entranced onlookers ('Cripes! will ye look at Timmy!) sat bedazzled on the ditch, their knees huddled up close to their collarbones as they prepared to make their own leap out onto the floor.

'House, byze,' roared Red Scissors, 'if it's mee coat ye want, ye can have it.' And the very sky lit up with the glow of his ugly broken teeth. By now the women were every bit as lively as the men and their faces began to glow like red tulips. At one moment they were as light as a swan's feathers. The next moment they were seen leathering the floor like high-stepping plough-horses. Such a pace couldn't go on all night for who on earth could keep up with the rattling heels of such unleashed abandonment? They'd be dead before midnight and there'd be more than a few corpses carried off to Abbey Acres graveyard when the early morning light came up.

# Shy Patsy

It was now time for the slow waltz: time to catch your woman around her trim waist and bring her in close to your heartstrings: time to put a stop to the steam rising up from the dance-floor and blinding the rest of the dancers: time to cool down the glowing cheeks of the baked set-dancers and to place your lips next to your dreamy one's forehead. And as the pink of the evening drew into the purple of night and before they completely lost sight of one another the dancers became a little more studious and a little more cautious. It would remind you of the horse-fair in The Roaring Town. For the men began to inspect the women and the women began to inspect the men. In a flash of intuition Little Nell's sisters (with a nudge of their excited elbows) could see that Shy Patsy's heartstrings were fit to burst from the force of the arrows that Little Nell had fired into him and that Little Nell herself (poor dear) was as earnest in her own desires for Shy Patsy. The quiet young man was wearing his best brown brogues – the 'brown ones' Little Nell would call them hereafter. He was dressed in his new sports jacket with the collar of his white shirt out over it and of course he had the richest dazzler-of-a-bike that she had ever seen in all her life. There were handsomer young boys than himself; for his nose was a little too hooked and his ears were a little too pointed and they stuck out sideways in two wide flaps – like an ass's. But, as Little Nell would tell the world hereafter, nobody could perform the wizardly steps like this young lad from The Quarries. The silky tidy movements of his nimble legs and his sudden wild dashes and his changes of pace as he swung her here and there in the latest quickstep won her tremulous heart utterly and completely.

Five years previously (at the tender age of sixteen) his tear-filled mother had waved him off, sending him to work for Bunnyfoot, an avaricious old landowner in The Limerick Glens. 'Fetch me the coppers from underneath the blue-gate pier,' said his master 'and go to the shop and bring me back the *Financial Times* till I see how my pile of money is growing.'

Just like Little Nell, Shy Patsy had worked as a pure slave from the break-of-day till the dead-of-night. From the very start his heart ached to be back home with his mother, she being a sick woman and with a hole in her heart and his father dead and buried from a fall in the river. Each night the boy cried himself to sleep abroad in the turf-shed where no-one could see him, so soft was his nature.

Five miserable years later he found he could bear this no longer. But, slave-driver though he was, Bunnyfoot eventually found a soft side inside in him as he sat up in his bed each night listening to the long-drawn-out sobs of the poor youth. He realized how much the lad ached to go home and see his mother. He took his coat and went to town where he strode into Slattery-John's shop. He bought Shy Patsy a most beautiful bike to ride away on and spend the weekend evenings with his saintly mother and walk once more with her to the spring-well across the fields and carry back the two buckets of water for her. Once outside his master's gate and as soon as he got up on the saddle of this mercurial piece of machinery, Shy Patsy rode like the wind and he never looked back till he reached his mother's half-door. And another thing – he never returned to Bunnyfoot with his precious bike (his hours of slavery had well earned him the price of it) and who could have blamed him for that? His mother, however, refused to allow her son's soul to fry hereafter in the flames of Purgatory and, though it made a big hole in her late husband's savings, she paid back every penny for Bunnyfoot's bike. Enough said.

# Shy Patsy Meets Little Nell

And now this shy young man was piercing with his eyes the blueberry eyes of Little Nell and he was admiring her soft lips with the natural redness of sweet cherries on them. Little Nell's eyes (it would sicken your stomach to look at the pair of them) were piercing into Shy Patsy's and from this night forth it would take a horse-and-cart to separate the two-in-one hearts of these young lovebirds.

And once again custom was seen to take over. For whenever such blossoming romances introduced themselves, the other dancers would steal craftily to the far side of the meadow where the bikes were thrown in a heap on the ditch. Out of this muddle of bikes (oh, the sly little hussies!) Little Nell's sisters picked Shy Patsy's brand-new bike. They quickly found the rusty old bike that Prayerful-Tim had lent their sister. They untangled the two bikes from the heap. They laid Little Nell's bike side-by-side with the beautiful bike of Shy Patsy and then their rascally cunning set in and began to weave its deadly charm. With ream after ream of brown twine and wire (found lying in the ditch) they tied the bike of Shy Patsy to the bike of Little Nell. They put triple knots in it (good and firm) so that in an hours' time when the dancing reached its sad and inevitable crescendo it would be impossible for the two little innocents to untangle the mess of their bikes. The girls rubbed their hands together and they congratulated themselves on having introduced their sister and Shy Patsy to indescribable realms of intimacy; for they knew that their two fluttery hearts would be forced to spend at least half-an-hour in each other's company. They could picture how the young lovebirds would be cursing them like blazes for having done such cruel mischief to their bikes. They could picture something else too – how their gentle fingers would interlace in their frustrated efforts to untangle the string and the wire. And where would they themselves be lurking all the while? Behind the bushes (the little hussies) and holding back their silent laughter as they peeped out at the young lovers breathing heavily into each other's ears and their lips so closely (oh, so very closely) alongside each other. Weren't these young sisters of Little Nell the wiliest little devils on God's own earth?

## The Harty Sisters

Whilst this match-making sorcery was going on there was yet another bit of trouble lying in store for the brand-new bike of the three Harty sisters from Growl River. It was always a major job for girls to guard their bike once they had thrown it on the ditch; their brothers were forever pointing out how a bike was the most valuable of objects on God's earth. So, if three sisters were riding their bike to the dance, it was vital for one of them to give the dance-floor a miss now and then and be on the look-out for some mischievous group of boys who'd like nothing better than take turns riding their precious piece of machinery and rattling it off of the ditches around the lanes in an effort to balance on top of it.

And now as misfortune would have it and such being the rascality of a few earnest lads with no bike of their own (and who had walked the long distance across the hills to attend the dance) the three Harty sisters found themselves tricked into being on the dance-floor at one and the same time. In the blink of an eye three impudent mountainy boys saw their chance. They snatched up the Harty's bike and began having the fine old time riding it round and around the hidden lane at the back of Judy's cabin.

The war and the ruction soon broke out: 'Nonie! Nonie! Come quick!

The feckin eejits from up-country – shit on them! – are riding our new hackle around in Judy's yard!' The three sisters left their stranded dance-partners sitting on their backsides in the middle of the floor and they raced into Judy's lane. They threw aside their ladylike demeanour and they lay into the miscreants with their flying fists. The laughter and the roars of the other dancers could be heard far and wide as they listened to the litany of inventive curses and swearwords and saw the three brave go-boys toppled from their perch on the bike and sent sprawling into the briars and the nettles. But before the night was over, these outraged young ladies and the three roguish mountainy lads would be seen walking arm-in-arm towards the dark corners of the ditch where an odd bout of shy kissing and innocent lovemaking would begin to torment the sleeping crows above in their roost.

## *Father Loveless*

You couldn't keep a good man down and you couldn't keep Father Loveless away from visiting the dancers as they started to leave the meadow. He prided himself on being the guardian of his flock's immortal souls and he drove his motorcar to the edge of Judy Rag's Meadow where he cut off the headlights and the engine. Armed with his powerful flashlamp (as well as a few mouthfuls of whiskey to warm his old heart) our holy huntsman clambered across the ditches, his eyes forever on the look-out for young sinners and his two ears cocked back like an ass, listening for the sound of a shy girl's giggles. What on earth (ah, cruel lamp-man and your prying eyes!) did you hope to find? Would your flashlamp catch out a brazen young girl smoking her father's stolen fag-butts, the cheeky missy? Or might there be (ahem!) a bit more for your old eyes to see? Perhaps you'd get a little glimpse of a young girl's garters or the shock of her bare speckled thighs? Or might you and your unseemly flashlamp reach the zenith (God in heaven forbid!) and spy out a pair of youngsters and they thrashing the wheat-field of love itself?

Father Loveless with his own personal renunciation of the marriage-bed and his own sacrifice of masculinity for the sake of the holy cloth came to Judy's meadow every Wednesday night. He was seeking out the Devil that he knew from his confession-box lay inside in the bodies of each of us.

From the altar rails every Sunday this holy man held up his trusty catechism and he denounced the sinfulness of Judy's Platform Dance and the lusts of the flesh that rose from it. But, though he and his fantasies bemoaned the simple enjoyment of the goodnight kisses, his very presence at the end of the dance didn't do him one pennyworth of good; he and all this flashlamp nonsense could go and drown themselves in the depths of Growl River (said all the young dancers). And the poor fellow succeeded only in driving the hot-blooded boys and girls further and further in over the ditches where they'd continue their intimacy in more remote trysting-places around the neighbouring woods and rivers. And it wasn't unknown for one or two mischievous young lovers (had they not an ounce of shame in them?) to let the priest and his poor aching soul see what the eyes of no man-of-the-cloth should ever have been let get a look at.

On this happiest and most memorable of nights his quest was to bear no fruit. Half-a-mile away (on the edge of Judy's callow-field) one or two young couples had already strayed to their chosen love-nest where they were content to while away a few precious moments smoking their hidden fag-butts and hiding the glow of them in case of the priest's lamp. In the darkness of the field their hearts were at play and their eyes had a hunger in them and their arms entwined in comfort around each other. Their simple few kisses were such that no flashlamp could ever destroy and their furtive little giggles of laughter touched only the nearby croaking frogs. The creamy moon nodded down its smiling face approvingly on their innocence. A few cautious timid kisses (they knew) would never set fire to their souls or land them in the bowels of Hell. Enough said.

## It Was Time to Go Home

There was darkness now all around Judy's meadow. It had won its fight with the full moon's opulence and the sparkling diamonds of the stars. The platform dance was over till next Wednesday. As bats and owls slipped out into the night so did the dancers scatter themselves like fieldmice across the hills. It had been like a dream from out of Heaven and the cycling girls shouted and roared like wild asses all the way back to their yard-streams, frightening the midnight fairies. They had squeezed the very last drops of merriment out of Judy Rag's Platform Dance. But whilst the girls sped their bikes down the mountainside and the boys strode their boots home through the woods of Lisnagorna, they left behind them the love-inspired Shy Patsy and his charmer (Little Nell) in the secrecy of their knotted bikes and their budding romance. A few little sighs seeped out of their tender young souls and an almost-sickly feeling of departing from one another flew back into them. They and their whispered poetry (little words of promised love pounding inside in their heads) had to go their different ways – she on Prayerful-Tim's rusty old bike and he on Bunnyfoot's razzle-dazzler. Their hearts beat fast and their pedals spun even faster as they rushed homeward like two small birds speeding to their separate roosts. Shy Patsy headed into the arms of his worried mother, who had stayed up waiting for him. She could tell by the glow in his eyes that all was not right with him. And she wondered. Little Nell proceeded towards the gloomy red gates that would imprison her for another year and maybe more. But in her mind's eye she could see a means of escaping from her perpetual drudgery. Shy Patsy would become her inspiration, her knight in shining armour. Prayerful-Tim had already drawn up his plans for her flight out of Tipperary and across the sea to England and on to London. Little Nell had built up a trust of late between herself and Sallyswitch and she would take his Kerry-blue cow to The Autumn Fair to sell. She would take the few silver coins that Prayerful-Tim had saved up for her and she would take a few more silver coins (these the old miser surely owed her and he would never miss them) from inside Sallyswitch's tobacco jar. But as she now whisked her rusty bike onwards she felt only the loneliness and the worry coming down onto her frail shoulders. She must put aside the wondrous stars and the smiling moon on high. She must put aside the silver clouds and the merry voices of the night-time ghosts following alongside her in the roadside bushes. Her world of beauty had stopped with the clock (like the magic for poor storybook Cinderella) and it would be replaced with her own fears for the laborious days ahead. God would bring in a new day tomorrow and Little Nell, after a few hours of fretful sleep, would stretch her tired toes and once more take her painful calf muscles out towards the pig-house and the six angry sows that were waiting to be fed.

And yet the platform dance had been a beautiful night for her (just this once) and had been worth all the endeavours of herself and Prayerful-Tim.

It had been a wondrous night too for her sisters and brothers and the other merry-faced dancers, their world ablaze with the fires of their laughter. They had jumped out from their home firesides and they had frightened Life itself out of its very wits. All too soon these years of their youth would flit away from them. One far-off day in the future they would find themselves sitting beside their turf-fire and stroking their little black dog absentmindedly. The women would be wearing the white wimple underneath their traditional black caps and the men would be sitting opposite them across the fireside. They'd have the aches and the pains from all the years of rainy field-wettings and they would hug close the potato-sack around their backs to keep the warmth inside in them.

Perhaps, as the girls now pedalled their bikes through the cool of the hills and the breezes of the Lisnagorna pine-trees around the hillside streams, one or two of the older folk in the nearby cabins would turn in their sleep and cock an ear, listening to the tinkling of the young girls' bike-bells. Perhaps they'd hear the laughter and the singing, floating on past their reverberating windowsills. Perhaps an old woman would recall the days when she too pedalled off to The Platform Dance in Judy Rag's Meadow. 'Oh-honey-oh!' she'd sigh to herself. 'Wasn't life grand in them days?'

For the next seven days of the week the boys and girls would continue to pray most fervently that the weather would hold tough and that the moon and the stars wouldn't let them down so that once again they could get for themselves another bit of Heaven's eternal happiness at Judy Rag's Platform Dance. We fill our glasses to the brim and we pledge our bumpers to the evening dancers. May the ash-trees come marching down from The Mighty Mountain before we ever forget such wondrous nights as this one. Blessed be the dance! Blessed be the music! Blessed be the poetry of big boots and swirling skirts and shiny-eyed happiness. Blessed be the love-light shining back and forth in the young eyes of Little Nell and Shy Patsy! And Teddy (one day soon to be born their son) would later agree to all of that.

# TWO

# *The German Blitz of London*

*When Teddy first saw the light of day
amidst the crippled ruins of London*

It was September in the year of 1940. By now the big war against The Germans had well and truly raised its ugly head on the streets of London where Teddy was born. The incessant roars of countless German bombers exploded their greetings over the night sky, indiscriminately attacking the railway stations and the power depots. It filled the streets and especially the home of Shy Patsy and Little Nell, who had recently arrived in London, with an unholy terror since everyone wondered if they'd still be alive the next day.

The Blitz started in early September and every morning scores of people (among them the newly-weds, Rita and Romeo, Little Nell's closest friends sixty yards away) were seen dead inside the devastated ruins when houses had fallen down on top of them in the middle of the night. That was when (unexpectedly and six weeks prematurely – a side-result brought about upon more than one of London's young pregnant women by the ferocity of the German bombers) Teddy decided to make his feeble entry into the world.

On the day before his birth Little Nell woke up at five in the morning to find her sheets covered in blood. Shy Patsy was left scratching his head: should he cycle off to work or should he stay and look after his young wife? Little Nell forced him out the door. Work was scarce for an Irishman newly-arrived in London, whose part in the war effort was about to take him away from her within a few short weeks. That afternoon and ten hours later she

9|2208749

found herself in The Royal Hospital on the broad of her back and Teddy's newborn self lying in an oxygen tent beside her and gasping his lungs out so as to catch his first few faint breaths of life.

Shy Patsy cycled the seven miles home at record speed. He threw his bike against the railings without so much as removing his cycling-clips and to his great alarm he found himself immediately surrounded and being greeted by his backslapping neighbours ('Good on yuh, Paddy, you're a daddy!'). With smiling faces they raised their glasses of egg-flip and Mann's brown ale and they toasted the health of Teddy, the new arrival. They spent the rest of the hour singing the praises of this shy young Irishman and his firstborn son. It was the one good thing that had happened for them that week amidst the bombed-out obliteration of their street.

On that same evening a far different scene was taking place above in The Royal Hospital: 'Take that little rat and his elongated head away from me!' croaked Little Nell. Harsh though it seemed, she had soldiered through the greatest of difficulties in forcing Teddy's tiny frame out into the world and by now she was worn to a thread. She turned her back away from her child and let the full flow of her depressed tears dampen the wall and the sheets.

## The Dilemma

The Bombing Blitz roared on with full force over the next few weeks and the people, forever defiant, cursed The Germans into hell. Whatever their own fate might be, there was a weak underbelly from the nightly attacks – namely the innocent children and their right to a future life and they would have to be ferried away immediately to safety. Little Nell now needed the wisdom of the biblical Solomon. She lay awake alongside Shy Patsy and she listened to the roars of the bombs – a horror far worse than those harsh bygone days working under Sallyswitch, her cruel taskmaster back home in Ireland. And the two of them realised that, if they were to save the life that Teddy had so nearly lost at his birth, they'd have to plan a quick retreat (however temporary) for this infant son of theirs. There was no alternative: Teddy would have to go (a tiny newborn evacuee) to his mother's own mother in Tipperary.

But Dowager, after bringing up her own fifteen children (and her husband dead), was by now a tired and stooped old woman. How could she be expected to cope with a newborn child, who by this time was able to roar like a lion throughout every blessed night? And besides this – Little Nell had learnt to love the very frailness in Teddy's tiny form, the so-called little rat. Her heart was full of him and she couldn't bear the thought of being separated from him. Was all her birthsuffering when her baby had threatened to tear the guts out of her now to be simply for nothing? Was she to have no little bit of motherly comfort from watching his playful development in the coming months and years? And yet she could picture (perish the thought!) another scene – a horrendous scene – losing her baby son altogether underneath the constant rain of the nightly bombers.

## Time To Escape From The Bombs

Broken-hearted and too tired to make the journey herself, she entrusted her baby to her younger sister (Polish 'n' Shine) with the instruction to run to the train-station as quickly as she could and from there deliver him safely across the dangerous sea and into the arms of Dowager, his grandmother. After all, Ireland was not at war with anyone else, thank God, and was as far away as the moon from the bombed-out streets of London.

Shortly after Sunday Mass a train left Euston with a woman and a baby on board and the prayers of a broken-hearted mother left behind them. Six hours later the cattle-boat was waiting for Teddy and aunt Polish 'n' Shine alongside the Holyhead quay. When the baby finally got to Rookery Rally he would be safe at last.

## Dowager

Dowager saw Polish 'n' Shine stepping down from the train inside in The Roaring Town. She had a suitcase and a hatbox and a tiny infant, not much bigger than a cat, in her arms. The old woman looked at this newborn soul and she blessed herself as the sun in her life began to shine once more. An untouched baby (she thought) that had just had a miraculous escape from the wrath of the German warplanes. With none of her own children still left at home (her last child, Una, had left for Dublin the year before), she snatched Teddy out of the startled arms of Polish 'n' Shine and she paraded herself and her new baby up and down outside The Tomato-Shop in Jinnet Street, showing him off to all the pig-sellers and farmers in his yellow fluffy-gosling suit and his milk-stained swaddling-clothes. You'd think her baby from England was a prince at the very least, the way she went on.

From the minute she brought the little fellow home she started pouring her very soul into him – her prayers and her whispering sighs. She never took her eyes off of him – coo-cooing over him, sighing and laughing at his every little gesture as well as the wet-crying of him throughout the early nights when the bombs were still rattling around inside in his infant head. And then she'd lull him back to sleep again with more of her recitations and poems and dydling rhythms. And next morning she'd hoist him up over the half-door for all the passers-by to see from their ass-and-cars as they hurried on to the creamery. And in the following springtime she'd be seen guarding his first footsteps away from the gander and the sow.

The neighbours all smiled and they whispered to one another: it was as plain as the nose on their faces that Dowager's heart, after the impoverished rearing of her fifteen children during her untimely widowhood, had suddenly turned as soft as Bog Boundless above at Growl River. She herself could have told them the very same thing: that she felt as though she was a brand new bride all over again. Blue-eyed Jack was no better than herself, all watery-eyed and dreamy-looking, the poor man. He never tired of hoisting the little fellow up towards the rafters ('Can you see Dublin?') and swooping him down again in underneath his wellingtons. The Old Pair treated Teddy, each in their own way, as though he was their very own child. It's a wonder that either of them ever got a blessed stroke of work done, so much did they spoil their little Englishman.

# THREE

# Father Chasible

*When Teddy went to the burial of his priest*

It was Springtime in the year of 1943. It was late in March and new life came into our midst, shivering anew all over Rookery Rally. Around every thatched cabin you could hear the re-echoing choirs of asses and horses, sheep and cows. And from the high-banked dung-heaps behind every hen-house you were greeted with the answering chorus of chattering hens, ducks and turkeys – even the snorting of the pig and the sow at times. The lanes were now fresh with several young flowers and Timmy's ditch on the upper side of the ash-pit where Dowager had just emptied her piss-pot was hidden in a long row of yellow and cream primroses.

By eight o'clock the early morning light of the sun had popped its head in through the window of The Big Cave Room where Teddy slept each night in the damp brass bed beside the warm body of his uncle (Blue-eyed Jack). Once more the big man, having brought back his seven cows from The Bull-Paddock to be milked, stamped his muddy wellingtons in through the bedroom door to rouse the little fellow from his sleepy nest. As soon as the child felt Blue-eyed Jack's beardy jaw rubbing a greeting against his own pink cheeks he hopped out of bed and he knelt down on the potato-sacking that covered the clay floor beside the bed. Once again the big man attempted to guide him in his babbling attempts at the very long list of 'God Bless' prayers that Dowager had been patiently teaching him since his second birthday. High above the empty fireplace, with its laurel branches and its

25

early bees, the bemused picture of the bespectacled pope in his purple and ermine robes looked down approvingly at this new child-saint making a mark for himself here in Rookery Rally.

# How The Days Flew By

Since his arrival as a newborn baby from London Teddy had spent two-and-a-half years with his grandmother and uncle (The Old Pair) and was well able to stray around the farmyard as though he owned the place. With his little stick he gave out his stern orders to all his subjects – to the hens and their chicks and to the ducks and the turkeys and the geese with their fluffy goslings.

But all of a sudden Dowager (who was perched on her chair at the half-door) saw him stumbling back towards her as hurriedly as his two short legs could carry him. To his shame he had just about wet his britches after seeing the sow and the gander making fierce war against each other and he was filled with the earnest fear that these two old ruffians might join forces and make a raid on his own feeble frame in spite of the fierce big stick he was wielding over his head. Dowager's heart did a small somersault of mock apprehension as he climbed up onto her bony old knees and then she wrapped her protective arms around him and she hopped him up and down several times in the folds of her black apron, all the time humming her warmth into him.

They sat there silently for a short while, the old lady wiping away his childish tears as best she could with the hem of her cardigan. By this stage of his life the old woman and the child were like the inseparable sides of a windowpane and she was well able to distract him from each of his daily worries. Once more she guided his eyes to what she wanted him to see in the early morning light. With her finger all the time pointing out this shape and this colour and this movement, the two of them sat watching the sun shining its long ribbon of yellow rays along the laurel hedge by the road. They watched it spreading its way across the stream's flagstones and wafting itself in over the box hedge that surrounded Dowager's little garden and the ruins of Darmidy's ancient forge. They watched it glistening on the fuchsia bushes at the pig-house ditch as it raced after the yard stream merrily gushing its waters into a little waterfall down by the rusty blue kettle. They watched it rise achingly above the misty blue pine-trees that crowned the surrounding hills of Lisnagorna.

As Dowager continued to stroke his curls the little fellow felt his fears becalmed for the tenth time this morning and he boldly ventured out as far as the stream where the ducks had decided to hold sway. From a safe distance (and with an odd look back at his grandmother) he gazed at them bobbing awkwardly on the rocks and looking for a suitable spot from which to tumble into the water. At the half-door Dowager kept her eagle eye on the increasing changes she saw taking place in this little English child – to think that he had been sent to her by Little Nell to prevent himself getting killed under the German's wartime bombs. But then (goodness me!) as though she had nothing better to do with her life she gave herself a good shake and she took her chair in the half-door and she prepared to get on with the busy chores of her day.

# *Blue-Eyed Jack*

As soon as Teddy had swallowed down his two eggs with the spoon of butter in them the 'two-men-of-us' (as Blue-eyed Jack liked to label himself and the child) walked down the road towards Mikey's stile, leaving behind them the old woman to clean the table and get ready the spuds and cabbages for the dinner. In their fists they carried their tap-tapping sticks and they marched along in a well-established musical unison, the little fellow taking long strides in imitation of the big man, who was (like Dowager) ever his teacher. In front of them were the patient cows, glad to be released from their chains. Soon both the cows and themselves were working up a good head of steam. Teddy stopped his wobbly legs from time to time to collect one or two flowers for Dowager's bedroom altar and Blue-eyed Jack made sure that he did not let his fingers roam too freely among the nettles and briars.

They reached John's Gate and they turned in towards The Bull-Paddock. The big man lifted the child up onto the bars of the gate, holding him firmly to his chest and they gazed out over the field, their eyes filled with the swirls of cobwebby dew. They entered the gate and Blue-eyed Jack picked up a shiny buttercup and he twirled it delicately around in his rough fingers. He pointed out its rich yellowness so that Teddy could absorb the glimmering rays of the sun in its cup. Then he picked up and showed him the contrasting clover that his cantankerous ass (The Lightning Whoor) loved feeding on, even better than the thistles. They were both looking for rabbits and those other lively creatures, the March hares, but not one of these little scamps were fool enough to pop out their heads when they saw the big-and-the-little-man coming their way. The big man broke the silence. He clapped his hands and from beyond the clump of trees at Corcoran's Well several crows soared aloft like a flurry of cinders on Dowager's hob and they floated away aimlessly towards The Bog Wood.

Suddenly the two adventurers heard the dull clangour of the church bells in Copperstone Hollow reverberating across the fields. 'Why, it's not even mid-morning yet,' thought Blue-eyed Jack to himself. 'Tom-the-bell-ringer and his sons would never be tolling their bells at this early stage of the day.' He knew it wasn't the time for the midday Angelus bells. It wasn't the merry bell-peals that attend a morning wedding. Someone must have died but who could it be? And he was left scratching his head.

Returning from their rambles, the big man led the little fellow out through the pig-house gap. He took off his own coat and he sat Teddy on the shiny side of his waistcoat and he rolled up his own sleeves around his leathery arms. He tested the edge of his axe with his sandpapery thumb and he began splitting his logs with a vengeance. The child kept well out of the way of the flying splinters. From time to time he held out his arms, crooking them at the elbow and he waited for a pile of the smaller logs to be stowed on him by his uncle.

'I'm at my work like you, aren't I, Jack?

'No better man,' smiled his uncle.

Teddy was well able for this sort of work. After all, he'd be three soon. Then he staggered down through the gap and he took his precious load of logs into The Welcoming Room, almost tripping up his old grandmother on his way in through the half-door. He placed the logs one by one in under the stool at the fireside and he counted all eight of them and Dowager looked on and she smiled to herself, well-satisfied with the care and attention that her little man from England was paying to his work with the logs and the new counting she was teaching him.

# The Lucky Child

The life of this little evacuee couldn't be more different from those other unlucky children his own age, who had been left behind in a state of dreamy delirium on the battered streets of London. 'Mummy! Mummy!' they'd cry, 'Gerry is coming! Gerry is coming!' and they'd press their tear-stained faces into their mother's blouse and they'd hang onto her with a grip of death in case a German bomb would fall on top of their heads. This fortunate little boy heard no merciless roars of the German planes or their cruel bombs ringing in his ears. He had no wartime nightmares to drag him screaming out of the horrors of a fitful sleep for he was living a life of absolute royalty. Each morning, even before he strayed out from behind the wrinkles of his sleep, he was greeted with a spoonful of butter topped up with sugar. 'Butter and sugar for Teddy – twenty minutes to sixty!' sang the voice of his uncle (the little fellow was never able to fathom out what hour this 'sixty' was). Then, after the customary prayers on the potato-sacking and as soon as he had scurried out to the front table there was placed in front of him a mug of the Kerry-blue cow's newly-arrived milk and two fresh eggs. These eggs had already been inspected by the ever-thoughtful Dowager. Her little finger had smudged them with a coating of hen's dung as well as a carefully-added white feather to show that The Little Red Hen had just dropped these special gifts from her fluffy bum and had delivered them this very second in the half-door for his breakfast.

# The Passersby

In addition to these daily trimmings with his uncle and grandmother there were (even at this unearthly hour of the day) the several passersby. There were the men on their galloping horses with their shirt-buttons loosened and their shirts opened out, showing off their hairy chests ('catching a breath of the mountainy air,' they'd shout in across the yard). Then there were the men inside their blue-boarded carts, lolloping their horse's hooves down from The Rebels' Den for their fortnightly trip to Curl 'n' Stripes' granary and their sacks of flour to make their next batches of soda-bread above in

The Hills-of-The-Past. Then there were the ass-and-car day-trippers with their rattling tanks of milk, taking the two miles' trip to the creamery gates – the old men holding onto their hats and the women continuing to curse their asses and laying into them like fair hell with their ash-plants. Then there was the accompanying cawing of the crows in The Rookery, who were by now outmatching the farmyard fowl and the two pigs in their raucous songs. If the child hadn't already been awakened by the laughing smiles of his two old guardians, this constant racket from outside the windowpane would certainly have alarmed his inquisitive little head and drawn him to the geraniums on the windowsill to gaze in wonder at the lively world beckoning him to come out and salute the day.

## The Roadmenders And Red Buckles

On this present morning he found himself greeted by the arrival of the roadmenders and the ditch-trimmers. They were easing their way up by John's Gate. They were armed with their billhooks and axes for trimming the trees and briars. They had their double-sized spades for distributing from the horse-and-cart several heaps of white stones into the potholes made during the previous winter and they were amusing themselves by pelting these stones into the holes from as far back as they could so as to outmatch one another. Leading this little party was Reuben from Temple Stile, whose brown hat was twice the size of anyone else's. It had been handed down to him from his grandfather and his father. And while his comrades (Red Buckles and Gus Gilton) continued their argument with the stones, he was seen putting as much vengeance into his work against Mikey's ditch-side briars as Blue-eyed Jack had done with the aforesaid logs. In contrast, Gus Gilton was wearing his father's grey cap – put on sideways at a rakish angle over one of his ears. He was a man of feather-light fingers that wrapped themselves each night around his red melodion whilst the children stood breathlessly under his bedroom window and wondered open-mouthed at the heavenly music that he drew from his bellows. Last (but by no means least) was the towering figure of Red Buckles. He had vein-stained cheeks on him that were as red as a horseradish and he had an unearthly laugh, so loud and ringing that it carried itself down as far as the metal bridge. Across his shoulder he was carrying his spade like a hunting gun and it was this giant-of-a-man that now came stamping his heavy boots in across Dowager's yard. His head was so high in the air (Teddy was to think in later years) that you'd wonder if he'd ever be able to get in through the half-door.

By now Blue-eyed Jack's logs were well and truly sliced and stacked against the pig-house wall and he was perched at the front table underneath the St. Brigid's cross where he was patiently building a house of cards for his 'little man' (a name he was forever calling Teddy). Suddenly in through the doorway came the heavy hobnails of the giant. 'God save all here!' he roared and he threw his cap on the nail beside the holywater font. Blue-eyed Jack made him a cursory bow and he beckoned him to take a chair and to shove up close to Dowager's fire. With more than a little apprehension he noticed that Red Buckles was holding in his fists a very long reins, which until now had been lying on the upturned ass-and-car abroad in the yard.

'Hand me out that old sow this very minute – and be quick about it!' yelled Red Buckles and the plates on the dresser suddenly shook with fright, for his voice was like a clap of thunder from up in the hills. 'I mean to put a reins round yeer sow's neck and carry her off with me to Fairyland,' said he and he spat into the palm of his fist and he rubbed the spit round and around. If the sow and the gander hadn't already caused Teddy some little discomfort in his britches, the arrival of Red Buckles surely ought to have done. But the brave little fellow instantly forgot his house of cards and he let them fall in a heap on the floor. In an effort to protect their sow he lurched forward and almost knocked the startled Blue-eyed Jack out of his chair. He rushed across the floor and he launched himself at Red Buckles, pummeling his two small fists into the giant's retreating fly-buttons: 'It's our sow! We want our own sow! It's not your sow!" he stammered. And although his choice of words was still somewhat limited, there was no mistaking the child's present statement as to which members of Rookery Rally's establishment were the rightful owners of this particular sow.

'Truly it's a brave little man ye have here,' laughed Red Buckles and all the while he continued to shout back mouthfuls of abuse and defiance at Teddy and to make such an unholy row with his fierce boots that Dowager had to put her two hands over her ears. 'Teddy, avic,' said the giant once more, 'that old sow belongs to me – I'm not leaving this floor till I haul her off with me to Fairyland.' And then he made a great show of dragging himself away from the child's clutches and the unmerciful beating that the tiny fists continued to rain down on him and he went on struggling his huge frame nearer and nearer to the half-door so as to get as far as the pig-house and do his wicked work with the reins.

In case the yard and the road hadn't heard enough noise this morning, the quarrel between the giant and the child was certainly livening up the day. Dowager tried to hide her tear-stained face but she couldn't prevent herself from a fit of silent laughter as she studied Red Buckles and his twirling reins and the look on Teddy's angry face and his manly little efforts to chastise the rascal who had dared come here to steal their sow. Blue-eyed Jack added to the fun by falling on his two knees in an act of solemn prayer: ' For the love of sweet Jesus, don't (I beg you, Red) take away our sow – she's the only one we've got.'

At last Red Buckles made good his escape into the yard and there was a lull in the storm for a minute or two. But then the rascally giant crept back from the pig-house gap and made one final raid in across the floor: 'That sow is not yours – I'm telling you she belongs to me, Teddy!' and he repeated all over again his threats against the harmless creature, who (abroad in her sty) hadn't the foggiest notion how near to disaster her life of happiness was becoming. But like all good sport the mock-battle came at last to an end. Red Buckles, depleted of all energy, took his cap from the nail and he went out over the flagstones, scratching his poll at the bravery of Teddy; he couldn't wait to make his report to Reuben and Gus.

The two of them by now had drained their bottles of milk and had eaten their doorstep sandwiches from the newspaper and had quinched their Woodbine fags. They were sitting on Timmy's stile and eager to devour the giant's latest bit of news. A minute or two later the laughter of the three men could be heard ringing all over the road as they made their way up towards The Hills-of-The-Past. When they reached Sheep's Cross they repeated this little saga to every man and woman they met – how Red Buckles had failed to lure away Teddy's sow with his reins and take her off to Fairyland.

'Becripes! – isn't our Little Englander the almighty man – what sort of small warriors are they sending us from across the waters?" said Moll-the-Man and she smiled and looked up at the sky.

'One day our Little Englander will grow up to wield a tidy pair of fists on him and he'll put every man-jack-of-us hopping off of the walls,' said By-Jiggery and he laughed and he shook his head. From that day onwards this new name ('The Little Englander') was given to Teddy and it would stick to him like glue amongst the people of Rookery Rally.

# Father Chasible And Some Very Sad News

With all the ructions safely out of the way, Dowager got on with her job of tending to the dinner and in half-an-hour she poured from her little skillet pot a feast of floury steaming spuds onto the front-table oilcloth. She ladled out a mug of milk for her two men (the big man and the little man, as she liked to call them). A slice of well-buttered soda-cake with a stretch of sugar on the top was placed before Teddy to help him grow as big as Blue-eyed Jack. Amidst the pealed spuds she added another helping of butter and milk, coupled with little onions or scallions and she mashed it all together to made a fine heap of champ for her little grandson. After he'd eaten his champ and the sugared buttered soda-cake and the big mug of milk he'd be good for absolutely nothing except lying on the ditch at the bottom of the yard and looking like a swollen fox after a fine feed of a hen.

It was Fatty-Matty's turn this week to bring back the skimmed milk and the salted butter from the creamery. Blue-eyed Jack and Teddy would be up and ready for the same journey with the horse-and-cart the following Monday. It was not until Fatty-Matty had dropped the milk-tank down on the flagstones that they heard the reason for the earlier tolling of the church bells: they had signaled someone's death, a fact that Blue-eyed Jack half-suspected all along. But who would have thought that their very own Father Chasible would have come to his sad end at so early a stage of his life? 'Didn't he make a very bad battle out of it?' sighed Dowager. She crossed herself and looked up sadly at the solemn face of Jesus in the Sacred Heart picture with his head to one side as though he was agreeing with her.

Here in Rookery Rally (known to some of the cruder men as the arse of the parish of Copperstone Hollow) the priest was neither loved nor hated – at least by the men. It was little they knew about him and Blue-eyed Jack and others like himself had more than one little thought at the back of their minds. They could forgive a priest for being far too busy to visit the likes of poor scholars (like them) up along the slopes. Hadn't Father Chasible a list of spiritual duties as long as your arm to be doing elsewhere? Every Saturday night there was a queue of chest-thumping women waiting outside his confession-box and they all anxious to pour their few miserable sins into his ears. It was to these poor innocents that he gave out the heftiest of penances – even making one or two of them walk barefoot to the well after hearing what amounted to just one or two little mischievous thoughts of impurity. There was more: hadn't the holy man spent several hours recently overseeing children for their First Holy Communion and their Confirmation? And what was that new-fangled Confraternity of his all about that he had to chair every month? And there was also the reciting of his holy breviary twice a day as he prepared himself for his death – a death he had hoped would come to him some day in the faraway future. Wouldn't all this have kept any priest on his tippy-toes? And at three in the morning (often during the harshest season of the year) he was known to get out of his bed and go and pray over some wretched man's dying breath. To see him at that hour of the night, you'd think he was no better than a poor farmer having to go and drag a newborn lamb from a ewe's belly.

But as kindhearted as Blue-eyed Jack always was, he had a further thought (may God forgive him!) sticking in the back of his mind. Father Chasible had always been ready to perform a few extra little duties among those who had a few spare sovereigns in their purse. In the company of these fine gentlemen he was seen to be as busy as a dancing master, saying his Masses for the souls of their ancestors and comforting their sick sons and daughters and putting in an appearance at their christening parties in their big houses and getting them to write letters to their kinfolk in The Land of The Silver Dollar so that they'd send back a bit of money now and then for the sake of the church and the altar. 'That (said Blue-eyed Jack to himself) is what wore poor Father Chasible away –chasing after a great number of imaginary rainbows that could do nothing for his soul – and may God be merciful to him.' The big man bowed his head and he said a short prayer for the holy man and he kept forever these irksome little thoughts firmly rooted in the deep caverns of his mind in case his mother would follow him out the door with her yard-brush and tan his backside for him.

# *How Did It Happen?*

No-one except Doctor Glasses and Molly-the-Housekeeper knew that Father Chasible had had a very weak heart for many years and had been given a mild stroke only two years before – the time he was said to be off on one of those mysterious Retreats to Mount Monastery down in Waterford. This very morning and as soon as he had finished saying Mass he went off riding his mare (Bessy) up towards Scenery Corner. He'd be back within the hour and sitting in his leather armchair in front of the fire with a warm glass of brandy in his fist – at least that's what he thought. But the sun was fiercely glistening into the mare's eyes and it caused her to give a few little dance-steps in the air and it startled the poor priest in his saddle. Suddenly he felt a fierce pain in his chest and without so much as a cough or a sneeze he fell headlong from the mare. The paving stones outside Bill-the-Bear's yard sprang up like a lump of iron in front of his eyes and they struck him on his skull and killed him on the spot.

On hearing this terrible news Tom-the-bell-ringer and his two sons took the pony-and-trap up to Bill-the-Bear's cabin. They found the settle-bed laid out on the floor and Father Chasible already stretched out underneath the blankets and the quilts. The reality that their poor priest was dead hit them in the face and their mood was as dark as an old slate, so much had the three of them loved him. They managed to haul him up onto the pony-and-trap and, almost forgetting to say thank-you to Bill-the-Bear, they made a slow and careful retreat down to the corpse-house. Molly-the-Housekeeper and her two daughters rushed out on the road to greet the three men and they thanked them for bringing the corpse back to the priest-house and they gently (but quickly) banished them from their sight. They were soon as busy as bees, for they too had loved Father Chasible excessively and no corpse was ever going to look grander than their holy man. They removed his day-clothes and they dressed him up in his starched linen alb and they wrapped the white girdle around him and they pressed his false teeth carefully back into his mouth to get rid of his surprised gaping-jaw appearance. He still had his crisp wavy hair but his face had the look of a sick lemon and Molly's daughters rubbed a little of their own face-powder on his cheeks (just the faintest deft touch) to give him a youthful look. For the next hour they continued to work on him. Finally they covered him with his best green chasible. They placed by his side the chalice that his mother had bought him the day of his ordination. Next morning they'd give him their last goodbye kiss when Tom came to nail down the lid of the coffin and they'd place a couple of shiny coppers over his eyes.

The rest of the women would be just as grief-stricken when they came across the fields to view the corpse and pay their final homage. Of course our men were always perplexed and saddened by a death (anybody's death) but it was the women (they said) who put on the long gloomy faces when a priest died and before the hour was up a crowd of them would be bursting in along the priest's yard and crying their eyes out like a bunch of defeated Trojans.

To see this had always brought out the bitter side in some of our men. Every blessed Sunday they saw their wives making a beeline up the aisle to get to the statues of Saint Patrick and Saint Francis. The saints' plaster toes were worn away from their kisses. Would you ever see a single man (said the men) getting up to such tomfoolery and kissing the feet (albeit a saint's) of another mortal man? And now, with the priest barely laid out in his coffin, it wasn't long before the first batch of women reached the door of the priest's house and lost their hearts when they looked down at the holy man's mortal remains. It was as plain as the nose on your face (said one or two of the men) that they were half-in-love with Father Chasible and not with their own man at home. And there was a good deal of head-nodding when the men recalled their wives' looks of mortification at Mass and how they had relished those tongue-lashing sermons when Father Chasible had chipped away at their souls and had whipped them up into a frenzy with the thoughts of hell's fiery furnace waiting for them if they didn't renege from their apparent sinfulness. Undoubtedly he had been a man gifted in chastising any acts of transgression with the greatest of thunder, hadn't he? And again – Dowager and her yard-brush (and the women like her) would have been called into play if these secret dark thoughts of some of the men were ever to be broadcast too loudly around the place.

As a rule our men never liked looking into the eyes of a dead man – their own death might come soon enough. And now they stayed abroad in the priest's yard and they knelt on their caps and they said their rosary, their fingers running absentmindedly through each of the beads. But little by little they began to re-write their priest's history-book for him and to give him at least some bit of credit where it was due. They recalled the way he used to dart across the fields when he first arrived here from Clare and how he blessed their crops of potatoes and their cabbages and turnips and their trams of hay. They remembered how he blessed their farmyard implements like their scythes and their rakes and their pitchforks when himself and his basket of eggs (and he singing like a boy) came riding home on Bessy from The Hills-of-The-Past after hearing old Gentility's innocent confession and absolving her from her invisible sins.

## Blue-Eyed Jack Does The Gentlemanly Thing

'I'd better do the gentlemanly thing and get myself ready and take Teddy across to the corpse-house,' said Blue-eyed Jack to Dowager. He quietly tiptoed into The Big Cave Room to check the roadworthy state of his bike and to put the rack through his hair in front of the broken bit of looking-glass. He was not looking forward one bit to this godforsaken journey, for he knew there'd be moaning and groaning throughout the parish for the next week-and-a-half.

Dowager washed Teddy's face, especially behind his ears. She dressed him in his grey Sunday shirt and his corduroy trousers – the ones his mother had recently posted from across the sea. Around his white socks she buckled on his brown sandals. The Little Englander would look like a prince among men if she was to have her way. In the meantime Blue-eyed Jack was out in the yard and wrapping the child's old blue jersey around the handlebars of the bike so that he could sit there comfortably for as much of the journey as he could bear. By the time they'd get half-ways to the corpse-house his little backside would be aching from the hardness of the handlebars.

Dowager showered the two of them with holywater from her font and they set off with the rest of the parish to pay their respects to their dead priest. Blue-eyed Jack cycled down to Kindy's Post Office and along The Creamery Road and over to Matt-the-Gatemaker's hayshed. By now his little nephew was getting sore and fidgety and the big man lifted him down from the handlebars and he threw his bike into the ditch. He placed Teddy on his shoulders for the rest of the way. Like any child lucky enough to be sitting seven feet up in the air Teddy had a majestic view of the hills and the pine forests of Lisnagorna and he could soon feel the boiling heat coming out of Blue-eyed Jack's body. From Matt's hayshed it was half-a-mile to the village corpse-house. Blue-eyed Jack took a shortcut across Hartigan's Thistle Field and it wasn't long before the steam was hopping off of his forehead and his two old shoulderblades were aching like blazes. They reached the grotto of Our Blessed Lady where he dropped Teddy down.

Together the two-men-of-us walked around the black-stoned Protestant Church and they stopped outside the corpse-house. In front of them The Copperstone Mountains gleamed like a huge wheat-field and a few chalky clouds skated across the sky towards Limerick. The quiet people outside the priest's gate had the darkness of crows about them and they looked at the two new arrivals with vacant stares. One or two of the older men from our own Rookery Rally nodded at Blue-eyed Jack and they smiled at The Little Englander. Inside the gate and on the gravel yard Teddy saw a group of men on their knees and they earnestly beating their chests and praying for the repose of their priest's soul. Molly-the-Housekeeper had a box of apples. With great abandonment she was handing the apples out to the children, who (like Teddy) had come to gaze on the face of Father Chasible for the last time and pay him their humble respects. The older women (too feeble to get down on their knees) sat on chairs along the outside wall. A few of them took delicate little pinches of snuff, which was an excuse for them to dab at their red eyes with their wadded handkerchiefs.

## Teddy And The Death-Room

Blue-eyed Jack took Teddy by the hand. They tiptoed shyly in through the hall doorway where the big man shook the hand of Tom-the-bell-ringer in commiseration. The death-room's walls were recently whitewashed and had no adornment. The bed on top of which the coffin was resting was a single iron one and behind it on the wall there was a large crucifix. There was one narrow low-lying widow for the daylight to peep in and a score of blessed candles had been lit all around the coffin to drive away Satan and his wicked spirits. There was a hushed and troubled silence in all four corners of the room and all that could be heard was the ticking of the hall clock and the occasional howling of Father Chasible's distraught little dog.

Blue-eyed Jack gripped Teddy firmly by the hand in case the sight of a dead man might frighten him. As with all things incredibly new, the little boy was intrigued by what he was seeing for the first time and he couldn't keep his eyes off of the dead priest. Molly and her two daughters had done a grand job (thought Blue-eyed Jack) in the way they had combed Father Chasible's glossy black hair straight back off of his forehead and allowed his face to dominate. The holy man had a serene smile on his face and the formality of his long white alb and his green chasible with the chalice beside him was every bit as clean and pure as the whitewashed walls. Teddy could see how the green-yellow fingers of the priest clasped his mother's well-worn rosary-beads and how his face (in spite of the dabs of rouge) seemed yellower than the wax on the candles. The dead man was propped up in his coffin amid the lily-white bed-coverings and Teddy, not knowing the meaning of a man's death and never having witnessed it before, half-expected him to sit up in that great big box and wave him goodbye. Blue-eyed Jack bent down and he whispered into the child's ear: 'Father Chasible is now in his long last sleep but his soul is wide awake and it has gone to live with God above in the clouds of heaven.' Whether the little boy understood a single word of this explanation is anybody's guess.

## Out In The Parlour

The two of them came out into the parlour where the little man was given his second apple of the day. Perched on a small stool in the corner he looked at the men steadfastly drinking their whiskey out of mugs and attempting to drive away their sorrow with a faraway look in their eyes. Up and down and up and down again went their Adam's apple like the handle of the pump at Abbey Acres. A death like this was one of the few good chances they'd get to escape from the women and put a few sly drinks in under their belts. Teddy could hear the rest of the men in the yard getting stuck into the final decade of the rosary. In between his own solemn sips of whiskey Blue-eyed Jack said 'Amen' and he finished his whiskey and led Teddy out and he knelt on his cap in the yard for the last few prayers. The child imitated his uncle and he knelt down beside him and he hit his chest with his fist whenever he saw the rest of the men doing it.

'Ah, the poor priest, (thought Blue-eyed Jack to himself) he is in a far better place than this – gone to greener pastures no doubt.' As always, a second thought took hold of him and he looked down at his little nephew by his side and he felt that the child also was in a far far better place than he'd have ever known if he had stayed back in England in the bombed-out streets of London when he was born and that the pastures here in Rookery Rally were far greener for him where no bombs or flying bits of masonry would ever prevail against him – a wonderful and fresh-springing life for any child on earth, thank God.

He shook himself back to life and remembered that his seven cows would soon have to be milked. He hurried out the gate and once more he lifted Teddy back up onto his shoulders. As he stepped along the road he was wrapped in a reflective silence. He was thinking what a sad old thing death was. They reached Matt-the-Gatekeeper's hayshed where he placed Teddy back on the handlebars of the bike and he pedaled on towards Abbey Cross. From there he'd have to push his bike uphill for the rest of the way home.

# That Evening

Later that evening Tom-the-bell-ringer and his two sons were given a bottle of whiskey and told not to come back till they had drank the last drop. They took their pickaxes and their shovels and they hurried over to the graveyard where one or two other lively men came and joined them in digging the priest's grave and to get their lips around the bottle of whiskey. Winter was not long gone and the ground in March was as hard as bell-metal and they had to use tremendous force with the pickaxes to get themselves started. It was hot and thirsty work and soon the bottle was half-empty. They took a few last swigs at it before jumping down into the half-made grave where they tackled the rest of the work with a renewed burst of energy. They'd been ordered to make the grave at least six feet deep so that the rats from Lord Elegance's lake wouldn't take it into their little heads to scurry out on future nights and annoy Father Chasible.

Meanwhile inside in Merrymouth's drinking-shop the rest of the men were seated on half-a-dozen trestles and wooden barrels and the place was filled with the smell of tobacco and stale sweat. There was a good deal of revelry and light-hearted music as they drank the health of the priest who'd be down in the ground next day. They couldn't have a proper wake in the priest's own house – it'd be talked of as nothing less than a sacrilege. Hammer-the-Smith and Gus Gilton (our two best melodion players) were on hand. The blind man (known as 'The Captain') was there to recite his own homemade songs. The Jug-Pussers and their riotous gob-music and paper-and-comb polkas were also a handy show. There was plenty of the 'holywater', namely the rawgut potheen that Merrymouth had cunningly mixed in with his bottles of whiskey. He poured it repeatedly into their bubbling glasses and it put them all in the best of humour for the rest of the evening. Their happy faces seemed to glow as the whiskey gurgled pleasurably down their throats and warmed their chests and hummed its way into their veins. They felt its hot sting and they smacked their lips and they tasted it with the tip of their tongues. It wasn't often that a priest died on them and they couldn't wait to see another holy man meet his death and give them the same great chance of having a proper pull at Merrymouth's mighty medicine.

# The Grey Daylight

It was a grey and spine-chilling morning that heralded in the next day – the day of the priest's burial. Misty clouds hung over The Copperstone Mountains, matching the frowning mood of the funeral, and a few spatters of rain fell on the trees and the bushes. Molly and her two daughters had been up since dawn, spending the time helping the funeral undertaker (Tim Clever) to deal with the coffin. They covered up any little gaps in the sides with pitch and stiff paper before fastening on the rolls of white satin with brass ornamental pins. The three women were worn to a thread. 'In his fine clothes and his satin-lined coffin we're going to send him up decently to meet his Maker,' they sighed. Then Tim and Molly smothered the coffin with fresh flowers (the dew still in their cups) and Tim's helpers took the coffin across to the church and they lifted it onto the trestles and they waited for the pallbearers and the mourners to assemble.

The priests arrived in their big black motorcars. They were more numerous than crows in a cornfield. They had come in from all over the county and as far back as The Mighty Shannon River and from Father Chasible's own native Clare. They sat in their serried ranks of importance with Bishop High-Hat and the monsignors and canons (with their ruddy well-fed faces and noses) all seated above in the front pews and the parish priests and the other clergy placed in behind them. They were dressed in somber black suits and they wore topcoats of sable serge. There was scarcely a woman to be seen – except for Father Chasible's saintly mother, who was weeping silently and with dignity. After all, it was a man's job to be seen burying the dead.

It was not until the following Sunday that a formal Mass was to be said for the holy man's soul. But inside in the dimly-lit church he was about to be canonized by Bishop High-Hat and the leading clergy, all of whom remembered him in his youth and prime. For a good quarter-of-an-hour they sang his praises and then they sat back and listened to the Latin motets being played by the village schoolmistress (Biddy Hollow) on the droning organ. A moment of silence followed, broken at last by the trembling hum of a solitary church bell in the steeple, its monotonous echo dying away across the fields as it was being pulled by the distraught Tom-the-bell-ringer.

The coffin was taken out and down the steps of the church. The chauffeur (Murty Horan) turned the hearse around in the direction of Father Chasible's final resting-place. The undertakers lifted the coffin into the car and the engine started up with a little tremor as Murty prodded the accelerator. The long sad cavalcade rolled respectfully out the church gates and the flowers shivered on top of the hearse. The funeral proceeded at a dirge-pace down the main street where house curtains were closed as a mark of respect. Mothers and their subdued babies came out to mutter a sincere and silent amen and the toddler who had been chasing the chickens peered out from under the bars of the gate. Old men (too feeble to follow) put away their pipes and they took off their hats and they bowed their heads and they blessed themselves. Men and their bikes followed along behind the cars and those who had no bikes brought up the tail-end of the procession and they walked along in silence.

Showered yet again with Dowager's holywater, the two-men-of-us headed down The Open Road. Teddy was excited to be off on yet another day's adventure and he held on tightly to a small bunch of flowers given to him by his grandmother. A few confused clouds lurked above the tall trees, not yet sure of their intent this morning. By the time they reached Ducks 'n' Drakes' cowshed the child's little legs were giving out on him and once more the shoulders of his uncle came in handy to climb up onto.

Reaching Abbey Cross they saw the hearse coming at a snail's pace along The Creamery Road towards the creaking gate that led into the graveyard. Almost motionless the procession made its way in along the avenue and across the stream. Blue-eyed Jack lifted Teddy down and, holding him by the hand, they pushed their way through the crowd. The child could see that today was different from other days – there were no loud shouts like you'd hear from a line of creamery carts every morning of the week when men's voices rang crystal-clear across the fields and valleys. Tom's tolling of the church-bell had ceased and there was a hushed and respectful sibilance as the mourners sought for an unaccustomed eloquence in their memories of the priest. Their stories were soon embroidered and some recalled Father Chasible's childhood and youth. Others remembered him at the hurling matches in Limerick when his face was red and sweaty from shouting and encouraging on his team. A few remembered his days as a fisherman above in Growl River and his sharpshooting of the grouse and pheasants alongside Lord Elegance. They all agreed – their priest was 'a tough yoke' and 'a grand bit of a man'.

Once inside the graveyard, Monsignor O'Reymus and his dour composure was to take charge of the burial obsequies. His purple stoll dripped down from his shoulders and his baretta hat was firmly fixed to his head. Teddy's eyes were captivated by the sheer height of the men towering above him and the look on their gloomy faces. He felt very small indeed and their hugeness frightened him much more than the priest in his coffin the previous evening. And then he saw the dark hole in the ground into which the priest was to be lowered and he was glad that he had Blue-eyed Jack's hand to hold on to.

The slow-moving crowd edged their way under the avenue's dusky trees and the surrounding ravens flapped their wings as though they were guarding the grave. Everyone was shuffling along to the graveside and even the older priests had stepped out of their cars and their boots crunched the gravel and kept up a trudging rhythm. Across the fence and poking out across the pastureland was the mansion of Lord Elegance and Lady Acceptable. His spacious lake was full of fat ducks and graceful swans and they paid not a blind bit of heed to the burial proceedings but glided along majestically and looked down at their reflections in the water.

This was a strange place for a small child to find himself in – a spot where countless tombstones filled the four corners of the graveyard, among them the spot where Dowager had buried Teddy's grandfather (Handsome Johnnie). He couldn't take his eyes away from the coffin. The priest's body (a mystery to him) was inside in that great big box and beside it walked the priest's mother and her hand was resting on the lid of the coffin.

The death and burial of Father Chasible was to be one of many new mysteries forcing their way into his daily life – the fact that the priest had been running around like himself only the day before yesterday and had been riding on top of his mare (Bessy) only a few hours ago and that he was now but a silent ghost and not a man anymore. Maybe (whispered Blue-eyed Jack in his ear) the dead priest was looking down on them from the clouds in the sky. Maybe his guardian angel was keeping a watchful eye on the small hole in the ground where his dead bones were about to be laid. An hour from now (he thought to himself) the shovels would be put away and the flowers would wither and crunch into powder and all this paraphernalia would cease until the next priest came to die. Father Chasible was now (he thought) just a light little breeze above them in the early morning light.

The mourners came as close as they could to the grave. They took off their hats and they bowed their heads. Blue-eyed Jack nudged Teddy forward with his little bunch of flowers to a place where they'd get a better view of the grave. The pallbearers gave way to Tom-the-bell-ringer and he and his sons passed the ropes underneath the coffin and they slowly released them and the coffin fell down onto the fresh earth with a soft thud. Monsignor O'Reymus stepped forward and, choosing a number of carefully opaque phrases to suit the holy mood of the day, he gave a suitable laudation and reminded the crowd that they'd one day meet their death like the good priest and that (like him) they'd all rise up again on The Day of Judgment. He sprinkled holywater down on the lid of the coffin and he handed the sprinkler to Father Chasible's mother to do the same. Tom threw his tear-soaked handkerchief into the grave and this seemed to be a signal for some children to come forward and throw their flowers down on top of their priest. Like the other children Teddy threw his bunch of flowers in also. The flowers deadened the sound of the stones and the clods of earth when Tom and his sons furiously started shoveling in the earth. The grave (thought Teddy) was a long way down. What was it (thought Blue-eyed Jack) but another scooped-out slit in the ground for each of us to fall into one day when we'd eventually come and be greeted by the men with the shovels and spades. Teddy looked on and saw that as the earth began to fill up, the grave began to look like any other patch of earth – except that Father Chasible was lying underneath the clay. And all the while the tall trees around the graveyard seemed to be shivering and their branches seemed to be careening forwards over the tombstones. The bright flowers were brought from the hearse and strewn on top of the fresh earth and then the shovels and spades were put to rest. The silent crows now flapped their wings amongst the long shadows of the tombstones and they flew away and they shook their raucous music from their throats once more. The crystal stream at the avenue entrance, which had seemed to stop flowing, now continued on its brawling way to join its own inevitable fate in The Mighty Shannon River. The parish had paid its dues to Father Chasible and the crowd began to struggle out the gate. A tiny robin, flushed with new life, flew back behind them and she perched herself on top of the grave, to feast and gorge on the new tasty worms.

## Time To Escape From It All

'Let the two-men-of-us go home,' murmured Blue-eyed Jack. In his haste to escape so sad a scene and to give Dowager all the news he forgot that he was walking too fast and when he looked back he saw Teddy dragging his struggling legs along after him and he whisked him up on his shoulders. All the priests' cars would soon be scurrying off to the priest-house where Molly and her daughters had a bit of a feast laid on and where Merrymouth had brought in a dozen bowls of hot punch to celebrate the return of the holy man's soul to God. By mid-afternoon the clergy would all be wobbling around on their chairs like saucers on sticks and Father Chasible would be forgotten.

Long before the two adventurers reached the cobbled yard Dowager had her ears pinned back. She'd been waiting and wondering and she sensed their coming even before they got as far as John's Gate. 'Well,' said she, as they entered the Welcoming Room and took off their coats, 'did ye give the poor man a decent burial?'

'Aye, faith – we buried him as good as any noble pope," said Blue-eyed Jack. 'Never in all my life were so many people crowded into one single space.' And before he could get an extra word in, Teddy burst out with 'I threw your bunch of flowers down on top of the coffin, didn't I, Jack?'

'You did very well, my child," said his grandmother, patting him on the head. And for the next half-hour she was inquisitiveness itself as she badgered Blue-eyed Jack with question after question (she always had her ears cocked into the wind for any bit of strange news). 'God rest his soul,' she said and her grey eyes clouded over for just a moment and then she got herself busy as though that was to be the last Amen to the funeral of Father Chasible.

## Evening And The Three Souls

After all the hustle and bustle of the day there was still some of the daylight left for the three of them to get a bit of peace and quiet. Teddy sat on his penny-stool and he listened to the sound of his grandmother's clicketty-clacketty boots scraping back and forth across the floor and he watched the way she waddled her backside like an old drake when she walked. He watched her turning over her soda-cake in the burner and inspecting it. Her gnarled fingers were hard and almost black and they never got burnt from the heat of the fire. With an air of triumph she rolled out the soda-cake onto the table oilcloth and Blue-eyed Jack cut the bread into thick slices with his sharp black-handled knife and he layered his bread thickly with butter and he covered Teddy's slice with the sugar. Dowager returned to her blackened canister on the fire, in which she had placed three eggs between a triangle of twigs. Fearlessly she put her fingers in through the flames and she took out the eggs when they were done.

Her little grandson listened to the fire's embers hissing and sizzling merrily. He could smell the whitethorn logs amid the turf-sods. He peered forward from his stool and he looked up the chimney to get a glimpse of the daylight that would soon die in the sky. He had forgotten all about the funeral of Father Chasible. Snug and warm beside the fire and his toes in the ashes, he was thinking of the cards that Dowager and Blue-eyed Jack would play when they finished their tea and the chance he'd get to lay out his own long line of miniature cards (the ace of hearts and the king and the queen and the knave) in all their beautiful colours. Their newness never failed to leave an imprint on him. The two candles were lit and they burned brightly on the front and back tables. Dowager cleaned the oil-lamp's glass bulb with a wad of brown paper. She turned up the wick and its light shone gloriously and spread out like the wings of a great big butterfly around the four walls. The beetles ran out from the logs and turf-sods in under the stool and they ran races across the floor. Dowager ran after them and she stamped them to death.

The rain outside came in suddenly from Kerry and it started raging in the yard. The hens and their ruffled feathers got a good soaking and they raced in under the eaves of the thatch and they set up an incessant cackling of alarm as the yard became flooded with torrents of russet rainwater. Teddy ran to the half-door and he stood on the bottom lat, his nose barely reaching the top board. Blue-eyed Jack lifted him up so that he could gaze across the yard and see the rain's little rivers. The sky (thought Blue-eyed Jack to himself) was offering its own tearful ending to this day of the funeral. The holly-bushes and the ivy and the pig-house fuchsias and the budding spring flowers in Dowager's tiny garden drank in the downpour and the battering raindrops clung in lines on Dowager's windowpanes and they gurgled their way around the little waterfall down near the rusty blue kettle.

But an hour later the dancing sunshine unraveled and it sliced its way across the sky's charcoal and it forced the rain to go and hide and the world started laughing again. The sheep and the cattle started bawling and the older children, who had been trapped inside and hunched over their fires, came twisting out from their half-doors and they shouted their relief and they ran across the haggart's late evening light and they climbed up into the nearest apple-tree.

Returning from the half-door, the big man and the little man joined Dowager and they silently ate their eggs and soda-cake and salty butter. The old woman smiled at her two men (her glow was always present) and then

Blue-eyed Jack wound up the gramophone and he took out the records (worn and scratched) from the bacon-box. Dowager stopped what she was doing and she listened attentively to the throbbing music. Whenever a new silver needle was required Teddy handed one to his uncle from the shiny tin box. Beautiful pictures flooded out from the turntable and they landed themselves inside in the heart of The Old Pair. Like the little white dog on the rotating label Teddy had his nose cocked almost inside the speaker and at the end of each record he clapped his tiny hands and he laughed happily and he picked out another record and handed it to Blue-eyed Jack.

## Time For A Toddler And His Bed

The clock on the dresser never stopped ticking. It was time for Dowager to march Teddy to the enamel pan where she washed his face and ears and the two sides of his hands and his fingernails and his legs too (especially the front and back of his knees). She brought him back to the fire and she knelt down between himself and Blue-eyed Jack on the cold floor. Together they said The Blessing Prayers, the little boy echoing his grandmother's words, and they included a solemn prayer for the cantankerous ass (The Lightning Whoor). Dowager gave Teddy the holywater on his forehead and she directed his fingers into making the sign-of-the-cross and she vowed she would make a solid saint out of him one day soon.

Blue-eyed Jack and Teddy stole out into the haggart where they made their rivers of poolie in the ash-pit at Timmy's ditch. It was cold out here and the big man sighed and shivered as he took a last look at the dimly-visible hills that sloped up towards the mysterious moon that seemed to penetrate the pine-trees of Lisnagorna and skip through the ragged clouds like a stray calf. How small are we mortals, he thought to himself, and his mind went back to Father Chasible. He brought Teddy back to his grandmother and he closed the wooden casement shutters for the night and he bolted the front door as well as the half-door. He turned down the lamp and The Welcoming Room grew remote and looked a little sad. The spiders in their corner webs held their breath before starting their night's work.

Dowager took the candle. She led Teddy by the hand into The Big Cave Room with its gloomy darkness and its smell of dankness and mildew. Except during his first year of infancy, he had always slept here with his uncle in the great big bed with the brass reindeers running across it. He'd place his little legs inside Blue-eyed Jack's legs ('Put your doggies in the nest,' his uncle would say) and the two of them would get warm and snug underneath their five blankets and they'd sleep the sleep of two fireside cats with their arms wrapped round each other to end their day. Dowager rested her candle on the tea-chest lid beside the empty fireplace with its laurel bushes and dying bees and she helped Teddy get up and hop into bed. The flame of her candle made a spattered fan all around the room. Her shadow loomed large on the wall beside the bed. The little boy closed his eyes as though he were asleep, a ritual they both liked to play. His grandmother fretted and fussed over him and she wrapped his limbs in tightly under the cold blankets. He nestled his head into the bolster and she piled the blankets up around his shivering ears. 'Are you warm enough?' she said and she told him to rub his feet together as hard as he could. He would soon be melting with the heat from all the blankets, she told him. She bent down and she gave him an embarrassing little hug and, with Blue-eyed Jack nowhere to be seen, she brushed his cheek with a shy little kiss. She tiptoed out the door, whispering to herself (thinking of the death of poor Father Chasible) 'Doctor, doctor, must I die?' – 'indeed you must and so must I'. She knew that after such an eventful day as the priest's funeral and with the sound of the breeze brushing monotonously against the back windowpane, Teddy would soon be lulled into utter oblivion and she smiled to herself. She left a red candle in a jam-jar on the mantelshelf and Teddy (if he kept his eyes open) could see above the jam-jar the picture of the pope's wine-red vestments. He could see the pope's face and finally his reading-glasses. If he screwed up his ears he could hear through the panels of the door the light laughter of his grandmother and uncle and the voices that he daily imbibed into his soul as they exchanged in undertones the last dregs of the day's gossip.

He would soon be three but he could still not get used to the dark and he was afraid. He closed his eyes to block out everything but he felt the room turning alive with its ghosts and witches and those cruel fiends (like The Boodeeman), whom the visiting card-players filled his ears with whenever they came in and sat around the fire. He said another little prayer to himself and then another one and another one in the hope that the little red candle wouldn't flicker out. In his half-sleep he entered his nightly world of Wonderland where he dreamt he had died and that he was lying in a big box alongside the priest. Vast crowds and their long sad faces were following close behind him and several yellow candles surrounded him as he was carried along the avenue towards the grave. But his head grew too tired to dream anymore and his young mind was as black as the blackest bag and like any young fish or bird he was soon sound asleep.

Dusk had crept in from The Mighty Mountain and had settled on the little farm. "Oh, honey-o, it's a bothering life!" sighed the weary Dowager. Blue-eyed Jack saw how tired his mother was and he gave her a dash of holywater and he handed her the green copper candlestick. He warmed up a hot jar of water to warm her backside in the bed and she crept off like a ghost towards her little box-room. Presently he heard her bed creaking as she lay down and turned herself round and around till she found the most comfortable spot to sleep in. The big man spread out the burnt embers of the fire with the tongs. He spread the ashes over the fire with his boot and he threw a few mugs of spring-water on the separated embers to quinch them. He wound up his pocket-watch and he turned out the lamp and he took the candle into The Big Cave Room. His spluttering candle-flame flared upright around the rafters and along the wall next to the hen-house, throwing up its shuddering shadows. He placed the candle on top of the tea-chest lid and he slipped out of his trousers and said a few whispering prayers to himself. In his shirt he crept in beside the sleeping child and the flames' tendrils had a sharp smell when he blew the candle out. He held the child's warm body close to his own. He could feel Teddy's heart beating and, like his mother and his little nephew, he himself soon collapsed in sleep.

## *Life And Death Had Now Shaken Hands*

The day of the funeral was the beginning of Teddy's life and a landmark he'd always remember, for until this very day he had known nothing of the difference between a man that was alive and a man that was dead. Father Chasible had met his death this week and Tom's funeral bells had tolled out their sad news yesterday and the mourners had said their farewells this morning. In contrast, it seemed as though the child himself had been born this very day – something to recapture in years to come. All around him stood the old men and women of the hills, who would leave their stamp on him. They were the grey shoots indissolubly joined to Dowager and Blue-eyed Jack and the little farm. And though his two guardians were at the very centre of a rippling pool and sent out rings of love around him each day of his life, these old folk too would walk around him protectively and keep guard over their Little Englander.

The previous unsteadiness of his infancy finally slipped away from him this springtime. In its place grew this little man. He was as yet unable to take his unaided adventurous footsteps out onto The Open Road where one day he would sport and play with the other children and the whole world would start to move in a new rhythm for him. The cockerels would crow in other farmyards and barndoors would slam in other yards and Rookery Rally would take The Little Englander to its hearts as they witnessed him growing stronger and stronger in mind and body. This night of the funeral, as he lay in his bed of straw, wood and iron (like the cow's calf in the manger) it was his task to live life to the full and do nothing except walk the fertile earth with Dowager and Blue-eyed Jack – far away from the war and the wrath of Germany – for the good of his young soul. The brass reindeers ran across the foot of his bed and the pope in the picture kept watch over his little nest. The child's heart was beating faster than ever and the blood was flowing merrily in his veins.

# FOUR

## *Gentility*

*When Dowager took Teddy
on his very first outing
across the fields
to see Gentility.*

It was the Summertime of 1943. 'Get up! Get up! Get up! I say'. Dowager nudged her little grandson from underneath his five blankets. 'Look out the window, Teddy. The sun's fat ball is already shooting its way in over the holly-bush and it'll soon be as big as a haystack.' She was always like that – herself and her big words. It was the month of May and Dowager was in a reflective mood. How grand it was (she thought wistfully to herself) to see once more the trees around her yard and her stream all bearded with green leafy buds and for once in her life to be looking up at those soft white clouds skipping across the clear blue sky from Kerry. Today was Monday morning and it was the day on which the women in Rookery Rally did their washing. Dowager had a number of sheets to deal with as well as the two white shirts that Blue-eyed Jack and Teddy wore on Sunday. She'd give her sheets and in particular those two shirts more than a dab of the Ricketts' blue and she'd make sure that her two men would shine like a pair of brass candlesticks. In spite of Teddy forever running around her black skirts and tripping over her boots and stopping her from her work, she was bent on decorating the bushes in the haggart with all the morning's washing (her old calico bloomers as well) before Blue-eyed Jack returned from the creamery and with the help of the sun she'd have the clothes all dried and taken in for ironing in no time.

# A Bright May Morning

This month of May was a generous one. It was a time for young lambs to finally make their way out from their sheds and leap all over the daisy-fields. It was a time for an old woman like herself to put on her best black boots and give them a good airing on the slippery slopes of Timmy's Field. It would be Tuesday tomorrow and she would follow her instincts and go off on one of her rambles as far as her old friend (Gentility). She would not go empty-handed; she would take Gentility a basket of duck-eggs and maybe she'd fill that same basket with a pile of cooking-apples as big as her fist and bring home the rusty bottom of her old friend's worn-out creamery tank, which she'd had her eye on for some time past. She'd give it to Teddy and he could use it as a bowlee-wheel and frighten the ducks and the hens (and maybe the sow and the gander) as he belted it round and around the yard with his stick.

# Gentility

The children in Rookery Rally called Gentility 'The White Lady' because of her snow-white hair and she lived in The Narrow Lane a stone-throw behind Fort Dangerous. Herself and Dowager had sat side-by-side sixty years ago when the school-house in Copperstone Hollow had first opened its doors and Whiskery Bob and his musical wife (old Biddy McCool) had welcomed them in and taught them to make the cambric shirt and to recite those long poems like 'The Ancient Mariner' and 'The Lady of Shallott'. Since that day they had become the best of friends and had always shared the little secrets of their uncomplicated lives. When they were children they shared the same spring-well. Their two thatched cabins lay in the same little haggart where they played their childhood games and lived each day like a pair of pet goats tied together. In that same haggart they had had their birth and continued to grow, knowing from second to second what the other one was thinking. Even now in their twilight years their souls were joined across the green spaces between their Welcoming Rooms and Dowager was as excited as a hen with an egg to be taking tomorrow's jaunt. It would also be an eventful journey for another reason; for it would not be too strenuous for Teddy to trot off behind her and develop his fragile legs like a little piggy running after its mother; it would give him the chance to take his first-ever walk across Timmy's Field and make further use of his two good eyes and stare at the great variety of newness that Nature would offer him on such a long walk and which May-time always brought in with her.

## Blue-Eyed Jack Was As Busy As A Gnat

Tuesday came in quicker than a dance-step. Blue-eyed Jack greeted it by being as busy as a gnat. He went out across the haggart singletree to fetch and milk his seven cows even before the earliest lark rose over the cowshed or the sun's early morning light got a chance to take the dew out of the grass. It was his task this week to take his horse-and-cart to the creamery in Copperstone Hollow with his own tank of fresh milk and the two tanks belonging to Fatty-Matty and Free 'n' Easy and to bring back the skimmed milk and the pound of salted butter.

He finished his milking and he made a beeline for The Open Road. It would be hard to keep up with him this bright May morning for among all the horses in Rookery Rally his mare (Moll) had the finest pair of legs on her and you'd give your two eyes to be looking at her. With not even a cup of tea to wet his lips the big man had soon raced her out passed The Kill and The Abbey Cross Post Office and had reached the front of The Creamery Road procession. In his wake and struggling vainly to match his speed was a pack of ass-and-cars and horse-and-carts on this jingly two-mile journey to the creamery gates. The younger lads had their caps on back-to-front or at a sideways rakish angle and they were always putting on a great big show – standing up in the carts in between the reins that restricted their shining tanks and belting (needlessly) into the backs of their asses or horses with cruel blows of their ash-plants.

Dowager knew that in an hour or two her son would be home and sorting out the three milk tanks. Then he'd take The Lightning Whoor up to Sheep's Cross to get himself a new pair of ass-shoes at Hammer-the-Smith's forge. The old devil had cut his front knees once too often as a result of his worn-out shoes and he had started slipping and sliding all over the road whenever he was carted up for her to make the trip to Curl 'n' Stripes' shop for her pound of sausages and the sack of flour. By now you'd swear he was kneeling down to say his morning prayers and he had become a pure laughing-stock in the eyes of everybody.

Dowager knew that visiting Hammer-the-Smith's forge was a job Blue-eyed Jack loved better than anything – listening to the roars of the bellows and the cling-clang of a piece of metal on the anvil and the hissing of his ass's new shoes as they were dropped into the cauldron of water. He couldn't help smirking when he pictured The Lightning Whoor and a shiny new pair of shoes on him. When the old demon got back home, wouldn't any lady-ass roll her captivated eyes around in her head like a pair of saucers and want to be nudging her ribs up close to his.

The big man was as regular as the clock on the press-cupboard and he'd be back at the metal bridge by now and maybe at John's Gate in a minute or two. Dowager and Teddy crossed the yard-stream and they listened for the sound of Moll's hooves and the rattling of the cartwheels. And then they saw Blue-eyed Jack and his pipe of tobacco-smoke coming on up the hill and the weary mare struggling to put one foot out passed the other. Teddy rushed down towards Mikey's Stile to greet his uncle. The big man whisked him up into the air and landed him on the lace of the horse-and-cart before the little fellow could even catch his breath.

## Dowager Was Excitement Itself

Dowager was as excited as a newborn calf at the prospect waiting for her today, taking her small grandson on an adventure hitherto beyond the realm of his tiny feet and turning over the pages in a brand-new storybook for him as he ventured through the hidden recesses of Curraghogue where the startled sheep and the bemused cattle might cast an eye at the two of them (she being so very old and he being so very young) and wonder who on earth was this strange little English child strutting along with Dowager and how the devil had he found himself so very far away from his native land across the Irish Sea.

This Tuesday was a fine springtime morning and the skies were aglitter and the little birds were chirping loudly on every laurel bush and blackthorn. Dowager hummed merrily to herself and she gave Teddy's sandals a good polishing and she especially attended to the heels – you could always tell a gentleman (she said) by the polished heels of his shoes. The little boy could throw them off when he was walking through the tall grass in Timmy's Field and he could put them on again before he got to Gentility's yard. Then she took down her message-bag from the press-cupboard and she carefully counted into it half-a-dozen duck eggs to give to her good friend.

She began making her preparations. Teddy watched her as she combed out her long locks of hair and they were as black as a crow's wing. She brushed each strand scrupulously till her hair was as shiny as the wavelets in River Laughter. She twisted it here and there and her mouth was full of pins and hairclips that she took from her box on her dressing-table, to keep it all in place. On special occasions such as this (known as her 'Gentility' days) she parted her hair from her poll down the centre to her forehead in what she called the Sunday way and then she rolled a long rope of it into a neat little braid and she pinned it to the back of her head.

Teddy was by now a very excited child. He ran into her box-room and he brought out the clothes that Dowager had laid out on her bed. She put on her blue-spotted skirt and the polka-dot blouse with the red-white-and-blue flowers on it and the red rim all around the edge. She coyly rolled on her best dove-grey stockings and she fixed them above the knee with the elastic. She put on her best boots, the ones with the laces in them. She put on her lightweight Mass coat, the one with the mysterious crossover ribbons on its insides that gave it a waist when it was tied. In front of the looking-glass she steadied on her basket-hat and it was as blue as the side-feathers of a jay-bird. She fixed it fussily at the correct angle. She hung her shawl loosely around her shoulders in case the rain came. It was as if she had turned the clock back and had dressed herself up for her own wedding-day and there was a silvery glint in her old eyes. She pinched Teddy's cheeks good-naturedly to give him the appearance of glowing health and then the two of them and their itchy feet set out across the yard and over the stream's flagstones. With their boots and sandals and their fine clothes weren't these two the most almighty swanks you ever set your eyes on!

# And Away They Went

They scattered the rough song of the geese and Dowager stabbed the road with her ash-plant as (almost of their own volition) her boots scooped up The Open Road towards The Easy Stile that led into Timmy's Field. On the far side of the ditch the smoke from Smiling Bab's chimney was as white as a mushroom and it spiraled its way into her pine-trees and it floated off towards Fort Dangerous. Dowager was already some distance ahead of her grandson, even though she was bent and stooped from the sciatica that had tormented her since the birth of her seventh son (Soldier Tom) who was fighting abroad on Africa's bullet-riddled sands against the Germans. Teddy was going to have the devil's own job to keep up with the stamp-stamp-stamp of her big boots. 'Wait for me! Wait for me! Why are you rushing away from me, Dowager?' moaned the little boy as she and her basket of eggs continued to outpace his short legs.

'Quicken your steps, child,' Dowager shouted back at his plodding sandals. 'Gentility and her flock of geese will be waiting for us at The Double Gap and it's now eleven o'clock. Can't you see how late it's getting?' But what did a child of his tender years know about clocks and the world's time? Dear God-in-Heaven, (his grandmother was thinking) the grasshoppers had already drunk up nearly all the dew from Timmy's blades of grass and in her excitement she began breathing quickly. Was there ever a child on earth (Teddy would have said, if only he had the words) who would want to be a toddler on a bright morning such as this? It would be many years before he'd be able to grasp the cause of his grandmother's agitation and the secret of the wondrous love that lay between herself and Gentility.

# Reaching The Easy Stile

They were near The Easy Stile where the last of the primroses were drooping towards the ditch. In their midst and sunning himself in his daily dreamland sat the ninety-year-old Corkscrew on his singletree. What a strange name was this! – Corkscrew. Three years ago he had been inside in

The Roaring Town Hospital for the one and only time in his life. He had refused to let his nurse (Black Bess) take off his trousers and give his bare belly the only wash he'd have had since the day he was born. Nor would he allow her to take the scissors to cut his toenails and she swore that they were six inches long and were curled up like skewers and that they reminded her of those corkscrews used by Curl 'n' Stripes in his drinking-shop when he was opening his bottles of stout.

Teddy's dumbfounded eyes pierced into the old man's face. It was covered completely with a white beard and was unlike any face he had ever seen in his short life. It was heart-shaped like the owl's ring of feathers that he'd seen in one of Dowager's prized picturebooks in the box under the hob. It was stained with the brown and yellow tendrils of the tobacco-juices from his pipe. The old man was wearing a wide black hat like the priests at Father Chasible's funeral and he had the sharp red eyes of an old goat staring out from that white beard of his. Dowager, as though she knew what her little grandson was thinking, said, 'Wouldn't you think that such a great white beard would itch the jaw off of poor old Corkscrew?' Teddy kept a wide berth away from this strange old man and with his little heart pounding in yet another bout of fear he gripped onto Dowager's hand and he quickened his pace considerably. He made sure to constantly look back over his shoulder and to keep his eyes firmly fixed on Corkscrew in case the old fellow might make a sudden jump down from his singletree and run after him and swoop him up in his clutches and carry him in over the ditch to some secret den amongst the trees.

## Timmy's Field

They were nearing Timmy's Field. It was a new world for Teddy. In earlier days he had stood on the ditch behind the cowshed whilst Dowager and Blue-eyed Jack were milking the cows. During the heavy snows of wintertime he had been taken as far as The Easy Stile where his uncle had held him up on the stick to watch the crowds of bigger boys engaged in the gliding-and-sliding races down Timmy's slopes; it was the only place in Rookery Rally suitable for a proper bit of winter sport. Smiling Babs' children were always into all sorts of devilment – like stealing the apples from Mikey's orchard or sickening their stomachs with the gooseberries and redcurrants from Cackles' back garden or pouring bags of flour into River Laughter to bring the brown trout up to the surface. One winter's afternoon when the snow had been at its thickest, they were at the height of their merriment; they came whizz-whizzing on their well-greased boards down the length of Timmy's slopes. But that was to be the day that their ringleader (Sweeney) was to gain an everlasting name for himself. At breakneck speed he arrived at the end of his run, where (to everyone's astonishment and unable to stop himself) he was catapulted several feet into the air and out over the ditch, landing in a heap on top of Dowager's cowshed. The cheers of the other children turned to instant tears when they saw how poor Sweeney had sailed into the sky as though he were a flaming rocket and how he was now lying senseless and half-dead and his wrists broken in two places. It took the bonesetter (Fingers Jack) the best part of a day to put right the damage and to make sure that Sweeney would be fit to join his father (Fiddler Joe) and pull up the turnips and spuds in the following harvest.

Teddy and his grandmother were now at The Easy Stile and Dowager was puffing and panting from all her efforts. She threw her leg out over the stick and she hopped along gingerly through the grass, which was already deep in places and still wet. 'Shy little rabbits will still have a few dewdrops to dampen their thirst with,' thought she to herself. From behind them Teddy could hear the cry of Cackles' ass and Cackles herself was heard shouting after her stray cows and the cows were making as much noise as herself, bawling and roaring in their search for their lost calves. He could hear Fiddler Joe repairing his gate with his hammer-and-nails and Mikey mending the boards of his horse-and-cart and singing away in that unmusical voice of his.

Swish-swish-swish! Dowager's long skirts scrambled through the crisp blades of grass. Before her eyes the sloping field seemed to touch the very sky and stringy gusts of fresh breezes ran down the field and they filled her papery old lungs. Amongst the sprawling black-velvet flowers and the early bees her little man and his unsteady legs found a new strength and he ran on ahead of her. He started to chase the white butterflies and to look for feathers to put in his grandmother's jam-jar on her altar. The old lady smiled to see how energetic he was getting, now that he had escaped from the farmyard. Father Chasible had died and was buried not long ago but today (she thought) her little man was bursting into life like a lovely May flower. It was the same with her own self. Away from the cares of yesterday and the washing of her clothes and the darning of her socks and the sweeping of her yard and the cleaning out of her creamery-tank, she found herself purring like a kettle on the fire. She was full of the most beautiful thoughts and was as happy as The Queen of Sheba. This very morning thousands of men might be fighting for their very lives in a cruel and meaningless war in those faraway lands, but she had time on her hands to relish the goodness and the beauty of this peaceful new day. It was the first time since the days of the snow that she could see her own shadow racing on ahead of her and she let out a deep sigh that was as good as a song. There wasn't a grey cloud anywhere and the gentle heat of the sun was on her brow and there was a glow on her old cheeks. Her little grandson was by her side and there wasn't a single German bomb to scare the life and soul out of him. Her thoughts (rapid as always) strayed back to her own childhood when she first strolled with Gentility through this very same field and her mind became torn with confusion – wanting to stay here all day long and lie down with her little grandson underneath the high heavens amid the new field-flowers – and yet full of a desire to hurry on out the gap at the top of the field and go and reach the smiling face of her beloved Gentility.

## The Hill Of The Goldfinches

At the top of the field there were a few furze bushes thrown across the gap to prevent Teddy traveling too far into the unknown and dangerous haunts that might lie beyond Timmy's Field. The child looked back from the gap and he saw the stooped figure of Dowager as she attacked the last vestiges of the slope. He saw the way herself and her stick kept waddling side to side in a steady rhythm like the gable-end of a cow coming up the road to be milked. They went through the gap and on into the second field and they paused a while to catch their breath. They listened to the little goldfinches singing in their hiding-places amidst the thistles. The field was alive with their song of greeting and it was the very reason why Dowager and Gentility had known since their childhood that this was their own Hill of The Goldfinches.

'Come down a little further into the valley and join us in our singing,' the little birds seemed to say. Dowager stepped forward and she clapped her two hands together: 'Shush-shush yeer singing and fly away with ye, my little birds!' she cried. With an energy that alarmed Teddy a pure legion of goldfinches glinted and swerved and swept aloft, swiping away the entire blueness of the sky and turning it into a blanket of green and gold. The happy child scampered down the field where he hoped one or two goldfinches (the old ones, said Dowager) might still be hiding in the long grass, too tired and too weak to fly up into the sky with their younger brothers and sisters. But the grass down there was deserted and Teddy gave up the chase and he made his way back to Dowager.

The two of them walked hand-in-hand to the lower end of the field and they bent down to look for daisies and buttercups to make a surprise gift for Gentility. Dowager pulled the odd wild hyacinth to enliven their bouquet – she knew how much Gentility loved the smell and the delicate pattern of these flowers. With the fairy breezes whispering in their ears, how much better it was for a child (she thought) to be out and about in the fields this blessed day than to be stuck like a prisoner inside the four walls of Dang-the-skin-of-it's school-house. If the war with the Germans continued to blaze away, the time would come (sadly and all too soon) when her little man would be forced to sit alongside the other children at a mournful desk for the whole of a bright morning such as this one. She was like a hen watching over her chick and she studied with amusement the little boy as he ran here and there and chased after the shadows of cotton-clouds as they raced over the field on their way to Galway and the sea. She had done the very same thing when she was a child and she laughed to see his futile efforts to stamp on them before they disappeared from The Hill of The Goldfinches and out across The Danes' Hill.

## Fort Dangerous

They edged their way towards Fort Dangerous where all sorts of witches lurked. Dowager gave Teddy's elbow a little squeeze and her voice dropped to a whisper. Here was the home of the little leprechauns (she said) and those other fairies that spent their time playing in the woods and rivers of

Rookery Rally. By now the little boy could understand some of the big-rocks-of-words that came spilling out each day from his grandmother's mouth; she had spent the past year filling his ears with the musical sound of her voice and her exciting stories – especially when she was dressing him on her lap in front of the fire.

They were at the entrance to the fort. She sat him down on the grass and she held him close to her skirts. They both felt a good bit tired by now and they needed a rest. It was a chance for her to recite some of her merrier tales to him – how the ancient Danes sailed across the sea in great big ships and how they lived inside Fort Dangerous and how they built their underground passageways into the nearby fields and how on their hunting and fishing days they went off visiting one another – just like herself and himself were doing this very day to Gentility – and how the ghosts of The Danes still marched up and down with the little leprechauns inside the ditch. She hardly gave herself time to catch her breath, so eagerly did she apply herself to filling Teddy's two ears. It was always the same way with her.

'What about the king of the leprechauns?' said Teddy; all her previous stories had had a king in them. Dowager looked around as though she was listening for the voices of some fairies and she whispered how the king wasn't any bigger than her own milking-stool and how each night the world's fairies came visiting him and brandished their brave little swords as they sat before his feet and waited for his commands – and that this little king had a silver hammer and a bag of golden nails. By now she had Teddy in the palm of her hands and his eyes were almost falling out of his little head. The king (said she) showed the other fairies how to hammer the golden nails onto the leather soles of the fairy-shoes. He taught them how to sew and stitch them roundabout before handing them out to the limping fairies that had done too much dancing the night before and who needed new shoes for the next bout of dancing.

In the following year (she thought to herself) she would have to tell Teddy far more gruesome tales in the hope that he would never go venturing too far from her yard and find himself wandering up around Fort Dangerous when her back was turned. There wasn't a woman in Rookery Rally who'd want to spend half the day (perish the thought!) running about looking for their lost Little Englander – only to find him vanished forever like some poor old dog running around in the hills. This time next year he'd be three-and-a-half years old and his grandmother would then tell him how Warts-the-Journeyman went into the fairies' fort to get himself a drink of spring-water and how he dropped his blue jug and how it broke and how the pieces stood upright as though by magic and how they cruelly pierced his jaw after he himself had stumbled and fallen. If that wasn't enough to frighten the living daylights out of her little grandson, she'd tell him about the ghost of the Kerry-blue cow and how the helpless creature got trapped in the fort's briars whilst searching for her lost calf and how she could be heard bawling hollowly by the drunken men as they took the short-cut home from Curl 'n' Stripes drinking-shop and how they blessed themselves whenever they spoke of this poor cow's ghost and vowed they'd never go that way again. 'Even if we can't see the leprechauns this morning, they can see the likes of us,' she added. 'If we go in and pick even one of their precious bluebells to add to Gentility's bunch, they'll come dashing out and throw chains of flowers around our feet. They'll bury us in the briars and spend the whole night dancing their wicked dances around us with their new shoes.'

Oh dear! Oh dear! All of a sudden she realized that she had gone too far – that she had let her tongue as usual run away with itself. She looked down and saw that her little man was frightened to the point of tears and he was holding onto her skirts for grim death. It was bad enough to have run away from the gander and the sow and to have gone to war with Red Buckles and to have seen Corkscrew and to think all sorts of fearful thoughts about what that old beardy-face might do with him if he got him in his clutches. But now there was this new fear – that the king of the leprechauns would send out his troops and that they'd pounce on himself and Dowager and that it would mean the end of both their lives and that they'd be the same as poor Father Chasible and thrown into a great big box in a hole in the ground. Dowager gave him a playful little shove and she started to laugh: 'Wipe your eyes, my little chickadee! There are more good spirits than bad spirits to protect us in this world. With a drop of my holywater from this little bottle of mine (and she tapped her pocket) we can beat the living daylights out of the king of the leprechauns and all his fairies if we ever have to.' This excellent news was just what Teddy wanted to hear and he at once wiped his eyes and he threw his fears to the winds and he put his head in his grandmother's lap and he stayed there a while. He knew that Dowager and Blue-eyed Jack would always have the answer to his childish worries. Enough said.

## *Climbing The Difficult Stile*

He suddenly sprung to his feet and he dragged his old grandmother away and on towards The Difficult Stile. She was satisfied with the way her words had redeemed her little man's spirits. In her heart of hearts she felt that he and his childish credulity would always pay heed to whatever she'd tell him. But if only she knew the real truth: that by the middle of next year Teddy would be far more sturdy and adventurous. He would want to go traveling further and further away with the rest of the children. And heaven only knows what worries that would bring to herself and her son.

They reached The Difficult Stile. The old woman lifted Teddy (one step at a time) up onto the ditch. She told him to wait for her and to hold onto the wire-fence. She hoisted up her own black skirts above her knees and she herself clambered up and stood beside him. She arched herself on tiptoes and she covered her crinkled brow with her hands so as to get the best possible view of this new and unbelievable scene. As soon as they dropped down into the lane, they'd find themselves in a long trench and the hedges would close up around them and deprive their eyes of any further spectacle of Rookery Rally's fine valleys and woodland. From this high perch she could now see The Roaring Town. She could see its Norman tower and the sharply-penciled spire of the stately church, which was slate-coloured like a rainy sky on the one side and dark blue like a sugar-bag on the other side. Far away she could make out The Holy Lake in the middle of The Mighty Shannon River and it was oily-looking and gleaming like a giant version of her looking-glass at home.

Teddy ('How tall I am – even taller than on Jack's big shoulders!') grasped Dowager's hand and he followed the line of her finger as she traced the different sights for him. The hens, ducks and geese back in the farmyard, and the men on their ass-and-cars and even old Corkscrew himself and all the rest of the world were a thousand miles away. Standing on the ditch and holding onto her hand he felt as safe as he had been earlier in the morning when he was inside the warm folds of her apron and she dressing him in front of the fire. It was a precious moment. For once in her life Dowager was able to share her happiness and her peaceful thoughts (albeit with a little boy, her grandson from across the waters in England) and she realized there might never again come a time as poignant and tender as this one. She seemed entranced with her life and her body swayed before the natural beauties of the world around her – the hills where the late morning sunlight flung itself in splashes from left to right across The Lisnagorna Forest and across The Three Heights and the mustard-coloured bushes that Smiling Babs and Fiddler Joe were forever trying to control. For a split second she forgot about Gentility. She forgot how she herself had been nagging the life out of Teddy to quicken his footsteps whilst they were down at The Easy Stile. Her good friend would have to wait a little longer before she could clap her tired old eyes on herself and The Little Englander. Teddy's grandmother was making the same mistake she always made – the one Blue-eyed Jack and his pocket-watch constantly told her about – forgetting what time of day it was, whenever she found herself gripped by a new and exciting beauty.

## Hurrying Along The Grassy Lane

She slid herself down the rough stone slabs on the far side of the ditch. They cut sharply into her leathery backside but she never felt a thing. She handled Teddy down carefully. With themselves and the duck-eggs safely down from the stile, they scrambled along the lane and Teddy balanced his sandals on the grassy tufts of the ridges before hastening to catch up with his speeding grandmother. Once more her boots stabbed the ground excitedly as she and her stick waddled on ahead of him. In the leafy tunnels surrounding the lane the big bunches of nodding bellflowers bent down and greeted them. A few cheerful little cliques of shy wren-birds ('Look at us! Follow us!') floated out from the silent briars. They shrieked and streaked ahead of them, summoning them ever onwards towards Gentility. It wasn't long before they'd be at The Double Gap and how pleased the old lady would be to see them. A visit from Dowager was the best of all possible visits and knocked even the previous monthly visits of Father Chasible into a cocked hat.

## Gentility Was Excitement Itself

Just like Dowager, Gentility had risen early this morning and had dressed herself fussily. Her eyesight had weakened considerably over the last few years. Yet in spite of this setback she had scrubbed and polished her boots till they shone. As soon as she had said her few prayers for the burning souls in Purgatory, she walked around her Welcoming Room and she hummed to herself and was as happy as an ass in a clover-field heavy with dew.

Suddenly she thought she heard voices. She and her great big boots took the shortcut through the grove to get to The Double Gap ahead of her visitors. Her heart was beating rapidly and she felt giddy from the beauty of her feelings. Her hens, which during the wintertime had looked tired and had kept to the yard, were once again the guardians of her poor old eyes and they fussed and clucked around her feet. Behind them and following in a royal procession (and all squawking at one and the same time) came her ducks and her geese and they almost frightened themselves with their own unusual excitement. Ahead of the hens raced Gentility's silky black dog (Sam). He nearly bowled her over when he understood that something strange was in the air and he spun himself round and around in an effort to bite off his youthful tail. Gentility paused in the middle of the lane and she cocked her head back like a mule and listened for the approach of Dowager's big boots. 'They're here at last! – I can hear them,' she murmured to her hens and she shielded her eyes as though the sun was in them, in an effort to concentrate properly.

Dowager ('We're almost there, Teddy!') could see ahead of her this skinny bird-of-a-woman and her grey skirts rustling and she now began to fret and fuss over the safety of her duck-eggs in the bag. She cast an eye at the huge nosegay of wild flowers that Teddy had amplified with foxgloves in the course of their journey up the lane. She was satisfied. They were not coming unprepared.

Teddy had never seen so many snow-white geese before as an army of them flapped their wings around Gentility's boots. Sam's eyes were shining like windows and he came lolloping down the lane and he wagged his tail furiously. Gentility (panting for breath) followed him with her great big strides and (like Dowager) her hair was pinned up in a bundle for this very special visitation. Her misty eyes had some difficulty making out the two wanderers until they were within an arm's reach. For the blink of a second her face seemed a little sad for she could never get enough of Dowager in her life. But then a warmth like a hot fire poured out from her. Teddy had never been on a visit before and he felt his own heart going pitter-patter and beating even faster than when he first came across the startling sight of old Corkscrew down at The East Stile.

'Dowager!' rang the raspy voice of Gentility, 'is it you that's in it?' She held out her limpid hands towards Dowager ('How good it is to clap my two worn old eyes on you!') and she gripped her old school-friend's elbows. She almost shook the arms off of her and a drop of salty water slid out of Dowager's eyes and it trickled down along her jaw.

## The Presentation Of 'The Little Englander'

It was time for Dowager to present Teddy to Gentility for her inspection. She gave him a little nudge and he stepped forward shyly and handed Gentility his bunch of wildflowers. The geese stood on tiptoes and they flapped their wings approvingly. Seeing the old lady and the black dog and the flock of noisy geese and the cackling hens and the throaty ducks and, behind it all, the white clouds and the haggart pine-trees and the forests of Lisnagorna on the hills – this was indeed a memorable morning for The Little Englander. Gentility stretched out her bony arms towards the little evacuee. She felt the curls on the child's head and the few bald patches interspersed among them (the result of the cattle-rash the previous year). She let out a long sigh: 'Ah, ye can't beat the youth – they have it all' and her two eyes grew wistful as she recalled the happy childhood days of herself and Dowager.

## Two Old Women Walking Arm-In-Arm

Step by step the two old ladies (their smiling eyes almost suffocating one another) walked in along the lane, linking arm-in-arm and they seemed to bow royally towards the cobblestones. Teddy struggled along behind their heels, as they headed towards the half-door, passing Gentility's small garden with its blackcurrant, gooseberry and redcurrant bushes in it and her American grass and her rows of pretty sweet-william flowers. Dowager handed Gentility her basket of duck-eggs. Then she looked back across the yard and she waited for her little dreamer. He was inspecting Gentility's black stockings and her pink bloomers drying on the gate and ballooning in the noonday breeze.

## Teddy Enters A Mysterious New World

Teddy followed the two sets of boots into The Welcoming Room where Gentility (in spite of her poor sight) had kept up a good fire with lots of logs and twigs that her nephew (Poesy) had prepared in readiness for today's visit. Since her father's death she had depended on him to come over in the evenings from his house in The Limerick Glens and tend to her yard and her small privet-hedged garden. She sat Dowager down in the place of honour (Poesy's rocking-chair). Dowager began testing its arms and teetering back and forth. Gentility sat down opposite her on her stool, the one she always sat on when her household chores were done and whenever she needed to feel the relaxation of the firelight. She began stroking her squinty-eyed dog, Sam, who lay faithfully at her heels.

Teddy sat shyly next to Dowager in the chimney corner. What can a child do at times like this and with nothing else to occupy his young mind? He looked up into the black furry walls of the chimney-hole like he did at home – to see if he could make out the square of blue sky or a cloud or two floating by. Turning around, his eyes took in the brown planks of wood in the rafters; they were like the boards on Blue-eyed Jack's horse-and-cart. He saw the picture of The Virgin and the little red lamp and the everlasting picture of the sad–eyed Sacred Heart and the crown of thorns piercing into his forehead and another crown of thorns piercing round his heart and the picture of the men saying their prayers at dinner time whilst they were ploughing and the dresser itself with the precious willow-patterned plates on it to liven things up a bit.

Gentility went into her bedroom to bring out her knitting. From the door she beckoned Teddy to follow her and Dowager gave him another little shove forward. He followed the old lady into the bedroom and he held tightly onto her skirts, for it was dark in there and he was once more a little unsure of himself or of where he was going. She rummaged about until she found her jar of humbug sweets. With her finger on her smiling lips she gave Teddy a few of them. He got used to the dull light and he saw that it was a huge room. Gentility showed him her butter-making churn, which was beside her piss-pot near the bed. The bed had a square frame to it and it had four wooden posts at the corners. It was at least as high as himself and he must have wondered how an old woman like Gentility could ever get up and into it at night until he saw a stool with some steps in the corner of the room. On a table at the foot of the bed was Gentility's washstand and it had a jug on it and her rosary-beads hung on a nail to bring her good luck. From her glass-fronted press she took out her pink-and-red wine glasses, which would later be filled with lemonade for the three of them. They caught Teddy's fancy, for he had never before seen coloured glasses of any kind. Then Gentility led him back to The Welcoming Room, all the time coyly holding onto him with her damp hands. She was carrying a pixy-tam that she had almost completed as a gift for Dowager. She turned around and saw Teddy's sad face and she darted back into her bedroom and came back out with a pair of blue mittens for him that she had been knitting for her own small hands against the cold of future mornings.

## *The Half-Door Beckons His Young Feet*

The half-door was beckoning to Teddy and he was let loose into the yard to make his own amusement. He would no longer have to sit and listen to the eternal gossip of two old women. Sam-the-dog was waiting for him in the yard and the child and his whimsicality chased him around the pig-house. Then he scurried after the two cats until they plucked up courage and sat with him on the upturned ass-and-car where he stroked their backs in the sun. The inquisitive chickens stood around his feet and then the fierce little warrior (no sign of Corkscrew here) bravely ran at them and they fled out over the dung-heap.

The ghosts of bygone children now followed him along on his rambles. He peered into the hen-house and the teachest where lay the snug and proud mother-hen with her tiny yellow fluffy chicks. She was keeping a watchful eye on this new visitor of hers. He walked around the hedge and looked for wildflowers to give to Dowager and Gentility; the crafty little devil knew that his gift would mean another handful of humbug sweets. He picked a bunch of yellow piss-a-bed dandelions and a few juicy dock-leaves to mix in with them. He walked on and he buried his nose in his bouquet the way he saw Dowager doing. Gentility would put his bunch in a glass on her altar in front of her Sacred Heart picture.

He played for a while behind the little scrape of stones that Dowager's ageless grandfather (Johnnie-be-good) had made on his hundredth birthday, a day prior to his death. He had been cleaning the horse-dung from the lane when God decided to come down and bring him up into the clouds. His children gathered round his bed and they offered him a glass of stout to revive his spirits and steady his nerves. He had never drank a drop of liquor in all his life and he hunted them from the room and 'take that old bog-water away with ye!' said he. God had seen enough and he smiled on Johnnie-be-good and carried him off with him to The Beyond. Teddy passed the hawthorn tree and came to a deserted shack where Gentility's two grown-up brothers (Dan-the-Lion and Pansy) had smoked their pipes a lifetime ago. These two shy fellows were far too polite to smoke tobacco in The Welcoming Room in front of their knowing father or their smiling mother and now their ghosts were following Teddy deep into the haggart.

Teddy climbed onto the rusty turnip-pulper. He looked back at the house-thatch where the smoke belched out from the chimney. Avoiding the nettles (which were as big as himself) he went into the tiny orchard with its three cooking-apple trees and he came to a lower gateway, rusty and creaking. He could see the deserted ruins of a second cabin where the sky peeped in through the rafters and onto the walls. He sat on the flagstones at the doorway where (though he would never get to know it) Dowager had been born on a cold November day in 1880. He stepped inside and the ghosts of bygone children led him on. The Welcoming Room was gone but the bedroom chimney was still standing and the fireplace was intact, the last traces in the lives of Dowager's mother and father (Tear-away Dan and Fancy-Nan). They had surrounded it with pink stucco and broken bits of shiny green glass to give it a bit of a lift and it had glorified their wedding-night with the warmth of its blazing turf fire.

## Two Old Ladies And The Hot Sun's Call

The hot sun was now putting its thumb on top of the pine-trees around Gentility's yard. Her loneliness of recent days had disappeared and was replaced by the gentle cordiality between herself and Dowager. It seemed not so very long ago that winter had roared around them and had trapped them inside their half-doors as they looked out helplessly at the echoing winds and the rain and the white flurries of snow. Now they could trip out the door. They could catch the lovely sunshine and enjoy the delicate beauties of Nature that had burst out all over their world. They sat listening to the fresh chirrups of the birds underneath the holly bush and behind the creamery tank and the fuchsia bushes at the pig-house. Their joyful old heads didn't know in which direction to point their ears and their eyes.

In less time than either of them would have wished the little wanderer came strolling back into their life. He was carrying his two bunches of wildflowers to give to his grandmother and Gentility. He shyly handed up the flowers to the two old ladies and there followed a bout of spontaneous laughter from Gentility and Dowager as they looked down at the little boy and his gift of yellow piss-a-beds and dock-leaves. Gentility placed her bunch in a jam-jar in front of her altar and she placed Dowager's garland on the windowsill for the time being and she bent down and abstractedly stroked Teddy's curls and she wiped her best chair for him with a wet rag.

It was time to prepare the table for tea. Gentility placed on a tray the pink-and-red glasses with the lemonade in them and she left the front window open to let in the yellow sunlight and the dreamy blue sky. She rolled out the soda-cake from the burner onto the table. She cut several long stretches of the cake and placed her best cuts of cold ham on a large plate in the middle of the table. The butter dish was nearby and the sugar too. She sprinkled it on top of the buttered bread for the little man (like when he was at home). She could see him squirming with delight when the soda-cake with the tasty butter-with-sugar-on-the-top oozed down into his throat. When they had finished eating, they tiptoed out the half-door and, fussing a good deal, they brought out the two chairs and the little penny-stool for Teddy into the centre of the yard. It was late afternoon and they were going to let nothing interfere with their enjoyment of the clear sharp sunlight, for within an hour they knew that the day's quicksilver light would change into a sparkling brass and then into a copper and finally into twilight.

Teddy sat on the ass-and-car with his new friends (the cats and their sharp claws) and their eyes were closed tightly to stop the sun getting into them and Sam was curled up between them and yawning happily. The chickens, ducks and geese were sleeping quietly underneath the ass-and-car and they seemed worn out from their day's work. And on the ass-and-car Teddy's childish daydreams went on and on undisturbed, unlike poor Father Chasible who was lying below in his grave underneath the clay.

The two old ladies sat on their chairs and they gazed up at the fuzzy pine-trees and the sunlight stroking the tops of them. It was as if the branches had stopped their waving in honour of this fine occasion and they both saw the slopes above the little farm grasping at the sunlight as if to devour it. From his perch on the ass-and-car Teddy looked across at the two of them. They seemed to have floated away from him and you would have forgiven him if he was thinking (child that he was) that Heaven had somehow come down into the yard and he half-expected that the dead Father Chasible would return from the clouds and dance his way in through the gate this very minute.

He came across the yard and he sat on his penny-stool. Gentility seemed to sense the quietness in him (he not being a part of their own high-sounding talk) and she placed him between her bony old knees and she gently rocked him to and fro. He was trapped there and had nothing to do but stare up at her – hard and deep the way children have done since history began. Her black stockings contrasted with Dowager's grey ones and the metal cleets on her outstretched boots reflected the sun's light. The smile on her face was like a pale angel's in one of Dowager's prayerbooks and it was directed not at him but across at his grandmother. From where he was (down between her knees) she seemed to be the tallest woman he had ever seen and she reminded him of one of Dowager's long-necked turkeys towering above the startled hens. Whenever she was talking she fidgeted a good bit and she wiped her hands distractedly against the sides of her crossover apron as though her fingers were covered in baking flour and her lips were fixed tightly together as she listened to what Dowager was saying to her. The hands holding Teddy between her legs were long with nails like a raven's claws and the skin on Gentility's neck was slack and shaky like a turkey's gobble. She had black cat-hairs on her chin and the trace of a blue-ashy moustache and, when her lips parted, her few remaining teeth were yellower than Dowager's and far more broken and she spoke out of the corner of her mouth. But (a fact which Teddy wasn't old enough to notice) she had far far fewer wrinkles on her face than Dowager, for she had never married and, unlike Dowager, she had never had the strenuous task of bringing up fifteen children together with all the added pain and suffering that such work entailed – and without Handsome Johnnie at her side to help her along life's long journey.

Oh, what we'd give to retrieve those vanishing shimmering afternoons and those shy unreal hours when the clock no longer seemed to be ticking – when Dowager and Gentility still reflected the fresh loveliness of flowers – when their hearty laughter still filled all four corners of the yard – when the melodic voices of these two old sun-worshippers had a grandeur in them whilst they were sitting on their painted chairs and imbibing the brightness of the daylight as though weaving themselves into some sort of charming embroidery. It was just another day up here in the hills around Rookery Rally – when hardly a word was ever heard tell about that blasted foreign war with its cruel bullets and its heartless bombs – the war that was weaving its own macabre embroidery all over Teddy's sad birthplace back in England.

The two old ladies' cheeks were soon as red as radishes as they washed the happy tears from their eyes. Then Gentility leaned forward and with an envious look at Teddy she placed her hand on Dowager's knee: 'It's been a long time since you and I were young like this little English child, hasn't it, Dowager?' And Dowager turned to her and said: 'Do you recall the time we went fishing – and how we put the holes in our sweet-gallons for the maggots to wave themselves in and out – and how we threw the rope over the bridge and caught the trout in our sweet-gallon to have them with those mushrooms we found in The Bull-Paddock?' On and on went their reveries and they couldn't talk fast enough as though these were the last words they'd ever speak and this was their very last day on earth. Not even Lady Acceptable or the little birds all around them could equal them in the courtliness of their speech: the land, the cattle and the men (especially the men!) and their sweethearts of old. 'Ah, ye can't beat a kiss from a man with the whiskers,' sighed Dowager and the two of them took a fit of laughing till their sides hurt. And all the time you'd hear the clicketty-clacketty knitting needles of Gentility as she put the finishing touches to Dowager's pixy-tam. 'Yes, Dowager, we too were young like the birds in the bushes.'

'Why shame on you, Gentility, we still are young birds – young inside our old hearts.' And once again they took a fit of merry laughing.

Then they rose from their chairs and they went back into The

Welcoming Room, for it would soon be time for the oil-lamp to be lit. They sat by the side of the fire for a minute or two and looked at Poesy's damp socks drying on the crane. Teddy followed them in the half-door. He could smell the spuds and the cabbages boiling in the skillet pot for Poesy's meal, when the fluffy floury spuds would be thrown out on the table. Sam the dog licked his lips in greedy anticipation.

## Time For Two Tired Souls To Bid Goodbye

It was late afternoon. The sun was far down and the sad moment of farewell had come. Quicker than you'd think, the sky was turning from copper to crimson and the blue was nowhere to be seen. Indeed the pine-trees were already black against the sky. From their grazing-fields beyond the haggart-stick the hens and ducks came in to roost for the night and to join the rest of the huddled fowl in the yard, who were now marching out from underneath the ass-and-car and moving of their own accord towards the hen-house. One by one and muttering to themselves, they all entered the doorway in an orderly fashion like good little schoolchildren.

Gentility took the tired little boy to see her fowl as they settled on their places along the sticks. They were sure that the fox and the weasel would try to call on them if Gentility didn't fix the hasp on the door as tightly as a drum. Even so, they would keep their ears cocked and in readiness. Through the dark scooping slits Teddy peered in to see them cooped up and to say his last farewell to them and Gentility fixed the hasp like the key of a dungeon. The younger and more innocent hens sat on the lower perches but the older ones (to whom God had given both wisdom and sense) hopped up onto the topmost roosts near the roof out of harm's way. A previous visit from the silent fox and the creeping weasel (both of whom had hoped to make soup out of them) had been lessons they were unlikely to forget and soon they were lost in their dreamland and even the crows were wafting down over the pine-trees to their own roost.

A ghostly coldness, brought on by the evening dew, was making its eerie way inside the half-door and Dowager started to get fussy as she looked out at the dusty blue in the trees and the darkening dusky sky. 'Do you think it'll rain before we get home?' she asked Gentility. She feared the threat of it and, not being well able to manage The Difficult Stile in the dusk of the evening, she fidgeted with her blue basket hat and she put on her coat. It was indeed a time of sadness and the previous heights of their conversation had turned into downcast eyes and a few brief mutterings. With something of a little ceremony Gentility made sure that Dowager had her pixy-tam and her basket fully laden with cooking-apples and a few sticks of rhubarb thrown in as well. She gave Teddy the blue mittens and the rest of the humbug sweets and she patted his cheek and she told him to be sure and come see her again. With a painful heaviness in their chests the two old ladies shook hands savagely, not wishing to let go of one another. Gentility's fingers dampened the foreheads of Dowager and Teddy with the holywater from her font and she rubbed the sign-of-the-cross on both of them to protect them from the wicked spirits and The Boodeeman.

Dowager was anxious to be off. The three of them went out the blue gate and onto The Double Gap and Gentility stood there to see them off. Then she waved her sock-hanky down the lane at their diminishing forms and she shaded her eyes to get the last remaining view of them. They could hear her rasping voice ('Good luuk! Good luuk! and be sure to coom again, let ye!') as she turned on her heel and went sadly back into The Welcoming Room to wait for Poesy. And she thought to herself: 'When will we ever have such fine old times again?' The last that the two wanderers saw was the smoke trailing out of her chimney.

Down the lane tramped the sandals and the great big boots between the flanking hedges. They were soon in tune with the growing dusk and their nostrils were filled with the honeysuckle's scent, which came on with the dew. The wren-birds that had invited them up the lane earlier in the day were silent now, having worn themselves to a thread from the many songs they'd been singing with their little stubs of tongues. Dowager had turned into a shrunken old lady and she was quieter than her usual self. However (had Teddy been old enough to know it) there was a bright wistfulness and a perfect contentment inside in her heart and she held him close to her skirts and she savoured her lovely private feelings for a little while, deliciously.

Once more Teddy's nerves were on edge; he thought of the fairies that might be out and ready to haunt The Hill of The Goldfinches as dusk came creeping in. Every little noise frightened him – whether it was a cow crackling her sleepy way through the thistles and nettles or the thousands of insects and their sharp nocturnes in the long grass. Dowager tried to distract him and she told him to crane his ears and listen out for the special sound that the crickets were making in the long grass (those that had escaped the beaks of the goldfinches). She whispered in his ear and reminded him that there was no full moon (not even a pale sign of her) and that the king of the fairies had not yet reached for his hammer and nails to mend the fairies' shoes. But Teddy still held tightly to his grandmother's skirts and in spite of her nearness and warmth the evening noises brought him the very same fears that he felt when the gloomy shadow of The Boodeeman stole into The Big Cave Room each night before Blue-eyed Jack came in to warm his feet with his own feet in the bed.

Dowager (though she didn't want to admit it) was herself a little bit afraid and she kept her eyes scanned on the horizon. They hurried towards The Easy Stile and she was relieved to see the wispy curls of smoke coming from Smiling Bab's chimney and the dim light of Cackles' candles gently winking across at them and the far-off view of The Roaring Town and a mist thickly scattering towards it and the street-lamps already flickering into the oncoming darkness. Somewhere amid those faraway gaslights she heard the mournful hoot of the evening mail-train, bound for Dublin and taking letters to loved ones in England, the former home of the little evacuee now trudging along beside her. In the last obscure ribbons of daylight they crossed The Easy Stile. Old Corkscrew had at last shifted himself off home. A few men were beginning their nightly work at rabbiting with their lamps. They were hauling their cumbersome bikes up along The Open Road, pushing them rhythmically with their heads inclined into the slopes of the hill. The smoke from their fag-butts hung closely around them and Dowager was glad of their brief company and she gave them a friendly little wave.

## Home To The Flagstones

The two adventurers reached the yard's flagstones, which had turned from white to blue where the stream's black waters were chequered with the first of the moon's reflections as though she herself had tumbled down into it. It was as though there was a permanent rope strung out between Blue-eyed

Jack and his mother. Long before their arrival he had heard their plodding footsteps coming down from The Easy Stile; for he had been looking out through the window. He ran out excitedly to greet them, mad looking for news and to see what his mother had brought back with her. Teddy and Dowager were just in time to ward off the rain that had been threatening to teem down on them.

They entered The Welcoming Room and Dowager was pleased to see that the fire had lots of logs on it and that the kettle was already steaming along like an old train-engine and that Blue-eyed Jack had also prepared the meat and the spuds. She unscrewed the lantern-cap of the oil-lamp and she filled the oil-reservoir and she dampened the wick and she turned up the screw and the flames filled every corner of The Welcoming Room, spreading out their edges like a great big eagle's wings. Teddy and herself fell on the feast of meat and spuds like two pure savages. The little boy scarcely had time to eat his feed as Blue-eyed Jack kept prodding him for some kind of news to be delivered to him from the child's growing vocabulary. Then Dowager knelt down between her two men (the big man and the little man) in a ring in the middle of the floor and once more she led the prayers and she said, 'Thank you, Lord' for getting herself and Teddy home safe and sound across the fields.

Night crept into the heart of the little cabin and it darkened its soul. Dowager put down her rosary-beads and she went out to the ash-pit and stooped to make her private river of poolie. She did it rapidly as all countrywomen did, alertly listening for the slightest sound of intrusion, but there was no other sound other than the trickling music of her free-flowing waters from underneath her skirts. Together with Teddy, Blue-eye Jack went out behind the hen-house and its dung-heap to make their own poolie. The winds whistled achingly across the dung heap and the hawthorn branches rattled off of the galavanize roof over the hens. The ducks grunted in protest and a gentle rain flattened the leave on the hawthorn. Blue-Eyed Jack buttoned up his fly and he shivered happily. The moon was now lighting up the fields around the little farm.

The candle-stick-holders went off in two directions. In her small box room Dowager got herself into bed and she found the hot jar thoughtfully placed there by Blue-eyed Jack early on. She placed it at her feet and she got herself comfortable. She would spend a little while yet saying her private prayers and she would soon be in the land of dreams with her rosary-beads wrapped through her fingers. When the dawn came up she'd be once more greeted by the newly-shod ass poking his head in through the broken windowpane and giving her his proud hello.

Her two men tiptoed behind the hob to The Big Cave Room where Teddy would soon wrap his feet in between his guardian's legs for the rest of the night when the big man hopped in to join him. Blue-eyed Jack came in and he tucked the child in under his five blankets, to be guarded by the brass reindeers stamped on the foot bed-rails. He dowsed him with the holywater to guard against The Boodeeman. He sprinkled it in the four corners of The Welcoming Room and again cursed away the wicked spirits of darkness. He went out and brought in a sack of turf and logs for the morning and he threw them in under the stool. He threw a mug of water on the fire's embers and he raked out the ashes. Then he headed into The Big Cave Room to join his little nephew. Sooner than you could blink Teddy had closed his eyes for the night. His uncle slipped out of his trousers and hopped in beside him and before blowing out the candle he turned and looked down at his little fosterling and he smiled tenderly at him. From a funeral the other day to a visit this very day – a great deal had happened for Teddy: Father Chasible lay beneath the heavy clay in the graveyard. Teddy was alive and well and he was blossoming like a new flower.

# FIVE

# *Rabbits Everywhere*

*When Blue eyed Jack and his double-barrel gun
took Teddy to kill his first rabbits.*

It was Autumn in the year of 1943. Blinded with smoke, Dowager was down on her knees at the fire. The wind seemed to be blowing directly down the chimney on top of her and with the lid of the sweet-gallon she was gently fanning the few sparks to get the fire going. To escape from under her feet and a lashing from her tongue Blue-eyed Jack was abroad in the yard and he was sweeping away some of the leaves and the fowl's slimy filth mixed in with the recent rain. In his mind's eye he was already planning his day ahead.

At this early hour the dusty rays of sunlight were waking Teddy up from his blissful dreamland in the four-poster reindeer brass bed behind the fireplace, himself and also the army of bees in the laurel bushes in the empty chimney in the Big Cave Room. This day was like any other day in the life of our young evacuee – a day for him to pursue his newest exciting adventures. In his shirt he stepped out into The Welcoming Room and (with Dowager's smiling face always there to greet him) he buried his curls in the black folds of her lap and she brushed his head with her blackened fingernails. For a second he warmed himself at the fire, which was by this stage a mountain of turf-blaze. There was little time for him to sit there, gawking up and out through the chimney-hole (his window-in-the-sky) and Dowager arranged his fingers into the praying position and she began the daily list of 'God Bless' prayers with him and even had him praying for the cantankerous ass (The Lightning Whoor).

On top of the twigs, and boiling along merrily in the black canister in the centre of the fire, Dowager had arranged his two eggs – the ones she had just brought in from the haggart and shown him – the ones with the little white feathers (the crafty old woman) and the bit of hen-dung stuck on the sides to show how The Little Red Hen had laid them freshly this minute. When the prayers were finished and his sainthood was well and truly established, she fished out the eggs from inside the flames with her crooked fingers and she placed them in front of him on the table. Once more she gave him a cut of soda-bread lavished with a coat of butter and she covered the top of it with a snowy stream of sugar. Wasn't he the spoilt little charmer? The Little Englander knew he was.

His grandmother wiped the table oilcloth and she put a wet rag across his face (not that it was dirty) and then she dried him good-humouredly and she patted his nose as though he were her favourite pussycat. She cleared away the delf and the cutlery and she washed them in her grey enamel pan. There came the rattle of a blue cart's wheels outside on The Open Road. It was Red Scissors and he was hunched down and hidden (the rascal) inside the boards of his cart with just the smoke (and nothing else) rising up from his invisible pipe. Dowager was always nosey, ('I wonder who that could be') and she paused on tiptoe behind Teddy and she looked hard at the cart to see who was in it and what was he up to, was he buying or was he selling.

## Teddy Gets His Young Brain Working

Teddy stood on the chair and he brought down the pack of playing-cards from behind the sour-milk jug. He placed them in a line on the table with all the red ones in one row and all the black ones in another row and he gathered all the picture-cards in a heap together. With all their beautiful colours, if only the king and the queen and the knave could have sprung into life and danced out onto the floor, what astonishing tales they would be telling him! Young as he was he had listened to so many stories from the visiting card-players in the recent evenings that he almost expected these cards to be doing this very thing for him.

For a while he concentrated on building a tower out of the cards, just as his uncle had shown him – only for them to come tumbling down in repeated disarray. He knelt on the chair and, with Dowager's guiding finger, he did his level best to read the Thomas Hood framed poem, an ancient school prize given to one of Dowager's own children (Una) in days long past ('the little house says stay and the little road says go'). He looked out over the red geraniums in the green windowsill boxes and he watched Blue-eyed Jack sweeping away the puddles of brown rain. He gazed at the chickens all huddled underneath the ass-and-car and at the wagging tails of the ducks as they stood awkwardly on the rocks at the edge of the swollen yard-stream before diving in.

These were mornings of golden silence with only the ticking of the clock on the press-cupboard. The older children had gone down The Open Road, reciting their Tables religiously on their way to Dang-the-skin-of-it's school-house. Now that he was three Teddy was old enough to feel a little sad not to be running out after them and he felt trapped like the fidgety little wagtails abroad in the cowshed. He was too old for his previous quaint habit of gazing ('who am I?') at his face in the looking-glass and Blue-eyed Jack peering in over his shoulder and saying 'You'll get a rash from that old mirror if you keep looking at it'. If only he could escape and go off on a journey to some faraway place like the thatched cabin of Gentility beyond The Hill of The Goldfinches!

## *Blue-Eyed Jack Was All Business Too*

Blue-eyed Jack came in the door and he wiped the sweat from his forehead and he took a mug of water from the bucket near the axe. He looked at his little man with those fleeting eyes of love that he and his mother always had for Teddy, so far away from the parents he'd never known – this present minute cowering from the bombs in a dusty London air-raid shelter. The big man kept reminding himself of his own good fortune (with no child of his own) – to have been destined to look after this little fellow from the moment he was born. Wasn't he the luckiest of men to be spending his days like this? Wasn't Teddy the luckiest of children to have been snatched away from the cruel fates of such a devastating war!

Earlier this morning and as soon as he had seen a gap in the night clouds and the mist rising up from beyond the haggart pine-trees, Blue-eyed Jack had quickly chased the sleepy blur out of his eyes. Unobtrusively and with no wish to disturb the sleeping child he had freed himself from Teddy's warm side. He came out in his shirt for his first drink of spring-water and he unbarred the window shutters. He put on his smelly old coat, the tattered one with the frayed lining, and he walked down the yard and out over the haggart stick. It was still dark enough for him to take the flashlamp with him and he headed down towards The Bull-Paddock to greet his cows and he buried his chin inside his coat collar and blew smoke out from his mouth.

Like all men Blue-eyed Jack was a killer. He was a heartless villain who said farewell to several fine crows, rats, mice, foxes and weasels or anything else that stood in his way. His snares and his traps were the bane of every rabbit that lived in Rookery Rally and there were enough of these little fellows above in The Valley of The Pig to feed the entire population. They were forever cannoning into each other and scampering away from the cheery-faced children sauntering along the evening fields after school was done. At harvest-time when the very last square was left in the oat-field and was about to be scythed down, Blue-eyed Jack was there at the ready and waiting to break the neck of any rabbit left behind and hiding in fear. As a warning to other adventurous creatures he hung the carcasses of crows on sticks in the field where his gun had brought them low, a stone-throw away from their home in the rookery – and he cut the tail from the cunning old fox and he nailed it to our hen-house door.

# Keeping Hunger Away From The Door

In the week before we got the monthly money from the creamery in exchange for our skimmed milk, the table might get a little short of the fat meat we all loved – that was until one of the two pigs was killed and salted and the other one sold in The Roaring Town. Of course we still had the neck of one or two hens to ring and we had a daily supply of their eggs. The frying-pan also had the odd few trout from the sally-hole in River Laughter and we had the juicy morning mushrooms from The Bull-Paddock to go with them together with the spuds and the cabbages and the turnips. And whilst there was scarcely any of this fine fare filling the bellies of the victims of war abroad in England, we could also add to our list the smell of a freshly-cooked rabbit – the finest white meat you could wash down your throat (said Dowager).

# Inside John's Gate

Yesterday the two-men-of-us had thrown themselves out the half-door in search of adventure below inside John's Gate. It wasn't a day for a child's growing imagination to be taken up with bunches of piss-a-bed wildflowers and silvery thistles or the singing of the birds. It wasn't a day to be seen chasing after cloud-shadows above on The Hill of The Goldfinches with Dowager. There was far more serious work to be done before the day was out and it would send rich feelings coursing through Teddy's veins. For the moment it was good to be near the wellingtons of his uncle and to smell the puff of his rich tobacco-smoke as they walked among the last of the flies that were drawing their richness from the cows' dung. It was good for Blue-eyed Jack (and the spirit-of-a-poet that was forever inside him) to be walking through a silence that seemed to saturate the inside of his chest to overflowing. And for Teddy, apart from his early visit to the funeral of Father Chasible, today was a chance for him to be away from tending to Dowager's hens and her ducks and her geese as they vied for pride-of-place in the yard. It was a chance (already well-planned-out for him by his uncle) to step aside from the black folds of his grandmother's apron and follow the big man into the heartland of Nature above in the hills. In many ways it would be similar to the time he had gone off rambling with Dowager to visit Gentility and enrich his soul.

The two-men-of-us continued to the lower edge of the farm and towards the wire fence that surrounded The Bog Wood. Blue-eyed Jack showed Teddy the rabbit-droppings. He pointed out their colour and their shape. They were the same as the black-puddings and sloes but much smaller in size. In his mind's eye our killer-of-a-man was already whittling the thatch-roof hazel-wands and was ringing the steel wire onto them to make his snare-stakes. He showed Teddy where he'd place these snare-stakes along the paths that the rabbits used when running out from the wood. He told him how the rabbit's neck would get broken when it struggled to get free from the snare. He warned him that the two of them would have to be out of bed even before the sun came up – that they'd have to race like the devil to reach the snares before the teeth of the wicked old fox or the beak of the hungry carrion crow had eaten their way into the rabbit's gable-end, for it was at that end of the poor creature that they'd strike first. Though barely three, the little fellow felt a great big weight growing inside him when he thought of these little rabbits and they dying like that and his thoughts went back to another death and the yellow face of Father Chasible on his deathbed and the rosary-beads entwined through his long saintly fingers.

They made their way back home to Dowager. In the haggart they came across a squealing rat that was caught in one of Blue-eyed Jack's traps at the side of the tar-barrel of oats and was trying to drag himself and the heavy trap to his comrades in the ditch. Its body left a trail of blood and the big man put it out of its misery with a few belts of a stick. For the rest of the hour Teddy watched his uncle on his chair in the yard as he fixed his snare-stakes with the wire and the hazel wands. Later in the evening and before the dusk set in they'd go down to the Bull-Paddock and they'd drive the stakes securely into the rabbit runs.

# The Big Gun Above The Hob

Blue-eyed Jack came back in the door and he cast a careless eye up at the ledge to the side of the hob. That's where he kept the horse's cropper and haymes and the ass's collar and winkers and behind them the goose-wings for dusting in the corners of the rooms and further back and hidden from view the double-barrel gun that belonged to Rambling Jack. It wasn't licensed and it was used (unlike Lord Elegance's sporting guns) only when food was needed to fill a man's belly and today would be a fine day for putting his gun to good use. The rains of the previous night had left the after-grass as juicy and sweet as could be and it made a perfect feast for the masses of rabbits living in The Valley of The Black Cattle less than a mile away.

# The Misfortunate Ferrets

Many years before the arrival of Teddy, the yellow musky ferret (Luther) had been the most favoured guest in The Welcoming Room. His boxed cage was at the foot of the press-cupboard and for a week or two after his arrival he was a source of daily amusement for Dowager's several children as he and his jingly bell patrolled up and down inside the box's wire netting. It had been Luther (rather than the gun or the snare) that was soon going to bring home a supply of fine rabbits for the table – though at first he'd be used for chastising only the mice and rats that were forever raiding the barrel of oats. At that time Blue-eyed Jack was not much bigger than Teddy was now. His father (Handsome Johnnie) took him and Luther up to The Valley of the Pig for their first ever rabbit-hunt together. Handsome Johnnie was carrying his shovel and his crowbar in case he'd have to spend the whole day digging Luther out, should he be fast asleep or altogether dead inside in the burrow or maybe getting too friendly with a dead rabbit and eating into it for himself.

Little Blue-eyed Jack was given the job of carrying his father's hat so as to catch the rabbits when they ran away from Luther and out into the nets already thrown around the mouth of the burrows. He would never forget that first day's hunting. That good-for-nothing Luther failed to chastise even a single rabbit and he almost died of shock inside in the burrow when he found himself coming face-to-face with half-a-dozen nimble rats as they went leaping out over his head. The poor fellow jumped two feet in the air and he fled from the mouth of the burrow and he never entered a burrow again. Indeed he was never seen again and some men at the drinking-shop made a laugh out of it and they said that Luther could still be seen running around the hills on the night of a full moon – even to this day!

Some years later Luther's successor (the faithful Velveteen) had a taste for freedom and was forever attempting to escape from his box. He had once got as far as the yard and attacked one of Dowager's geese only to get his neck and throat severely slashed by the angry gander. Blue-eyed Jack was left with his two sides bursting from fits of laughter as he captured the mystified ferret and put him back in his box. But there was no stopping Velveteen and a few months later he made his escape once too often. Stylish was one of Dowager's younger sons and a veritable rascal amongst his brothers and sisters. At times he got bored easily and was constantly looking for a new way of amusing the household to while away the morning. One morning he left the hasp of the cage open whilst The Old Pair were abroad milking. Whereupon the grateful Velveteen made a sudden unwelcome appearance onto the middle of the floor. He got alarmed when he heard the screams of the children and he scurried up the sides of the dresser and he smashed at least half of Dowager's best plates. By now the children were frightened out of their wits and they ran hysterically round and around The Welcoming Room, the girls holding onto their skirts in case the little devil ran up their legs and got intside their knickers. Dowager raced in from washing out the creamery tank and she saw the sudden cause of the ructions and she pounced on Velveteen with thoughts of chastising him with the scrub-brush. In her haste her grip was far too low down on his back and the desperate creature twisted his sinewy body and he bit into her little finger with his steely teeth and he held on to her for dear life.

Blue-eyed Jack came in the half-door. He saw Velveteen dangling in mid-air and his poor mother's face whiter than a sheet. He ran to the fire and he pulled out a blazing sod-of-turf with the tongs and he roasted Velveteen's backside with it before throwing him out onto the dung-heap behind the hen-house. That's when Reynard (for once a welcome fox) arrived on the scene and made off with a tasty morsel for his family's supper. Not one of the children mourned for the loss of Velveteen: 'What possible use (blasht the pair of them!) were either of our two fine ferrets to anyone?' cried Dowager as she wiped the tears from her eyes and nursed her broken finger (it had started to swell up). 'First it was Luther,' said she. 'What a brave little ferret he was supposed to have been until he pissed himself whilst running away from a few lousy rats. And then it was Velveteen and his love for amusement outside the confinements of his cage'. But for once in her life Dowager found that she was merely talking to herself; for by this time Blue-eyed Jack had taken his bike from the hen-house wall and was racing like the wind to Doctor Glasses' front door to tell him to come quickly and deal with his poor mother's broken finger before she died altogether on himself and the other children. And then where would they all be?

# *'Let's Shake Hands With The Open Road'*

Blue-eyed Jack was now anxious to be out on The Open Road before the rabbits had finished their breakfast and he lifted the gun down from the ledge. He hated to see it lying up there and getting rusty and he fondled its hammer absent-mindedly. Dowager gave him a wink and she ran to the triangular box above her bed. Though they were dear to buy, she took down a box of shiny-tipped red cartridges and brought them out to Blue-eyed Jack. You could see how proud she was of her son and his gun. For whereas other hunters might sometimes be a little messy and their guns be known to damage the body of a rabbit to such an extent that their women couldn't sell it at the shop, Blue-eyed Jack had a shooter's eye and a pin-point accuracy that was every bit as sharp as his mother's tongue.

He let Teddy roll the cartridges around in his fingers and feel their shiny smoothness and admire their fierce red colour. He told him to put the box in his pocket and to hand the cartridges to him when they got out on the road and were up near The Hills-of-The-Past. Apart from wanting a few rabbits for the pot he had the usual desire to increase Teddy's daily education for him and before this day was done he'd be sure to point him out a number of new sights – among them the rabbits' long ears and their smoke-coloured tails and the streak of ginger running down along the length of their backs.

There was another side to this day's hunt (he knew, but kept it to himself): this year those infernal rabbits had broken down every single ditch in The Valley of The Pig. They had destroyed the two cabbage-fields of Ned-the-Herd and this same fellow swore that it was as if a storm of hailstones had hit his barley-field, so much ruin had the little devils caused him.

Up until today it had been a good life for rascals like our hillside rabbits – with all that fresh vegetation to feast on to their heart's content. When the sun came up each morning you'd see them out at their play amongst the little finches that came across from The Hill of The Greenfinches to sing in their ears and whip cheekily across their backs and annoy them while they were busy chewing on the succulent groundsel and the white-starred chickweed. It was, however, going to turn out a very different story this morning. It was going to be a day for Man and his mighty big gun – a day when the younger more foolish rabbits would introduce themselves to Teddy at their peril – instead of being careful and cautious like their wise old mothers had warned them to be.

The two hunters were almost ready for the road and Blue-eyed Jack sat with his small nephew in the light of the window. He showed him how the gun worked and with the joined-up length of rags he carefully greased and oiled it so that it was now ready and primed for the hunt. He warned Teddy that, if he was to go off hunting on this great big rabbit-hunt, he would have to be quieter than a mouse in case the rabbits cocked up their ears and heard them coming up around Moll-the-Man's yard. And then there was another problem: Lord Elegance might be out hunting like themselves for he loved to feel the air of the hills getting inside his old lungs. And these fine-weather days gave him the chance to be using his gun on his pheasants or his wild ducks or his laughing partridges. Nobody with a stem of sense would want to come face-to-face with this nuisance-of-a man (said Blue-eyed Jack, half to himself) especially if they were carrying Rambling Jack's unlicensed gun and with no rightful excuse to be killing the lord's precious rabbits. 'I'll be quieter than a little snail,' said Teddy. Then Dowager came out to the half-door and she blessed her two great hunters with a shower of her holywater from the font.

## 'Time To Introduce Ourselves To Some Fine Rabbits'

'Let the two-men-of-us go and kill a few fat rabbits for ourselves,' said Blue-eyed Jack, looking down tenderly at Teddy and wiping away the few drops of holywater that were hanging on the bridge of the child's nose. He'd bring home at least one rabbit for the pot and maybe another one for Smiling Babs and (if luck prevailed) a third one to give to Cackles or to sell below at Curl 'n' Stripes' shop. The big man and the little man headed across the flagstones and they took The Open Road that led into The Hills-of-The-Past, which would still be loud with the song of the wrens and the corncrakes. Struggling to keep up, the little boy bravely attempted to copy his uncle's manly strides and he toddled along beside the flapping wellingtons of his uncle. From the high trees in the rookery a few crows spiritedly cawed after him and little gushes of wind came down from the hills and welcomed him and they climbed up his trouser-legs. Once again, as on his visit to Gentility, there was the smell of various grasses and the quietness of the sunlight and his young eyes were all the time looking out for the whiteness of a rabbit's tail. In his imagination he soon saw several rabbit-tails and their owners all hunched up in the haunting shades of the bushes (the little liar!)

Blue-eyed Jack held the faithful gun slanted downwards. He puffed pensively on his pipe and his brows were drawn together almost in a frown. The tobacco-smoke drifted back over his shoulder and was like pure honey to the little hunter. The present season was one that the big man loved, when the farming was all done – misty October and the wind-raking breezes all over the ice-grey sky. He knew every blade of grass, every haw-berry on the ditches. He felt akin to all the swallows that were readying themselves to fly off to faraway places heard tell of only in his books. And though the children called this upland 'Rabbit-Land', some of the old people called the place 'Heaven' for its fields were the greenest on earth and there were no sowthistles better in the whole of Ireland for greasing the bellies of our pampered rabbits.

## A Big Man's Serious Reverie

Blue-eyed Jack slackened his pace to that of the child. He was thinking to himself how big and strong Teddy was growing and how in one or two year's time he'd be starting out to the school-house of Dang-the-skin-of-it. But would the little fellow still be left here? With the hands of the clock on the dresser ticking the hours and the days away, he dreaded the thought that this war with the Germans might end sooner than anyone imagined. It would mean that Little Nell and Shy Patsy would come racing across the sea and snatch Teddy back to a dreadful life on the gloomy streets of London. And just as one or two rabbits would die under his gun this very day he knew that his own heart would surely die if such a day ever came for this little boy to be suddenly taken away from him – so much had he grown to love him. They strolled on and he sighed heavily and he spat his tobacco-juice out disdainfully. Such a cruel fate, this blasted war – to have sent a baby boy to him and Dowager from across the waters and one day to be wrenching him away whenever that day should come. Dowager too must have had these disconcerting little thoughts whilst sitting opposite him at the dying fire in the quiet of each night. And neither of them could deny that behind their daily joy there was always this one great dread and they dared not mention it (not even to one another) for it was far too painful to endure.

# Teddy Was Learning To Be A Hunter

Teddy was running on ahead of the big man and he was trying to leap out over the fresh heaps of dung from the horses and cows. Blue-eyed Jack had to bend down and whisper a few more admonishing 'shushes' into his ear and remind him of his promise to keep as quiet as a snail. A small hunter needed the eyes of a great big hunter (he said) and to be always on the lookout for Lord Elegance in case he popped out his head from the bushes to steal their gun away from them. He himself would be unable to hunt for the rabbits (he said) without the help of Teddy. And then he called him 'My Little Patroller' – a phrase that had no meaning whatsoever for the child.

Teddy, without understanding it, could feel the mystery and the intrigue and he continued to be as dutiful as ever as his eyes skimmed the length and breadth of every bush and field – so much so that within the next few minutes he had made out several fabled sightings of the dreaded Lord Elegance inside the bushes. 'Will there be many rabbits when we get to Rabbit-Land?' he wanted to know. For he tried to picture what would happen when they got there. Blue-eyed Jack had described earlier with the movement of his hands how a pile of rabbits would do somersaults in the air when they heard the sound of the great big gun.

'You'll see a much greater number than the fifty you and your grandmother know how to count up to,' he smiled. As though mulling over the seriousness of the child's question, he got down on his hands and knees and he cocked his ear to the ground and he nodded his head in satisfaction: 'Would you believe me, Teddy,' he whispered, 'I can hear the hammering of a little rabbit's heart in Ned-the-Herd's Field. Again he smiled to himself and his little fellow-hunter felt the excited hammering of his own heart and he was reassured.

Higher and higher the two hunters trudged, breathing in bellyfuls of mountain air and they turned into a grassy lane and were screened off from the world of Rookery Rally. The trees here were shot through with the lovely autumn colours of a dead pheasant and yet these same trees seemed a bit sad as though they had eyes of their own and were disturbed by the arrival of Man and were scrutinizing every move the two hunters were making. These were the glades under whose canopies the Rookery Rally children roamed and lost themselves in earlier September when they brought out their jam-jars in search of wild berries for their mother's tarts. At milking time they'd return with a good deal more juice sprinkled down along their dresses and trousers than was in the jam-jars.

The big man paused, panting for breath. He saw that it had been a long journey for Teddy and that his short legs must be sore and weary by now and he lifted him up on the broad of his back. As they went on he continued to point out this tree or that tree and which ones shed their leaves and which ones didn't and which berries were good to eat and which were bad ones and which trees made good firewood and which did not. All this was said in the faintest of whispers since the long-eared rabbits were able to hear a tiny twig snapping or a leaf falling from a mile away (he said) and even now they might have heard the approach of the two hunters' wellingtons. It was just as well that they were on the right side of the wind (he said), for every rabbit depends on its sense of smell and, if they knew that the hunters were near, their little rabbit-feet would be thumping out furious messages to their brothers and sisters from field to field. That's what he said. But how much of this went straight into one of Teddy's young ears and straight out the other ear is anybody's guess.

## Time For Those Shiny-Tipped Cartridges

Blue-eyed Jack nudged Teddy to give him the cartridges from his coat-pocket. The child handed him the cartridges, knowing by now that they meant death. It was hard for him to understand what was going to happen to one or two specially chosen rabbits within the next hour. He knew that at this very moment they were hopping around in the field and hadn't the foggiest idea that death was on its way and that it was waiting for them round the corner. Very soon they would lie still in the posture of death like Father Chasible in his great big box. Without knowing why (and how could he?) the excited spirit of a primitive little hunter began to rise up inside in his chest – the spirit of the blood-letter being fostered within him by his guardian on this day of the huntsmen.

# A Sight, Better Than Silver Or Gold

They veered through Sandy Dough's Field and they tiptoed catlike along inside the ditch, the big man's eyes forever searching the fields. He put Teddy gently down from his shoulders and he clambered over a nearby gate. He silently lifted the little hunter over and onto the ground, careful to avoid the mud at the entrance. They continued up the hill towards Tom Yawn's Hill and came to a sudden halt a few feet inside the briary gap. In a pool of red sunlight on the level heights Blue-eyed Jack pointed to a strange burrow in the middle of the field. He crept furtively up to it and he beckoned Teddy to follow him and come near. 'I have something to show you that no-one else has seen and it is far better than any silver or gold,' said he. Teddy stooped down to look inside the burrow. And there he found a small wonder indeed – a nest of baby-rabbits with their bodies hairless and their heads as pink as newborn mice. Nearby and hidden from view and powerless to defend her innocent babies there crouched an alert mother-rabbit, shivering in the ditch and boring her fierce eyes into the hunters. She had seen how Blue-eyed Jack had pushed aside the surrounding mounds of rabbit-fur that was topped with bits of dry grass so as to make a safe hiding-place for her little family.

For Teddy here was a sight every bit as enticing as the Maytime chicks that he had seen in Gentility's teachest. His eyes sparkled and almost fell out of his head and he yearned to bring one of these little creatures home and look after it as a pet. He would have given up even his toy farm of berries and his rusty bowlee-wheel for just one of these small creatures, but Blue-eyed Jack, though he was equally wonder-struck, didn't let him take so much as one of them from its delicate nest to stroke. In church-like silence they stayed a while longer, gazing down, and then Blue-eyed Jack and Teddy and his heavy heart put back the dry grass and the rabbit-fur just as delicately as they had found it. 'Sleep well, my little ones, in your dark place,' said the big man and he dragged Teddy away.

# Reaching Tom Yawn's Field

With velvet feet they moved along the side of the ditch beneath the sun's shadows and Teddy was thankful that his uncle had not thought of killing the baby-rabbits. Blue-eyed Jack kept the barrel of his gun hidden so that its shinyness would not be noticed by any watchful rabbits. And in return for his kind treatment of the newborn rabbits the big man's prayers were now answered. In front of him on the downward slope of Tom Yawn's Field lay a great big rabbit, stretched out in all his glory and sunning himself in the noonday sun. He was sleeping like a baby, his white belly moving in and out like Hammer-the-Smith's bellows. Blue-eyed Jack's nerves tautened the same as a hunting-dog. Never again would he get a chance to catch himself so handsome a rabbit as this – and with such little hardship to himself. He lifted Teddy down from his back and ('shush, my little fellow!') he perched him on the side of the ditch so that he could behold what he himself had seen – this big buck rabbit to whom death might shortly reach out its hand with the unexpected arrival of Man and his swift-striking wrist. After the excitement of the baby rabbits this was yet another picture for a child's awestruck wonder. He gazed at the grey-and-brown fur of the rabbit. He gazed at its white belly and its tail and the way the gentle breeze made the fur move along its sleeping back. Up till this minute life had been ever so good for this rabbit with its belly full of the dewy juices of these hills.

On fairy feet the big man crept out from the ditch. His back was bent double like a ferret's. And soon – in less time than you'd dance a jig-step – he snapped the hind legs of the rabbit. With its incredulous muscles and its disbelieving eyes-of-death the rabbit scarcely had a chance to give Blue-eyed Jack the fierce kicking he was half-expecting from it. And with one swift clip behind its ears he took away its life. He looked back at Teddy with a wrinkle-of-a-smile on his lips and he whispered, 'Dowager will be as happy as a sandboy – this fine rabbit will make a tasty soup for this week's dinner,' and he held his rabbit aloft in triumph and returned to Teddy at the ditch.

He reached into his pocket for his penknife. He cut an incision through one of the rabbit's hind legs so as to put the other leg in through it. As he didn't want to reach another field further along the lane that might be full of rabbits and to show them the sight of this dead rabbit hanging down from the barrel of his gun, he wrapped the dangling rabbit around the overhanging branch of a tree, to come back for it later in the day. The big man stood looking at Teddy. The child was looking into the dead rabbit's eyes. He saw that they were no longer soft and warm like the eyes of a dog or a cat. Blue-eyed Jack knew what was in the little boy's mind: the rabbit's eyes were steely and already frozen in the bleak sterility of its sad sad death.

## Entering Ned-The-Herd's Field

They left Tom Yawn's Field. Teddy with his finger on his lips strode prudently along beside his uncle, half-running to keep up with the happy man's dancing feet. His little heart was again hammering inside in his chest for he had witnessed the death of a rabbit at very close quarters. And then Blue-eyed Jack led him across the lane to a much wilder place behind Ned-the-Herd's Field – to the secret home (he said) of all the world's rabbits – Rabbit Land. And suddenly their eyes were full of rabbits. Blue-eyed Jack let out a sigh of pure pleasure and he clutched Teddy nervously by the arm. Rabbits, rabbits, rabbits and even more rabbits – as countless as the thistles and clover that grew in Smiling Babs' Field and with the dew still soaking into their long brown backs. And the two hunters turned into a pair of church statues and it was as if they were two shapes frozen in the wind.

Blue-eyed Jack lifted Teddy up to get an even better view and there was a look of the purest incredulity in the eyes of the little hunter – a stifled look, which could only belong to a small child as he gazed for the very first time on such a field. He knew by now that Death was very close and was only a few seconds away for one poor rabbit. 'If only ye little rabbits were aware of our coming and the presence of our great big gun (he would have said, had he the words in his head), how frightened ye would be and what wings ye would put upon yeer four feet!'

In their crouched position the two hunters could see the way the very young rabbits kept close to the side of their mothers. They could see how the mothers had their ears forever cocked and their eyes fully alert. In

94

spite of this there were some very careless adolescent rabbits and they were hopping around haphazardly in the grassy dew (the silly things) and there were a few more of them lying down luxuriously in the sun and making a great show of their enjoyment and there were yet more of them even more foolish and they were sporting with each other: they were well and truly ripe for a hunter's gun. 'What do we care?' they seemed to say. 'We young rabbits love the cool breezes in the tall grasses and we love the petals of the sunlight on our tails and we hate the cowardly shadows of the ditches.'

Teddy could see how some of the rabbits spent their time twitching their noses and then rubbing them through their paws. He could see them stretching out their sinewy backs and their hind legs one at a time. He could see their white bellies as they reached up to nibble at one or two tasty leaves. They looked full of health and they were already fat like their mothers and it was as if they couldn't eat another single bite. Tomorrow, however, one of them would no longer be sunning himself in Rabbit-Land. He'd be in Dowager's black pot.

The big bucks were far wiser and that's why they had lived for such a very long time. They sat as rigid as could be and they kept away from the middle of the field. Some of them seemed to shiver and quake as though they had already spotted the gun and their eyes were constantly fixed on the mouth of their nearby burrows. Perhaps they knew that one of their younger brothers and sisters would this very day meet its unexpected wintertime and die. 'Run, young rabbits, run! Come back to the ditch, you foolish young rabbits, come back!' they seemed to say.

Blue-eyed Jack (with Teddy as always trying to imitate him) edged himself across the grass and he hugged the little man to his side and they lay there, perfectly still for a long time as all hunters should do. (Dowager had always said that the patience of a true hunter ought to be written on a stone monument). In the meantime the older sentinel rabbits had stopped eating and were sniffing at the air. They stood stiffly on their tails. You could see their forepaws hanging down limply in front of them. They buried their ears into their backs and they pretended that they were some new kind of plant. And, just as the heron below in River Laughter knows how to stay stock-still when seeking its prey, they didn't move a single muscle.

# Teddy Is Prepared For His Kill

Once more Blue-eyed Jack's jaws tautened involuntarily as he prepared his gun for the rifleshot. He knew the drill: he would ready his aim: he would calculate the distance: he would steady his eye. He blessed himself and he said a silent prayer to Saint Jude the patron saint of all lost causes – just in case he'd miss with his cartridge. As soon as the first volley of the gun went off there'd be no second chance to get a crack at these rabbits – they'd fly like midges for the rest of the day.

'I must aim for the head,' thought Blue eyed Jack to himself. If he hit his rabbit in the back leg the poor creature would crawl away and die a miserable death inside in one of the nearest burrow. He raised and lowered his gun so as to get the most comfortable position before separating life from death in his chosen rabbit. He made Teddy tiptoe down the lane and wait for a signal from him. 'When I give you a nod of the head, you must clap your hands three times and be quick as a wink about it,' he whispered. 'It's only right and proper to give our little friends a fighting chance to run and escape with their lives.' He knew what would happen: the rabbits would look up to see where the clap was coming from: they would avoid the shame of being gunned down before getting at least a half chance to run from the bad man and his wicked gun. The sportsman in Blue-eyed Jack had always urged him to hold back his shot till the rabbits were speeding their way to their burrow and (besides) this would be the utmost test for the accuracy of Rambling Jack's gun.

Before sending Teddy off on his hand-clapping mission he pointed to a solitary rabbit a short distance away from its companions. And then – it was as though he were asking his little man to choose an apple from the barrel in Curl 'n' Stripes' shop – he asked him if he'd like him to kill this rabbit with his gun. It was a rare and decisive moment in an impressionable child's life. And Teddy nodded his assent.

The hunter fixed his eagle eye on the rabbit and he loaded up two cartridges and he readied his gun for the kill. Teddy was shuddering with new feelings, something akin to purest excitement. For the first time in his three-year-old life he could sense a strange kind of fear growing inside him – the terror that was about to be instilled into the kingdom of the rabbits.

He had never yet seen how a gun did its lethal work and with a child's inbuilt curiosity he wanted to know how the shiny cartridge was going to kill his chosen rabbit and how it was going to turn what was a breathing soul into just a piece of dead flesh that'd be as still as the stump of an old tree-root and as lifeless as Father Chasible and the chicken on which Dowager had done her work with her short-handle axe last Christmas.

When he was safely down the lane Blue-eyed Jack gave him the signal. Without a shadow of guilt Teddy (the little Judas) then destroyed the tombstone silence of the hills by clapping his hands three times as instructed. 'Am I being a good little hunter?' his eyes seemed to say back to his uncle just as all the rabbits' fear-filled eyes looked up the field towards the sound from his clapping hands.

'Here come Man and his great big gun. We must run – run faster than the speeding bullet from the gun,' they seemed to say. And then, as he watched the panicking tribe of rabbits eating their way down the field, Teddy's shivering temples felt their frightening hearts inside in himself and his very spirit began to struggle to get out from his body and skedaddle down the hillside along with them.

# Teddy And The Loud Gun – And The Kill

It had taken but a second for the field to come alive with the running feet of the tail-bobbing rabbits as they scattered in zig-zags and bumped hysterically into one another, forgetting what their mothers had taught them when they were little. Among them there were a number of rabbits that had been hiding themselves in the long grass. They suddenly belched forth from their hiding-places and not one of them had time to give a squeal or a cry as they sought the safety of the ditch. In the midst of all this wonderment Blue-eyed Jack's face had darkened and he became filled with that age-old inspiration to kill and kill again with his double-barrel gun. There followed the double whiplash sound – crack! crack! – of the reverberating gun as it abruptly punctuated the whole of Rabbit-Land. It was like the roar from a great big cannon. It was as if the hills would fall down on top of Teddy's head. So frightened was our little hero that just as with his past fears of the sow and the gander and Old Corkscrew and the leprechauns in Fort

Dangerous and The Boodeeman in The Big Cave Room – he almost died on the spot.

The bullet had gone straight into the head of the little hunter's chosen rabbit – the one that had been foolish enough to look around and ponder over the sound. He had faltered close to the ferns near the ditch as though (what was it?) he was trying to scent the breezes behind him. 'Too late! Too late!' sighed the older rabbits from the safety of their burrows as the young simpleton kicked his legs in a mid-air leap and with an unuttered gasp fell down limp and dead. There were a few splashes of blood on the ferns and one or two of his fluffy tail-bits floated towards the two hunters and their gun-stenched nostrils. At the sound of the gun the crows and the jackdaws had flown off to safety, screeching maniacally from the top of the trees and with Death echoing back up at them. Teddy could see the smoke rising up from the gun. He could smell its cordite and its gun-grease. And then there came into him that unreal mood – a strange and almost overpowering feeling – a feeling that always comes to a child after the killing of a rabbit – and it was accompanied by the field's silence condemning the very sunlight to run away and hide from Rabbit-Land.

From every ditch and every burrow a hundred pairs of eyes peeped out and brothers and sisters looked at the pathetic dead form of their lost companion (Tombstone Teeth). They recalled the recent joys they had shared with him when he had felt brushing against his chest the hilly breezes that whistled down the length of Ned-The-Herd's Field and they were all left bereft and weary-eyed to see him lying out there pathetically on the hill and he mistily dead. The air had become a barren and bleak place. There was nothing but the crackle of the grass under the feet of Blue-eyed Jack as he stood up and brushed the wet leaves from his threadbare britches. Teddy stood next to him and then he felt a bout of curious energy coming to birth inside in him and he ran scurrying down the length of the hill-space to gaze upon the shot rabbit.

The little hunter reached the poor creature. His eyes were at once entranced and he felt the unexpected pain of a deep sorrow inside in him when he saw the blood on the grass and the ferns. The rabbit's glazed eyes seemed to stare back up blindly at him (is this what it's like to be dead?) and its teeth gaped helplessly and senselessly like the white tombstones below in the graveyard. Teddy thought he saw the traces of a few tears in the eyes of Tombstone Teeth and he knew that it was his very own clapping hands that had helped his uncle to kill the poor creature. He saw where the rabbit had been shot above the eyes. He saw the bloodstains dripping onto the fur of its white belly – this still-warm belly which he longed to touch but knew that his fingers would get no joy from stroking or hugging it, unlike the fur of the playful kittens on the ass-and-car back in the farmyard.

And now (if only a three-year-old child could have put it into words) he had the feelings of a real killer just like Blue-eyed Jack with his gun and like Dowager the time she sawed off the neck of the goose in The Welcoming Room and the time she went out to the haggart to kill a fat duck, resting her two knees in the middle of its back and its chest puffed out with air. How he had pleaded with her that she might spare the poor duck, but its life was soon to become nothing but a mere myth. And now once more – the alarm following this poor rabbit's death stirred itself inside in his chest and it troubled him and he was too young to know the reason why.

There was more to come: the second bullet from the gun's double-barrel had bounced off of the first rabbit, hitting another rabbit nearby. And now it was shaking and jerking the last few breaths out of its dying body. Blue-eyed Jack ran down the field towards where Teddy was standing. He was just in time to catch hold of the little hunter's arm and to prevent him from getting too close to this poor rabbit. Its fiercely kicking feet would have clawed the arm off of him and drawn more than a little of his English blood from him. And what would Dowager have had to say about that when she saw the pair of them sloping guiltily in over the flagstones later in the evening and The Little Englander with his arm hanging off of him?

Blue-eyed Jack stood over his nephew and (as with the rat caught earlier in the trap in the haggart) he put this rabbit out of its misery, clipping it behind its ears. He lifted both rabbits up by their hind legs and he ordered Teddy to touch the warm fur and to stroke the silky smoothness of each forehead. The little hunter did so. He saw the blood streaking all over his hands. Blue-eyed Jack dabbed some of the blood on the child's neck. He wiped more of it across his cheeks. 'Now you have become a real true hunter,' said he. But the pain inside in Teddy's chest would not go away and he thought of all the other rabbits still alive and he thought of these two rabbits – Tombstone Teeth and his brother, dead beside him. As young as he was he could fully understand and have feelings for the eyes that would no longer see anything and the ears that would never again hear anything and the teeth that would no longer chew the dewy grass and the fur that would never again feel the drenching rain lashing into these two small rabbits.

With his penknife the big man cut holes in the hind legs of both rabbits and he asked Teddy to load the dead rabbits onto the barrel of the gun. They were not too heavy for a child to carry and there they lay, side by side in death and as close together as fleas on a dog's back. Blue-eyed Jack placed the gun on his shoulder and the two hunters headed up towards the gap and out onto the lane. For Teddy it had been the very same as another funeral, as he trudged along beside these two dead rabbits that had been enjoying the sunlight for the very last time this afternoon and that were now (unlike himself) as still and as dead as Father Chasible below in a black hole in the graveyard of Abbey Acres.

Suddenly they heard the shouts of Ned-The-Herd, who had been checking on the health of his black cattle. Blue-eyed Jack looked in that direction and gave him a wave of his hand to show that he understood the reason for Ned's shouts. At the edge of the field was yet another rabbit – a rabbit with some strange mystical powers of its own. It was sitting bolt upright without a care in the world. Its forepaws were curled across its chest. Had this rascal-of-a-rabbit no fear of Man and his big gun? Blue-eyed Jack continued to chew on his bottom lip: either the rabbit had been born deaf or his two ears had been suddenly damaged by the sound of the gun. And then he began to smile. And then he began to grin. And then he burst out laughing at his own stupidity so that Teddy thought a bit of crabapple must have got stuck in the big man's throat. 'Go fetch me that rabbit,' he ordered his young hunter.

Teddy ran down the length of the field but was beaten to it by Ned-The-Herd. Blue-eyed Jack himself came running close behind the little fellow's heels. The three of them could see that this young rabbit was as stiff as a board and as dead as could be – even though it hadn't a single drop of blood on its face. Ned-The-Herd touched the rabbit with his wellington and the poor creature keeled over with its forepaws in the air. It had been wedged into a tight hole in the ground just like a cork in a bottle of stout and unable to move a single muscle when it heard the terrifying sound of the gun. The shock of the exploding cartridge had simply stopped its poor feeble heart and prevented it from racing after its brothers and sisters. Blue-eyed Jack handed the rabbit to Ned-The-Herd. After all, the two-men-of-us had three fine rabbits of their own to bring home to Dowager – the two on the barrel of his gun and the one that was hanging on the branch of a tree outside Sandy Dough's Field. Three rabbits were more than enough for anyone. Unless you were a living legend, the whole of Rookery Rally knew that it was harder for a hunter to kill three rabbits than it was to put The Hills-of-The-Past inside in your back pocket. Fair play to you, Blue-eyed Jack! Fair play to you, little Teddy! You have three fine rabbits to take home to Dowager on your very first day out hunting and won't The Open Road be full of the tale of it and won't The Little Englander strut himself up and down among the hens and geese for the next week-and-a-half!

And yet Blue-eyed Jack could see that Teddy was feeling both the joys of the kill and the sadness that came from the sight of death. 'With so many rabbits up here in The Valley of The Black Cattle and with mother-rabbits bringing baby-rabbits into the world quicker than the blink of an eye,' he whispered, 'these three rabbits won't even be missed.' He gently ruffled the little man's curls and he promised him that they'd return in a week or two's time and that they'd put the fear-of-god into the heads of yet more rabbits with their gun and their cartridges. And as with Dowager's comforting words and his former fears of the leprechauns in Fort Dangerous, these re-assuring words drove Teddy's sadness away from him and it was replaced by the thought of how happy and dumbfounded his old grandmother would be at the sight of them and their dead rabbits. She would give one rabbit to Smiling Babs and another one to Cackles or to Gentility. Teddy hoped that before they crossed the flagstones and the yard-stream he'd be able to add to her happiness by gathering yet another big bunch of wildflowers with the help of his uncle. What a bright contrast these flowers would make to the fear-filled gaze of his three sad rabbits.

## Two Tired Hunters Were Homeward Bound

They left the gap and the grassy lane behind them. They found the third rabbit on the tree where they'd left it. The big man cut two sticks and he paired them into spits – one longer stick for himself and a shorter one for

Teddy and he placed the smallest rabbit on the child's stick. The two hunters swept on with their sticks hoisted over their shoulders and the bloody rabbit-heads dangled down in two neat lines like a Monday washing-line. With what powerful strides did the little hunter clutch his rabbit-stick as he strolled alongside his uncle's flapping wellingtons. Soon all his recent sadness was gone from him and there was almost a rabbit-hop to his triumphant jauntiness, so fluttery did the merry heart under his coat start to beat. Blue-eyed Jack's own spirits were also bathed in a cool beauty, so much happier was he with the capture of his rabbits and his mood (as always) continued to thrive as his nostrils breathed in the refreshing breezes that rustled their way down from the hills.

They chatted away in the language that a three-year-old child understood and they saw in their mind's eye the face of Dowager. She'd have a big fire blazing for them and so eager were they to get back home to her that they gave little heed to the damp mists that were beginning to fall around these shadowy fields in The Valley of The Black Cattle.

Blue-eyed Jack made a turn into a lane to the right of Moll-The-Man's hayshed. He was on the lookout for an ash-tree with a curly bend to its root and he came upon just the right tree. He marked it with a few drops of rabbit-blood. He would come back one evening and he'd cut it down. It would make a fine hurley-stick for Teddy and Big Tall Paddy in Brindley's Grove would fashion and plane it for him. What joy there would be for the little man when he found he was the owner of his first-ever hurley-stick, the reward for all his fine day's hunting. Before they re-entered the homeward trail Blue-eyed Jack cut another small branch from a tree. When it was trimmed and paired it would make a walking-stick gift for his mother so that she could chastise her cantankerous ass (The Lightning Whoor) and belt the sides off of her cows at milking-time when they hit her across the jaw with a lash of their shitty tails.

The afternoon was turning into evening and the hunters found they were not alone. In nearby fields the countless shadows of black crows and jackdaws were returning to their prickly nests and seemed to give the pair of them a raucous song of farewell. And then – there was silence – the silence of the two hunters' tiredness and their former chatter and jauntiness gave way to trudging steps. And then – at Scissors' Well there was the sound of the cold mountain stream running sluggishly along inside the ditch.

They emerged from The Hills-of-The-Past and this churchyard atmosphere again intensified. The smoky clouds of the earlier day grew foggier by the minute, peeping down over the tops of the high trees and the sky that overlooked faraway Clare looked pure grey-rat in colour. At last they glimpsed the vague outline of The Roaring Town and the winking bluebell-coloured lights that were already beginning to light up down there. Nearby they saw the first of the Rookery Rally cabins and the trails of smoke rising up above baking fires and then fading away into the sky like the light of this rabbiting day. Teddy soon heard the familiar rattle of the milking-buckets and the chains and tackling of Sam-the-horse as he entered Fiddler Joe's yard. All around these little thatched cabins he heard the last calls of the geese coming into the shed and the last footfalls of the horses, asses and cattle and the last squawking of the drakes like some rusty old bicycle chain as all these silhouettes ambled in to the different farmyards and haggarts.

And then he saw the first of the evening rabbit-lampers and Ayres 'n' Graces leading the swaying pack of them as they came trudging up towards Sheep's Cross on their night's rabbit-hunt. Once again (as when he came home from Gentility) they were pushing their bikes and leaning their fists on their saddles and their newfound buttercup lamplights shone on the road ahead of them. Teddy (as any child would have done) made a noble effort to lift his rabbit-stick as high as he could and he took on a somewhat pompous and assumed carelessness as he passed them by and he gave them scarcely a sideways nod of the head. 'Tis The Little Englander and his rabbit,' they said. And they smiled at one another.

## The End Of A Little Hunter's Big Day

The blue-glow dusk had well and truly settled in and the dew was heavy on the fur of the three rabbits. Before they reached the yard-stream Dowager heard the footfall of her two men for she knew the sound of her son's big wellingtons as well as a bad halfpenny. She left off darning the socks and she stood at the half-door with the lighted candle in her cupped fist and she listened to the little breezes outside as they shook the geraniums in her green window-boxes. As though carried on the wings of the wind Teddy came echoing in across the flagstones towards his grandmother and (tired as he was) he ran straight into the black midnight of her apron as she in her turn rushed out excitedly to meet her little hunter.

Were he to bring her a dozen bunches of bluebells or buttercups the old woman could not have been more pleased with the withered little nosegay of wildflowers that he handed her and she wrapped her twilight hanks of hair around him and she gave a little yelp of delight when the child held up his stick and pointed to the rabbit on it. 'See what we two-men-of-us have *brang* you, Dowager, (grammar was still a mute point) and look at the big rabbits we have shot and killed for you,' he said proudly. Then out from the semi-darkness behind the pig-house fuchsia bush darted Blue-eyed Jack and along with him was his big stick with the two rabbits on it.

When Dowager realized that there were three dead rabbits (a sight rarer than swallows in wintertime) she blessed herself and she raised her eyes to thank heaven for this new miracle. 'From what far-off place have ye wise men come? What great big journey have ye been making? ' she said in wonderment at her two noble hunters and she led them in through the half-door. She couldn't wait to get her ears round the rest of the day's news. She eyed Blue-eyed Jack suspiciously for a second – as though he had robbed one of the rabbit-poachers – and yet she knew in her heart that the big double-barrel gun had been invented for none other than the hands of her lovely son.

Teddy was as pleased as a tinker at Puck Fair and his grandmother ruffled his hair and she told him what a fine little hunter he had been and she hugged him for the second time against her black skirts. Blue-eyed Jack had two pockets full of pine needles and he threw a few handfuls of them onto the fire and Teddy watched as the flames climbed up frantically and caught hold of the other twigs and the dry turf and left little fires of laughter on the soot at the back of the hob.

The big man put the gun and the box of cartridges back safely in their hiding-place. Dowager blessed her two hunters with a shower of holywater. She sprinkled some of it on the floor and in the corners of The Welcoming Room to ward off the fairy-men of the night and those wicked spirits that Father Chasible (when he was alive) had told them were alive and kicking and always wandering across Rookery Rally and Copperstone Hollow in an effort to ruin our souls.

She was as busy as a gnat as she ran hastily this way and that, tripping over the horse's tackle where it lay beside the bucket of spring-water. She made several trips to the dresser and she laid out her delf and her cutlery. She kept her eyes on the fire to make sure that it was nothing short of a volcano and you should see the dance the bread she was baking now made as it hopped out onto her fire-stained hands when she tossed it from palm to palm to see was it ready for dispatching from the burner. Her black kettle was puffing with steam in readiness for Blue-eyed Jack's well-earned mug of tea and soon she poured the tea out, good and strong the way he liked it (in spite of the wartime scarcity). She got down her blue jug and she filled it with milk from the gallon and soon Teddy had a fine white moustache above his upper lip and his two guardians began to laugh and hold their sides in earnest. The three of them were in the very best of humour as they sat for a while round the blazing fire and toasted their shins.

It was time for Dowager to get out the soda-cake and cut thick slices of it. She covered each slice with layers of the blackcurrant jam that Smiling Babs had brought down to her, knowing well that the two hunters would be starved to death when they got home. There was a short spasm of silence as they sat at the table and leathered their way into the soda-cake and into a second feast – the apple-batter turnover that Dowager had baked earlier in the day from Gentility's apple-gift and which soon danced its way in several belches down into their stomachs. Dowager picked the blackcurrant skins from off of her toothless gums and Blue-eyed Jack heaved a sigh of pleasure ('oh-honey-oh!') and he got up and went to the white enamel bucket behind the door and took down the grey pewter mug from the nail. The spring-water tasted powerfully good and he helped himself to three flowing mugs of it and he drank into himself the peace that was being made by the ticking of the clock. He felt restored and replenished and he came and sat down beside the child near the fire. He took out his tobacco pipe and soon ('I have hunted well') he was blowing rings of its honey smell up into the rafters. He looked back at the three rabbits hanging on the back of the door and said: 'I must remember to take one up to Gentility tomorrow.' As an afterthought he said, 'Who on earth could refuse to take a gift to an old woman that was born in the same haggart as my own mother? And he and his mother both laughed.

He looked across at Dowager and they smiled at one another. 'Ah, it's me that's thinking what sweet-smelling rabbit-soup we'll be having in a day or two,' said he. He knew his mother would be busy as could be tomorrow. With

Teddy at her heels she would take her enamel pan and her gutting knife and she'd strip off the fur from her rabbit and would slit the skin up along the legs as far as the rabbit's elbow – a strange and new sight for the child to behold. The child and his innate curiosity would see the way his grandmother grimaced up her mouth as she blew air in under the rabbit's skin and ballooned it up and how she stripped the fur from off the belly and dragged it out over the rabbit's head so that she could sell it in Curl 'n' Stripes' shop. And while she was skinning her rabbit she'd paint a picture for Teddy to contemplate – a picture of the black skillet pot that'd be simmering on the hob next evening with the rabbit cooking inside in its depths. There'd be onions and cabbage as well as the spuds to fill up their plates and you can imagine how the rabbit-meat would be flaking off of the bones. Dowager liked nothing better than seeing her two men swallowing down a fine feed of rabbit and wiping the soup-stains from their oily mouths onto their sleeves after cleaning their plates snow-white with a sop of her bread.

Meanwhile on the back of the front door the three rabbits hung down their heads. Their limpid eyes seemed miserable even though they were dead and a little pool of dark blood gathered on the floor beneath them and it continued to drop down onto the axe-handle near the stool with the bucket of well-water. Teddy and his innocence gazed at the sleep that ends all sleeps and he thought about the three rabbits' deaths as he gazed at their button-eyes and their floppy ears, dangling there like a sock-ball at the base of a stocking. At three years of age he knew that life was not a plaything. This day of the hunt he had seen a few small rabbits alive and kicking and running towards the ditch when he clapped his hands. The next minute they were gone from the earth – as dead as dead could be. For them there'd be no more leaping around the fields and no more nibbling at the grass and he looked at them in disbelief for a considerable time, fascinated by their faces.

Blue-eyed Jack put some pink poison-paste on a few cuts of bread and he went out and he put them behind the horse's cart but not too near the hen's galavanized sheeting. During the night the rats would have a fine feed of the poisoned bread and that would put a stop to them plaguing the haggart where they were forever trying to get into the straw-covered pits of the harvested spuds and turnips as though the berries of the hawthorn tree weren't good enough for these little devils. Smiling Babs' cat (Hen-chaser) would pay a visit to Dowager's yard overnight and she would see the dead rats. She would drag them daintily up outside Dowager's half-door to show her when she arose from her bed in the morning. When she opened the door she'd find the results of her son's poisoned bread – a carefully arranged line of dead rats lying on their delicate backs for her to inspect and when Teddy rose from his own little nest he'd find himself gazing at yet another death – the death of the ugly pink-tailed rats.

Blue-eyed Jack got up and he stood at the door and breathed in the sweet scents of the dying day and he listened to the yard stream prattling away. He went with Teddy to the ash-pit to make their poolie and his big wellingtons broke the misfortunate backs of a few snails in the darkness. They came in and they barred the door for the night. Teddy could hear the bad-tempered gander making its way in from The Bluebutton Field (lucky if the fox didn't grab him). Blue-eyed Jack wound up his pocket watch. With tired and grainy eyes all three took the holywater in readiness for bed. Blue-eyed Jack got a mug of water and threw it on the fire to douse it. He raked up the ashes with his foot before hanging his socks on the crane. The Old Pair, armed with their two candlesticks, quenched the lamp and again retired to their separate rooms. Dowager was soon whispering a load of her prayers from her mother's prayerbook. The other two prodigals were in the cold depths of The Big Cave Room, their eyes penetrating into its dark recesses. They knelt on the damp potato-sacking and said the prayers that Teddy was learning – The Our Father and the Hail Mary. They got into the musty bed in their shirts and they rubbed each other's feet together and soon they'd be as snug as piglets around a sow and the child would feel the warmth of the big man's belly ('give me some more of the blankets!') as they listened to the faint drizzle of the rain and the wind tossing and turning in the haggart trees. The Little Englander would soon be asleep and dreaming of faraway fairy kingdoms and sunny fields that once were a home to these three dead rabbits.

In the meantime the rest of Ned-the-Herd's rabbits had no delusions about Man and what he could do to them. Like Teddy, they too were fast asleep in the blackness of the night. Galvanized with fear, the baby-rabbits clung close to their mothers inside the briars of the ditches and they thought of Blue-eyed Jack and they thought of Teddy too and they thought (above all) of the fierce supernatural powers of that great big double-barrel gun.

# SIX

# Dowager Takes Teddy To His First Mass

*Teddy went to the Church for the first time
and he met up with some new friends.*

It was July in the year of 1944. Sunday was the day for the crispness and the newness. It was the day of the well-ironed white shirt and the hard white collar. It was the day of the dark suits and the day when men put on their respectable cap (they had two) and practiced shaping them at the correct angle and not with the peak cockily opened at the button like the townies or rolled around back-to-front like a box-player. From Rookery Rally and from The Valley of The Pig and from The Valley of The Black Cattle and from Growl River itself they were going to Copperstone Hollow to meet their God in the little blue-and-white church humbly situated behind the huge dark church of 'the foreigners' as Dowager insisted on called the rich Anglo-Irish gentlefolk, who lived within our reach. It was the one and only day in the week when everybody put their faces on show before the eyes of the parish and not like an outing to a hurling-match or a Fair Day when it was only a man's pig or his bullock or his horse that held the centre of the stage.

The evening before Sunday Mass Dowager took out from the base of the press-cupboard the two polishing-brushes and the rag and the polish tin. This was the press-cupboard where Blue-eyed Jack oftentimes took out his shoe-last and his hammer, his cleets and his nails to repair the boots, dipping the pieces of leather into the water so as to soften them and then trimming and pairing the soles into shape with his penknife.

Polishing the three sets of boots was a job Dowager loved to be doing and doing well. And if soldiers from an army were to arrive in the yard and test her skills she'd knock them all into a cocked hat with the sheen and the shine she put into these boots and it was the heels ('you can always tell a gentleman by his polished heels') that got most of her attention. And while she was at it (just like her father before her) she'd be whistling a sibilant little whistle through her last few teeth – a tuneless and silent little whistle that you'd recognize through the wind of it. Then with an air of satisfaction she'd lay the three sets of boots out in a neat row before the fire.

## Getting Ready To Go Meet God

There followed the ironing of the Sunday clothes. The old woman heated the iron on the hot coals and she took it up to the light of the lamp to examine it and she spat on it. She wrapped the handle in a thick wad of brown paper and she began to iron with gusto, all the time talking away to herself. Soon you could smell the fresh linen and her Bird's starch and the aftermath of her little bags of the Ricketts blue. First of all she tackled her black skirt and then her best blue calico blouse – the one with the white dots on it. Then she tended to the two shirts of her big-and-little men and she placed all the warm clothes, almost lovingly, on the back of the chairs in front of the blaze to air.

Saturday evening was the time when men put the razor to their jaws (it was the only time they shaved – and Blue-eyed Jack was no exception). He left his cheeks as clean and as smooth as a little child's face and as shiny as a sweet-gallon for there wasn't a man in Rookery Rally who would go unkempt before his God. The big man rolled up his sleeves. He turned down his collar to leave his neck free. Teddy, like a young puppy, was always tripping beneath his feet when he saw his uncle propping up the broken bit of looking-glass on the window-shelf in The Big Cave Room. He watched him waxing the cut-throat razor on the leather belt and testing its sharpness with his sandpapery thumb. Blue-eyed Jack spread his legs wide apart and then he went to work with the soap and the razor. He always left a few whiskery cat-hairs, too sacred to touch, in under his eyes and he told Teddy that if he didn't leave them there, the next thing he'd be doing was shaving his two eyeballs and this piece of information caused the little boy to wonder if any of the other men in Rookery Rally were shaving their eyeballs these days.

When the mission of shaving his stubble was completed Blue-eyed Jack sluiced the water several times over his face and he inspected his jaws in the looking-glass. Like his handsome father before him he was proud of his flowery-coloured skin and he came out to The Welcoming Room and he took another gaze at his face, looking down at his reflection in the bucket of water on the stool, with Teddy peering down behind him. Then he showed his face to his mother and asked for her inspection and Dowager ran her hands across his skin and then she laughed in admiration and said: 'Y'are as smooth as a pig's bladder' and the two of them took a fit of laughing and Teddy laughed too.

After that, Blue-eyed Jack took the chair out into the yard and he rolled his shirt down to the waist and he washed his belly and his armpits with lashings of carbolic soap. Again and again he sloshed the water over himself and as he washed, he whistled a few bars of music from some old tune of his father's and his mother smiled out the half-door at the sight of him standing there in the yard – to see the power in his big body – and she thought lovingly of her own dear husband (Handsome Johnnie) now lying cold below in the graveyard, in whose mould Blue-eyed Jack had been fashioned.

The big fellow flung the soapy contents of the pan down the yard towards the hen-house-door, hoping to scatter a few rats that might be on the prowl and looking for an egg or two to take back to their family. Finally he tucked in his shirt and he hitched up his galluses and he came in the half-door and sat by the fire and dried himself with the rough towel. For a little while he aired his belly before closing up his shirt and then he took the rack and combed back his hair. To complete this trim-up he cleaned his teeth with the soot from the hob before spitting into the fire. At last he had completed his reverent preparations for next day's journey to God's house and he felt that he could put himself on show next to any beast or man the length and breadth of Ireland.

In the meantime Dowager selected her best walking-cane – the one with the shiny ivory handle. When it came to next day's Mass it was not for her to make use of her faded ash-plant or the sally-switch that she'd be using on the backs of her cows the following Monday. Like her son, she paid special attention to her appearance so as to put her best side out. She put a towel around her shoulders and neck. Then she washed her long black hair in a warm pan of water and it fell in tangles all around her cheeks, almost reaching the bottom of the stool on which she sat. She rinsed it time after time and she came and sat near the fire beside her big-and-little men. She looked steadfastly into the fire and she teased the hair into layers to dry it. The laughing flames danced before her eyes and they seemed to be looking back at her and her face was suddenly shone through with flickering light. This rich ropey hair of hers was her finest feature, like some indescribably sunlit river, and she was very proud of it and was forever fussing over it with the pins and redesigning her long tresses into new coils – a feat of almost mechanical engineering. And for next day's Mass she'd be plaiting it into a rope and twisting it up into what her dear departed husband had once called her precious loveknot.

Blue-eyed Jack loved to see his mother looking so well these days after her many years of toil bringing up her huge family with no husband at her side to help her. He knew the reason why she was so joyful – the arrival of her little man from England, who had filled her with an intense happiness these last three or four years and it was true for her – it was as if she had become a new bride all over again.

## Teddy And The Dreaded Bathtub

Next, it was time for Dowager to tend to her grandson. From as far back as he could remember (even before the death of Father Chasible) the child had had this awful dread of Saturday evenings. It was the time when Dowager brought in from a nail in the cowshed the big grey bathtub – the one she used for washing her sheets in. His fear of the bathtub was almost as bad as the fear he'd felt a year ago – the time of his first haircutting. It was just after Blue-eyed Jack had finished mowing the hay. There were times when the big man was the most prime of all mischief-makers and he

111

had told Teddy it was time to cut his hair with 'the machine'. Whereupon the poor child nearly died of fright; for the only 'machine' he had ever seen was this rusty old mowing machine – the one that slew countless frogs at harvest time. And he was sure that his head as well as his hair was about to be shorn clean off of his body.

Dowager now placed the bathtub in front of the heaped-up fire. Blue-eyed Jack filled it to capacity with clattering cauldrons of hot water from the bubbling crook. Teddy tried to hide in under the table for he knew that he was about to get an unmerciful scrubbing. His uncle made a grab at him and after much effort removed the little fellow's shirt and trousers, leaving him in the middle of the floor without a stitch on (like Reckless Rody the time of The Platform Dance).

The big man marched him over to the tub before he'd get his death of cold and he held him by his two heels upside-down and (with much laughter and shouting) he threatened to plunge him down repeatedly into the water so that his hair and ears would get the washing of his lifetime. This was far from a laughing matter as far as Teddy was concerned. You could hear the hapless screams of the little fellow and also (Dowager putting her hands over her ears) an added number of new ('feck' and 'shite') swearwords that Teddy had learnt from the visiting card-players and poachers during their evening visits. If you were pushing your bike up the hill from below at John's Gate you'd think one of their two pigs was being led out to be slaughtered.

To put an end to the child's tears Blue-eyed Jack soon changed his tune (enough was surely enough) and he started dipping the struggling child a little more gently – even sympathetically – into the water. Then Dowager came and took over and she put some of her best elbowgrease into the act. Between the two of them Teddy was eventually a mass of frothy soapsuds, which found their way into his eyes and began crackling inside in his two ears. It was no use his crying any more for he knew that his old grandmother was now in command and that she was bent on making him thoroughly presentable next morning. Her Little Englander had to be seen as a prince-among-men in the eyes of all and she'd make sure that he was.

To distract Teddy from his misery Blue-eyed Jack brought out the broken bit of looking-glass and he showed him his new angelic face – his china blue eyes and his pink-spud rosy cheeks, all seraphic-looking after the ritual of the bath. And even Teddy (for all the harshness of Dowager's scrubbing of him) had to admit that it was well worth being covered in soapsuds if he was to turn out so fine and decent-looking a gentleman as this.

As soon as the nightmare was over he was toweled and dressed in his shirt and britches and he sat for the rest of the evening in between his grandmother and his uncle. He was as snug as any little kitten, close beside the big turf fire, and he felt as good as he'd ever felt in all his life.

## Smiling Babs Was Busy As Well

Nor was it simply in Dowager's Welcoming Room that all the hustle and bustle went on each Saturday. A stone-throw away from Dowager lived Smiling Babs' brood of six children (the young rascals, as Dowager playfully called them). For once in their lives they'd have the misfortune of putting on their Mass boots when all they ever wanted since the day they were born was to run across the universe in their bare feet as Nature had intended. Saturday evening saw the steaming shirts and frocks and the copiously sweating chin of Smiling Babs as the good woman ironed the pile of clothes and rested them on the back of the chairs in front of the fire. The girls had the rags and the curl-papers and the hot tongs put into their hair – to be paraded up the church aisle with their ringlets of hair flowing back like a horse's mane in all directions. Each girl would be dressed in her best cotton frock and each boy in his best corduroy britches.

And whereas Fiddler Joe (the father of this happy flock) was busy testing out the harness and the axle of his pony-and-trap, Rambling Jack (another stone-throw further up the road) was busy with his bag of spanners and wrenches and his bicycle plasters and his adhesives, the smell of which filled his yard. He adjusted and wiped his saddle and he straightened out the odd spoke and the two wheels between the spokes. With his gentle fingers he trailed his inner tubes through the pan of water and he tested each of them for the odd little hole, spitting on the tubes and feeling for the bubbles of air where the latest puncture might be. You could almost hear the whistle of his hot pump filling up the hard tyres with air before he bounced his bike off of the yard in readiness for next day's Mass. The fuss the whole crowd of us were making in our attempts to uphold God's holy day would make you think that Bishop High-Hat himself was coming to say a Mass over us.

## *Dowager's Serious Reverie*

In a few months time when the autumn days would come to greet us Teddy would have reached the age of four. Dowager realized that his bath-time days were over. A certain sort of shyness had crept into her little man – a shyness at being stripped naked of his shirt and britches on these dreadful Saturday evenings and she hated to see him running around The Welcoming Room looking for a straw to shelter under and hide his private credentials. A new washing arrangement would start the very next Saturday the minute Blue-eyed Jack started showering himself abroad in the yard with the cold water from the yard stream. Teddy would follow him (he'd need no encouragement) and he'd wash himself likewise. After all, he had so often (with nothing else to do) sat upon the upturned ass-and-car in the yard and watched the way Blue-eyed Jack threw the cold water over his head from the stream after an afternoon out in the meadow and his one and only wish (wasn't it always the way?) was to follow in the big man's footsteps. It was going to be the happiest of all days for the little man – the day on which the continual war between himself and the bathtub would finally come to an end. At the stream – and after a few fox-like yelps out of the brave little fellow – the washing of his upper body and hair would become a matter of pure routine from now on.

But poor Dowager couldn't help heaving one last little sigh of regret. When it came to Teddy she always had the feelings of a mother-hen for its chick and she knew how much she was going to miss this Saturday-night ritual of her grandson's bath-time and those quivering feelings of affection that she hadn't felt since the days when Una (the last of her own fifteen children) had been a child the same age as this little fellow. She was going to miss rubbing him down with the hot towel until he looked as though he'd hopped out of a magic bandbox. She was going to miss the banter and the teasing between the two of them after the toweling was over when she would put on that dumbfounded air and that puzzled expression of hers and ask Teddy the same old questions over and over again from one Saturday to the next: 'Who is this brand new angel we have here in our midst? Where on earth has my little man, Teddy, gone to?' Could it be possible… was it… surely not… her very own Teddy that was here before her? These last few years she had spent so many pleasant moments after his bath-time hopping her grandson up 'n' down off of her bony old knees. She and her cleeted boots had rung out those nursery rhythms, which she was in the habit of whispering into his ears ever since the days of his babyhood – and in a voice that was as soft as a bog and as caressing as a lullaby.

There was another thought going on at the back of her wise old head this springtime and she felt the guilt of it: it was time to let her grandson make his first appearance at holy Mass and to be seen walking down the aisle alongside herself and kneeling before his God. And just as important – it was time for him to come eyeball to eyeball with some of the neighboring children when he went into the church each Sunday. For up until this year both Dowager and Blue-eyed Jack had sheltered him as though he were a priceless jewel to be forever enclosed and protected by the two of them. It couldn't go on forever like this. His legs were sturdy and strong enough to let him run off out the half-door and meet up with the other children from now on. These adventurous little devils would lead him around like some small puppy and into those new and hitherto unknown mysteries of their childhood – out into the fields and the woods and the rivers. The older ones (under pain of an instant death) would guard his safety every second of the day and she hoped and prayed that he would no longer find himself labeled 'The Little Englander' – but would grow into being a proper Little Irishman like the rest of the children in Rookery Rally.

## Father Accessible

Sometime after the death of Father Chasible, we had been introduced to a new priest (Father Accessible) and he'd been here since the last eight months. Monsignor O'Reymus had brought him to us from Clare beyond the river. Before his arrival the church had been in the hands of a crotchety in-between man (Father Abstemious), who was well into his eighties and nobody knew why on earth he had been sent to Copperstone Hollow to hold the fort and plague the likes of us. He was frail and he was doddery and he took the best part of the morning to say his Mass and for a finish we were all sick to death of him. Of course Teddy (as young as he was) could have gone to hear the old priest's Mass if Dowager wanted to take him with her. He was old enough and had learnt a list of prayers as long as your arm and there were lots of other children his own age, who were going to church with their mothers. However, this wise old woman thought that the sight of this sour old priest (him and his ferocious red eyes that looked just like a ferret's and which pierced into the heart of the entire congregation) might put the fear of God into her little man and add yet another unnecessary ogre to the long list of wicked boodeemen that filled his dreams some nights. But Father Abstemious was at last gone to his eternal reward, having died in his bed with a cup of tea dripping all over his saucer, just as the housekeeper (Molly) was coming in the door to give him his egg and his buttered toast. Once again the sunlight shone in through the church gates and up onto the altar and Dowager decided (just as she had with the bathtub) that it was high time for a change: she would bring Teddy to Mass the very next Sunday.

The new priest (Father Accessible) had been with us as a curate some twenty years earlier when he was just a strap of a lad. The minute he arrived back as our parish priest the news went round as quick as a jig-step – how he had now become as fat as a harvest frog and that he was a right good jovial fellow. Above all (and more power to his elbow for saying it) he could deliver his Mass in less than half-an-hour and the parish jumped for joy and they clapped their fidgety hands. His sermons too were short and sweet and full of good sense and he could whip his congregation into a fervor that we never knew existed before. In a short space of time he put a head of steam into the heart of the parish and at the same time he showed that he was a smart enough man not to spend his Sunday morning constantly reminding us that our lives were an everlasting tug-of-war between ourselves and The Devil.

Like the rest of the dewy-eyed women, who began flouncing round him like a rash of measles, Dowager took a shine to him at once. Though money (just like Blue-eyed Jack's tea) was a good bit scarce during these wartime years she still managed to fish out a few handfuls of coins from her jug on the press-cupboard and she didn't even bother to count them. She couldn't wait to get her ass-and-car over to the church and give the money to the new man so that he'd say one or two Masses for the soul of Handsome Johnnie. And one more thing – the whole of the parish knew that she was worried sick over her seventh son (Soldier Tom). It was not long after he had left Dang-the-skin-of-it's school-house that Tom had made a name for himself as the tamer and carter of wild asses up around Temple Cross. Rookery Rally, however, was always going to be too small a place for the likes of him and he went off to join Teddy's mother across the sea. By now he was twenty-four and getting a good deal more adventure than he'd ever bargained for, fighting for his very life against the German hordes on the desert sands of Africa. Dowager knew that her gift of the coins to Father Accessible would protect her soldier-boy from a savage death and would bring him home safely to her. She also knew that the priest's Masses would bring herself and her two men (the big-and-the-little) nothing but good fortune throughout their lives. Enough said.

## *It's Sunday – Let's Go Praise The Lord*

Now it was Sunday and up in the luminous sky and all over the misty pine-trees the larks were singing and the cattle below in The Bull-Paddock were gleaming inside the ditch at John's Gate. Blue-eyed Jack went down to The Bull-Paddock with the reins and the winkers to bring back Moll-the-mare and tackle her for Mass. His seven cows had seen his breezy coat coming down along the misty field and he had heard one or two of them coughing as the clouds of steam poured out of their nostrils. They followed along behind him and they found their own way out through John's Gate and on up The Open Road and into the cowshed for aching out the milk from their swollen udders.

Whilst The Old Pair were milking, Teddy waited inside by the fire. Once again he did his own particular weather-watch by looking up and out of the chimney-hole to see if the early morning sun had started to shine. On the back of the two chairs was his shirt and that of his uncle. Dowager had given them another good airing and she had given her grandson one of her own small holy-books with shiny pictures of the saints in it for him to be looking at and in case he felt lonely when they were abroad in the cowshed.

The perplexed cat (Hen-chaser) came down from Smiling Bab's yard and looked in through the cowshed doorway and listened to the milk as it hissed into the buckets of Blue-eyed Jack and his mother. The Old Pair rose up from their milking-stools and they carried the foaming buckets of hot milk in past the log-pile. The buckets were covered with several early-morning flies and the big man drained the milk into the creamery-tanks. Teddy (aware that this was going to be an exciting day for him, his first ever journey into God's house) was held upside-down so as to dip his mug into the tank and get himself his first drink of the day. They were already in a great hurry to bolt the green door and get their heels out into the yard and up onto Moll-the-mare's horse-and-cart for Mass. There wouldn't be time to bother with the breakfast until they got back home. Even before Blue-eyed Jack had time to take the cows back down to the Bull-Paddock, Dowager had dressed Teddy in his finery – the white socks and the brown sandals and the blue shirt with the red tie and the navy blue suit. Once more she caressed the shirt tightly into his little body and she straightened his tie with care and she fussed over the curls on his head and she spat on his fringe to keep it down. Finally she brought him up to the half-door and she showed him his blue eyes and his rosy cheeks in the broken bit of looking-glass. He was ready for Mass and there'd be no other child as well-turned-out as himself this day.

She greased the toecaps of the three sets of boots with a dab or two of the lard left over from last year's killed pig and she fussed over her own blue-basket hat and the coat with the inner ribbons on it. Turning away from her two men, once more she coyly put on her best dove-grey stockings (the ones she wore when visiting Gentility) and she put on an extra bit of style (her grey wedding-gloves) and she dabbed a bit of perfume on her hanky. She sat impatiently at the half-door and she waited for Blue-eyed Jack to fix in the stud at the back of his white collar. Her silvery walking-cane was at the ready and tapping on the floor and there was a look of godliness in her two old eyes.

## Moll-The-Mare

Moll-the-mare was harnessed and carted in the yard. Blue-eyed Jack gave her a good dowsing with the holy-water and added the sweetness of his tongue to put her in the best of humour so that she'd shorten the journey with the fine cut of her hooves. Then it was jiggey-jiggedy-jiggedy and away the three of them sailed to Mass, frightening the odd solitary crow as they passed over the flagstones and the stream.

The pale day grew more freshening by the minute and Moll soon warmed to her work and she and the cart seemed to be in a perfect musical harmony. Teddy listened to the heavy rattling metal wheels and the clanging song of Moll's clouting shoes and the harness-rapping rattle of her tackle and chains. Nor did the occasional protruding bush cause the sound mare any bit of trouble. It was only when they reached the metal bridge that they heard a love-like whinny from Moll and she paused at the very next gateway and she looked in across the field where Fandango (her ploughing partner of old) was buried. She remembered those earlier days when hoof-to-hoof they had ploughed the furrows of Blue-eyed Jack's seventh field before Fandango took the ragwort poisoning and died on her.

Then, a gentle tap of the whip and off the little party went again. Teddy was as quiet as a mouse and he was soon almost dizzy from watching Moll's feet spanking off of The Creamery Road and the silver of her shoes that was glinting up into his eyes. From his high perch on the straw sacking of the cripplers' lat-board he could see in over the ditches and from time to time his grandmother fussed over him and she wrapped the soft tartan rug more firmly around his cold knees. In front and behind them was the sound of several other horse-and-carts and pony-and-traps, all in an urgent hurry to get to Mass on time. The occasional whip punctured the quiet air and some of the ponies almost kicked themselves in the chin as they set fire to the road. Everybody was as clean and shiny as a new pin in their Sunday finery and, though he was too young to understand it, their faces were cocked stubbornly high and with an important-looking air about them. The girls and their mothers wore their best feathery hats and they looked as colourful as rich garden flowers and their necks nodded delicately in rhythm with the dancing hooves and the jingling harmony.

From behind the carts you could hear the whizz-whizzing of the bicycle tyres and the rattle of the mudguards as a stream of bikes came dashing passed, young men steering in and out between the carts in an awful hurry to reach the church before the rest of us. The tails of their coats rippled in the breeze and their neck-ties streamed like flags behind over their shoulders and they were wearing their best check caps with the peak sharply down over their eyes so as to ward off the wind. Those with no caps were said to be dressed 'in their hair' and they had plastered it down earlier with the pan of soapy water so as to keep their hair-quiffs in place like the rowdy townies from The Roaring Town. As they passed by, they almost brushed against Blue-eyed Jack's boot-laces where he was seated on the lace of the horse-and-cart and Dowager kept on turning around (back and forth, back and forth – the nosy old woman) to see if she could name any of the young men that were cycling out passed her and hiding their faces underneath their caps. She was such an inquisitive old soul and she kept on nudging Blue-eyed Jack and questioning him as to 'who was in it?' Finally she spotted the brothers (Larry and Harry) who had nearly killed each other during that dreadful Civil War of '22 – the war that had nearly wrecked the soul of our land. As more and more cyclists passed by her, she began to put a few names to their faces and Blue-eyed Jack smiled to himself, seeing how she was able to bring up from her vast mental treasure-chest a number of hidden gems from the past pedigree of each of the passing cyclists.

## At Copperstone Hollow And Joe-The-Cart's Yard

They reached the church and the village of Copperstone Hollow and the big man turned the horse-and-cart into Joe-the-Cart's carpentry yard. Here was the man that could make you an ass-and-car. He could make you a pony-and-trap or even a stagecoach. He could paint and lacquer the same machine in black and gold and as good as ever was seen on any church saint or angel. Teddy's nostrils were filled with the smell of the new timbers (salmon and almond in colour and juicy with resin) and in between the heaps of logs and planks there were showers and showers of curly pig-tail shavings.

To get his hands on so much timber Joe-the-Cart had roamed through almost every forest in our land, so much had the call of wild nature gotten a hold of his soul and he had such beautiful pictures in his head that he could make a book out of them. There were half-a-dozen hens picking their way through the yard and Moll-the-mare scattered their shivering cackling with her striding hooves. Blue-eyed Jack roped her to the stake and he put down a few handfuls of hay in front of her and he untackled her from the cart.

Teddy jumped down. He went rambling among the carts that were strewn here and there in various stages of completion. Some were fully finished and had the red paint on their frames and wheel-felloes. Blue-eyed Jack remembered those previous creamery mornings when he had passed the gates of Joe's yard – only to see him clouded all over in sawdust amidst the music of his hot saws and pounding hammers and his head held low and his hands working precisely and with the conviction of an artist. In the eyes of the big man Joe was a craftsman that sculpted rather than built his carts, in spite of the size of his great big sausage fingers.

But today Joe-the-Cart's yard was quiet and lifeless in honour of Mass and his God. The two-men-of-us walked round and around the yard, admiring Joe's finished carts that lined the walls of the yard. Blue-eyed Jack had to laugh to himself. For all over the place he saw the finest of carpentry tools, dropped from Joe's hands and hidden amidst the sawdust in the exact spot where the great man had last been using them. So intent had Joe been on the details of his work that he hadn't had time to stoop down and pick them up. It seemed he had eyes only for a tool when he needed it and tossed it aside when he didn't need to use it the rest of the day. Enough said.

Dowager and Teddy went up past the Canadian cottages that Tiny-Man had built for the miners the year they came here to dig for the lead and zinc over at Billy's Cross. Blue-eyed Jack went out the thorn-bitten gap at the back of the carpentry yard to ease his bladder. He was careful not to spill any of his poolie on Joe-the-Cart's rows of cabbages but to give the dewy grass and the surprised dock-leaves at the edge of the field a good soaking. The chill of the early morning ran into him as he drew the air into his lungs and he lit the remains of a Woodbine fag and he pulled hard on it. This was one of thos precious moments in his life and he looked down the field towards the swollen river. The limp mist that protected the village was lifting slowly and whirling its way towards the surrounding hills and up into the pyramids of pine-trees that studded them before meeting up with the grey-white clouds that floated like pillows above The Mighty Mountain.

The big man came back through the gap and he left Moll-the-mare chewing at her hay in the yard. He heard the roar of Father Accessible's motorcar as the holy man drove up the street in a fog of a hurry. He blessed himself at the rare sight of such a fiercely speeding machine ('that fellow will get himself killed one of these days') and he said one of his silent prayers to Saint Jude, the patron saint of all lost causes. Bikes and carts and traps all stood reverently aside to let their priest pass by and the men lifted their caps and they saluted him respectfully.

Not far behind the motorcar came the metal sound of The Bellaboy's great big cleeted boots as he strode up the middle of the street. His big bullet-head ('clear the way, lads! Clear the way!') and his lumpy face was positively smoking with a fog of sweat and steam, so hot was he in his haste to reach the church gates. He had walked at least five miles across the fields and he had no way of knowing (other than the sun) whether he was in time for Mass or not. Sunshine was a rare sight at times in Copperstone Hollow so that the Mass could be half over before The Bellaboy got inside the church door. Once Mass was finished, this mountainy man wasted not a single minute talking to anyone but he would stride home belligerently over the same arduous fields, content that he had come face to face with his beloved God in the church. He was often soaked to the skin before he got back to his yard and whenever he met other travellers on the way, he'd give his shoulders a good shake and tell them that a few drops of rain wouldn't melt the likes of himself as he was neither a lump of sugar or salt.

## Doctor Glasses From Cork

Blue-eyed Jack reached Our Blessed Lady's flowery grotto where the old pump used to be. A number of villagers were stepping out smartly from their doors as though the church at the top of the village was on fire. The wind from the hills threatened to knock them back on their backsides but they leaned forward and they clutched at their hats and caps.

The big man shook himself when the sound of the Mass-bell's metallic clang started pouring out its monotony around the village that was normally as dead as the winter's butterflies. The bell was fifty years old and had been installed to replace the original bell. A wild witch-woman (so it was rumoured) had once stood her ground against the unquestionable powers of the parish priest. As Dowager was often heard to say – it was a case of this woman's curse waging a battle with the priest's curse – as though any curses had ever done anyone a single bit of good (said Blue-eyed Jack). Neither the priest nor the witch-woman saw out that same year – she, getting herself bewitched into a great big quarry-hole where a big rock fell and killed her and the old church-bell falling down on top of the priest's head and killing him stone-dead when he was ringing it to call the faithful to prayer. Then Dowager would let out a little sigh of regret; for the peal of the old church-bell had been far more musical than the present one.

Blue-eyed Jack was standing unseen and a little way down the street from his mother and Teddy. The old woman was tapping her cane on the street and she was twirling its silver handle with her gloved fingers. She was engrossed in conversation with Doctor Glasses and she seemed to have forgotten her immediate duty to hear Mass, as though it would wait all day long for her. The doctor was holding his hat in his hands out of respect for her and his eyes were shining with amusement. He was the only man in the parish that wore a pair of spectacles to help his delicate eyes and in his green suit he looked very much taller than Teddy's grandmother.

He patted Teddy on the head and he told him what a fine 'big little' man he was (whatever that meant!). Then he bowed towards Dowager: 'Why – you're as solid this morning as a church steeple, my good woman,' said he. Dowager looked coyly down at her bootlaces. 'Aye, faith – indeed and I am.' She stretched herself up to her full height and she laughed archly up at him. 'You'll never make a brass farthing out of me, my good man,' said she. It was true for her: the only time Doctor Glasses had ever been summoned inside her half-door was a year previously when Teddy got the cattle-rash that took away half of his golden curls. (Whatever would Little Nell have said, if ever she got the chance to cross over the sea?). The doctor smiled and he placed his hands on Dowager's two shoulders: ' God bless and preserve you for the health that's in you, Dowager – you'll outlive half the parish,' said he. He himself was a college-man and yet (for a country-woman) Dowager hadn't an ounce of fear of him and his high schooling, when there was scarcely a living soul that'd raise their eyebrows above knee-level in the presence of such a fine gentleman as Doctor Glasses. He never tired of hearing Dowager's sharp and frank turn of wit and the politeness that crept into her voice on these Sundays when they would meet. It was the same way she'd talk whenever she came across the likes of Lord Elegance or the town 's butcher if she was trying to get a bargain from him. And this fine speech of hers contrasted well with the fierce cursing she could do when tending to her cattle or her fowl.

From a distance Blue-eyed Jack could see that his mother's polished tongue was equal to the lilting voice of Doctor Glasses – with his Cork accent and the way he made his voice rise up and down like a choirboy's song. He could see his mother good-humouredly prodding the doctor with the tip of her cane. He could hear her asking him whether he preferred our County Tipperary or his own County Cork. She knew that Doctor Glasses' heart had been left behind him long ago on the banks of The River Lee. It amused Blue-eyed Jack to see that the shine in his mother's boots (as well as the music of her tongue) was able to match the shine in Doctor Glasses' own patent-leather shoes and (better still) it tickled him to see the way that Teddy for once in his young life was struck utterly dumb at the changes in Dowager's voice and how he wasn't able to do anything other than pierce the doctor's glasses and moustache with a child's innocent and astonished eyes.

Doctor Glasses raised his hat in a salute to Dowager and he skipped up the street and he hurried round the dominance of the huge Protestant church (God's other house) towards our own little wooden church.

## The Church Beckons Clattering Boots

The tramping feet and well-cobbled boots could be heard scraping persistently up the street as the crowd streamed towards the church and they crunched the white gravel that circled around inside the railings and they ushered themselves in through the church door. One or two of the older women still wore their shawls and their plain dark bonnets were tied down with a bit of string under their chin. All the women and the younger children made their way down along the heavy plank-boards into the belly of the church and they headed for their usual seats in the side aisles around the altar. The pews were soon heaving with the number of them and you could see the cocked hats of the women, low on their foreheads, and their gloves slimly around their wrists and a brooch or two on the lapels of their coats. The older children made a bid for the stairs that led up to the gallery and they smiled down at their mothers.

Further up and near the incense and the polish of the altar were one or two reserved pews for the rich farmers and the gentry of the parish and also the schoolmaster and his wife, who had given the church handsome sums of tythe-money the previous Easter. Dowager made a note of the good quality of their clothes – the women in their stiff skirts and petticoats and the men in their fine waistcoats. These rich people had nothing to be ashamed of and they each went smartly into the benches marked with their names and they sat themselves as close as possible to the priest, underneath the auspices of Saint Patrick, their favourite saint. Neat as a pin, their faces bespoke their worth and their importance amongst us. They were in the church to be seen by the likes of us. Not for them the part of the lowly Galilean at the rear end of the church!

All of our women were in a tearing great hurry to get inside the church. But until the bell stopped ringing, Blue-eyed Jack and the rest of the farmers remained leaning uncomfortably in a long line and scuffing their boots against The Conifer Wall outside the church. They talked quietly about recent deaths and about the farming and the hurling. They talked about the never-ending war across the seas and they cursed the men that had ever started it. Their Woodbine fags were fiercely aglow as they gave a last few pulls on them and inhaled vigorously. The bell finally stopped ringing and the four corners of the village could rest their ears from it now, thank God. The men plucked up courage and they sidled in the gate – some of them with shamed faces and downcast eyes in anticipation of what Father Accessible might say to reprimand them. They placed their pennies on the card-table at the door where the balding figure of young Freckles Moneybags (the bank clerk) stacked the coins into neat piles; for it was not by prayer alone that we took our first steps towards the gates of Heaven.

The men plodded sheepishly up to the holywater font and they ceremoniously blessed themselves and they showered the water on the men behind them and they took off their caps. Most of them were wizened-faced from the windy weather and the sun. Blue-eyed Jack noticed that a lot of men were as bald as old vultures – so little daylight had their heads ever seen from under their weekday caps – with only a few little wisps of white fluffy moss standing out from the sides of their heads and ears. In one or two cases amongst the older men the dye of the band inside their hats had turned their hair a faded shade of green and yellow and sadly (without their knowing it) had made them look unusually comical.

# And What Of The Men?

Once inside the door, the men stayed as close as possible to the back of the church and they were afraid to push themselves up to the front light of the candles in case anyone would see them and their shyness. It was as if they preferred to do their praying abroad in the open spaces near the church wall. They put one of their knees on their caps and they leaned their elbow on the other knee and, awestruck with reverence in the presence of God's authority, they took out their first-communion rosary-beads and they began praying like fair hell. The loop on their beads gradually grew less and less slack as with closed eyelids – their big knuckles folded tightly over their beads – they prayed sibilantly for their dead mothers, the only saints they had ever known. From time to time their nostrils sniffed at the cold air of the doorway, as though to hide a tear. Or they stared bleary-eyed at the statue of The Mother-of-God, as though they might feel the touch of her coming down and into their souls for just this one brief instance in their lives and there was the odd bout of coughing and sneezing and wiping of nostrils onto their delicate trouser-legs.

They knew their place and it was here at the back of the church like fretful children on their first day at school. They were resigned to being locked in here for the moment – here in God's silent house where no bird of the skies ever came in to sing its song. And Blue-eyed Jack was mindful of his father's stories when they were abroad in the bog – how men, women and children had once danced and sung and had sported and played – here on this very spot many years earlier, before this little wooden wonder-of-a-church was built in honour of our God. He reached into his pocket and he pulled out his rosary-beads and absentmindedly he let it drip-drip-drip through his fingers.

Like the rest of the men he hung his beads on his bedpost for the rest of the week. He now thought of his God and he thought of his mother and he thought of his father and he thought of little Teddy too and he wondered how the child would end up after this cursed war against the Germans came to its end and whether the steam train and the big ship would steal him away – the only little boy he'd ever known and loved, almost like his own son – and whether The Little Englander would be dragged back to a new

126

and strange world to the parents he had never set eyes on in those gloomy bombed-out streets of London.

'Look at us poor scholars, all trapped in here,' he thought to himself – 'all waiting for the priest and his sermon, as though we were back on our benches inside the school-house door'. He wondered, as he did every Sunday, what sort of greeting Father Accessible's sermon would have for himself and the rest of the congregation, though he knew that the priest was a harmless man. As a long-standing rule the men had always been in dread of any sermon whatsoever and many of them believed that they were half-ways along the downhill road to the fiery furnace. Blue-eyed Jack scratched his head and he asked himself what sins the likes of himself had ever committed. He hadn't stolen a cow from Fatty-Matty or a horse from Moll-the-Man. And what with the plough and the hay-fork, he hadn't had time to go bad-mouthing another soul or to molest another man's wife, for fear that an army of her brothers would come in the half-door one night and beat the shite out of him – or kill him outright. He tried to forget how his old heartbeat was starting to stutter from some unknown and imposed sins as he inhaled the moist atmosphere of the candles and the incense. He tried to quell his mixed feelings of anger and piety as he gazed out the stained-glass windows at the vague shapes of the green pine-trees and the yew bushes that fringed the church and within the pin-drop silence of the church he could hear the branches creaking and rustling painfully.

## Teddy Was Afraid – Yet Again

In the meantime, Teddy could be seen squashing Dowager's hand tightly in anticipation of what was about to happen in this strange big house. Never having been inside a church before, his darting eyes kept turning round and around in his head like two saucers and he kept gaping from one end of the church to the other. Like any unfettered country child, he couldn't help marvelling at the immense brightness of the place. His young brain was beginning to suffocate from all the information he had to start taking in – the lemon-and-white walls and the high windows with the dazzling coloured glass in them, stained red and blue and green. They made the coloured stones from River Laughter, with which he often tried to draw cattle and sheep, look very dull indeed.

And as though he were a lost lamb, Dowager dragged him along with her down the aisle and she ushered the two of them into her selected pew and they knelt down silently before the beautiful banner of Saint Anne. His grandmother told him that it would soon be time for him to start reverently whispering his list of all the prayers she had taught him and his eyes continued to scurry everywhere but most of all upon the showpiece of the church, the altar itself. It was ablaze with countless candles and they shimmered and darted about playfully on their wicks with a number of orange and cream flames. These big candles made a shabby show out of his grandmother's pair of candlesticks back home and in front of them there were two big jars and in them were huge bunches of red flowers (none of his piss-a-bed flowers or his dock-leaves here). On either side of the altar there were two life-sized plaster statues of saints in smoky brown robes tied with thick white string. Above the altar was the beautiful statue of Our Blessed Lady and she was wearing her long blue and white garments, flowing like the summer skies, and there was a dead snake from his storybook twisting itself round her feet and her lovely ginger hair was covered with twinkling stars. Never in all his born days had Teddy seen anything as magical as the smile on her face. Together with everything else inside the church you couldn't blame him, if (young as he was) he was already wondering whether Heaven was anything like this magnificent place. If it was only half as good (he thought), then he wanted to go there as quickly as possible and live there forever and ever alongside his old grandmother. For the first time in his life he hadn't had a moment to spare a thought for Blue-eyed Jack – so utterly imbued was he with all the new beauty around him in this holy house of God.

Suddenly he was brought back down to earth. He looked up and saw a number of children's predatory eyes staring down at him from their lofty perch in the gallery. He remembered his visit to Gentility and he began to feel as uncomfortable as he had felt the time himself and Dowager passed by the leprechauns in Fort Dangerous when he had half-expected those fearful fairy-men to step out from the gap and make a grab at him and carry him off. It was just as well that his fingers were again locked in Dowager's or he'd have died on the spot at the sight of so many children's eyes glaring down at him and not one of them saying a single prayer.

# New Friends And Their Smiling Faces

He felt a gentle tap on his shoulder. In the pew behind him there were five of Smiling Babs' children. They were Cull and Patches, Bucko and Norrie and Darkie – and they were all smiling kindly at him. The youngest of the girls (it was Darkie) gave him a shy little nod of her head and a comforting little smirk as if to let him know that the church was a safe place for him and that it was in no way as frightening as Fort Dangerous and that he'd still be alive and kicking when Mass was over and done with. She could not have chosen a better moment to re-assure him of his existence and all at once his happiness bounced back into him and he gave her one of his own awkward little smiles in return and he never looked up again at the balcony.

At this early stage of his life his innocent eyes would not have noticed that these five children were somewhat different from himself. The two girls were wearing their cotton frocks and the three boys were wearing their plain brown corduroys. He was wearing his navy suit and a grown-up red tie and a blue shirt (all sent to him by his mother) and these boys were wearing grey shirts and they had no ties around their necks. The five children knew, of course, that Teddy was a different child from them and that he was the foreign little gentleman, the one known to them as The Little Englander from over the waters. It was as though he had come from outer space and throughout the Mass they would stare into the back of his head and they'd be wondering if all Little Englanders had those bald cattle-rash patches that Teddy had amidst his curls!

# Hosannah! – Let The Holy Mass Begin

Tingaling-tingaling! The little tea-bell was ringing at the side of the altar. Everybody rose to their feet. The walls of the little church were echoing with the fine singing rhapsodies of 'Faith of our fathers – we will be true to thee till death' and there wasn't a soul that didn't mean every single word of it. Mass was about to begin. The leading altarboy had his eyes firmly fixed on the metal crucifix at the top of a nine-foot pole and he was the first one to come into view, padding along in his black plimsoles, which squeaked on the polished boards. He marched very slowly (as instructed) and he gave everyone plenty of time to fix their eyes on their crucified Saviour at the top of the pole. He turned in towards the tabernacle and he bowed. A woman a few rows in front of Dowager started digging her elbows into her neighbours' ribs, reminding them that this saintly young fellow was her one and only beloved son. Behind the leader came a younger boy and it was his job to swing the long-chained thurifer with the burning charcoal and the incense in it. The little devil blinded the eyes of half-a-dozen rich farmers in the front pews with clouds of smoke and they coughed and they sneezed like blazes and they cursed him down into hell. Then came the swishing cassocks of four very small boys. In their slippy-slappy pumps they made a thumping sound like a field of young rabbits. They quickly reached the altar-steps and they rushed around fussily to their selected places at the sides. Their hair had been well-groomed by their mothers and had been pressed down into their scalps with the soapy water and (a fine touch, this) they were wearing white gloves that were as snowy-white as the starched cloth on the altar-rails. 'Ah,' said Dowager, sighing her approval of them, 'aren't they the little purity-boys!' For these celestial seraphs appeared to shine like gold in the light of the candles and she gave a sideways look at her grandson and she wondered if he had the makings in him of a fine young priest one of these days?

## Teddy's Transfixation Time

Teddy was by now transfixed, for he had never seen anything so immaculate as these apple-cheeked boys, except for the ginger-and-white calves inside at The Roaring Town Showground. And to crown it all, the six altarboys were wearing a set of red cassocks (redder than the rabbit-cartridges) instead of the drab black ones that Father Accessible had condemned to the depths of a wooden chest in the sacristy behind the altar. The high crucifix glistened like a piece of gold and Teddy gazed at the figure of poor Jesus hanging there on his cross on top of this pole and he wondered why on earth he had let himself get killed without putting up a bit of a fight. And although the adults' senses had become somewhat numbed at the regular sight of this crucifix, Smiling Babs' children were now full of remorse, for it was only recently that they had helped the mad-woman (Slipperslapper) to drown the tinkers' flea-ridden puppy in River Laughter and they were unable to get the thought of the poor puppy out of their minds, remembering how it gasped its final breath from inside the mouth of the potato-sack. Its drowning had been their first great big sin and as they looked up at the cross they remembered what had happened to their beloved Saviour on Calvary Hill and the cruel whipping of him and the crowning of his head with the wreath of thorns. It was too much for their tearful eyes – to see the image of him up there on that great big pole and the way he cast his sad eyes down on them and the outpouring of his love for themselves and the rest of the crowd in the church. "Faith'n if I had been in Jesus' shoes,' whispered Bucko to Darkie, 'I'd be damned if I'd let a pack of eejits nail me to a tree,' and his mother gave him one of her sharp smiles and she patted him sympathetically on his head. His brother and sisters nodded their approval of this angry statement and then they joined their hands reverently and they began saying their morning prayers.

## Out Steps The Holy Man Himself

The women craned their necks towards the sacristy door to catch a glimpse of Father Accessible and one or two of them looked back towards the rear of the church to see could they spy out their own coy man. Some of them were sick and tired of their men's coarseness and their cursing and their fighting and they hated their love of strong drink, whenever their man had the price of it in his pocket. There were times (they'd tell you) when they'd need a mighty strong rope to tie their last cow to the bed-rails if the blasted drink got a hold of their man – for fear he'd take the beast to town and sell her and drink the price of her before he got back home.

Sh! Sh! – who's this? It was the two men carrying the acolyte candles and out behind them (like a pure gust of wind) swept Father Accessible himself, the women's pride and joy. His bloodhound eyes darted all over the church and he bowed to the left and to the right and his smile was as broad as Galway Bay. His fine robes (again the saucer-eyes of Teddy) out-glittered all the rest of the church's glitter.

Though he was a man of small height he was neat and he was trim and his long fingers poked out from the sleeves of his thickly-starched alb. He was a bit on the fat side around his middle and he'd remind you of a plumped-up cushion (thought Blue-eyed Jack). His hair was snow white and it was swept back straight and his ruddy face was as shiny as a sweet-gallon and as smooth as a well-stretched balloon out of The Daffy-Duck's Circus. He was highly scented and he did not smell (thought the women) like the rest of the men with the smell of tobacco and the even staler smells of strong drink and piss coming out of their clothes. In contrast to the altarboys and their dull black plimsoles, his shoes were polished to death and they were pointy like the ones in Fanny Farthingale's Dress Shop in The Roaring Town. Teddy (and those saucer eyes of his) was wrapped with attention to the holy man's appearance and he made a note of everything like most small children would have done when confronted with a new and dazzling spectacle.

As soon as they clapped their eyes on Father Accessible, the women looked as though they had been drinking hot punch and their cheeks were on fire. From the day he arrived in the village he had wrapped his arms around them all – like a pair of angel-wings – and as a result of his inspired performances at Mass and the velvet tones of his sermons they had given him the whole of their hearts, if not their souls (which belonged to God alone). To be fair to them, most men (in spite of their long-held doubts about those they believed to be their higher and betters) didn't mind the holy man one bit and by now they had given him the title of Speed-the-Plough, he being the fastest man in Ireland when it came to saying his Mass. Today would be no exception and their priest would be in and out of the church in no time at all as there was a hurling-match for him to attend later that afternoon.

After a moment's silence Father Accessible made the sign-of-the-cross and he began his Mass in a deep and sonorous voice. Teddy felt his heart fluttering nervously. It was like the fear and foreboding he had felt in The Valley of The Black Cattle when Blue-eyed Jack made him stand stock-still during the closing stages of the rabbit-hunt. In spite of the nearness of Dowager, he was very much alone and he felt as remote as he had ever been in the depths of The Big Cave Room during the darkness of night. He gave a pleading look up at Dowager but her face and eyes seemed to be lifted up high like a sparrow soaring into the air. Her lips seemed to take on a delicate smile as she hurried through her well-memorised prayer-book verses and, as rough as her tongue could be when giving out to her cattle, her soul must have been as white as the driven snow in these precious few moments of her life.

It wasn't fear alone that was overwhelming the child. He felt a strange elation – too confusing for so young a child to comprehend – as he continued to gaze up into his grandmother's face. It was as though he too was about to get himself lost in holiness and to surrender his bewildered heart and soul to the very angels that were attending this Mass somewhere in the invisible enclaves of the church. Like the five sets of children's eyes behind him, he turned his gaze towards the altar and he spent the next five minutes staring at the dangling legs of Jesus on the crucifix. It must have been very painful for poor Jesus to find himself hanging up there and with the coldness creeping up along his bony legs and he without a stitch of clothes on him like himself at bath-time. He looked sadly at the few drops of painted blood on the side of Jesus. Dead as a doornail (poor Jesus!) like the rabbits hanging on the back of the door at home and their blood dripping down onto the floor. He hit his breast a few belts like he'd seen the old men doing when they entered the church door and he joined his hands solemnly and he pointed them up towards Heaven like Dowager had taught him – the same way as the hands were doing on the statue of Our Blessed Lady amidst the altar's candle-lights. Dowager looked sideways at him and she saw how the reverence was getting a hold of him. She gave him a gentle prod and she whispered into his ears and she urged him to say a special prayer for the dead sawyer (Larry Cash), who had been killed by the fallen tree in front of his demented son only the week before last. 'Pray, Teddy, that his ghost may rest happily in his grave.' The child lowered his eyes like the rest of the people around him and he began to say his prayers with an earnestness that must have frightened the life out of the Devil himself.

## *Those 'Purity Lads' – The Altarboys*

The next twenty minutes went by like grease lightning. Father Accessible and his altarboys (for all the strange droning Latin they were rattling off) might as well have been speaking in Chinese or Japanese for Teddy didn't understand a single word of it. That didn't matter a bit as there was so much more for him to be taking in. With the speed of a whip the green chasible over Father Accessible's long white night-shirt made a number of elaborate sweeps to charming effect and his two arms spread themselves out wide like the wings of a great big butterfly. He must have borrowed Doctor Glasses' spectacles (thought Teddy), for these were now perched on the tip of his nose in readiness for reading from the great big red book – the biggest book that the child had ever seen. The holy man turned the pages with the deftness of a card-dealer and he began to work himself up into a great big fit and to breathe in-and-out heavily through his flared nostrils and his lips and his tongue were fizzy and flustering with white spittle.

The altarboys almost matched him in their alertness, grace and speed. Each of them bobbed up-and-down off of their knees and they twisted and they turned as they marched to the left and then back to the right like a troop of Dowager's ducks. One of the four little boys became the man of the hour when he went up the four steps to the right-hand side of the altar. With much pomp and ceremony he lifted up the unmercifully heavy book and he carried it achingly down the steps on his tippy-toes before staggering back up again and placing it on the gospel side of the altar. It had been a difficult enough job coming down the steps but the work was twice as hard going back up again. On both stages of this painful journey he could see neither head nor tail of his feet through the immense size of the book and he was in mortal dread of falling down and breaking his neck and making a holy show of himself and his family. Teddy (and yet another bout of those saucer eyes) held his breath. This great big book had toppled more than one small altarboy of late and it was a test of the strength in that little fellow's arms and wrists to see if he was up to the mighty task. But the well-fed lad that he was, little Murty O'Hooligan proved more than able to carry out his charge and he did it manfully so that one or two of the congregation had a mind to clap their hands. Once again Dowager saw a mother's bosom heaving with pride as she dug her neighbours in the ribs and whispered, 'That's my lovely son up there' and proudly pointed her cocked finger in the direction of the altar.

## Time For The Lofty Sermon To Save Our Souls

It was time for the sermon. Father Accessible raised his hands and he bade us to put away our rosary-beads. Until that moment we had been up and down off of our knees like bouncing balls. We all sat back and we folded our arms and we waited. The priest solemnly folded his own arms inside the wings of his chasible and he gave us an all-round gaze for a couple of seconds as though he was about to mesmerize us like the ferret and the rabbit. And though it pained Dowager a good bit (she being such a wonderful talker) that she now had to sit down dumb and listen and that she couldn't even get a word in edgeways, she really didn't mind a bit listening to the likes of Father Accessible. He was no mere plaster saint (she thought) but a real flesh-and-blood holy man and she knew that today he'd be giving everyone the fine old time of it – as good as a deathbed sermon. But the priest knew (in spite of his genuine holiness) that in his sermon his voice was the one and only voice to be heard and there couldn't be any objections from any of us – that he had all the answers and was able to have us eating out of the palm of his hands. And now he showed that he had one or two extra strings to his bow and that he could well have fashioned out a career on the stage for himself. On Saturday evenings he would practise a few smouldering glances in front of the mirror. He would point his index finger up towards Heaven. He would pause for a second or two to bring about the suspense we all loved to hear and look at and these little tit-bits were sure to add to the sublimity and the warmth in his words.

When the men heard what he had to say to them they were quite content to remain in their dark hiding-places at the back of the church and were no longer anxious to make a run for the door and the drinking-shop across the street. They could see that Father Accessible was the direct opposite to Father Abstemious (whose sermons could make an old horse cry); for their new man spoke from his heart and he carefully selected the right words for each and every occasion. There wasn't a proud bone in his body (thank God) and none of that dry and unwanted dominance that the congregation had come to expect from one or two visiting priests and missioners. And before he was half-ways through his sermon the congregation were all gaping up at him (the men too) in pure admiration at the way he was able to demolish them with the purity of his words. Dowager smiled at Teddy and she whispered: 'He has the mouth of a solicitor on him – he's even better than our gramophone.'

The previous Sunday ('Put off thy sandals, for thy feet are on holy ground') he had made saints out of even the most hard-hearted of men.

Today he spoke of the forgiveness of Jesus as well as the pure love that he had had for all the nations of the world. He managed to stir both of these themes around in the same mixing-bowl. Dowager and Blue-eyed Jack felt such a powerful amount of God's love pouring into them that they believed the entire world was soon going to be saved from sin and turned into a far brighter place – in spite of all the killings and bloodshed going on in the blasted war across the seas.

Father Accessible's voice now rose and then it fell like the stormy waves as he began telling the tale (oh, how we all loved a tale!) of the ten diseased lepers that Jesus had cured whilst they were lying outside the walls of the city – a sad group of outcasts from the rest of mankind. The packed church loved the way he told it, letting his words waft arrow-like across the pews and filling their souls with fierce emotion. In the space of a few minutes he almost had the entire congregation in a flood of tears and he himself seemed close to shedding a drop or two of his own when he came to the bit about the thankless nine lepers who (unlike the tenth leper) hadn't an ounce of charity in their entire bodies and hadn't bothered to make the few steps back to see Jesus and say thank you to him for curing them of their disease. On that roasting hot day inside the city walls of Jericho (said the holy man) it had been the saddest day (barring the death of Lazarus) in the whole life of poor Jesus. It was at this bit of his sermon that Father Accessible made one of his more famous pauses. He lowered his head and he gave everybody time to reflect on their own thankless natures. It was plain as the nose on our faces that not a soul in the church loved an ungrateful wretch like those bleddy lepers and for a finish up there wasn't a man, woman or child that didn't prick themselves hard and feel a refreshing burst of moral magnanimity. Indeed everyone vowed that the very next Sunday they'd put at least a dozen pennies (instead of the miserly six) on the card-table outside the church-door. A wise man and no fool was our Father Accessible, the rascal.

## The Skill Of The Priest's Big Joe

With the sermon over, the priest shook out what looked like a rich man's handkerchief and (far from blowing his nose with it) he took to drying his hands after washing them from a small jug of water. A minute or two later he used the same hanky to wipe out the inside of a big golden cup, repeatedly inspecting it to see had he done a good job on it. The holiest part of the Mass (and Dowager gave Teddy another little nudge) was the mystery of mysteries when the priest bobbed up-and-down and then unexpectedly bobbed up-and-down a second time in what looked like an unnecessary bout of the fidgets. One of the altarboys lifted up the holy man's chasible as high in the air as he could and Teddy peered to see what was underneath it. When the priest lowered himself and hit his knee against the floor Teddy could only see the back of his head and the series of wrinkles on it. As soon as the priest disappeared from sight, a huge gong was heard echoing alarmingly round the church as the leading altarboy hit it with his drumstick. To the bemused Teddy it seemed as though the genuflecting priest had blindly (but more than skillfully) felt his way around the floor with his shoe in a search for the solid gong and that he had given its metal rim a right good crack of his big toe to make such an almighty din and the child and his imagination was left wondering what a marvel-of-a-man this Father Accessible must be to be able to make such an almighty racket with his big toe. It was then that the priest rose higher than ever in his humble expectations and his toe-and-bell skills drove clean out of his mind the lack-lustre sounds of the previous meaningless Latin phrases.

The glory of it all ('Look at him, he's at it again, Dowager!') was that Father Accessible performed this wondrous exercise for a second time. But this time he went down so fast that Teddy thought he must surely have fallen through the floor-boards – only to see him come back up once more (thank God he was safe!) after his toe and the gong had boomed out their second message. Oh, the almighty power that the priest had in that big toe of his (if only Father Chasible could have come back to see it) – to be able to perform such a wonder and bring the gong to life not once but twice!

## The Sacred Moment – The Body Of Christ

Shortly after this surprise, the altarboys unravelled the white linen rail-guard. This altar-cloth had a line of red crosses on it and the Limerick lace all around the bottom and it was now turned inside-out all the way round the curved rails. The rails had no drawing power whatever for the men and they were nowhere to be seen. But the women and their clicketty heels headed to the front of the altar where they each received the Body of Christ in the form of a small round wafer. What were all these holy women thinking about as they knelt at the rails with their fingers and rosary-beads entwined and coming heart-to-heart and soul-to-soul with Jesus, their Saviour?

A minute earlier Teddy had seen Father Accessible consuming a very large white wafer ('Dowager, look at him eating and giving none of it to us') and again his grandmother had given him another little nudge: 'Shoosh, child! It's the Body of Christ'. On each of the women's tongues the priest placed a small silver wafer and Smiling Babs was now getting one. Teddy looked back at her five children and they had serious faces on them and they were peering anxiously down the aisle to see could they spot their mother coming back from the rails and that they hadn't lost her. Dowager was anxious to go up to the rails but was frightened to leave Teddy alone, this being his first visit to Mass. She knew that he was a nervous child at the best of times (it must have been those war-bombs still rattling around in his head at night) and she thought he might make a bolt down the aisle to follow her or maybe run back to Blue-eyed Jack among the men at the door.

## Distractions, Distractions, Distractions

With so many sensations occupying his young mind Teddy was growing tired and like any small child he took to staring out the stained-glass windows at the haze that was creeping up from the river. He looked at the sheltering trees in the swishing breeze and he looked at the solitary cloud lagging behind them and he looked at the slight blotch of sunlight trying to burn its way through that cloud and through the trees and get in through the windows. Nature was calling him to come outside and join up with her. He was brought back to his senses when Father Accessible ceremoniously blessed his people and complimented them for their devotion to God and begged them to continue on the true path of righteousness throughout the week. They all smiled and they did everything except clap him on the back. They knew he had the power to prevent them from working on a Sunday and that he gave them lee-way to do so only when the hay or the barley was about to get drenched during harvesting days.

# *Out In The Blessed Sunlight*

Mass was finished. Dowager took Teddy by the hand, careful not to lose him amongst the crowds that were piling out into the aisles. To avoid getting entangled in the mad rush, she took him to the statue of Our Blessed Lady. She lit a candle and she gave it to him to hold and she made him say a short 'God Bless' prayer for the repose of the soul of his grandfather (Handsome Johnnie). She took the holywater at the font. She sprinkled a fair share of it on Teddy's brow to guard him from The Devil and to keep him out of harm's way.

In the meantime the men were standing once more at The Conifer Wall. You could hear their murmuring voices (like a thousand swallows on a foggy morning) as they pulled on their Woodbine fag-butts and put as much smoke to the heavens as the incense inside in the church had done. The women in the doorway were themselves chattering away like ducks in the rain. Teddy shuffled along in his sandals behind his grandmother and he heard once more that meaningless phrase – 'What a fine big-little man our Little Englander is growing to be!' – from one or two of the older women. He didn't really mind this since he was again out in the light of the sky and into the fresh air. He was at one with the trees and the surrounding hills and his tongue and heart that had been locked inside in a bird's cage inside in God's holy house were both free again. He spotted Blue-eyed Jack and he ran across the street to him and the big man whisked him high in the air and spun him round and around.

# *Home Again Home Again, Moll-The-Mare*

A moment later Moll-the-mare began to make her way home along The Creamery Road. Before they reached their yard-stream Teddy noticed yet another of Dowager's misty smiles on her face and her lips were turned sharply inwards in satisfaction. She had a good feeling inside in her chest this cold morning and she knew she had done the right thing in bringing her little man with her to hear his first Mass. From now on they'd be going to Copperstone Hollow every blessed Sunday to meet up with their God.

# Time For Teddy's Own Celebration Of Mass

But that wasn't the end of the matter: with Mass over and as soon as the mare was untackled and the fire was lit and the breakfast of eggs and leftover rabbit-soup had been swallowed down, Teddy climbed out over the haggart stick, closely followed by Blue-eyed Jack. It was time to start his own brand of Mass and not leave all the show to Father Accessible. His wily old uncle would prove to be as good an assistant as those stately altarboys. The child and Blue-eyed Jack made a raid on Dowager's washing-bushes where she had left one or two of his old shirts to air and he picked out the one that was the most raggity. It would make a suitably long robe like Father Accessible's vestment – even though it wasn't half as fanciful.

Teddy put the shirt on and it made him look like a second-hand scarecrow as it trailed over his feet and out along the ground. Blue-eyed Jack wrapped a bit of twine around the shirt's middle to look like a priest's girdle. To impress the inquisitive ducks and hens the big man found an old bucket behind his mother's garden. He turned it upside-down so that the little child-priest could stand on top of it and be seen by all his flock when the time came for his lofty sermon. He gave the little man a few practice runs at this delicate operation and he held onto his little fingers and helped him to balance daintily on top of the bucket in case he'd fall out on top of his nose and break his neck.

The solemn moment arrived. Teddy and The Old Pair got into a line, the new child-priest fussing them into position as they made a slow procession around the haggart. Thinking that they were going to get a feed of oats, the ducks and the hens took it into their heads to follow along behind them. It was a grand and glorious sight for the crows in the rookery to behold. The holy trio returned to the altar (made from a few lat-boards and half-barrels) where it was time for the child-priest to say his Mass.

The Old Pair sat down cross-legged on the grass and they told the new child-priest to get started and be careful with his long shirt. Dowager said he had the makings of a fine priest like Father Accessible. At the instigation of Blue-eyed Jack Teddy tried his hand at spouting a few introductory verses of his own bog-Latin ('a-table and a bush! – a table and a bush! a table and a bush!').

'Speak oop!' urged Blue-eyed Jack – as though Teddy wasn't roaring

loud enough by this time. Indeed any crow or tinker who cared to pass by
at the flagstones would have been frightened to death and would have made
for the hills straightaway.

The little priest went on bowing and smiling across at the dung-heap
and making a number of charming salutations and greetings to the farmyard
fowl and all this pleased The Old Pair greatly. He even waved to the sheets
on the washing-bushes. He stretched out his arms to their full width and
(with Blue-eyed Jack prompting him with the bigger words) he began
shouting out a long list of Blessing Prayers – even adding a few of his own
to the ones Dowager had taught him. (Each prayer had to be repeated after
him by his guardians).

'Blessed be the stars of the night'. (Blessed be the stars of the night).

'Blessed be their sister, the moon'. (Blessed be the moon).

'Blessed be Little Nell and Shy Patsy across the waters'. (Blessed be
Little Nell and Shy Patsy across the waters).

'Blessed be Dowager and Blue-eyed Jack'. (Blessed be Dowager and
Blue-eyed Jack).

'Blessed be me'. (Blessed be me).

And then (in a moment of pure inspiration) he started blessing every
creature in sight around the haggart. He blessed the hens and then he
blessed the ducks and then he blessed the geese. He blessed Smiling Bab's
wildcat (Hen-chaser). The Mass concluded with Teddy's lofty sermon – a
supremely powerful and irresistible burst of gibberish from his perch on
his wobbly upturned bucket. Dowager and Blue-eyed Jack dropped to their
knees. The pair of them clapped their hands and they whispered and sighed
and they said that their little man had the look of a blue-eyed angel, despite
the bald patches amidst his curls.

With compliments such as these ringing in his ears the little priest gave
the final 'Amen-amen-amen' and the three of them joined their hands
together and they made their final procession around the haggart. Teddy
took off his big shirt and the twine girdle and he became himself again. His
innocent version of Mass was over. And if that most celestial of all earthly
luminaries (the bespectacled pope) had hopped out from his picture-frame
and jumped into the haggart that very minute he'd have been forced to shake
the little man warmly by the hand and invite him to come back to Rome
with him – for tea and a bit of soda-cake (added Blue-eyed Jack).

## The Silent Witnesses

Unbeknownst to this merry little threesome there were five of Smiling Bab's' children hiding outside at the flagstones. They had witnessed (and wondered at) this tidy little performance of Teddy's new Mass. Full of excitement, they scampered home to give a full report of it to their mother. Teddy's flight of fanciful ecstasy was going to keep everybody amused for the rest of the week since the news of his haggart Mass was to spread like a homespun song up and down the length of The Open Road. He had no time to play with his berry farm or his bowlee-wheel. He had no time to take his pretend tea with his new friend, little Darkie, in her cubby-shop in the dyke. He was as busy as a gnat saying Masses for the likes of Gentility and Slipperslapper and for Cackles and for Smiling Babs and her children. In the end it was agreed that (at least for these few days in his short life) he was the new patron saint of The Open Road. And even Father Accessible finally got to hear of his Mass one morning whilst he was swallowing down his two duck-eggs and his glass of buttermilk.

# SEVEN

# Teddy And Patches Go Fishing

*When Teddy and his new friend*
*went off with Blue-eyed Jack*
*to catch the great big fish in River Laughter.*

It was August in the year of 1944. Blue-eyed Jack rubbed the sleep from his misty eyes. As early as five o'clock (long before any cockerel crew or a beam of light had slipped through the window to caress his pillow) he was lying awake restlessly underneath the blankets and quilts beside the warm body of his sleeping nephew. He was listening to the incessant rain coming in from Kerry and in across The Forest of Lisnagorna and making its dreary descent on Rookery Rally. The black night would soon be carved open and out of it would come the dawn and after that would come the various sounds of the little birds in his yard trees and the farmyard fowl would join them a minute later, chorusing faster and faster even before leaving their roost. Then the daylight would lighten and throw a white sheet across the back wall of The Big Cave Room that separated himself and the child from the hen-house. And only then would our cockerel (Rampant) crow and crow and crow till he was as hoarse as an old drake.

Half-an-hour later Dowager was seen disappearing out the half-door, even before the big man had time to reach for his britches on the bed-rail or put his nose out the bedroom door. She was just in time to watch the faint light of the moon disappearing dismally and taking with it the half-hearted stars. Such precious moments as these were the best time in her daily life. She was just like her sentimental son and she loved these unreal mysteries in her world – the times when she was on her own and in her private small fairyland of half-hidden shapes among the surrounding trees and when she was listening to the lively music of her yard's ever-rolling stream, now heavy with flood-water from the black night's rain.

She emptied her piss-pot onto the ash-pit near the woodpile behind the pig-house and she waddled down the yard towards her hen-house. She opened the sheltering door and she removed the big stone that protected it. She carefully inspected and counted her thirty hens and her twelve ducks (her geese slept in the cowshed these days). The hens were well-used to her arrival and they greeted her sleepily as always and the ducks muttered their annoyance and un-tucked their heads reluctantly. Neither the fox nor the weasel had come to greet them during the night (thank God) and the old woman blessed herself as usual. Making her way back to The Welcoming Room she noticed how the blackbirds and the jackdaws were already making a day of it, scuffing with their beaks amidst the yard's debris. Not to be outshone by the likes of them the little robin was giving air to his own sharp energetic notes in among the silver spider-webs on the pig-house fuchsia bushes. Even before Dowager reached the half-door, those hitherto unfriendly ducks had beaten the hens to the yard and were already dabbling their webbed feet in the stormy waters of the stream.

The old woman almost bumped into Blue-eyed Jack who had at last made his way guiltily in and out from the pig-house gap at the upper end of the yard and was carrying on his back a sackful of logs, twigs and thorny bushes for the day's first fire. The two of them went in the half-door silently and with the broken bits of candle they started to tend to the fire. And then the big man took the two buckets to the well for the first of the day's six buckets of water.

## It's Time To Take Teddy To The Big Pool

Today was going to be the day when Blue-eyed Jack would see to his rods and his tackle and his jam-jar of fresh pink-and-blue maggots. He had made plans for a day's fishing-trip with Teddy so as to add to his growing education. From the moment he woke up his mind had been full of the fine fishing the two-men-of-us were going to do this day. Following the night's non-stop rain, River Laughter would have lost its smooth-sliding look; it would be swollen to the gills with flood-water from The Hills-of-The-Past as well as the odd branch from trees trying to hold her back. The brown trout would rise up to the surface to get themselves a breath of fresh air and our two fishermen would be there at the river's edge and would greet these little creatures with their fishhooks. Blue-eyed Jack would make sure that Teddy's shoulders carried his own small fishing-rod, cut from a hazel-tree, before they reached the bank of the river.

The Art of Fishing and Blue-eyed Jack were like the two sides of a windowpane (they were inseparable) and he loved nothing better than to sit on the bank of River Laughter and look down at those big brown trout and see the way they looked back up at him. As with his days spent among the rabbits in The Valley of The Black Cattle, he loved the closeness of the hunter and the hunted. His mother and Teddy would never go short of a bite to eat as long as he could slip his rod and line into a river.

# Fatty-Matty

There were times when himself and Fatty-Matty were just as close as that – like the days last June when they felt it better to go fishing in places where Mother Nature was not their mistress but where the laws of Lord Elegance prevailed – inside in the privacy of his lordship's ornamental lake. That's where these two great poachers saw the finest of rainbow trout swimming during the early evening when the mayfly and the swarming midges were at their busiest on the surface of the lake. That's when they threw their lines with a skill that Lord Elegance would have been proud of and brought home no less than half-a-dozen trout apiece for themselves. In doing so, Blue-eyed Jack brought a smile (and even a little laugh) out of the lustreless eyes of Fatty-Matty, who had every reason to feel sad, having recently lost his noble plough-horse (Fandango).

It was in Fatty-Matty's yard and before the eyes of a great crowd of openly-weeping men and women that this noble beast had met with his untimely death after a false feed of poisonous ragwort. The last we saw of him was his dilated nostrils and a river of sweat running down his two sides and the brave and unnatural efforts he kept making to stagger across the yard and to put his head in over the half-door and give his last hoarse farewell to Fatty-Matty's wife. It would break your heart to see it and Fatty-Matty had aged overnight. His eyes became red and his face grew green from all the crying he had done and it was only the regular fishing of Lord Elegance's lake in the company of Blue-eyed Jack that had set him free and put an end to his grief and saved him from utter madness.

## Handsome Johnnie

This present week Blue-eyed Jack had seen fit (the same way as Fandango had done in the yard) to pay homage to his own dear father (Handsome Johnnie) and go down to the graveyard in Abbey Acres and kneel on the spot where the good man had been buried. Over the last sixteen years it had always been the same story – to the day and to the hour, if not to the minute. At four o'clock the big man would kneel on the grass with his thoughts and his prayers and his rosary-beads, making his private pilgrimage to the man who had been the best of all fathers. Handsome Johnnie had coughed up the last bits of his liver inside in The Roaring Town Hospital at that very hour (four o'clock) on the last Thursday in August 1928. Always the finest of singers, he had sung his last farewell verses ('The Bird in The Gilded Cage') to the doctors and nurses that gathered at the doorway. And though all of his thirteen children, barring his beloved Blue-eyed Jack, were later to travel three of the world's continents, they stood with Dowager at the dying man's bed-head that very same sad evening and they listened to his final quavering song as the other patients rose up from their beds and drew near to his bedclothes to hear him. The only thing missing was his battered old concertina that would lie forevermore dusty under the bed at home in The Welcoming Room. It would have broken your heart to see such sorrow for the loss of so fine a father and husband as Handsome Johnnie. Enough said.

Having paid his respects to the man, who (together with Dowager) had instilled in him his deep love of rivers and woodlands, Blue-eyed Jack tore himself away from the graveside. He hopped in over the wire fence leading to Lord Elegance's lake. He stood there, alone with his thoughts, looking at the black Japanese swans sleeping beneath the willow-trees in the last of the day's sunshine. He hadn't been there since his last trip with Fatty-Matty.

He gazed at the pintail ducks and the foreign-looking geese from Canada and Egypt and he watched those big rainbow trout as they leaped dolphin-like into the air in their search for the plentiful gnats. He smiled to himself, for he knew something none of these trout knew – that the greatest of all the trout in Rookery Rally was a fish he called The Rogue. Rambling Jack and Saddle-the-Pony had seen this monster-of-a-fish (perhaps the two of them were just a little bit drunk) leaping a foot out of the water and with a size on him the length of your wellington (they said). The Rogue, however, didn't live in Lord Elegance's lake but a mile up along River Laughter.

## The King Of The World's Fishes

Teddy was playing with his coloured cards on the upturned ass-and-car in the yard. He knew nothing about this great big fish or the fact that this very afternoon Blue-eyed Jack would lead him a mile upstream through the tangled reeds and through the rushes to that secret cavern known as The Big Hole where The Rogue held sway over all his minions. Although he was looking forward to this fishing encounter, the big man couldn't get the thought out of his head – how this cunning rascal-of-a-fish had broken Saddle-the-Pony's best hazel rod in bits. He knew he would need a wrestling arm's strength in his own struggle with The Rogue and that it was a battle he simply had to win – for the sake of the little child – the new fisherman.

## Blue-Eyed Jack Had A Serious Thought

Ever since Teddy's introduction to Father Accessible's Mass, Blue-eyed Jack had been planning to take him on this fishing trip. Unlike Dowager, he felt that with all the recent images of holiness being hammered into the child's poor little skull whilst Mass was being said (and even during his make-believe haggart Masses) it was high time for the child to feel the refreshing breezes of Mother Nature seeping back into his soul before they got completely knocked out of him. Any fool (and it was no sacrilege to say so) could see the increasingly dazed look on the little man's face the minute Moll-the-mare was tackled and carted up for Mass. What with all the statues, the dazzling candles and the flashing sheen of the holy priest and his altarboys, strange and unreal must have been the thoughts rattling around inside that little head of his. It was time to present him with a few more earthly images than all this – such as the majestic scenes he'd be seeing this day along the riverbank, from where he'd carry home the echo of the river's purling music inside in his child's soul. It was better to fill his bedtime dreams with pictures of the muddy trout that spent their lives playing beneath the water's surface in The Big Hole. The Rogue would add a new and far different richness to Teddy's developing nature; he would balance things out a bit between the Church's dazzle and ceremony and the natural world around the child. Of course Blue-eyed Jack didn't breathe a word about these heathen thoughts of his to Dowager for fear she'd chase him round the yard with her yard-brush for the dozenth time and chastise his sore backside all over again for him.

## Jobs To Be Done

First of all (and with the sun trying to eat away the last of the mist) the cows had to be milked. But even before Blue-eyed Jack could reach for his coat, Teddy had already loosened himself from his sleep and with a leap out of his body he was into his wellingtons and standing at the half-door. Before Dowager had time to get to the two of them and dowse them with the holywater, the morning breezes were washing the two cheeks of her son and grandson as they headed down The Open Road under the gloom of the trees and veered towards John's Gate and The Bull-Paddock. Though Blue-eyed Jack loved to walk barefooted through the morning grass and feel the dew between his toes (a sure cure for corns and bunions, he said) there was no time on this fishing day for them to take off their wellington and let the coldness climb up their legs. There was no time to look up at the battle between the clouds and the sun above the pine-trees in Lisnagorna.

The big man was thinking how his cows hadn't yet eaten all the mushrooms that had grown overnight amidst the early spider-webs. He was thinking of Dowager's big frying-pan. He was thinking of a number of trout lying on their back in the middle of the same pan. He was thinking of the dab of butter and plenty of salt thrown in around the fish and the melting juices of the fish mingled with these mushrooms from The Bull-Paddock and the whole meal washed down with a mug of hot milk and pepper. There was a smile on his face. He sat Teddy in the shelter of the lowly dangling boughs of the oak tree. Seeing the two would-be fishermen, the cows were stirred out of their dreamland and they came loping languidly towards them.

As soon as they had closed the gate behind them, the two-men-of-us led the lazy-eyed creatures up the road and into the cowshed, their breath steaming out of them in a fog of steam. In no time at all the milk was streaming into the buckets of Blue-eyed Jack and Dowager. The Old Pair kept Teddy busy hopping from one leg to the other as they laughingly squirted streams of warm milk into his surprised face. They got him to say his Counting List (he was well past a hundred by now) and to say a few of his 'God Bless' Prayers and they got him to repeat his former Nursery Rhymes and to sing the few verses of 'I have a bonnet trimmed in blue, do I wear it? – yes, I do'. Blue-eyed Jack told him that the longer he went on singing, the more and more milk they'd get from their cows. Then they drained their heavy buckets through the muslin cloth and into the tank and the three of them went back into The Welcoming Room.

## Teddy's New Friends

It is high time at this stage to introduce Teddy's new friends – the ones that he had met at his first Mass and had royally entertained thereafter with his own brand of Mass. They were the children of Fiddler Joe and Smiling Babs and they had always been were very fond of Blue-eyed Jack. Before the arrival of Teddy the older ones had constantly pestered him for his news and his stories. Some might say they were trying to dodge from the regular drudgery of their own domestic chores above in their yard.

In the last few years, however, – ever since Teddy had got used to his new feet – they had kept themselves away from the yard. They knew that Teddy was different from them, he having come here from England and they being the children of The Old Sod (Ireland). Their mother (Smiling Babs) was the wife of Fiddler Joe and he was the only man known to play the fiddle left-handed on one of his two homemade fiddles – each fiddle known for its three separate woods and the family's hand-me-down glues.

149

Whereas some mothers had as little as three or four children to their name, Smiling Babs could hold her head up high the length and breadth of Ireland. Year in and year out she had produced children like card-tricks and she was healthier than any sow or cow, thank God.

What a fine healthy bunch her eight children were at this stage of their life (there were six more to follow!). There was an air of the tomboy about each of them. They had skin as brown as a rusty nail. Their feet were as hard as leather from running around barefooted up-and-down the flinty roads whereas Teddy lived mostly in his socks and his sandals. The youngest three (Cull, Patches and Darkie) were not old enough to take the three-mile trek to Dang-the-skin-of-it's school-house whereas Bucko, Golly and Gallant had their heads down on the desk every blessed day trying to get The Sums and The Dictation into their aching heads. Any day now Norrie and Sweeney (the older two) would be off working for one of the rich Anglo-Irish farmers still left in Ireland – Norrie serving her time in the kitchen and cleaning out the ashes and Sweeney doing odd jobs in the farmyard and garden and out on the land. This springtime holiday (along with their brothers and sisters) the two of them were having their last few weeks respite in between the former imprisonment of the school's walls and starting out to work to bring home their few shillings to Smiling Babs.

The Young Rascals (as Dowager with a shake of her head was forever playfully calling them) were seen racing all over The Valley of The Pig from one day to the next and terrifying the river and woodland spirits with their wildness and ensuring that the poor old ladies in The Hills-of-The-Past (including Gentility) never got one wink of afternoon sleep. You'd see them tearing off to the foot of the highest tree in Red Scissors' Lane where Sweeney was the first to storm the ascent and reach the very topmost branch. From his lofty perch he let out a war-whoop that sent cats and dogs scurrying for their lives and then the devil lifted the leg of his trousers and let fly a fine stream of his hot piss down on his younger sisters and brothers as they struggled to climb up the tree after him. Were you there, your two ears would be completely deafened and you would soon have learnt the finest set of swearwords in Ireland from the mouths of the soaked children (feck! feck! and feck you all over again, Sweeney!) as they screamed up at him from down below.

After this bout of amusement was over, the children ran hell-for-leather down to River Laughter's metal bridge and they paddled up-and-down its rocky bed without even a flinch from their bare toes. They collected the pink, saffron and lavender stones so as to draw the faces of their mother and father on the flagstones in their yard and put their parents in the best of humour for the rest of the day.

Inside in Timmy's haggart an hour later this same army of Nature's children lay down in the afternoon heat on top of that poor misfortunate man's trams of hay and they made wells in them and flattened them entirely. Then they chased each other down The Open Road and they leaped in over the singletree to their secret grove where they sat like a line of crows on top of the fallen pinetree. All of them (even the youngest) began smoking their fag-butts (stolen from Fiddler Joe's canister). They let the smoke out skillfully from their nostrils and one or two of the older ones produced smoke from their two ears as well. That was all the excitement for just one day and it was surely enough.

In due season, however, their restless spirits would make regular raids on every orchard the length and breadth of Rookery Rally or they'd trot off with their jam-jars to gather blackberries and deliberately destroy their faces with red juices as though they were returning from some far-off pig-killing or were a new breed of Red Indian recently come to dwell amongst us.

There were times when their wild actions became almost wanton – just a little bit short of vandalism and downright cruelty. They let loose the fat sow of Shy Dennis and they opened Red Buckles' gate to see his alarmed calves race away from the sow and run hysterically round and around the field. They threw the chicken down Moll-the-Man's chimney while she was saying her rosary and they pelted stones at Gret's two pigs and they ran amok amongst her revered flock of turkeys. They chased their ass (Slowcoach) and they tried to get up on his back and ride him through the dock-leaves in The Thistle Field.

But their mood (like Ireland's weather) could change at times and suddenly grow very soft. The younger boys would walk down The Thistle Field to pay a polite visit to their two sisters' cubby-houses in the depths of the dyke and they'd drink their pretend tea from rusty tin cans. Norrie and Darkie would make bangles and necklaces from field flowers and place them on their brothers' wrists and necks and spend the rest of the day dreaming their lives away on the flagstones above their yard-stream playing with the brown-and-ginger caterpillars that lived at the foot of the oak tree and letting them weave their lazy dances in and out across their legs. Or they'd drift off in ones and twos and collect handfuls of horse-dung and mix it with the mud from the rainy dykes and ditches and invent make-believe farms with red hawthorn berries (for cows) and fir-cones (for horses) and white berries (for sheep) before squashing one or two of these berries into the surprised ears of either Darkie or Cull.

For a finish all eight of them would climb wearily up the ladder in the evening and lay themselves down on top of Mikey's hay in his hayshed and amuse one another by quietly singing their end-of-the-day school songs (like 'Barbara Allan' or 'Come with me over the mountain') before sending themselves home to bed like worn-out birds to their nests. And if Father Accessible's lavish Mass had been a spectacle to dazzle the baptismal eyes of Teddy and rattle the brains inside in his developing head then the antics of this colourful group of children were more than a match for it. Enough said.

## They Come Calling On The Little Englander

And on the day of the fishing (and at the recent instigations of Dowager and Smiling Babs) five of them and their bare feet came padding in across the flagstones. They treaded their way tentatively up through the pig-house gap where Blue-eyed Jack and his axe was chopping up several logs from the wood-stack. It was almost half-ways through the morning and Timmy would soon be down to take the milk to the creamery. The little group of visitors stood there, giving one or two shy and peculiar glances at Teddy. Likewise he stood there like a statue and looking back at them and he wondered about them and why they had come visiting. Himself and themselves were the very same as starey-eyed cats and for a while nobody said a single word. Together they began to watch the big man as he lay siege to the rest of the timber.

By this time of the day Blue-eyed Jack had worked himself into a great ball of sweat. After a little while he stopped to wipe his brow. To tell the truth he was enjoying his work far more than he would have imagined when he'd staggered out of bed earlier in the day. And now it was his turn to take a good look at these friendly children; for (like his mother and Smiling Babs) he thought today was the day to bring Teddy in tune with other children and the best way to achieve this was to get both camps to come and help him at his work. He began to pile some of the smaller logs into the arms of Teddy, Patches and Bucko and he told them to fire their loads in under Dowager's stool near the fireplace. She would now be able to keep up a blazing fire for boiling her spuds and cabbages (he said) and feeding her two pigs and her fowl.

The three older children, seeing such a great big heap of sliced logs lying higgledy-piggledy all over the sawdust, immediately rushed to Blue-eyed Jack's side, anxious to get their teeth into the work. He gave Sweeney, Golly and Gallant a few weighty armfuls of the bigger logs. He told them to start making a second wood-stack near the pig-house wall and balance them neatly and carefully into level rows and show him the metal of their arms. It was a job they got to grips with only too well and as a reward for their labours he took from his coat pocket a package of fags. They were made of stronger tobacco than his usual Woodbine fags and were stronger too than the fag-buts that the children often stole from their father's canister to smoke in Mikey's grove.

Blue-eyed Jack laid two of the fags on the chopping block and with his penknife he divided them ceremoniously into four halves. The three big boys sat down beside him against the pig-house wall with their arms folded across their knees. There was no room for Teddy or for Patches or Bucko and for the first time in his life (though he couldn't understand the reason why) the little man felt strangely uncomfortable and confused.

He saw his uncle lighting up the four fag-halves and he watched him hand three of them to Sweeney, Golly and Gallant, keeping the fourth one for himself. The boys energetically puffed and coughed on their strange new fags. They watched the fag-smoke rise up in lavish plumes and float off over the wood-stack in mysterious little wisps. It made them feel that their heads were growing heavy and were hanging loosely on their shoulders. From time to time they sucked their cheeks inwards and breathed in and out through their nostrils like Blue-eyed Jack.

In spite of themselves, they were soon swallowing huge heaps of smoke. They closed their eyelids as if nothing strange was happening to them but their eyes began rolling round and around in their heads and they thought they could see coloured dots across the back of their eyeballs. Blue-eyed Jack (the old rascal) chuckled to himself. But then (for his heart was as soft as a bog) he capped off the morning's smoking by teaching them to make wide circles with their lips and form smoke-rings. They were soon making them bigger than himself. The art of smoking was a tremendous success and everybody (including Teddy) began to laugh and clap their hands excitedly.

## A Summons From Smiling Babs

The gathering at the woodpile, however, was suddenly interrupted by the loud clanging of Smiling Babs' tin tray against her flagstones. In times of emergency this tray was her natural weapon. It acted as a warning bell to tell her children to hasten home at rabbit-speed. Sometimes it was just a ruse of hers – to put an end to her rascally children galloping all over the countryside and to bring them back for the most mundane of tasks such as shoveling out the dung from Slowcoach-the-ass's stable. But they had already dealt with this task the day before last and the stable was as shiny and new as a church window. However, it still needed a few cartloads of ferns to make the ass's stable-bed as comfortable as Lord Elegance's.

With a skip and a jump Sweeney led his four brothers home from the woodpile and out into The Thistle Field where the dull-blinking Slowcoach was chewing his way through a few choice nettles. With the reins and the winkers safely on him, they returned to their yard. They backed him in under the shafts of the ass-and-car and they harnessed him tightly with the bellyband. Fiddler Joe had made the sharply-pointed stakes for the four corners of the car and he carefully handed two sharp billhooks to Sweeney and Golly and warned them about the danger when the time came for them to cut down today's heap of ferns. Before they could head off to The Bog Wood, their mother ran out after them and she fingered the sign-of-the-cross on their foreheads and also on the head of the ass and then Slowcoach made his sluggish way out of the yard. The five boys left Cull and Darkie behind them in the capable hands of their older sister (Norrie) and they took their way down The Open Road.

# Lord Elegance's Private Domain

This was not one of those blazing hot days of the previous June when they had spent their afternoons filling their tar barrels at the metal bridge and throwing their buckets and reins repeatedly in over the railings above River Laughter. Now was the time to make (what we all did from time to time) a stealthy raid into The Bog Wood. The wood was one of Lord Elegance's private realms and the ferns were more than plentiful in there and the children could bring home load after load on poor old Slowcoach's ass-and-car. Like his lordship's ornamental lake, The Bog Wood was a place forbidden to all of us. In the eyes of little Patches (who hadn't been down there before this day) it was another secret part of his childhood fairyland. Once September came round and the season of hay-and-wheat was finished and all we had to think about was killing the pig and worrying about the harsh winter ahead and the job of warming the family fireside, Lord Elegance would open up The Bog Wood to everybody to go and collect their kindling and chop up the fallen branches.

Though it was still August, one or two of us (including Blue-eyed Jack) were making stealthy raids on it after dusk and loading up the ass-and-car with as much ferns as we could. Our animals' winter bedding would be made a bit more comfortable by topping the usual rough corn-stalks with this soft touch of Lord Elegance's greenery. With all this urgency about bringing home the ferns, you'd think it was a palace we had in mind for the likes of our Rookery Rally animals!

# Blue-Eyed Jack Wastes No Time

Meanwhile, having listened to Saddle-the-Pony's dispute with The Rogue and the way the monster had broken his rod, Blue-eyed Jack was anxious to make tracks to the riverbank with Teddy and to make him aware of the importance of a fishing day and what lay in store for him. He was sitting at the breakfast table and swallowing down a huge mouthful of bread and butter and licking clean the edge of his butter-knife when he harmlessly let slip how there was a fish of monstrous size living in The Big Hole less than a mile up

River Laughter – a fish that none but the mightiest of hunters could ever be seen trying to catch. Then came the solemn pause in his voice and then… came the great big lie! He told Teddy that he himself had made several attempts at catching this fish and had failed every single time. 'This monster goes by the name of The Rogue and he is the king of all the fishes in Ireland,' said he. He gulped down his tea without so much as batting an eyelid.

'We must catch him! We must! We must! We must!' yelled the little man, jumping up from the table and forgetting the spoon in his upturned egg.

'And let me tell you this,' went on the big man seriously, 'three fine hazel rods has this wicked fish smashed on me (and this was an even bigger lie!) and he is indeed well-named – The Rogue. Only last year he damned near pulled me into The Big Hole and he was about to swallow me up entirely when Saddle-the-Pony came and rescued me in the nick of time.' There wasn't the trace of a smile on his rascally lips and at this moment it was this big man more than anyone else, who should have been performing above on the Dublin stage. Was there a man in the whole of Ireland who could lie like Blue-eyed Jack?

Teddy saw the big man get up from the table and go into The Big Cave Room. He reached behind the bedpost for what he called 'the medicine' – his two hazel rods, just in case one of them was to get broken by the huge fish. Teddy forgot all his other daily niceties, such as feeding the ducks and the hens with Dowager and trying to draw a picture of her face on the flagstones. Indeed everything else was cast aside and swallowed up as quickly as Blue-eyed Jack's bread and butter and his little heart was pounding away like a rabbit's. With a pleading set of eyes he clutched at his uncle's sleeve: 'And you will let me go fishing with you, won't you, Jack?'

Blue-eyed Jack pointed his finger at him and he gave him an unusually threatening look: 'I might take you with me. I just might – but only if you're as good as gold and as quiet as a church mouse.' It was the very same tale as the day when they went hunting the rabbits. And once more the big man saw the fretful trace of doubt creeping into Teddy's face. He bent down gently and then he threw the shrieking child up on his broad shoulders and he spun him round and around the room breathlessly. Teddy finally knew that the two-men-of-us were definitely going to go on this very special fishing-hunt – a great big hunt for the king of all the fishes in The Big Hole and that it would be yet another glorious day's outing for him.

# Dowager Plays Her Part Too

Dowager was standing beside her two men. She was thinking (just like her son) about her big frying-pan and the trout and the mushrooms that were going to fill it. She followed her son into The Big Cave Room and she threw open the lid of the piano (Old Harpy) that Lady Brindleton had bequeathed her on her deathbed and which nobody ever played. Inside the lid was where Dowager stored her icing sugar and her nutmeg and other spices, as well as her flour. She pulled out a large folded satchel. She blew the dust off of it and she wiped it clean of its flour-stains. She handed it to Teddy. She had been planning to use it as his future school-bag should the war go on for another few years and The Little Englander find himself trotting off to join up with Rookery Rally's own home-grown scholars.

'I'm relying on you, my little hunter,' said she, 'to fill this great big satchel with the silver-bellied trout and to bring them back to me this evening.' The child, as always, was only too ready to obey her commands and he snatched the satchel from her. He knew what he would have to do: obey Blue-eyed Jack's instructions at all times (as with the hillside rabbits) so that they'd catch The king of the fishes. Blue-eyed Jack knew they'd need the patience of all the saints if they were to snare The Rogue and a few of his friends. How else were they going to fill a great big satchel like the one Teddy was to carry?

# Maggots, Maggots And More Maggots

Beyond the woodpile and close to Timmy's ditch there was a pile of stale manure that had been gathering from as far back as Blue-eyed Jack could remember. Each springtime and with the sweat and the steam rising up from him, he would skim the top off of it and fork out the sharp-smelling matter and shovel it into the horse-and-cart. Then he'd take it across the fields for spreading. This monstrous slimy mess was known as The African Sink and its blue mire stank to high heavens. It was rich, however, in the number of oily maggots deep down in its middle.

Teddy had been warned never to go near it. If he climbed up on top of it (said Dowager) his two legs would be swept out from under him by a family of wicked spirits, who were far more deadly than The Boodeeman and he'd be sucked all the way down into darkest Africa (wherever that was) and be swallowed up by the Monster-of-all-monsters, The Devil. A child of almost four didn't need to be told this story more than once!

From the haggart-stick Teddy and Dowager stood looking at The African Sink. The child was holding onto his grandmother's hand with the grip of death and watching his uncle at his work. Blue-eyed Jack had brought out a jam-jar and he drove his four-grained fork repeatedly into the dung around the edges of The African Sink, trying to bayonet his way through its fermenting fumes and find the best possible maggots for this day's work. Finally he saw what he was looking for (a huge heap of maggots) and he picked out the longest and thickest ones. Some were blue-headed and some were pink like the chickweed blooms amid the potato-stalks and they glistened and wriggled around his wellingtons. He soon had a big pile of them. 'Food for the line that's going to hook The Rogue,' he laughed, thinking how these maggots would herald a rich day's fishing for himself and Teddy.

The jam-jar began to fill up nicely with the selected maggots. The big man looked across at Teddy and he showed him the wrigglers, swarming like the pile of twisted rabbit-guts whenever Dowager was cleaning out one of her rabbits at the table. Meanwhile the old woman was kept busy chasing away the army of inquisitive hens and ducks that had followed her out from the yard and were scurrying around her son's wellingtons in search of the odd maggot he might let drop.

If there was one thing that Teddy feared (apart from a long list of leprechauns, boodeemen, Fort Dangerous, Corkscrew and Warts-the-Journeyman) it was the sight and touch of a maggot. At potato-picking time Blue-eyed Jack was up to his usual devilment, pelting maggots at him when he least expected it – simply to hear him pour down on his head those foul curses that he'd learnt from the visiting card-players. And that's when the row would always rise up as the pious and holy nature of Dowager attempted to prevail against her son: 'Is it for Heaven or for Hell that we are rearing this child of ours? How can I make a saint out of him, if this is the way you're going to blackguard his innocence?'

And now, seeing how the little dreamer had wandered off from The

African Sink towards the safer puddles and how he was gazing down into the reflections of the clouds, the rascally Blue-eyed Jack picked out the juiciest one of his maggots and he fired it at the child's head. And whatever bird, hen, duck or insect happened to be nearby, they were surely frightened to death by the profundity of the curses ('feck! feck! and feck you again!') that the little man rained down on the head of Blue-eyed Jack. And while the big man had a pain in his sides from his fits of laughter, Dowager was far from amused ('Will this bleddy eejit ever learn to watch what he's doing – himself and his stupid maggots?') and she walked away out of the haggart in absolute disgust.

## Let Two-Men-Of-Us Go Fishing

It was time to leave The African Sink and Blue-eyed Jack put the jam-jar of maggots into his coat pocket. He checked the flexibility of his two rods and he checked his tin for the soundness and suitability of his fishhooks. Ruffling his little man's curls, he took him by the hand and said: 'Let two-men-of-us go hunt the trout and bring the king of the fishes back to Dowager and put a smile back on her angry old face.'

There was something missing (Teddy's little fishing-rod). Blue-eyed Jack noticed one or two dark clouds suddenly appearing over the child's eyebrows: 'Did you make me a fishing-rod?" asked the little man. The big man was stung by his own forgetfulness and he assured the child that he'd have a fishing-rod before they were at the metal bridge. After a quick dash of holywater, the two hunters set forth and headed for The Briary Stile, which would lead them to the river and The Big Hole.

## In The Depths Of The Bog Wood

Meanwhile Smiling Babs' five children were busy too: they had got as far as the entrance to The Bog Wood. They spent the whole time looking anxiously around them to see if Lord Elegance was about to spring out and seize them by the throat before they could open and replace the wire fence behind them. Little Patches and his vivid imagination began to see several changes among the silver birch trees surrounding them. He believed that messages were being passed along from tree to tree by the woodland fairies: 'The children are coming! Slowcoach is coming! They are here! They are here!'

His big brothers set to work and (as with their handling of Blue-eyed Jack's pile of logs) they were soon showing the stout metal in their arms as they stacked the ferns higher and higher in the ass-and-car, filling the four corners first. Quicker than you'd think, they tied the reins criss-cross over the finished load. They led Slowcoach out to The Easy Tree – the tree where Rookery Rally's children from days gone by made their first attempts at tree-climbing when they were coming home from the school-house.

A few paces away from them flowed the majesty of River Laughter. It beckoned them to come down and cool their aching bodies. Thanks to the floodwater that followed the recent rains, the river was deeper than usual and had risen even higher than Sweeney's knees. They took off their short britches and they began gingerly paddling about in their shirts underneath the echoing bridge and its dappled shadows. It was like a bit of paradise to them. It wasn't long before they started cupping their hands and firing water into one another's eyes. Then, in case their shirts got soaking wet and their mother had to lay into them with the yard-brush, Sweeney gave the order to remove these obstacles. And without a stitch of clothing on them they entirely forgot their good manners, making grabs between one another's legs at what they called their private credentials before falling in a heap and screaming abuse and foul language to the skies above them. What Slowcoach-the-ass thought of all this rude rascality has never been recorded. Asses were never so impolite as this.

## Along Came Slipperslapper

Slipperslapper with her ass-and-car was crossing the bridge on her way home from The Roaring Town. All of a sudden the bold boys ran out from their hidey-hole and they saluted her most regally. Brazenly they showed her their backsides before giving her dazed old eyes the full manifestation of their private credentials. The poor old soul clung onto her hat and almost died of fright at this manly gesture and she gave a fierce lash with her ash-plant to the misfortunate back of her startled ass (Flat-foot).

It had all been laughter and smiles up till then. But even in the children's newly-found paradise a touch of boredom was likely to creep in and raise its ugly head. They recalled the story of the biblical baptism of Jesus that had recently been taught to them at school and Sweeney shouted out: 'Hey, byze! – it's high time for Patches to get himself baptized in The River Jordan'. And then – he made a sudden rush at his delicate little brother. Golly was next in line of command and. sensing that this was going to prove a bit of further amusement, he joined in with his older brother. They took a leg apiece of their terrified younger brother (you'd think Patches was a turkey's wish-bone!) and they tipped him upside-down above the river. You could hear the little fellow's shrieks above at Sheeps' Cross.

'One – two – three!'

They ducked his head repeatedly under the water and they held him down for as long as they thought fit. It was a miracle he didn't drown, what with the gallons of water he was swallowing. He must have had half-a-dozen fishes inside in his belly!

'Ye basthard! Ye basthards!' was all that poor Patches could stammer as he eventually freed himself and fled from the river. He snatched up his shirt and britches and, not bothering to put them on, he raced up The Open Road in the direction of his home and his saviour – his mother. With blinding tears running down along his cheeks, he passed out Slipperslapper and her ass. This second bout of his nakedness ruined her day completely and she'd be sitting up in the bed for half of the night, thinking about it.

## Poor Patches

Blue-eyed Jack had been busy cutting Teddy his first fishing-rod from a clump of hazels at John's Gate when he saw the hasty flight of Patches. The little boy had the look of a demented pig after its slaughter: 'The basthards have just baptized me in The River Jordan,' he cried and he was shivering from head to toe with the cold and the fear. The big man helped him into his short britches and Teddy helped him into his shirt so that Patches was decent-looking enough by the time they'd finished with him. But his little heart was still trembling like a lost lamb's, when Slipperslapper and her averted eyes raced on passed, her whip still leathering into the confused back of poor demented Flat-foot.

'You'll get a fishing rod, Patches. I'll cut it for you myself if it's the last thing I do,' said Blue-eyed Jack angrily. 'And I'll tell you something else – you'll spend the rest of today fishing with the two of us. By God-in-Heaven won't your four lousy brothers be the scalded cats when they see you coming into the yard this evening and the fine fishes you'll be bringing home to your mother and father?'

## A Time For Children's Guilty Reflection

Patches' big brothers began to realize the terror they had struck into him and they called a halt to their merriment in the river. In silence they put on their shirts and their short britches. They led Slowcoach out onto The Open Road and they headed up towards John's Gate.

They were just in time to see three noble hunters lightly tripping down the hill towards them in the shape of Blue-eyed Jack and Teddy and ('do our eyes deceive us?') their little brother, Patches. Without so much as a look or a word the three fishermen passed them straight by. And Patches (how quickly children seem to forget their wounds!) was no longer shuddery but had a fresh smile on his jaw and he held his nose high in the air. As soon as they reached The Briary Stile Blue-eyed Jack turned round and he shouted up the road: 'Ye'll be wetting yeer britches tonight when Fiddler Joe gets a hold of ye. Yes, by God, yeer legs will be red raw from the fine belting he'll give each of ye.' Such steely talk was uncommon from a kindhearted soul like the big man. But it was no laughing matter the way they had half-drowned their little brother and the poor child not yet old enough to defend himself. The big man vowed he'd never offer them a single one of his half-fags again.

All the children's good work in The Bog Wood now counted for nothing. The shame-faced crew struggled sadly on up the road and into the yard, their eyes staring down at their toes. They were just in time for the bit of dinner and the loaded plates of champ and mugs of milk. Whilst they were coming up the road they had had time to think about what they had done. They were no fools and had made a pact with one another: it was best to let Sweeney to do all the talking when asked by their mother where on earth their little brother had gone to.

## Sweeney, Ever The Diplomat

Sweeney coyly explained to his mother how poor Patches had fallen back on his back into the river while they were pretending to give him a religious baptism the way Jesus had once been baptized by his cousin, John. With the delivery of this bit of news his brothers had to smile and wink at one another; they knew that Sweeney had hit the nail right on the head. For their mother loved Jesus more than words could say and she'd be as pleased as punch with this biblical tale of events.

'And where is he now?' she asked.

'He's below at the river and he's gone off fishing with The Little Englander and Blue-eyed Jack'.

'Aren't men awful eejits,' she muttered to herself, shaking her head. 'Surely Blue-eyed Jack knew better than this and that it was time for the poor lad's dinner? I'm surprised at himself and yeerselves. Patches will be starved-to-death by the time he gets home.' Without another word (which could have complicate matters a good deal further and reveal their act of treachery) the children heaved a sigh of relief and they raced through their plate of champ and milk. Smiling Babs cleared the table and she picked out the two largest spuds she could find from the skillet pot and she cut them into quarters. She added a plate and a knife and a fork and a small bottle of milk and she stowed them in her shopping bag. 'Go down to the river, let ye', said she, 'with these spuds and milk and see that yeer newly-baptized brother is well-fed and watered.'

At this, the rascals nodded their heads vigorously and their mother smiled at the readiness of her good-natured children to make amends for their thoughtlessness in letting their little brother go off fishing without them. Little did the simple soul know that her children had made a right old ass out of her!

Before they reached the half-door she added: 'There's to be no roaring or yahooing whilst ye're down at the river (do ye hear me?) for ye'll have to be as quiet as the grave if ye want Blue-eyed Jack to catch his fish.' Again the four heads nodded spontaneously. And then their mother had a second little thought: 'Who knows – ye might yet be able to redeem yeerselves from the worry ye've caused me in losing Patches – ye might even bring back one or two little fishes for the frying-pan.' The children couldn't wait to get out from underneath her feet and they ran towards the yard at considerable speed. They had escaped their mother's wrath.

## Onwards, Onwards To The River

Onwards towards the river tap-tapped the other three merry sets of fishermen's feet. The two-men-of-us were carrying their fishing-rods on their shoulders and Patches was carrying Teddy's big satchel for holding the fishes. The master and his two pupils were now enjoying the almost-poetic essence of this soul-calming day. The bushes were still wet with the night's lodged raindrops and they looked like pieces of diamonds. The sky was light and blue and the clouds had been scattered away by the high winds. They passed Mikey's gate where the ghost of the slain woodcutter (Larry Cash) would sometimes appear and frighten the dancers coming home from The Platform Dance-in-Judy Rag's Field on summer nights. They reached The Briary Stile. They heard River Laughter brawling and sobbing, long before they could watch her fighting her way towards The Mill and Halting Cross to meet up with other rivers.

Blue-eyed Jack knew every inch of this river – all the little turns and twists and the deep rocky pools and the sally-holes. He knew the clear shallow stretches and the little sandy beaches. He knew the spots where (undisturbed by any other mortal) you could sit yourself down with a canister of tea and hang your legs out on an over-reaching log across the water and eat your fill of hazelnuts and blackberries. He knew those rare shady parts under the remote oaks and beech trees where no man (other than Rambling Jack and Saddle-the-Pony) had ever clapped their eyes. These were places where you'd see him sitting on the shiny side of his waistcoat and shivering with delight and conversing with those river fairies (the ghosts of his ancestors) who forever seemed to accompany him on his mystical rambles into the heart of Nature.

One at a time he took the hands of the little boys and he led them up and onto the stile. The far side was covered with nettles. He jumped down into them and grasped them firmly in his fists so as to clear a path for the children to get through. They eased themselves over the wire fence and he swung their legs and their unsuspecting shrieks out over the nettles. From where they were standing they could see the two pillars of the bridge above their heads where children returning from the school-house would look down at their own reflections. How privileged (thought the big man) were the two little fishermen to be standing here this Saturday afternoon and watching the river's silken curves. Ahead of them was the little tributary stream that flowed down from both their farmyards. Back and forth leaped Blue-eyed Jack over it, carrying each boy across amid their further shrieks of laughter.

They knelt down and they cupped their hands and they drank the clear water. The real journey had now begun. They were on their way to the innermost haunts of River Laughter, leaving behind them The Open Road and the world as they had known it. The ghosts of former fishermen came out to greet them from Mikey's Ferny Field and they beckoned them onwards towards the mysterious Big Hole. The children walked in front of the big man, hugging the green fringes of the rippling river. They listened to the rustling sounds of the spiky ferns, which were so tall that the boys felt almost lost. A few yards away from them the fishes were playing amid the swaying rushes and darting around in their underwater kingdom.

Man had rarely come this far up the river. At the height of summer, however, a few older boys might come here in secret to find a little bit of paradise and to bathe naked in the sally-holes and frighten the little fishes. The big girls might come here also at other times. It was a clothes-free place; it was full of frivolous fleshy glances on those hazy afternoons – a place to which boys might scurry down amongst Mikey's cattle (carefully avoiding his big red bull) and sit amongst the hidden oak-trees on the river's bank and steal scandalous looks at the fleshy young girls bathing without a stitch of clothes on. In a similar way girls might go down and spy on the boys. And then you'd hear the screams of recognition (the girls) and the folded arms and the cupped hands (the boys). Was such unbridled laughter and such cursing and swearing ever heard tell of before or since in Rookery Rally? The poor little fishes hid themselves deep in the rushes, deprived of all their heavenly peace and quiet.

## This Hidden World Of Childhood Dreams

Teddy slipped out of his sandals. He handed them to his uncle to hold, wanting his bare feet to feel the grass. So intense were the young fishermen that their heads were almost falling off of their shoulders from looking around at all the aspects of this great big river. Blue-eyed Jack thought it best to hold them by their hands and keep them away from the edge of the water – in case Patches got himself baptized all over again. With this hilarious picture in his mind he couldn't help from quietly laughing to himself.

The two small boys were now as far along the river as they had ever traveled and Blue-eyed Jack and his sharp eyes told them that they were coming near The Big Hole. The river opened into deep pools and Mikey's oak-woods loomed above them. Across the river were the ruminating cows and horses belonging to Joe-the-Buckle, gazing across at them. And once again – how much better (thought the big man just as Dowager had done on her visit to Gentility) for Teddy to spend a day here in the wilderness – journeying to The Big Hole and swallowing in the song of the river and its pristine scenery – how much better than squeezing his shy shoulders (when the time came) into the back benches of the school-house and singing his droning Tables – how much better for him to be learning from Nature than all the knowledge being drummed in between the ears of other children at the hands of Dang-the-skin-of-it with all his lofty Poetry and his Euclid.

## The Big Hole Itself

The big man stopped dead in his tracks. They had reached The Big Hole. He put down his rods and he rubbed his hands together. His heart could have danced a jig when he thought of the many trout that caroused around in rings, paying their respects to the king of the fishes. The three fishermen (the big and the little) leaned down. They peered in over the edge of the pool, blue like the reflected sky and its ripples shining like a hundred silver coins. Perhaps The Rogue was looking up at them. Perhaps he saw the eyes of these fantastically shaped giants looking down into his eyes? Blue-eyed

Jack placed his two rods against a tree. There was a sudden chill in the air and the little birds kept breathlessly still and they wondered at the strange fishermen entering their world. Death was nearby (they knew it).

Blue-eyed Jack scraped away some broken sticks from under his feet. He brought a few clumps of musky ferns and he laid them on the ground. He settled Teddy and Patches into their leafy hidey-hole on the sloping bank. He made the little boys as sheltered as could be amid the long-shadowed trees where no wind or rain could get at them. The children sat there obediently and they wondered what was going to happen next. Blue-eyed Jack looked back at them and he smiled: they were sitting stock still like two young stags on the shiny lining of his warm waistcoat and were far enough from the fishing-hole to be safe from his flying rod when the time came to fish. For once in his life there wasn't a word out of him. He felt the eyes of the riverside fairies peering down impishly at him from the gaps in the treetops where the hazy sunlight spread its tentacles of soft warmth and reflected itself in the yellow wrinkles of the pool. He was lost in his dreams of the river's greatest treasure – The Rogue.

## The Other Children Head For The Briary Stile

Leaving behind them their yard and their father (Fiddler Joe) to fork out the ferns from the ass-and-car and deal with Slowcoach's stable, Sweeney and his three brothers had by now made their speedy way in over The Briary Stile. In no time they reached The Big Hole and they hid themselves a short distance away from Blue-eyed Jack. They did not know what to expect from him. They plucked up courage and they gave a few little coughs. Tentatively they held aloft their mother's shopping-bag on a stick as a peace-offering to Patches and their old friend, Jack. Sweeney gave the nod and they plucked up enough courage to emerge from the ferns: 'We have brought you some spuds, Patches,' they whispered, remembering their mother's warning not to disturb the fishes and seeing Blue-eyed Jack with his finger on his lips. 'We're sorry for baptizing you in the river and all the trouble we have caused you. We have brought you a bottle of milk as well, Patches.' The list of their sorrows went on and on; they knew when to make the right crestfallen gestures and to divert their eyes and to hold their heads low (the crafty little schemers!).

It didn't take much to soften the heart of Blue-eyed Jack and he shoved Patches forward to take the shopping-bag with the food in it. The happily reunited children now felt a bit more comfortable in themselves. They sat cross-legged on the sheltered bed of ferns and once again Blue-eyed Jack smiled on the six of them like a loving father. They looked like they were back in Dang-the-skin-of-it's school-house and preparing themselves for one of the great schoolmaster's lessons to worry its way down into their heads.

## It's Fishing Time

It was fishing-time. Their eyes were fixed on the big man. They could sense the growing excitement oozing out of him and the thoughts in his mind – to catch The Rogue and fish him out onto the bank and into the satchel and to have him on the dinner-plate in the evening. Their silence throbbed softer than a sleeping infant and they wondered if the same silence filled the watery souls of the fishes. The Big Hole was far deeper than the waters beneath the metal bridge where they had once helped Slipperslapper drown the flea-ridden tinker's pup (and, oh how sorry they continued to feel for that former crime of theirs).

Blue-eyed Jack cut himself a squid of tobacco with his penknife. He rolled it around in the palms of his hands the way his father used to do. He lit his pipe and the honeyed smoke filled the children's nostrils as they watched him drawing in jaw-filling puffs of smoke beneath the lid of his pipe and banishing the flies, a number of which were by this time out and about.

He had a great deal to consider. He knew that after the night's heavy rain this was the best time for him to come fishing; that the trout would be full of false confidence: that they would sink down to the bottom and hide themselves from the eyes of Man. He knew that the longer they stayed below the surface the more their eyes would become unfamiliar with the increasing sunlight of the day. He knew that the younger more innocent trout would be more than likely to take his bait of maggots, being unable at first to see the line and its hook when they came up to the surface to greet the light.

He studied his rod and he studied his line. As soon as he had captured enough fishes to put into the satchel, he'd let the children join him in his fishing. But until then he would fix the rods of Patches and Teddy as deep as he could into the mud of the bank. Sometime later he would put a few lush maggots on their hooks and help them to throw their lines.

With his tough leathery fingers he delicately skewered one or two wriggling maggots onto the hook. He stepped out into the freezing water and onto the boulders around which the river spilled. He could sense the thumping hearts of the fishes as they heard the soft thud of his wellingtons above them: 'Here comes Man. Here comes our greatest enemy. Here comes his inevitable rod and his line.'

Blue-eyed Jack looked along the edge of the pool at the bubbles around the gleaming stones where the inexperienced trout danced through the blades of the rushes and the water chuckled playfully and avoided the strong tumbling currents at the centre of The Big Hole. 'Before this afternoon is finished these young numbskulls will dance to a far different tune. They will find themselves on the end of Teddy and Patches' fishing rods,' said he to himself. He continued to gaze into the heart of The Big Hole where that great big fish and all the older lazy-eyed fishes were now looking up at him and giving him nothing less than the evil eye. Their tails were no longer swaying. Their bodies were no longer dancing. Their very souls were frozen in time. They knew that the mental battle of wits had already begun – the battle between Fish and Man.

The hunting now began in earnest. It gladdened the hearts of the children, who were hoping they'd see a great big trout hanging off of the big man's rod. And while they were patiently waiting, they lay back on their bed of ferns and they gazed up at the passing clouds and the shapes in the topmost branches of the trees that were confusing their eyes.

Suddenly Blue-eyed Jack heard the plop of a solitary trout rising up from the far corner of the pool. He looked towards the spot. He got ready to cast his rod. A rustling bird warned the unwary trout of the line's perilous approach and it swam down through the water, disturbing the peaceful pool. It scurried further and further down to join its companions, avoiding the clumsy stones. Blue-eyed Jack's line followed it across the pool as though he knew where it was heading. He knew these trout – the ones who hid themselves behind little tussocks of grass, the ones that slid in behind the rocks in the middle of the pool, the ones that sought out the far bank's protection.

Now came the waiting. And then came the hoping. And then followed the uncertainty and the frustration. The children saw the changes in Blue-eyed Jack's face. They saw the tension building up in him. His eyes were constantly reading the language of the pool. He was thinking of nothing but this single runaway trout. Swift action was needed if he was to snare his first catch of the day.

But what was going on in the mind of this poor trout? One minute himself and his natural cunning were making a desperate dart for safety and trying to reach the reeds and hide. The next minute (thanks to his hapless irresolution – or was it his poor eyesight?) he found himself turning back towards the savage hook and its mesmerizing feast of maggots.

Blue-eyed Jack's rod suddenly grew taut. The runaway fish had caught himself on the hook! It looked back helplessly at its comrades in the reeds. The children sat bolt upright and they watched. And then they saw Blue-eyed Jack yank out a fine white-bellied trout – the end of its unrestricted liberty. Teddy and Patches slipped down the bank. For the little man it was another new death (just like the rabbits) to add to his growing education as he saw the speckled fish thrashing about on the end of Blue-eyed Jack's line. With a flushed face the big man took the sad-faced fish off of his hook. He threw it high up the bank towards the children. For a few seconds it tumbled about like a lump of jelly in a vain attempt to flop back down the bank and get itself into the river.

Teddy picked up the slippery fish. With the help of Sweeney he fumbled it into his satchel. A moment passed and then he and Sweeney nearly jumped out of their skins. The dead fish seemed to have come back to life – twitching and fluttering about inside in the satchel with the final hammering of its little heart. That's when Teddy felt the true horror of its death – felt the fish's last seconds of its precious life. And once more those mixed emotions came back into him that he had formerly felt when the shot rabbit met its death in The Valley of The Black Cattle and an aching sadness was in him for the death of the fish. There was no way his four-year-old mind could tell anyone. There was going to be no more playfulness for this misfortunate trout: there was going to be no more races up and down River Laughter towards the metal bridge. This very evening this fish would lie on the burning frying-pan together with the delicious Bull-Paddock mushrooms. Mixed with these inexpressible thoughts was another little thought for Teddy: he had become a hunter not only of rabbits but of fishes and he was bursting to race off home as quick as the wind and show Dowager what the two-men-of-us had caught for herself and her frying-pan.

# Will The King Of The Fishes Win The Day?

The rest of the children looked on with their hearts in their mouths as they watched Blue-eyed Jack fixing yet another maggot on his hook. Continuing to puff-puff-puff on his pipe, not once did he give the children a look back. He was absorbed in his efforts to penetrate the mind of The Rogue and to understand the thoughts that were inside the great fish's head when he saw the rod and the big wellingtons of The Man above him. In former days perhaps the great fish had seen a certain fisherman in one of his dreams – had seen the very fisherman that would one day come looking closely for him – the fisherman that would prove to be the fiercest of all threats to his life.

Luck and good fortune had always been on The Rogue's side. He had the finest of hiding-places in The Big Hole. He had always avoided racing away with the younger fishes through those bright green runnels and rushes. Like the older and wiser fishes, he spent most days resting peacefully and sleeping for hours on end in his cavernous palace behind the rocks. But not even this mighty fish could sleep away the whole of his days and when the early evening's light came achingly calling him he would be forced to rise up for his daily feast of midges and gnats.

Assuredly there wasn't an ounce of fear in him. And though he was certain of his own importance, he was never rashly over-confident. In many ways The Rogue and Blue-eyed Jack were very much alike. The big man felt that this battle with the king of the fishes would not be easy to win when the evening light drew them both inevitably together.

Bit by bit Teddy's fishing satchel grew fat with more and more trout. Himself and Patches were kept busy running up and down the bank to watch Sweeney and his brothers catching the somersaulting fishes as they tried to roll their way back towards the river. The bigger boys threw the fishes indiscriminately into Teddy's satchel. He felt them twitching helplessly about in its dark depths. He couldn't help shuddering and finally he gave the wretched satchel to Patches to carry. The poor fishes that had been swimmingly around indefatigably in the river's dense throng now found themselves in another dense throng – they were dead in the satchel.

## Time To Cry Halt And Rest A While

It was time to call a halt in this battle with the fishes and Blue-eyed Jack climbed up the bank. He took Smiling Babs' shopping-bag from the shade in the ferns and he gave it to Patches. The older brothers looked at their little brother as he unwrapped the spuds and (though they had had their dinner only a short while ago) they had the appearance of avaricious dogs. Blue-eyed Jack took out the doorstep sandwiches that Dowager had wrapped in layers of newspapers – the bread and dripping ones for himself and the bread and butter and blackcurrant ones for Teddy. And again there were the sad-looking eyes of the older boys, whose daily soda-bread saw butter but never a trace of blackcurrant jam on it. Blue-eyed Jack led the six children a little way up the river where they sat and acted as if they had nothing better to do than while away the day without a care in the world – just like the fishes themselves would now be doing, thinking that the fisherman had gone off home. 'Young fishes,' the big man shouted back at The Big Hole (for there was no need to whisper this time), 'we're off home now, but we will be back again tomorrow.' Under his breath he added: "We'll be back a lot sooner than any of ye think.'

With the children he went further along the bank of the river. He knew a few rocks, dotted beyond the bend, and an overhanging branch of a tree where they could sit and dangle their legs above the water and wiggle their toes in the pebbles. It was a sandy secluded spot – a place where it was good to sit and eat. He bade the older children lie down by his side while Teddy and Patches leathered into their bit of dinner and milk. The children sat there quietly, listening to the bubbling song of the river. Blue-eyed Jack finished his sandwiches and he stretched his arms behind his head. He looked around at the serene hills and the changing patterns of the clouds and he breathed in the fresh breeze that whistled down on him through the treetops. A little bit of lethargy crept into the children's spirits and gradually they dozed off into the lost land of their innocent dreams and they were thoroughly at peace with the world and its solitude. And the big man smiled down at them.

## The Big Hole Beckons Yet Again

It was time to return to The Big Hole. Blue-eyed Jack put the milk-bottle away and he wiped his mouth with the newspaper. He led the children back for his stealthy battle with The Rogue. There would follow the finest fishing the children's eyes would ever see – the song of the rod and the cunning of the huge fish and each one of them prayed for the death of The Rogue.

Blue-eyed Jack put a few more maggots on the rods of Teddy and Patches and he showed them how to study the pool with their eyes and search for their trout. He helped them cast their lines out as far as they could. Sweeney and his brothers looked on rather helplessly and their spirits felt chastened following their previous baptism of Patches. Teddy and Patches soon became a part of the river and their eyes were glittering with concentration. Was this the day when they would catch their first fish? With a certain amount of patience – and the fact that they had the best maggots from The African Sink – they caught a fish apiece and it was a picture to see the astonished eyes of two small boys as they whispered: 'I have caught a fish! I have caught a fish!' Blue-eyed Jack made sure that each fish wasn't so large as to pull the children back into the water and perform yet another ceremonial baptism on Patches. He helped them yank their precious fishes out and into the air. The two little fishermen stumbled up the bank and helped each other to hold down their still-living fishes before throwing them into the satchel. This day was an almighty triumph for them. Even that wild child (Sweeney) was forced to throw up his hands in admiration and raise a smile to his lips.

## Battle-Time At Last

Daylight was passing quickly. The children saw that Blue-eyed Jack and The Rogue were going to be tied into a single knot before long. The big man tipped the rest of the maggots out onto the newspaper. He selected six of his best blue-heads (all fat and juicy). He wrapped them around in a ball like twine and he skewered them firmly onto his hook. What a feast was in store for The Rogue! He took a last look inside the satchel and counted eight fishes in all: one for Daisy's brother (Mattie) who was at death's door with the leukaemia: one for Cackles, who was recovering from a mild stroke: one apiece for Rambling Jack and Saddle-the-Pony, the only other men ever to lay eyes on The Rogue: two for Smiling Babs and two more for Dowager. Blue-eyed Jack had no fish in the satchel to call his own: he was hoping to catch the king of the fishes and keep him for himself. The children could picture him hopping down to Curl 'n Stripes' Drinking-Shop later that evening and showing off the greatest prize of all time to the mesmerized drinkers. Those starry-eyed old men would be talking about it till kingdom come.

Blue-eyed Jack cast back his rod and he whipped it with a rustling crack out into the very centre of the pool. His nerves were stretched to the point of bursting. The cunning crows woke up on their dreamy branches and with their cries they warned the fishes that danger was nearby in the shape of the line with the blue-headed maggots – in the shape of the fatal hook and The Man. The big man kept asking himself a number of questions: Had he cast his line too soon? Had he cast it too ungainly? Had he cast it far enough out into the pool?

Down, down, down swam The Rogue, all the while eyeing the line. His minions swam down alongside him. They rested on the sandy bed and avoided any noise they might make against the stones. There was an unreal tranquility as Blue-eyed Jack stood frozen on the bank the very same as a heron. Likewise stood the children and the ghosts of previous fishermen and the feverish river fairies that forever lived on the river's banks. They were thinking of nothing else but The Rogue and The Man – and The Battle.

## A New Fear

Something like fear had taken a hold of each child. Only Rambling Jack and Saddle-the-Pony had ever seen The Rogue or knew how big such a monstrous fish might be. Maybe he was huge enough – maybe he was savage enough – to drag Blue-eyed Jack down into The Big Hole and drown him on the spot. Maybe he'd have jaws big enough to gobble the big man in one gulp (thought Patches). And they began to bless themselves and give The Rogue imaginative and magical powers of his own. Sweeney whispered that The Rogue might make a rush out at any moment and devour them up – one and all. And Golly swore that even if The Rogue were to die at the hands of Blue-eyed Jack's rod, he'd be sure to come back as a ghost that night and haunt the daylights out of every one of them for the rest of their natural lives.

## The Great Big Fish And The Great Big Man

The unsettled sun continued to drag itself along into the late afternoon. The children were just as unsettled as the sun, not knowing if they were about to see the end of the mighty fish's life. And then there followed the quick action of the mighty fish. And then there followed the even quicker action of the big man and his line. And then the children saw Blue-eyed Jack laughing to himself as his line sprang taut: 'I have snared you at last, my beauty,' he said and his smile was as blissful as a child with a full bag of sweets. And then there followed a most peculiar look in Blue-eyed Jack's eyes – a look of remorse and (could they believe their eyes?) a look of sympathy and sorrow for so great a fish.

'Ah, my most beautiful fish!' cried the big man when he saw how the mighty fish had been tempted by the amounts of juicy blue-headed maggots rolled around on the hook. The Rogue's jaws were irretrievably embedded on the hook but there was a great deal of life still left in him. The battle reached new heights as the fierce fish struggled and thrashed the surface of the river in an effort to escape with its life.

A curse on that blasted hook! It was what he had always feared. It was what his clever mother had warned him against when he was a young fish. A minute or two later the children saw the rod bending into an unearthly curve (almost to the point of breaking). And then they saw the final trust as the line sprang back in a quiver. And then they saw the upward trust of the rod into the air – and an enormous fish sailing aloft with it.

Were children ever before so greatly enthralled by life and its mysteries?

They gave a sigh of pure relief when they realized that as monstrous in size as the mighty fish was he was nowhere big enough to devour even The Little Englander – let alone drag Blue-eyed Jack down into The Big Hole. Then the older children began to have another little thought to themselves and it was a wise one: might not The Boodeeman and the king of the leprechauns and The Devil Himself all be just a number of tall tales told to frighten the lives out of innocent children like themselves? They kept these wise thoughts to themselves and they told none of this to Teddy or Patches. After all, they themselves had had to put up with all these fears long enough.

## A Man And His Head And His Heart

In spite of the look in Blue-eyed Jack's eyes and his mixed emotions of happiness and sorrow over the great fish, it was time now for the mighty creature to die. It had come down to this: one minute he was swimming about in the river: the next minute he was flying through the air and wrapped foolishly around the branch of a tree (where the line had pelted him) and left swinging about like an old clock's pendulum. The children crowded underneath the body of The Rogue and they gazed up at him. Blue-eyed Jack stumbled frantically up the bank towards the fish – to see its size at first hand and to compare it to the flagstone sketch made by Saddle-the-Pony. It was indeed The Rogue. And then… the eye of the fisherman looked into the eye of the fish. And then… the eye of the fish looked into the eye of the fisherman. The children saw it all. Fishes were meant for the frying-pan. Fishes were meant for the delicate blending with a handful of mushrooms from The Bull-Paddock. Above all – fishes were meant for a man's belly. One thing was sure and certain: fishes were never meant to be returned to the river. It was a thing unheard of in the whole history of Ireland.

There followed a moment which was pure magic for a child to behold – a moment of acute sorrow and joy – a moment when Blue-eyed Jack reached out his hand towards the mighty fish. It was almost too much for the big man's heart to withstand. Carefully and slowly he freed The Rogue from the hook. Almost reverently he touched his poor hurt jaw. 'Ye great big fish,' said he as he lifted the king of the fishes down from the tree. He stepped carefully down the bank and he gently placed the great big fish back into The Big Hole.

The Rogue looked back up at him and he circled around for a moment or two on the disbelieving surface of the pool. It was hard for the befuddled eyes of the children to take it all in. The king of the fishes raised its exhausted head aloft as though he were saying (like Fandango at Fatty-Matty's door) a grateful farewell to Blue-eyed Jack. It was an unspeakable and precious moment – a moment of pain and relief for Fish and Man – a moment of such privileged personal intimacy between the hunter and the hunted that no other human being should ever have been allowed to stand and witness it. And then the great big fish sank down into his underwater kingdom and was gone.

## Dowager's Fears For Teddy

Meanwhile Dowager was waiting at the half-door and listening for the footfall of her two men. She had been on her own all day and there had been a sadness in her – to see Teddy and his newly-developed freedom and the way he was growing closer each day to the bigger boys. But (she told herself) isn't that what she had wanted all along? And yet she felt she was going to lose her little man if he grew more and more like other children – if he were to go off galloping all round the map with them. She felt a little ache creeping into her heart from the top of her ribs.

## Time To Depart From The River

It was time to depart from the river. Blue-eyed Jack climbed up onto the bank. His eyes were misty with his tears and they were difficult for him to hide. He picked up the satchel of fish and he retrieved his silent rod and line. He swung his rod over his shoulder in an effort at manliness and he led the children towards the metal bridge. Unlike him, the children's hearts were light and airy, thinking of the great day's fishing that had been done. They were anxious to tell Dowager and Smiling Babs all about The Rogue but Blue-eyed Jack warned them not to tell a living soul about the battle –

the battle that his rod had just won – the battle that his heart had just lost and how he had let the great big fish get away with its life; he'd be the laughing stock of the whole of Tipperary.

They reached the echoing railings of the bridge. The peace of the fishing day had ended. The secrecy of their magical world was again marred by the sight of the cattle in The Bull-Paddock and they all bawling to be milked. They made their way over The Briary Stile and out onto The Open Road, the big man lumbering along and the children scurrying ahead with their tales to tell. At John's Gate Teddy said goodbye to the bigger boys and Blue-eyed Jack gave them their two fishes wrapped in newspaper. Their heels were soon out of sight as they raced with their prize on towards the avid smiles of Smiling Babs and her outstretched hands.

The two-men-of-us crossed over The Bull-Paddock and they picked up the pink-gilled mushrooms, as many as they could find. Blue-eyed Jack peeled each one from the centre to the edge to see if they were good enough to eat and between them they filled their pockets. The big man led his cows out through John's Gate and they trudged up the hill-slope. They crossed the flagstones and were just in time to see the moping hens following the ducks into the hen-house, leaving behind them their dusty beds under the hawthorn bush. The pulse of the day was now gone and the sky's wine-colouring had rolled down through the last of the day-clouds. Spears of gold, bronze and red added to the over-painting of the dying blue sky but already the grey and navy clouds were sailing in over Lisnagorna.

Smiling Babs' children had no time for singing their lullabies in Mikey's hayshed. They were tired out from the long day and within an hour they had sunk down into their own sunset and were lying in their settle-beds. In the darkness of the bedroom they said farewell to their day's bit of paradise.

Dowager gutted the two fishes and she washed them in the cold yard stream. It wasn't long before the frying-pan was got out and sent sizzling with plenty of butter and fat from the dripping-bowl on the press. Teddy and Blue-eyed Jack had gluttony on their minds and their stomachs were turning over with the hunger. Their nostrils were soon filled with the sweet and succulent smell of the trout and the mushrooms and the salt and onions and mashed potatoes. It'd put a smile on the walls of The Welcoming Room. Soon the three plates were empty and wiped clean with a sop of bread as the last of the trout-meat was wolfed down. It was a pure joy and Teddy felt like a prince.

He had scarcely time to finish his meal, so many were the tales he had to tell Dowager, all of them greatly exaggerated as he threw his arms out wide to indicate the size of some of the fishes he and Patches had caught. Not a single word did he utter about the mighty king of the fishes and the way Blue-eyed Jack had placed him gently back in The Big Hole.

# Night-Time

Night entered the yard and it peered into The Welcoming Room. Dowager lit the oil lamp and the two candles. The three of them knelt down in a ring and they said their fervent prayers to guard them from The Boodeeman and the other wicked spirits that rambled through the world for the ruin of their souls. Blue-eyed Jack raked up the ashes and they each took the holywater from the font to protect them in their sleep. With the two candles they headed to the left and to the right – Dowager to her little anteroom and the two-men-of-us to The Big Cave Room next to the hen-house.

Blue-eyed Jack blew out the candle on the corner of the teachest and Teddy snuggled down under the cover of the five blankets and the wadded quilt. He shivered deliciously in the damp musty sheets that he wrapped around his ears. He put his two small feet in between Blue-eyed Jack's legs and he rested his head against the big man's chest. The darkness of The Big Cave Room seemed to be piled up in the four corners and the stars shone dimly in through the broken-glass window. The moon tangled itself amid the trees of the haggart and the faint glimmer of curly black clouds showed where the cowshed was and the wind shrieked on the hen-house galavanize. Being so close to his uncle The Little Englander felt very brave and believed that he could take on a great big lion if he ever saw one.

Blue-eyed Jack lay awake for a long time. It had been a good day's fishing – a load of dead trout and some of them already eaten. But there were many more trout (thank God) swimming happily this night beneath the rushes of The Big Hole and he was already mulling over in his head another fishing trip with Teddy. He wrapped his little nephew tightly to him, protecting him from the wind and the rain and from The Boodeeman.

Teddy and the bigger boys had learnt a great deal this memorable day. They had seen into the gentle soul of the big man. The Rogue was once again swimming safely in The Big Hole. This mighty fish was thinking (you and I might like to believe) of The Man and his great kindness – of The Man who had gently lifted him off of the hook – of The Man, who had reverently placed him back in his home. The king of the fishes swam happily among his minions, deep in his kingdom in the moonlit silvery pool.

# EIGHT

# Rambling Jack's Pig

*When Teddy went to kill the great big pig.*

It was September in the year of 1944. Blue-eyed Jack was awake early as usual. He could hear from behind the hen-house wall the self-satisfying quack-quacking of his mother's ducks telling the hens it was time to stop dozing. Careful not to disturb his little nephew he went to the back window. The dark night clouds were grudgingly scurrying away over the dimly-waving haggart pine-trees, whispering him a greeting and beckoning him to get started. He breathed in a deep mouthful of air from outside the broken-glass window. The misty ass (The Lightning Whoor), in between munching the juicy thistles, was standing at the stick and looking straight across at him from the depths of the haggart. He turned his back away from the big man and trotted off across The Bluebutton Field in search of his companion, Moll-the-mare.

Blue-eyed Jack couldn't help coughing from the dampness of The Big Cave Room. He returned to the potato-sacking and he knelt down beside the bed. The bespectacled pope in the picture peered down at him as he sibilantly started to say his morning prayers. Then, stretching his arms ('oh, honey-o!') the big man staggered out in his shirt to The Welcoming Room with its vacant echo of the previous night. He reached for the mug on the nail and he dipped it into the white enamel bucket and swallowed down the cold water. Then he washed out his mouth with some soot from the hob and he put some water into the tin pan and with cupped hands washed his face. He looked at his reflection in the broken bit of looking-glass. Then he combed his hair with the soapy water.

He stuffed a piece of bread and butter into his mouth and he opened the latch of the full door and the half-door. He walked out into the freshening day, going out through the pig-house gap to make his water. The leaden-coloured yard was already changing as the stormy rain of the previous night had turned the stream into a musical torrent, making a little fountain below at the rusty blue kettle underneath the hedge.

He made a few quick runs to the woodpile and returned to the half-door with an armful of logs and twigs before running back for a final armful of turf. Then, grabbing his coat and his mother's rain-hat in case the rain should come back, he headed down to The Bull-Paddock to fetch the cows. The raindrops dripped down on him from the trees in The Rookery, falling on his shoulders and hat and breaking the otherwise purity of the new day's silence. He passed Mikey's Stile and saw the thick columns of whitethorn smoke rising up from Mikey's chimney and drifting into the breeze, making the air fresh and perfumed. At last he began to feel he was alive.

He took off his mother's old hat and he bared his face and neck to the cool cut of the early morning light. He opened John's Gate and walked across the Bull-Paddock where the mist had gone off towards The Bog Wood. He whispered a few words of endearment to Moll-the-mare and The Lightning Whoor, who by this time had reached the friendly mare and was striking up an animal conversation with her. The words of the big man were such that only the three of them were ever likely to understand them. He walked on through the dewy silver of the grass and finally made his way towards The Danes' Hill, whistling silently to himself, so delicately that only the sharpest of ears could have heard him. One thing he was sure of – that the sun herself would be peeping out from behind Lisnagorna before he had the cows back in the cowshed and ready to be milked.

## *Everybody Has Work To Do*

Not just for the big man, but for Dowager too, such day-to-day moments as these were precious. After the great Fishing Day, she had Teddy to herself for a while with most of the nearby children out of sight. Sweeney and Norrie were taking their first stab at work with Lord Elegance and wouldn't be home till the weekend. Four more of Smiling Babs' children (all except

Little Cull and Darkie) were heading down the road to the school-house to attack the complicated lessons of Dang-the-skin-of-it. Among them was Patches, struggling at the tender age of six to keep up with the others on the long three-mile haul across the fields. Before Teddy could get a chance to strike up a chat with either Little Cull (at the flagstones) or Darkie (in her cubby-shop), Dowager sensed that she had a chance to break him away from the ever-increasing influences of the other children and bring him back to the folds of her black apron and walk and talk with him as they used to do.

With Blue-eyed Jack gone off for their cows, she was never a one to lie frowning in her warm bed, listening to the sorrows of the wind and rain outside her window and she hopped out onto the floor and looked around her. She had enough kindling, thanks to her big man, to light her morning fire. She had enough logs and turf to last her till the evening and Blue-eyed Jack had been thoughtful enough to take out yesterday's ashes. She lit a candle and she placed it on the hearth to see what she was doing. She broke into pieces some hawthorn sticks across her knees and arranged her fire, carefully building a small pyramid of smaller twigs around a few loose wads of newspaper. She threw a few bits of broken candle into the middle and poured some kerosene onto the wood. She put a match to the fire and she began impatiently shuddering the lid of the sweet gallon back and forth to fan the fire to life. The dust from the ashes kept flying up her nose: 'The Devil himself wouldn't light these sticks,' she said (and that's what she always said). Very soon a huge feather of black smoke rose up the chimney to meet the sky and you could hear the merry hissing noise that the twigs were making, as the flames finally vomited upwards. With her face surrounded by smoke, she continued to fan the sparks and her fire eventually snapped and crackled into a most delightful blaze that lit up the four walls and mirrored itself in the blue plates on the dresser and danced back at her from the Sacred Heart picture. Like Blue-eyed Jack, she had a good feeling about this day – she had come alive.

Herself and her stooped back hobbled off down the yard to greet her fowl. The little privet hedge surrounding her small garden glistened with raindrops. The ducks, full of gratitude for the rain and the gurgling sound of the swollen stream, rushed out and passed around her legs, almost knocking her off her feet before bobbing up and down in the stream. One or two of them waddled up to the half filled tar-barrel that had drowned the rats and they jumped in and flapped their wings. The goose-pimpled hens, shivering and dismal-looking, lay close to the protecting wings of the cockerel (Rampant) and they huddled against the croaking hen-house wall or hid themselves underneath the upturned ass-and-car.

The old woman returned in the half-door. But even before her clickety boots had reached the door of The Big Cave Room, Teddy made sure that he kept his eyes firmly shut and he pretended he was fast asleep. His grandmother, her hand on the latch, paused for a moment. Then the little man could hear her heavy breathing as her clickety boots came across the floor. Though he hadn't yet opened his eyes, he felt that she was smiling down at him. She had brought him his customary spoonful of butter and sugar and she whispered in his ear: 'Slugabed, the day is half gone and it's twenty minutes to sixty – arise from your nest!' The 'sixty' had always been a coy expression of hers ever since his infancy. He took the spoon and, with one eye opened, he smiled up at her and then her clickety boots went back out the bedroom door. Cocking his ear, he listened to the din outside the windowpane (like a rusty old bicycle chain) of the ducks and geese as they vied with each other to see who could sing the loudest.

The bespectacled pope in the picture looked down disapprovingly at the sleepy-headed child and made him dash out of bed and follow the faint echo of the clickety boots as far as the blazing hearthstone. He ran into his grandmother's apron and together they ran through his list of Blessing Prayers and he recited for her his growing list of poems and nursery rhymes. His grandmother asked him to count the number of turf-sods and logs that were piled in under the stool, to see if he had added them up correctly. She pulled his blue jersey down over his ears to keep him warm against the increasing cold of the moving year and a look of gratitude fled from his eye and into his grandmother's eye and then it came back again.

Blue-eyed Jack wasn't yet home with the cows. Teddy and Dowager had their mugs of milk and their well-buttered slices of soda-cake. Then the old woman hurried out to the haggart and she brought back his egg with the stains of chicken-dung and a small white feather on it – just dropped from The Little Red Hen's backside (yet again, she said). Like Blue-eyed Jack she was good at telling her whopping big lies and the egg was often one that she had taken down from the dresser before wobbling excitedly to the table to tell her little prince that his favourite hen had obliged him once more.

# A Time For Childish News

Before the big man had chained a single cow to the cowshed chains, the child and the old woman washed their faces and they sat down by the fireside, exchanging bits of childish news with each other. This morning it was as if Teddy had never been away from his grandmother's side or had never been gallivanting his days away with the rest of the children. She took down her goose-wings – the big ones for herself and the little ones for Teddy. They began their daily task of looking for cobwebs and spiders in the four corners of each room and God help any beetles that were bent on playing hide-and-seek in among the turf-sods and logs! But (thought Dowager to herself) what was a day's working and tidying the house, compared to these moments when she had Teddy all to herself? In these few minutes, when the big man was still off chasing his cows, she prayed that he would stay out a little while longer and give her time to go on teaching the child and pouring into him her wealth of stories and poems – would give the little fellow (you might have said) time to imbibe the sweet music that was in her voice. As with her privet-hedged garden, she was happiest when giving him her care and attention, for in her eyes he was by far the most delicate and precious of all her flowers.

The lessons for the morning, however, were interrupted by the sudden sound of Blue-eyed Jack's wellingtons. With the cows safely chained in the cowshed, he came in the half-door, greedily looking for his egg and his milk. He took off his cap and threw it on the nail and he bowed to his mother and his nephew ('God bless the work,' he said) before putting the kettle of water on the crane and wetting himself his first cup of tea. Then, standing in the middle of the hearth, he lifted up his coat-flaps and he turned his back to the fire and gave his backside a right good warming.

# Children Head For School, Teddy Sits At Home

It must have been very troublesome walking to school on wet days such as this – especially for little Patches. The weather was always unpredictable and there would be other wet days when he and his brothers would be soaked to the skin before they reached the school-house door. The sympathetic Dang-the-skin-of-it had rolls of newspapers ready to stuff down the back of their jerseys so as to soak up the wetness. Even when the rain did not prevail, the grass in the fields (especially in Joe-the-Buckles') was often two feet high and Golly had to take off his coat and hold it in front of him like a shield, while his brothers marched behind him like a flock of young ducks.

For Teddy a morning like this was also a bit of a nuisance for this day promised rain and prevented him from playing in the yard or the haggart or The Bluebutton Field. Trapped inside in The Welcoming Room he couldn't dangle his legs from the upturned ass-and-car and watch the antics of the hens pecking at the grain and puffing out their chests importantly with one eye always on him. He couldn't run at the ducks and geese with his stick and ('Look at me!) frighten them off over the singletree and out into the haggart. From the half-door he asked Blue-eyed Jack to bring him in a straw from the thatch so that he could try blowing some sort of music on it. He had heard from Darkie that you could make music that way. He'd also heard how Sweeney and Golly had the art of straw-blowing off to a fine art and could catch young frogs at harvest-time and put straws into their mouths and blow them up till they burst in pieces. At least that's what the ever-boastful Sweeney had once told Darkie, making her scream her head off. Teddy hoped that by the afternoon he'd get a chance to run out and meet Patches coming home from the school-house. His little friend would be armed with all the news of what was happening in his important new life and tell him all the learning that was being driven in between his two ears in that great place of mysteries three miles away.

'You'll get a rash from looking into the flames of the fire,' said Dowager and Teddy went off into The Big Cave Room where Blue-eyed Jack was rummaging through his bicycle tools – the pump and its adaptor, the yellow box with the tyre plasters. He placed Teddy on his shoulders and wrapped his little legs around his broad neck. On the ledge underneath the thatch he kept a hidden box of his treasures, his precious sets of cigarette-cards and he picked out the set called The Bicycles. The two-men-of-us went out to the front table and sat underneath The Saint Brigid's Cross. Apart from Father Accessible's vestments and Dowager's Infant-of-Prague statue, Teddy's astonished eyes had never beheld anything so beautiful as these delicately-painted cigarette-cards. They portrayed cyclists in their bright uniforms on their coloured bicycle frames – blue, gold, red and silver. They outshone even the coloured court-cards, stored on the press-shelf behind the sour-milk jug, which were a part of his daily efforts to build himself a card-house.

One after the other, Blue-eyed Jack brought down his other sets of the cigarette-cards and he laid them out in rows on the oilcloth. There were Soldiers to gaze at. There were Birds and Animals. There were Kings and Queen. With each of these sets the big man managed to distract his little man from any brooding he might be doing, now that he was on his own and without his friends. He had his own way of enriching the little fellow's daily life and broadening his education and he encouraged him to study each set of the cards and ask him questions about them. It was as if he was unveiling his private secrets to Teddy and only too glad to be doing so, having no son to call his own.

Behind the unused piano (Old Harpy) was where Blue-eyed Jack kept his bicycle, known as The Twenty-Eight-Wheeler. He used it some Sundays to cycle off to hurling matches and harecoursing (even as far off as Kilkenny, some twenty miles away). And, oh what news he'd have to tell about the unusual strangers he met on his travels and in great detail he'd describe the mysterious hills and valleys and the flowers on the bushes and the passing clouds of those afternoons in faraway places.

He wheeled the big bicycle out in front of the fireplace and he turned it upside-down on its saddle. It was time to tend to its roadworthiness, since it was forever at risk from the sharp stones on The Open Road. Teddy sniffed the air. He could smell the oil, as his uncle oiled up the metal parts and tested the brakes. He could smell the gluey adhesive all around The Big Cave Room, as the big man removed both of the tyres and ran them through the pan of water, (all the time looking for air-bubbles) to see where the little punctures were so that he could stick on the plasters and dust them with the white powder.

Finally his pinched fingers made the air in his bicycle-pump come out hissing like the hooting coots on Lord Elegance's lake. And, as with the hunting of the fish and the rabbits, this was a time for a child's composure and reflection with nothing to distract him from his thoughts. When his uncle was finished tinkering with his bicycle, he took it out to the flagstones and he tested it by hopping it off of The Open Road. Then he sat Teddy up on the crossbar and soon the two-men-of-us went whizz-whizz-whizzing up and down The Open Road and you could hear their laughter as far away as Copperstone Hollow.

## Sister Rosamunda

There were two surprises the next day (Friday). Sister Rosamunda came home from The Missions in Africa, having been granted permission to cross the dangerous wartime seas and be at her father's deathbed, for the poor man was to be waked that night and buried the following day. Happily the holy nun brought with her a small brown suitcase. It had come for Teddy and inside it was a fine new suit of clothes, which Little Nell had sent home with the nun. Dowager insisted that her little man dress up straightaway in the fine new suit – to see did it fit him and what he would look like in it. She stood him outside the half-door and she cocked her head to this side and then to that side and she joined her hands in prayer and she said he looked like an angel in her holy-book. Blue-eyed Jack scratched his head and he frowned and wondered who on earth was this little gentleman ('it couldn't be Teddy, could it?') and then the three of them burst out laughing.

## And In Came Rambling Jack

At that very moment there came the second surprise of the day as into the yard stepped Rambling Jack and his famed greyhound, Zippity. The man and his dog were like the two sides of a shirt (inseparable) and Zippity slept in Rambling Jack's bed each night, sloped across his feet to keep his toes warm. The hunter had come down to take back his unlicensed gun, the one Blue-eyed Jack had used in The Rabbit-Hunt in The Valley of The Black Cattle, for he was about to go shoot a few rabbits for himself: 'The skillet-pot is empty at long last and not a single rabbit have I had time to go kill this blessed week,' said he. 'And another thing I'm telling ye – I'm down to the last fletch of fat bacon and my old stomach is getting weaker by the minute. It's time I was taking a good look at one of my two pigs.'

'Aye, faith,' said Blue-eyed Jack. He knew what was in the wind. In a day or two he'd have to take his reins and his sharpened knives (the long one and the short one) and stick them in the throat of one of Rambling Jack's two pigs. Several households along The Open Road (including Dowager's) would get plenty of Rambling Jack's pig when the killing was done with and the big man smiled to himself. The spuds, the turnips and cabbages, the eggs and the soda-cakes were all highly valued, but when the fat pig was washed down with lashings of fresh milk, it was a match for the rabbit (if not better) as we prepared our bodies for the harsh winter ahead.

The pig was the most delicate of creatures and a damned nuisance to rear. He would simply fade away and die on you if you ever changed his diet and that would be nothing less than a tragedy. There was nothing we liked better than a good fat pig and to get out teeth into a plateful of greasy bacon with a few inches of lard on it. Many of us were eating up to three pigs a year and the eyes of Doctor Glasses were by this time red-raw from the tears he kept shedding when he saw so many of us dying young on him from all the fat bacon we were stuffing into our bellies. But the warning words from the good doctor continued to fall on deaf ears. We were a stubborn lot and we loved nothing better than to boast how we were pampering and fattening up our pigs before finally gobbling them down.

# The Role Of Blue-Eyed Jack

As a result, there was always a set of men's feet trotting in Dowager's half-door, demanding the attention of Blue-eyed Jack when the time came for a man's pig to be killed. Besides that, the big man was forever busy – either trimming or pairing a walkingstick for some old women or giving a haircut to a man stepping out to his wedding or getting called out to burn the midnight oil and follow after a neighbour's runaway cow. How often had he tended to a neighbour's newborn foal at two-in-the-morning, the Zane Grey novel still open and unread on the cowshed window-ledge? How often, whilst Teddy slept like a baby and kept the bed warm for him, did he help a neighbour to nurse an infant lamb on a cold winter's hillside? All this was somewhat of a surprise, for Blue-eyed Jack had awkward fingers on him that looked like helpless sausages and he could never open a packet of Woodbine fags or fish out a match to light up a smoke and they were forever bleeding on him from careless cuts. However, he had superb dexterity in his wrists and colossal strength in his two arms and shoulders and all this would come in handy as he struggled with Rambling Jack's angry pig when all the poor pig would want to do was run as fast as his little legs could carry him and get to hell out of Tipperary and to the other end of the earth.

The big man took his coat from the back of the door and he stepped up the hillside with Rambling Jack. It was mid-afternoon and the children had finished this first week's lessons at two o'clock and they were finding their way home along The Open Road. Like Teddy – Dowager too – they were always a curious bunch and they ran alongside the two men and they followed them into Rambling Jack's haggart. The two men hopped out over the hen-house dung-heap and they went across to the pig-house for a final inspection of the doomed pig. Golly and the others stood watching them. They knew that one morning soon would be the day for the sticking of Rambling Jack's pig and suddenly they were anxious to know which one of them would become the envy of every child in Rookery Rally and get himself the creamy bladder from the sad pig's belly.

## The Inspection Of A Pig

The men were leaning in over the pig-house door. With eyes of scrutiny they were musing over the girth and stamp of this fine pig. They took in the whole animal and they calculated how much he weighed and how much meat he would produce when he was slaughtered, singed of his hair and his guts cleaned out. This pig was indeed a magnificent animal.

Blue-eyed Jack was pleased with all the preparations for the killing. Rambling Jack had brought back from The Roaring Town oceans of salt-blocks and had stored them in the turf-shed, for it was as cool in there as in any of his other out-houses. He had tested the ass-and-car to make sure that there was enough clean straw and that there were holes enough in the new galvanized sheeting on the floor of the car so that the gallons of pig's blood could run down into the runnels. One or two women from The Hills-of-The-Past would come down to help the men and they'd bring out their pans and buckets and place them under the cart. They'd be working at a devilish speed, collecting the pans of blood and taking them into the house for the filling of the pig's guts and the making of the black puddings and sausages.

There and then Blue-eyed Jack made up his mind: he was going to take Teddy to his very first Pig-Killing. Before shaking hands with Rambling Jack or leaving his haggart, he asked for a small enamel pan to be got ready for the little man – to help him work alongside the women and catch the blood while the pig was in the act of dying.

## Pig-Killing Day Arrived For Teddy

The day of the pig-killing was near. On more than one occasion Teddy had heard pigs squealing at the hour of their death. Patches had told him that Simon-not-so-simple had had his pig killed just a few weeks ago and that himself and Bucko had been present to see the violent struggle between Man and Pig. It had needed four strong men and their well-heeled wellingtons to drag the demented animal out of the pig-house and up onto the sloping boards of the ass-and-car. Blue-eyed Jack had been the killer of that pig, said Patches. His big brother, Sweeney, had been given the pig's bladder and Patches and his brothers had spent the livelong day racing around The Thistle Field with the smokey-white bladder floating behind them on a long string and up in the wind. All this was breathless news to Teddy's ears and he felt his heart stirring with a pride in his uncle (the killer of pigs) and he wished with all his heart that he too could get his hands on a pig's bladder like Sweeney had done at Simon-not-so-simple's.

## It Was Saturday

When Saturday morning came sailing in on her rosy footsteps Teddy peered round the corner of The Big Cave Room and he ran out and stood in his shirt beside Blue-eyed Jack outside the half-door. Something exciting was in the air – he could feel it. The big man placed his hands on Teddy's shoulders and his face beamed down at him. He suddenly lifted him up in

191

the air, his head almost touching the overhanging straw of the roof-thatch: 'Teddy, avic, there's to be a killing today,' said he.

'I know. Patches told me. It's the pig. Where will it be?' asked Teddy.

'Above at Rambling Jack's shed. I have seen this pig and he's as fat as a fool. He's ready to be killed and we two-men-of-us are the very ones to throw our hands into the work'.

Teddy's heart was almost up in his mouth: 'And will Rambling Jack let me come with you?' he asked cautiously.

'Why – they'll find no better man to hold the pan as steady as you and to catch the pig's blood as smartly as you,' said Blue-eyed Jack with an air of tenderness in his voice.

What great joy filled Teddy when he thought of the bladder: 'And will I be getting the bladder, like Sweeney did at Simon-not-so-simple's? And will I be running around the fields with it?' He was bursting to know this and many more answers to is persistant questioning.

A child like him could play the livelong day with a sock-ball made springy with a few corks in it. He could watch Patches rolling down the hill his bowlee-wheel made from the rusty rim of an old creamery tank. But far higher in his imagination was the racing he could do across The Bluebutton Field and down into The Bull-Paddock, if only he had a pig's bladder to call his own and wave it behind him on a piece of string. It was the prize of all prizes and he couldn't wait to go and help kill the pig and get a hold of the shiny bladder. Blue-eyed Jack spun him round and around: 'Of course you'll have the bladder and I myself will pump it up for you tomorrow after Mass – be sure of that.'

## The Big Man Sharpened His Two Knives

The big man was sitting on his chair in the yard. Though it was early in the day, he had a bottle of stout at his heels – to give him courage and wrath against the pig and to increase his desire for killing it. His way of dealing with the pig was different from other men: he'd be using no mallet or sledge-hammer to stun the animal and he wouldn't be using the rifle like one or two men had done in previous years – it would spoil the bacon. The pig (pure and simple) had to be stuck in the throat with the thick short-handled knife and then the long-handled knife (which was fifteen inches in length) would be directed down the pig's windpipe until it pierced its heart so that it would slowly bleed to death. In that way Rambling Jack would get the best possible meat for himself and we'd all be better off when the day came for him to share it round with the rest of us.

Not wishing to interrupt his uncle from his work, Teddy said nothing but stood a good ways off on the flagstones across the stream. The sun was shining on the glinting knives, turning them from blue to silver and they continued to hold his attention. He could imagine the fierce cutting edge of these butchering knives and their power to take away the life of one of Rambling Jack's two pigs. He looked away and he walked out over the singletree and into the haggart and he climbed up into the lower fork of the hawthorn tree and hid himself there for a while and began thinking of the pig's death.

The hens, ducks and geese had learnt wisdom over the years and they ran a safe ways off from Blue-eyed Jack's knives and they watched him from underneath the ass-and-car. The big man whistled silently to himself, his pipe sending up a constant fog of smoke into the trees. He tested each one of his knives in turn, sharpening them rhythmically on his sandpapery thumb. He took down the long reins from the roof of the pig-house and he placed it beside the leg of the chair. It'd be used for hog-tying the pig from back leg to front leg. He would need the help of four strong men to drag the animal across the haggart and lift him up onto the sloping boards of the ass-and-car.

## The Children Arrive On The Singletree

Golly and Gallant had come down to watch Blue-eyed Jack at his work. They were sitting on the singletree outside Mikey's grove. They saw the reins and they saw the knives and they knew that this was the day when one of Rambling Jack's two pigs was to meet its death. And though they shrugged their shoulders to show their indifference, they had two very long faces on them. Things were going to be different from now on, they could see: The Little Englander was old enough to be taken to his first pig-killing and it was going to be him and not the likes of them that would be marching up the hill to help Rambling Jack. It was also going to be him and not the likes of them that would get the pig's bladder at every pig-killing from this day forth. An unusual anger started building itself up inside them against their little friend. But (bladder or no bladder) all was not lost and they knew there would be meat (and plenty of it) for their family to eat for at least the next month and they sped off home to their mother to give her the glad tidings of Rambling Jack's pig. Not once did they think where Teddy had gotten himself off to or where he might be hiding himself this morning. Not once had they thought of looking for him in the depths of the hawthorn tree. For all they cared, The Little Englander could go and rot in the depths of hell.

## Teddy's Childish Sadness For The Poor Pig

Although he felt sorry for the pig, Teddy wasn't going to show it. The hunting of little rabbits was one thing (fishes too), but the killing of a pig was a far more important matter. He had never before seen the death of such a great big animal and he couldn't help wondering which of the two knives Blue-eyed Jack would be using first. His uncle, not noticing the sad look on Teddy's face, took back the chair into The Welcoming Room and he put the reins and the two knives into his sack. He brought down his bloodstained apron from behind the horse's tackle on the ledge beside the hob and he took down his good supply of hazel wands, which he had whittled into sharp points at either end. They were to keep open the pig's belly when it had been slit down the middle and hung upside-down on the ladder, to drain.

## The Two Pig-Killers Set Sail

The two pig-killers (the big-and-little-man) were now ready to go off and meet up with this great big pig. Dowager came out and she wiped her hands on her apron. She shook some of the bottle of holywater on her two men's foreheads and she bade them God speed. She put a special little dab on the killing hands of her son and then the two-men-of-us headed out the back car-way through the cow-dung and puddles in Timmy's lane and they stepped up The Open Road without giving so much as a glance back at Dowager. She looked admiringly after the two of them.

Teddy's previous fears for the pig were soon replaced with light-heartedness. After all, (he kept telling himself) it was he that was going to get the bladder. Like the hunting of the rabbits and the fishes, it was to be another day's exciting hunting for a child like himself to go and kill an animal for the dinner-table. They passed by Smiling Babs' gateway and Teddy saw the other children sitting outside on the ditch. The little man was full of self-importance as he passed them by and he fixed his two eyes on the road ahead and he never gave them a look back. He could feel the dirty looks they were piercing into the back of his neck at not being able to go with him and get their hands on another bladder. He knew they were angry with him. But what did he care? He was entering a new and exciting world and going to a place where a pig was about to greet his uncle's knives and meet Death.

## Envy Has No Place

Smiling Babs had little sympathy for her heap of sulky-eyed children. They had been given (and had destroyed) more bladders than she could even count: 'It's no use crying over spilt milk,' said she. 'Go down to the well with the buckets, let ye, and bring back the water – and don't go baptizing Patches all over again.'

In a few minutes the children had shaken themselves out of their lethargy. It was true for their mother – it was no use reflecting on their sad fate. They ran down The Thistle Field and hopped over the wire fence and into Mikey's yard. They had the place to themselves as the old-timer was in town selling a few of his cattle. In their jealous rage they took their vengeance out on his two old dogs and they started kicking them round and around the yard until they were half-dead. This seemed to satisfy them for a while and they brought back the water from the well.

## Above In The Killing Yard

Blue-eyed Jack and Teddy were now in Rambling Jack's yard. As well as the hunter himself there were three other men there to meet them. There was Timmy and his father (Stonemason Tim). There was also Red Scissors, who was always ready to help a man kill his pig. He was bigger and heavier than any pig. The four men were dressed in their filthiest raincoats and they greeted Teddy ('And how is The Little Englander today?') most affectionately, although he had never understood the grand title that people bestowed on him.

The three men had spent the last hour calculating the pig's condition and giving Rambling Jack the benefit of their wisdom. They needn't have bothered. For, unlike other men, the hunter had his own particular plans for both his pigs. The pig that he had destined for the market was now having a right royal life of it. Rambling Jack had been fattening him up to a fine finish (to show him off to the Limerick buyers) by feeding him each day not on the customary few miserly slips of strained cabbage-water but on a good shake of oats and cabbages as well as the best of turnips and fresh milk. As for this day's sad pig with the death-sentence marked out on him Rambling Jack had spent this past week easing up on the amounts of food he threw into his trough. Of course he didn't starve him altogether in case his body would fade away too quickly and lose the eventual quality of the bacon. But for the last two days he hadn't fed the poor creature a morsel of food and there would be no trouble with his innards and he'd have scarcely an ounce of dung inside in him when it came to opening him up and cleaning him out.

Rambling Jack brought out a table and he placed it next to the ass-and-car, on which the pig would soon be tied down to die. Blue-eyed Jack laid out his two knives and a towel and a basin of hot water for cleaning and scalding his surgical hands. The operation was about to begin. He took off his coat and he hung it on a bush. Then he put on the leather apron. Rambling Jack filled the cart with a mountainous mixture of new hay and straw, to soak up as much blood as possible and sieve it down into the buckets below.

The men tied a belt of string tightly around their waist, to make sure that their raincoats were tight on them and wouldn't go flapping about or get chewed away by the pig in the coming battle (it would be a formidable task to get the creature out from the pig-house). And just as in any tug-of-war, they now needed their best-footed wellingtons on them so as to get the best possible grip in the spongy straw when they were dragging the pig out by his two ears and tail. For if the mighty animal knocked one of them down within such a confined space, that man was as good as dead and buried in his grave, so great was the rage of any pig in the face of its imminent death.

## The Men Loftily Salute Their Pig

'Ho there!' said Rambling Jack loftily. 'Bring forth this squealer-of-a-pig, let ye,' and the men smiled at one another. It was always the way Rambling Jack introduced the act of killing his pig – by fashioning some bit of formality to the greeting they were about to give the illustrious creature. And Stonemason Tim was not slow either to take up the pompous introduction: 'Let the pig's gruesome squeals awaken the sleeping world,' he offered, giving his own singular bit of style and humour to the day's main event. A moment of light-heartedness such as this was important to the men since it wasn't the easiest or most pleasant job in the world for them to be standing here and so closely wrapped up with Mother Death.

'Enough of yeer nonsense', said Blue-eyed Jack, half-laughing. 'Let's be introducing ourselves to this noble pig.' He was growing impatient and was anxious to get on with the work of dispatching this animal. In spite of the many pigs he had slaughtered, he was always a little nervous prior to each new operation. He remained standing next to the ass-and-car with his implements of death (the two knives) while the four men walked stealthily across the haggart towards the pig-house door.

## The Thoughts Of A Singular Pig

And what (you might ask) were the thoughts inside in the head of this misfortunate pig? Already Teddy could hear a loud bawling coming from the other side of the pig-house door. If he'd been able to peep in through a slit in the door, he'd have seen the poor quavering creature all red-eyed from weeping as he recalled the days of his wobbly and bulging-eyed piggy childhood – those bygone days that he spent fidgeting happily in the straw alongside his mother and his many brother and sisters. How he had loved the huge expanse of The Nettle Field behind the pig-house. And, as with the newborn calves that Teddy had witnessed tearing The Bluebutton Field asunder this springtime, this pig could remember how Rambling Jack had opened the gate for him and his brothers and sisters and how the hunter had propelled them nervously out into the grassy world to a place they had never seen before or even knew existed. From the dark pig-house to the bright sunlight and out towards Freedom underneath the vast blue sky – what wild joy had been his! And what nimble dance-steps had he performed around and around The Nettle Field – as though it were his last days on earth! It had almost been too much for him to cope with – as though he'd been granted a hay-shed full of hay or a garden full of turnips for his breakfast.

He had been the most likeable of little pigs, always following Rambling Jack about like a lost puppy and running absurdly in giddy fits across the haggart, panting hoarsely as he jigged himself round and around and tried to catch a hold of his tail. His display of sheer happiness, (the good-natured little piggy that he was) had put Rambling Jack into fits of laughter. What's more, he was as clean as any cat and you'd see him snorting and almost laughing in his excitement at having the run of the yard alongside the other little piggies. He'd be twirling that curly tail of his as it shivered along behind him and you'd hear him grunting good-naturedly and trying to talk back to Rambling Jack in that hoarse young voice of his. His caring mother had always protected his pink skin from the harsh rays of the summer's sun and how he had reveled in the cool mud at midday, rolling around alongside her and his brothers and sisters.

But what could he boast of now? 'I am a noble pig and I am about to die. But once upon a time I had such a number of callers trotting across the haggart almost daily and leaning across the pig-house door and admiring my fine comely features, whilst Rambling Jack fired fistfuls of oats and turnips into my trough. Now all that I've got is this terrible fear – the fear that I felt the day I was born and was looking around me for the very first time at the strangeness of my new world. I have this fear of a wild thing called Man, whom I knew would come for me one day and would slaughter me with the knives and make a feast of me for men and women throughout the coming wintertime. And I see how clever I was to have had those terrible fears. But it is too late for me now. I will never again look across The Nettle Field at The Forest of Lisnagorna. I will never again run after the goose and the gander the length of the haggart.' Enough said.

# *The Gruesome Sound Of The Wellingtons*

He heard the approaching footsteps bringing him his irretrievable destiny. He heard the peg being lifted from the hasp and staple of his door. There was a shaft of light. The glare of it filled his eyes. He saw four enormous shadows across the straw-strewn floor and the huge black ghosts of Man-the-serpent hovering in the white light of his doorway. The killers closed the door noiselessly behind them as though they were trying to hide their guilt. The pig was surrounded by four sets of wellingtons. Rambling Jack held the reins in his outstretched hands. The pig saluted them all with a river of his piss down into the straw. The four killers (big strong men, bent on his destruction) glared at him. He glared back at the killers. And all the weeping he had been doing of late came suddenly to an abrupt end. His eyes had huge sparks of red fire flying out of them – sparks of raw hatred taking over from his fear. He realized that, unless he could make a dash for freedom and get our passed their wellingtons, he was going to be singing a far different tune from his piggy-day tunes before the daylight closed in on him and his life disappeared forever. And, as with a man on trial for his very existence, a river of pure sweat suddenly broke out across his forehead.

It wasn't just the pig: the sweat was soon hopping off of the four men's foreheads. There was none of the polite oink-oinking piggy-cries in the days when this pig was getting his buckets of mash and gruel thrown into his trough. His new warlike screeches made the four would-be killers regret getting out of bed this morning – at least for a second or two. Then Red Scissors forced all the great weight of his body in behind the pig and he grabbed him sharply by the tail. That was enough to distract the pig. The other three men rushed in at his head and, whilst two of them snatched him by his two ears, Rambling Jack managed to throw the reins around his front fetters and to push him backwards. This was the last thing the pig had wanted and his legs got caught up in the reins and he fell ignominiously onto his back.

Panting and puffing, the four men dragged the helpless creature down the length of the haggart towards the ass-and-car. Their wellingtons were covered in the pig's fresh dung and piss. The hysterical ducks and hens ran for cover and looked on in astonishment from the comfort of the ditch. Would it be their turn next for the executioner's knife?

## The Murdering Cart Awaits

At last the killers reached the cart and at the same time the women that had come down from The Hills-of-The-Past (their protective arms around Teddy) were listening to the pig's screams from the safety of the turf-shed. Gus Gilton (the box-player) was passing by from his home in The Valley of The Black Cattle and he swore that he heard the pig saying his prayers for a speedy end to it all. Teddy peeped his inquisitive nose out from the door of the turf-shed and he saw the thrashing of the pig's legs and its enraged mouth hissing out frothy white streams of spittle like a demented rattlesnake out of a story-book and he kept on trying to strike at Man whenever he got half a chance and his gable-end continued to let flow whatever dung was left inside of him. Teddy had never seen such a tussle in all his young life.

The men managed to raise the giant pig up onto (his bed of thorns) the slanting boards of the ass-and-car. Rambling Jack took the long reins from the table and he used it like a lasso on a wild horse and with the help of the others he hobbled the helpless creature's four fetters, back and forth and down the middle, and then he bound the reins tightly to the body of the cart. With his trapped legs pointed towards the heavens, it would be the pig's last glimpse of the blessed sunlight. Blue-eyed Jack put on his bloody apron and he inspected his cauterized knives and once more he tested their sharpness on his thumb, as though to occupy himself. The time for the pig's butchering was now.

It wasn't just the ducks and the hens that had run for their lives. The crows had seen that the pig's end was nigh and they had fled up into the ditch-side trees. Their echoes remain there to this very day as they cried and cried over the helplessness of their brother, the pig. It was like a strange dream and the women (along with Teddy) took a few steps out from their safe hidey-hole in the turf-shed and they stood watching this unequal contest between Man and Pig.

The men scooped away the hay-and-straw mixture where it had been ruined by the pig's dung. They replaced it with copious fresh handfuls, soon to be reddened by the pig's steaming blood and they looked admiringly at Blue-eyed Jack and the pig and waited for him to begin. There'd be enough meat soon for the king and queen of England to share (thought Stonemason Tim to himself), if either of them could distract themselves from the blasted German war and come over the waters to visit them.

# The Killer And His Knives

Blue-eyed Jack took the short brown-handled knife from the table. He put his arm around the pig's neck, all the time searching with his fingers for the well-known vein in the pig's throat. The flesh was as soft as a mouse's belly and it hid the vein. He continued to smile into the eyes of the pig and he held its soft ear in his fist, almost lovingly and caressingly. And just as he and Fatty-Matty had once whispered into the ear of Fandango the day they were coaxing him away from that faraway horse-fair in Galway to come and live with them, he again whispered his charmed words ('Oh, how lovely thou art!') into the pig's ear and he tried desperately to convey a small bit of calmness and relaxation into the creature. In this way the pig would die a better death (he thought) and not spoil the blood for the meat. His gentle words (you may be sure) were flung back ragingly into his face by this ungrateful squealer-of-a-pig.

Blue-eyed Jack had been dispatching pigs ever since the year Handsome Johnnie died. He got up onto the ass-and-car and he knelt down over the glazed eyes of the pig. The reins had prevented any sudden movement out of the animal so that by now the heaving and the weaving had just about stopped. With his index finger and thumb the big man continued to probe for a spot to puncture. He had the air of a surgeon about him, searching for the death-spot in the depths of the pig's gullet. The pig saw the glint of the knife and he knew that his hour had come. Blue-eyed Jack marked off a small triangle of flesh and with the flat of the knife he slipped an oblique cut into the largest bloodvessel in the pig's neck, just underneath the jaw-line. He gave the knife a twist and the first hot flush of blood pumped out, steaming hot in the cold air of the haggart.

The blood (as Teddy now saw) was as red as Dowager's geraniums or the ruby trappings of the bespectacled pope in the picture in The Big Cave Room and it flowed freely and it stained the upturned soapy-white belly of the horrified creature. And though the pig tried to bounce up-and-down on the cart in the face of its impending death, in these dying agonies its screams could do nothing but grow fainter and fainter. Blue-eyed Jack looked at his pocket-watch for a minute or two for this pig had to die slowly (if not calmly) so that the meat would not get spoiled. It was time for the long knife (the black dagger) and he plunged it deep into the pig's throat, as far down as his raging fears would allow it to travel. Mercifully – the pig was dead. From below on her flagstones Dowager cocked her ear in the wind and she made the sign-of-the-cross on her chest and she said, 'Ah-ha! They have killed their pig at long last, thank God.'

Seeing that the blood was starting to run down through the straw on the cart's slats, the women rushed down the haggart with their buckets and pans and they placed them underneath the front of the cart and they made a chain of buckets towards Rambling Jack's front door. They pushed Teddy and his pan forward and they settled him down low between the wheel and the lace of the cart.

## Teddy's Immense New Feelings

His heart was thumping wildly and the flesh on his back felt strangely sweaty. His recently uplifted spirits when asked to come to the pig-killing were replaced by new and complicated feelings – of childish wonder at the changes taking place (with a living pig becoming a dead pig) and his own natural pity for the poor manacled creature lying their miserably in all its ropes and impaled on that horrible long knife. And were it not for the promise of the bladder, a little voice inside in his head would have escaped from his dry throat and cried out, 'Untie the pig, Jack! Let him go free! For god-sake, let him go free!'

Not to disgrace himself opposite the men and women, the child held his pan out dutifully underneath the hole in the galvanized sheeting and he began to collect the sticky carmine ribbon of blood as it drip-dripped down from the pig's belly and oozed its way into his marble-stained pan. The little hunter from the rabbit-hunt and the fish-hunt at The Big Hole had no time to think about the pig's bladder but to concentrate on filling his pan with the blood and let not a drop of it spill. Yet in spite of himself, he couldn't get rid of his sorrow for the poor pig and a heavy sickness rested itself in the pit of his little belly – even though the killing of the pig hadn't raised a single eyebrow from any of the big people around him. He could see that there was much more blood (the cart was drenched with it) than he'd seen at the killing of the rabbits. He tried hard to hold back his tears and to act the part of a brave little man – that's what Blue-eyed Jack would have wanted from him. As the blood in his pan rose up to the top, the women took him and his pan to the door of Rambling Jack's house. He kept his eyes diverted from the cart. When he returned to collect his second pan of blood he saw that the pig's eyes were sad and leaden in the loneliness of its death and at the same time it seemed as though it was lying in a peaceful state of sleep – lying hopefully in some faraway piggy heaven. Only then did our little man realize that he had been crying silently and he wiped away his tears – now that the pig was dead and no longer in any pain.

## *The Women Are Hard At It*

Inside in Rambling Jack's house the women started running to and fro with buckets of spring-water from the well and putting on burners of water on top of the blazing turf-fire. When the pig would be cut up, the pieces would have to be completely scalded in a bath of boiling water. They had brought down with them a box of tapers, like the ones used for lighting the altar-candles at Mass and everything was in place for the singeing with the tapers and the scraping of the pig's bristles with their box of sharp razorblades.

With their ensanguined hands bespattered in the pig's blood the men wheeled the cart up to the front of Rambling Jack's house, careful not to disturb the weight of the pig's carcass. Rambling Jack brought in his ladder from the hayshed and he leaned it against the back wall of his Welcoming Room, a few feet away from the pile of furze bushes that he kept in the corner for the evening fire and the singeing of the pig's bristles. They carried in the dead pig (it was heavy work) and they hoisted it up on the ladder and they tied its fetters firmly to the rungs, the hind legs up at the top. Blue-eyed Jack carefully slit his knife down along the length of the pig's belly from the groin to the neck and he thrust in his hands and he pulled out a huge mass of entrails. He hung them (still warm and sticky and stinking to high heaven) on his arm and he shouted to the women to hold out their hands and they ran forward immediately. They didn't mind a bit. There'd be meat in plenty from now on (enough to feed the pope) when all this work was over and done. They unravelled the guts one at a time in a silent and orderly fashion (like a skein of wool) and they placed them neatly into several buckets. There was to be no wastage.

Meanwhile the carrion crows came circling their way down from the haggart trees and they hopped around the ass-and-car. The dead pig was gone from the cart and they strutted their way impudently up to Rambling Jack's door and they waited patiently. He came out and he threw the unusable bits high into the bushes. The crows flew away and were silent for the rest of the day, gorging themselves to their heart's content, before the rats from the hayreek could come and pay them a visit. The women washed and scrubbed the guts several times over and they placed them in a boiling cauldron to make their puddings later. Then Timmy and Stomemason Tim inserted the hazel thatching-wands from side to side (half-a-foot apart) to open up the belly and keep the pig's sides apart. The drying out of the insides could now begin.

## Teddy Sees The Poor Spread-Eagled Pig

Once the ceremony of opening up the pig was completed, the men had a chance to wipe the sweat from their foreheads and there followed a moment or two of quiet calm as they silently surveyed their pig. By this time Teddy was sitting on a stool by the fire and reflecting as usual. He looked at the spread-eagled body of this pig that had been running up and down the haggart in days gone by. The colour of its body was no longer the pink of that former little piggy but was as pale as Father Chasible's corpse – almost as yellow as the corpse of Danny-go-slow, which Teddy had seen the other day with Dowager as it lay in its open coffin outside The Roaring Town Hospital. The child crept forward and he looked into the pig's glazed eyes. Despite all the gory mess, the dead creature looked like a glassy-eyed saint in one of Dowager's holy-books. Unlike the dead rabbits that he'd seen hanging down from the back of the door, this death had been far more cruel and fierce than the death of any rabbit or fish and the picture of it was to stay lodged inside Teddy's head, never again to be erased.

Finally Rambling Jack took the centre of the floor. As the owner of the pig, it was his duty to perform the last ritual and he pushed a spud into the dead creature's mouth, making it look farcical and comical in its death. Then he folded a fistful of wispy hay into a tight ball and he thrust it up into the pig's backside so as to block it up completely. There followed a bit of smiling devilment as the men took a look at the sad face of Teddy in the corner. At the instigation of Blue-eyed Jack (that rascal of all living rascals) Teddy was given strict instructions to report the news of this final little ritual to Dowager as soon as he got back home: 'Dowager! Dowager!' he was instructed to tell her, 'we put a spud in the pig's dead mouth and we stuck a sop of hay up into his arse (be sure and say 'arse' and not 'backside', they said)'. The big man could picture the greeting that Teddy would get from his shocked and angry grandmother at the use of such foul and dirty language and Blue-eyed Jack (the old devil) would stay laughing for the rest of the week.

By now the women had gone back up into The Hills-of-The-Past, having drained and cleaned the pig. The next day the men would deal with the precise cutting up of the meat and would salt it into curable fletches. The women would return for the scalding and the singeing and the scraping of the pig. It was of great importance that the pig was cleanly razored or people might talk to each other and whimsically (sneeringly, some would say) suggest that you should take your razor with you when sitting down to eat the bacon of Rambling Jack as there'd be a bit of scraping to do first.

## The Men Are Hard At It

Meanwhile the men left the carcass to dry out, with the hazel wands across its belly, and they sat down around the fire. They treated themselves to one or two bottles of stout and they opened up a package of Woodbine fags. By that time Teddy was fast asleep in the corner of the hob. The big man, remembering his promise to the little man, took the creamy bladder from the pile of entrails and he washed it again and again. Tomorrow he'd blow it up like a balloon and he'd make a present of it to Teddy and help to bring back his cheerful spirit after the pig's cruel death. He could see it all this minute: the outstretched hands of the child and the eyes full of gratitude and the hands wrapped around the bladder's smoothness and the legs ready to gallop out the half-door on feathery feet to race the bladder all around his little world and all the muted hens, ducks and geese, the cows and their calves, staring in wonder at this strange new sight, The Little Englander and his bladder.

The pig's blood was still on the killers' stained wellingtons and the smell of the killing lay deep in their nostrils. They badly needed the extra refreshment of the lively medicine that the drinking-shop of Curl 'n' Stripes had ready to pour down their dry throats. Blue-eyed Jack gently lifted his little man and he put his coat around him to keep out the early evening chill from his bones. By this time the sun had grown pale, lending the air a tepid softness. And the whining voices of faraway farmers could be heard as they led their cows back to the fields to trudge their way towards the ditches for shelter during the night. The gliding and swerving of little birds was coming to a close and flocks of them were scudding back to their nests in the treetops and hedgerows. Blue-eyed Jack carried Teddy on down the hill and he quietly dropped him in the half-door to Dowager, who had been waiting for the last half-hour for the return of her two pig-killers.

The big man smiled down at his mother and he handed her the pig's bladder. He took his bicycle pump off of The Twenty-Eight-Wheeler and he placed it on the table so that Teddy would see that it was there to pump up the bladder when he woke up next day. The big man would pump it to bursting-point and make the little man the finest balloon you ever did see so that he could run off and frighten every cow in sight. Dowager saw that her little hunter was worn to a thread, as though he'd been on a visit to the moon and back. She knew this would happen and she had placed a hot jar in her bed. For this once in his childhood he would sleep beside herself in the bed, just as he had done when he was a tiny infant fresh over from England. He wouldn't know whether he was alive or dead, such being the weariness of any young pig-killer.

The rest of the men had followed Blue-eyed Jack down The Open Road and were sitting on the singletree in Mikey's grove, waiting for him. The big man rushed out the half-door and he joined up with them over the stream. They were determined to race each other to the door of the drinking-shop and get their teeth into their first pint of stout (the 'black doctor') and wash away the smell of Death.

# And Morning Strolled In All Over Again

When morning burst forth on Rookery Rally, Dowager was greeted by her over-excited grandson; he had seen the bladder lying on the table. He hadn't forgotten the commands of Blue-eyed Jack and in a rush of colourful language he told his grandmother the story of the pig and he described the way Rambling Jack had pushed the spud into the pig's mouth and the way he had stuck the sop of straw up into its arse. And though Dowager (the good woman that she was) attempted to show how cross she was ('That's enough of that sort of language!') she had to turn in towards the fire to avoid being seen with scarcely-controlled laughter around her lips and a look of tenderness in her tearful old eyes. Blue-eyed Jack ('The heavens to you, Teddy!') couldn't stop from laughing and he patted Teddy on the head to show how much he approved of the way the child had described the unruly ceremony of the spud and the straw and the dead pig. After a little bout of silence The Old Pair looked at each other across the firelight and took another fit of laughing and Teddy joined in.

Dowager would have liked to go up and help the women with the work that was still to be done. But there was Teddy to think of and for once she left him in his dreamland at the fire while she fussed over her list of jobs: the clearing out of the ashes and the lighting of the fire and the preparing of his egg from The Little Red Hen. She knew that Smiling Babs and her sister (Cackles) would both be on hand to join in with the rest of the women.

# The Ladder And The Scraping Of The Bristles

The men had been up early and had laid the ladder and the pig flat on its back on the floor. They spent the next hour using their sharpened knives to scrape away the coarser bristles from the body. Then the women knelt on either side of the pig and started the more detailed scraping with their razorblades, just like they'd scrape the feathers from off their chickens. They were like a team of old barbers (scrape scrape and scrape again – you could set it to music) until they had meticulously scraped off the last of the bristles and the pig's flesh was as smooth as a sweet-gallon.

They arranged the pig's smaller morsels in rows on the table (including the bits of its heart and liver) and they spent some time cutting them up into little pieces to be put into the puddings along with the pig's blackened blood. Each of them had raided their press-cupboards for spices such as the red and black peppers and the cinnamon, the cracked oats and the caraway seeds. If Dowager had only been able to go up and join them, she'd have taken a few bits of chopped onions to give an even more mouth-watering flavour to the puddings. The cauldrons of water were kept boiling over the blazing fire and poured into Rambling Jack's tin bathtub. Finally the job was over and done and the puddings were tied and placed in the tub and the women rested. The hungry smell filled the hunter's Welcoming Room.

The following few days saw the men getting back into action. Rambling Jack removed the pig's backbone and then the men cut the body into several fletches. They brought in the rock-salt from the turf-shed and they applied it vigorously, salting it into the hams and the knuckles and the joints. They kept aside the fat from the steaks of pork and they softened it into bowls of lard for the women to cook with during the coming months.

Rambling Jack had the loan of The Bonesetter's curing barrel. He had already stored it behind the half-door, ready for the bacon-fletches to be placed into it. During the next eight weeks he'd keep the meat inside in the barrel. He laid the fletches into the barrel and arranged them in between inch-thick layers of salt and oaten-straw with a little well-water to make up the best possible brine solution. He left an inch or two of empty space at the top of the barrel and he placed some clean potato-sacks over the last layer of bacon. Then he fixed the lid tightly in under the barrel's lip so as to make the whole thing airtight. To give a good finish to the job he placed some large stones on top. His bacon would last for the next two years. He'd hang half-a-dozen fletches of the salted meat on the hooks in his rafters and he'd put the three biggest fletches on the nails over the hob's canopy so that the smoke from the fire would turn them a light brown. You would never see a fly go near them and his fletches would be so well cured and hardened from all the work done on them that you could make a fine pair of boots out of the skins – and still be able to eat his bacon! Enough said.

# A Time For Another Dance

The Open Road might well have held a dance in honour of Rambling Jack. For throughout the next couple of months they'd be gorging themselves senseless on pork and steaks and puddings and spuds and cabbages and turnips. They'd be in savage health with their bellies extended on them like the pig had been a week or two before its untimely end! And Teddy and his uncle would spend a good deal of time looking at Dowager and the way (without a tooth in her head) she could crunch a pig's ear with her hardened gums and feel the juices of it every bit as goods as her son and grandson. The all-round feasting in Rookery Rally would go on and on until Rambling Jack's barrel was deserted and it was time for Blue-eyed Jack to go back up the hill with his knives and kill another misfortunate pig.

# Children And Their Listlessness

While all this was going on, Smiling Babs' children sat listlessly in Mikey's grove. They were too sad to even smoke the fags they'd stolen from Fiddler Joe and they were itching to get back at Teddy and get rid of the envy and anger they felt in their hearts. If anyone now had a plan against Teddy it would be Sweeney. He could imagine how the little man would be running his races round and around the fields – himself and his blasted bladder. Sweeney would come with his brothers and they'd waylay him. They would snatch away his bladder and they would burst it maliciously and they would laugh and mock the life out of The Little Englander. Afterwards they would be caught out and they would take their punishment from Fiddler Joe's shaving-strap. It didn't matter. Teddy would sob in Mikey's grove behind the singletree and he would remember the sad look on the pig's face before its death under the cruel knife. In his own small way he would have his own heart pierced (like the pig's) with a hitherto unknown sadness and for days to come he would look as sad as the pig had done. Not even Dowager's warm breath into his ear and her caressing arms around his neck would be able to soften the hurt that was about to enter his soul in ways far more cruel than the stealing of his bladder.

# NINE

# Teddy's First Trial And Tribulation

*A sad sad day
when Teddy's joy came face-to-face
with sudden heartbreak and gloom.*

Nothing in the whole wide world could have prepared Teddy for the day that was about to enter his life. It was a dark day and it was a dirty day. No matter what any one in Rookery Rally might have said, the difference between The Little Englander and the other children was marked out not only in the style of the clothes that they wore (and now Teddy had the additional brand new suit brought to him by Sister Rosamunda) but by one fact alone: the other children were from the true Old Sod (Ireland) and Teddy had come to live amongst them from the land of John Bull (England). Nothing had changed in Rookery Rally until he came here from that strange foreign place where (some children had heard) Ireland's long-established enemies spent their lives.

Up until the day of the pig-killing it had been a case of 'so far and so good'. With his cute little curls and the bald patches from the cattle-rash and his attempted doughty swagger and speech Teddy had grown into the hearts of us all and it seemed as if he had been living here forever. This year he had already had his fourth birthday – although nobody on our Open Road kept a track of anyone's birthday. They'd tell you they didn't know the birthday of their hens and they didn't know the birthdays of their geese and their ducks. And anyway – how on earth could a mother be expected to recall the birthdays of all her children when Mother Church had forced her to have so many of them? But there was one date that every mother did know and that was the baptismal date of her child when the little infant was taken to the house of God to be entered into the fold of the Christian Family and get filled with the grace of The Holy Spirit.

Matters were different, however, between Dowager and the rest of the women. Out of respect for Teddy's mother (Little Nell) and her English ways of doing things she never forgot a single one of Teddy's four birthdays and on each occasion she gave him a big bowl of jelly and a plateful of sweetened rice from the burner with all the little crispy brown bits round the edge. Lady Acceptable brought him up an orange on his latest birthday and she smiled down at him from her brown mare. 'This child is going to be heard tell of one of these days, mark my word,' said she to Dowager – and for Teddy each of his birthdays had proved to be nothing short of a royal treat!

## An Inevitable Contrast

There couldn't be more of a contrast between himself and the children close by. The little thatched house of Smiling Babs and Fiddler Joe was chockful of children (there were eight of them so far and six more to follow). There was no room for labeling any of them a little prince like Teddy or for spoiling the youngest two (Darkie and Little Cull). Instead there was the handy ash-plant always ready and able to redden any of their legs if needs be. There was also the yard-brush and the shaving-strap for the older children should any of them step out of line or break the family household law as laid down by Smiling Babs, namely to respect your father and your mother – and to love your neighbour as much as you loved yourself.

The older children (Sweeney, Golly and Gallant) could now see the lie of the land. Every day they had seen Teddy wearing his grey flannel trousers and his polished brown sandals. At Mass each Sunday they had seen him with his long grey socks and the two blue hoops on them. They had seen him wearing a white shirt and a tie and a brand new suit – all sent from the mother that The Little Englander never even knew existed. In contrast, Smiling Babs' children wore hand-me-down clothes, a thankful present from one child to the next and (as with all big families) there wasn't a single shoe to their name throughout the weekdays. Their legs were a mixture of briar-cuts and cow-dung, at least until after the Saturday night's washing in the yard stream. But they were happy young souls just the same – that is until they saw Teddy running off with Blue-eyed Jack to the pig-killing in Rambling Jack's haggart and coming back home with the pig's bladder all to himself.

## Dowager Brings Out Teddy's New Suit

The day after the pig-killing (Sunday) Dowager brought out the new suit and she dressed Teddy for holy Mass in a style worthy of Lord Elegance. There was a blouse-like shirt with buttonholes around the base and these fitted into buttons at the top of the trousers. If only she had a box-camera she'd have taken him out to The Easy Stile in Timmy's Field and turned him into a brown photograph, so proud was she of her little man.

When Mass was over and done with and Father Accessible had hurried off to yet another hurling-match, Dowager made sure that everyone outside the church gate had a good look at her English grandson in his new suit. She took him for tea and a piece of cake into the parlour of her niece (Mary-the-Linnet, the schoolteacher) where Teddy made a few circles round the room and showed off his foreign finery. Mary-the-Linnet was sure she was in the presence of one of the new saints (she said) and she asked Dowager if the child had just come down from the skies.

If people had only bothered to think (like Sweeney, Golly and Gallant had been doing), they'd have been able to spot these differences between a spoilt little boy from over the seas and the wild, adventurous lives of the other children. They'd have seen the development of an almost-biblical tale resembling the story of Joseph and his coat of many colours and the envy it had caused in his brothers. From there it would have been a small hop to understand the anger in these boys and how jealousy would raise its ugly head one fine day and would sow the bad seed inside in their hearts.

## They Too Had Once Had Their Bladder

Yes, these children had been given more than one pig's bladder over the years and had filled The Thistle Field with their war-whoops as they breathlessly raced it up and down until it burst on them. But it was Teddy (yes, Teddy of the very fine clothes) who had gone a step further and had been given Rambling Jack's pan for the pig's blood – the pan that not one of them had ever had the privilege of holding, it being a task for grown-up men and women right up until now. They could scarcely keep the bitterness out of their eyes. The rusty bowlee-wheel from Timmy's creamery tank and the sock ball with the corks in it to make it bounce and the skittles on the flagstones – all these playthings and pastimes could go bury themselves in the river as far as they were concerned: 'We want the bladder! We have to have the bladder! By hell or by crook we will not sleep a wink till we get a hold of the bladder!' That was the song that had been in their hearts from the moment they heard the recent squeals of the dying pig. What an unbelievable shock lay in store for Teddy, finding for the first time in his brief life that he was a complete outsider from across the sea and a victim (like the pig) instead of a little prince.

## The Thoughts Of Smiling Babs

Though it was forbidden by Father Accessible to do a stroke of manual work on a Sunday, Smiling Babs and Fiddler Joe found themselves above on The Three Heights (a humpy field) and labouring away in silence. They were digging up their spuds and hoisting them into the ass-and-car and the rain was pattering down gently around them. Smiling Babs knew her weather and she could see by the look of the sky above Lisnagorna that the sun would soon be trembling its way through a vent-hole in the clouds and all would be well and her children could then go off from under her feet and enjoy themselves for the rest of the day abroad in the fields.

# Teddy In His Usual Dreamland

Meanwhile Teddy was living in his own day-to-day dreamland and he knew nothing of the sinister feelings of the bigger boys. He returned from Mass and he had his buttered egg and the two slices of soda-cake and he washed it all down with his customary mug of milk. Then, without a backward look at Dowager or Blue-eyed Jack, he went strolling up The Open Road to see Patches and Darkie and Little Cull, his newfound friends. He'd tell them all about the pig-killing and he'd ask them to come and play with him when Blue-eyed Jack pumped up the bladder in an hour or two's time. In the meantime maybe they'd let him joint them in The Thistle Field and share a pretend mug of their tea out of the tin mugs in the cubby-shop. The day would be like any of the previous days and the little man would also mix in with the bigger children and try to imitate their way of walking and talking. It was as if he was their little brother – except for the fine clothes that he always wore. In the last couple of months they had let him sit with them in Mikey's hayshed as they sang their songs to end their day. They had recently let him enter the orchard of Ducks-and-Drakes and share their stolen apples with them. He had raced his flaggard boats with them down along their stream as far as the spring-well where they'd caught a tiny trout for him and placed it in the blue canister to take home to his grandmother. He had done everything except smoke their stolen fags with them and cough up his guts. And none of this would have happened if Sweeney and the rest of them hadn't promised Dowager that they'd be Teddy's protectors and take care of him as good as his very own guardian angel. These happy-natured boys were only too glad to see him tag along behind themselves, together with Patches, Darkie and Little Cull – up until now.

And in ways far different from Dowager they had already taught him a great deal. It wasn't only the visiting card-players that used coarse language and tried to influence his developing speech (the rascals). Sweeney and Golly had taught him to curse and swear every bit as competently as themselves and they called him their bold little trooper. He could say new words like 'piss' and 'shite' instead of 'poolie' and 'dung'. The words 'feckin' and 'basthard' were two favourite words among all of them (even the little ones) and Teddy had been quick to adapt these words too. And just as they delighted in annoying Patches (like the time they gave him his cruel baptism in the river, simply to hear the foul language pouring out of his mouth) it would be Teddy's turn next to get a taste of their cruel medicine.

# Children At Their Daily Play

Sweeney and Golly and Gallant prodded their way through the ragwort and they strolled down The Thistle Field, puffing merrily on their half-fags. They knew that Smiling Babs and Fiddler Joe were two fields away and busy with the spuds and couldn't see them smoking or acting as if they were newly-established grown men. The three of them walked as far as the wire fence bordering Mikey's hay-shed. They took huge long steps like those other children did when they came down from The Hills-of-The-Past to Curl' n' Stripes' shop for their father's package of biscuits. From time to time they'd stop like these mountainy children and they'd give a shrug of their shoulders and they'd spit at a fly in the cow-dung. Teddy and Patches, Darkie and Little Cull walked reverently a few paces back from them and they made the same long steps as the big boys and they also spat at a fly in the cow-dung from time to time.

In the meantime Blue-eyed Jack had found the ball of twine and with the pump he had made a good job of blowing up the bladder. He hadn't an inkling of these boys' bitter feelings from the moment they'd seen Teddy trotting off to the pig-killing and causing them to believe they'd never get another bladder. Neither had Dowager a notion of the poison she had created by dressing Teddy up in his new suit for Mass and displaying him all around The Open Road as though he were a new brand of priest. 'What's an old bladder to the likes of them anyway?' Blue-eyed Jack would have said, for he had pumped up several bladders for them in the past. In fits of wild laughter the bigger boys had always burst them as soon as they got tired of them – partly to drive Patches and Darkie and Little Cull clean out of their minds with rage and see them spitting fire and lighting the field with their cursing and swearing ('Ye pissy load of old feckers!').

A few years back, their aunt (Polly, the left-handed fiddle-player) had brought them a china doll from The Land of The Silver Dollar. They soon twisted the arms and legs off of this doll and then they smashed her to bits with the hammer to see what made the squeaky voice come out of her belly and up into her mouth. They had even run off with Fiddler Joe's flashlamp and smashed it on the flagstones to see if the graphite from the batteries could write letters or draw their mother's face on the flagstones the same way the coloured stones from River Laughter did. No – Blue-eyed Jack had no worry over the bladder; he was giving it to the child who had never had one before and he couldn't wait to see Teddy running the length of The Bluebutton Field with his new plaything and the long string flying away behind him in the breeze.

From the half-door he could hear the sudden roars of the children from across the valley. Like a crowd of springtime lambs they were running themselves silly all over The Thistle Field in ways that Teddy found unbelievably admirable to watch. Their cartwheels and somersaults frightened the young calves and the sluggish cows so that they hurried off to the far ditch and hid themselves in the briars. Golly chased Slowcoach-the-ass into the lower corner near the stream and he caught him by the two ears. Sweeney got up on his back and he tried to steer him towards the younger children and frighten the life out of them. Teddy (the little dreamer) continued to watch in wonder and awe. Sweeney had become his everyday inspiration.

For once in his life the ass (Slowcoach) wasn't as slow as his name implied. He kicked his hind legs into the air and he pelted the astonished Sweeney off of his back and into the nettles. The laughter of the other children brought a furious redness to their big brother's cheeks and he tried to laugh it off. But it had only added to the temper that was already bubbling up inside him against The Little Englander and his stylish clothes. The three older boys grew tired of their playfulness and they came and joined Teddy and Patches, Darkie and Little Cull. Turning to his little sister (who was about to enter her cubby-shop and lay out her neat row of tin mugs) Sweeney whispered in her ear and asked her to make him a special mug of her pretend tea. Darkie (like any coy little girl would do) turned away from Teddy and the other boys and she sat down on her haunches and let loose a stream of warm poolie from the private spout between her legs.

# The Jaunt Of Jaunts From A Pissy Mug

Teddy didn't know what to expect next, for the bigger boys had never before played in the cubby-shop. Sweeney came back with the mug of poolie and he held it out towards the little man. With his forefinger he gave it a stir and he gestured how men all over the world used the yellow stuff to brush their teeth and had been doing this very thing since the days of Adam and Eve: 'Surely you know this much, Teddy,' sighed Sweeney with a sad shake of his head. 'It's at least a hundred years ago since The High-Talians and The High-Gyptians started washing their teeth with piss. This was a very strange puzzle to Teddy, who hadn't yet started school or got to know such mighty wonders as this. Dowager had never informed him of these faraway races and he didn't want to show his ignorance in front of the other children.

Golly nodded his head fiercely in support of Sweeney's bit of wisdom: 'Believe you me, Teddy – the poolie is just the job for dealing with the teeth – ask Blue-eyed Jack or anyone else around Rookery Rally if you don't believe a word I'm saying.'

As if that wasn't enough, Gallant then jumped forward to put in his own pennyworth: 'It's the poolie – and by cripes, nothing but the poolie – that those important fellows like Doctor Glasses and Father Accessible have been using from as far back as I can remember – and that's what has given them their fine set of white teeth. It's high time, my young English friend, for you to wise up and act like a man – trust me, Teddy, trust me'. By now their talk was as good as a sermon.

And then Bucko stepped forward with the last few words: 'Poolie – everyone in the history books has known it all along – is far better than any soot for the job of cleaning out those hidden little bits of bread and cabbage when they get stuck in the back of the teeth and (what's more) it's bound to give a man's teeth their natural whiteness.' The four rascals dipped their fingers into their little sister's mug and they pretended they were cleaning their teeth with her poolie. Following their example, Teddy (the poor simpleton) dipped his finger in likewise and he began rubbing his teeth with the poolie – back and forth as they had shown him. He completely forgot that Dowager had trained him to brush his teeth with the soot from the back of the hob.

'That's the way to do it, Teddy! That's the style of it!' smirked Sweeney and Golly. The Little Englander seemed to be making a very fine job of it. Suddenly the entire Thistle Field (the cows and their calves too) burst into fits of uproarious laughter and even Slowcoach-the-ass was braying as never before and singing his ass-songs of pure derision. There followed several bursts of delirious cartwheels and somersaults up and down the field at the sight of Teddy cleaning his teeth with Darkie's poolie.

The big boys left Patches, Darkie and Cull to comfort the little man and tell him the reason they were all laughing. They suddenly ran up the field and went skipping out over the ditch towards The Heights to help Smiling Babs and Fiddler Joe load up the cart with the spuds. Clearly this mean little trick of theirs had made them as happy as a hedgerow of sparrows; they felt they had successfully vented their anger on The Little Englander – that they had given him a thing or two to remember them by. Patches, Darkie and Little Cull sat down beside the tearful Teddy. They told him at length how their mean-spirited brothers had made an awful fool out of him – how they had tricked him out of pure spite and for nothing else but their own amusement into washing his teeth from a mug of the filthy poolie.

## Teddy's Pure Sorrow

Teddy was completely confused. He couldn't fathom out why these big boys should have wanted to bring so much sadness on him. With childish temper he threw the mug of poolie at his three young friends and he ran off home as fast as his legs would carry him. He dashed across the flagstones towards his grandmother with the tears hopping from his eyes. He burst in through the half-door: 'Dowager! Dowager!' he cried. 'Those pissy load of old feckers – Sweeney, Golly and Gallant – made me drink a mug of Darkie's piss.'

'Enough! Enough!' said Dowager, putting her hands to her ears when she heard the filthy language pouring out of her grandson's mouth. It was sad (but she knew it might happen one day) that on top of his prayers he had learnt such a fine set of swearwords – in spite of all her daily efforts. And she felt she might have to run for the soap and clean his mouth out for him. If she wasn't careful it would not be too long before he was every bit as proficient as Sweeney in everything he said and did. Indeed all that was missing from this mimicking little jaybird of hers, as Blue-eyed Jack later remarked, was a cocked hat on the side of his head and a pipe sticking out of his mouth.

'But they did do it – they made me drink it!' he wailed. 'And now I'm going to die like Rambling Jack's pig.' For a short while Dowager said nothing and Teddy lay sobbing in the folds of her black apron. She pondered the pain he had had to endure and she went on stroking his curls and she tried to force back the anger that was boiling up inside her. 'Hush! Hush! my little goose,' she said as she tried to soften his fears and his belief that he would be taken away from her and carried off by the angels to an imminent death.

Little by little she got the truth out of him – the dipping of the finger into the mug and the brushing of the teeth with the finger and the roars of laughter from the bigger boys. At last she knew that the drinking of Darkie's poolie was his own childish exaggeration of the truth. Only a small drop of the filthy stuff had gone down his throat (she said) and it wouldn't kill a fly (she added). 'Oh, how could you have told me such a great big lie, Teddy!' Her little man would be given a somewhat stiff Penance from Father Accessible when he went to make his First Confession a year or two from now – that's what she told him.

## *Dowager Reproaches Herself*

The whole episode might have been avoided (thought Dowager) if she herself hadn't been such a careless old fool. From now on she'd have to re-arrange her little man's activities. Perhaps she could take him on one or two more of those charming journeys like the morning when they'd gone to visit her old friend, Gentility. Perhaps she could infuse in him those happy memories of when he had run ahead of her like a new calf, full of admiration for the birds in the sky and the racing clouds across the glorious sun above on The Hill of The Greenfinches. On the other hand, if the big war with The Germans went on for a few more years (she knew) he'd have to take the road to Dang-the-skin-of-it's school-house and mix in with the other children (the rough and the smooth alike) and then there was no forecasting what might happen to him. No longer would she have him in the palm of her hand or be able to guide his footsteps along the right path. And she shuddered to think of the filthy language he'd be learning from the older children and the dirty mean way they might go on treating a child somewhat different from themselves. The Little Englander indeed!

She shrugged herself out of her daydreams and she got busy. She went to the dresser and with tears in her eyes she handed him the sock-ball she'd been making for him out of Blue-eyed Jack's old socks. Inside the folded socks she had put three of the blackened bottle-corks that she had burned in the fire for smudging away the bald cattle-rash marks amid his curls. A moment ago the child had been angered, – bewildered and humiliated – at the way the bigger boys had made a proper fool out of him but now he brightened up considerably.

As with other children, he could change with the weather and at the sight of the sock-ball his memory of recent events in The Thistle Field was suddenly as fleeting as his tears. He remembered the delight he had felt when the bigger boys threw their own sock-ball onto Smiling Babs' thatch and then caught it as it made its uncertain way down through the straw. He remembered how Sweeney had sent Patches and Little Cull around the back of the house ('Be ready to catch it!') when Golly pelted the ball high over the thatch, sending it sailing passed the chimney. His two brothers had raced round to the back of the house to see if their little brothers had caught it before it could hit the ground.

Dowager waved an admonishing finger at Teddy as he scurried out the half-door with his new plaything: 'Take care, my little man, that you don't throw it up onto our thatch and destroy the bit of roof over our heads!' Teddy carried his sock-ball out across the haggart stick and over the dung-heap to the back of the house. Then The Devil came chasing around the corner after him and put a slice of hell's devilment (if not downright disobedience) into the child's head. He passed by The Lightning Whoor who was braying in through the broken-glass window of Dowager's bedroom. He stood looking up at the back of the roof, which at this point was almost touching the ground. He forgot the wise advice of his grandmother. Inside his head he heard again the harsh sounds of the bigger boys' laughter echoing across from Mikey's grove at him. He had no way of punishing the likes of the big boys and their cruelty. With a child's misguided logic he threw his sock-ball up contemptuously onto the thatch roof in an effort to hurt somebody (anybody at all, even poor old Dowager). But each time he made his throw, the sock-ball seemed to punish him by zig-zagging down the thatch in such a teasing way that he couldn't catch it and it ran out passed him onto the grass. And then it played an even better trick on him – it stayed hidden forever in a hole in the thatch, refusing to come down and amuse him anymore.

## A Playful Blue-Eyed Jack Returns

Blue-eyed Jack came back from The Bull-Paddock after returning his cows to The Danes' Hill. Dowager was too frightened to tell him the news of the bigger boys' mean trickery against Teddy. She knew that if her son got wind of it he'd take his ash-plant up the road and redden their legs for them. The big man hopped out over the haggart stick. In his hands he was holding the pig's bladder, all pumped up and shining. It was as big as a milk-bucket and was creamy and white and it had little blue and red veins running up-and-down it. He twirled it aloft a few times and then he stretched it out towards Teddy. Though he had lost his sock-ball in the thatch the child's mood changed yet once more and he ran happily to his uncle. He had never seen a pumped-up pig's bladder before and he couldn't imagine how such a great big shape was only yesterday inside in the belly of Rambling Jack's dead pig. And now he was as cheerful as a cock-sparrow as the two-men-of-us hurried back into Dowager inside in The Welcoming Room.

For the next half-hour the big-and-little men played with the bladder, keeping one eye on the blazing turf-fire. Time after time they tapped it up to the rafters and they caught its delirious joy when it came back to them like an old friend returning from a long journey.

Dowager found herself laughing heartily when she saw how her two men were having such a blissful time of it and how Teddy seemed to have forgotten his recent shame over Darkie's mug of poolie. Even the rafters seemed to share in the all-round hilarity of the three merry souls. Never before had The Welcoming Room witnessed such fine fun – not even on those days when Blue-eyed Jack used to make sudden rushes across the floor and (oh, the squeals of the surprised child!) knock Teddy off of his feet and pelt him up to the rafters with 'Can you see Dublin? – Tell me if you can see the great big city'. No – there was nothing that could compare with the playful pig's bladder.

Dowager took down the ball of twine from the press-cupboard. She tied it stoutly around the bladder. She wound it ceremoniously around the child's wrist, keeping her eyes on it so that both the wrist and the string were bound safely together and the bladder would stay fast friends with Teddy when he went running across the fields with it. The two-men-of-us walked out the half-door and out across the haggart stick. Blue-eyed Jack led Teddy towards the gap where he had been feeding the calves earlier on. For a second or two he watched the little boy running joyfully round and around The Bluebutton Field with his bladder. He watched him making his way down towards the broken tree. He watched him going out the gap that led to The Deer Field and The Bull-Paddock. It was the last sight he had of him until later on in the day. Not for one moment did he think that the bigger boys were holding so fierce a grudge against the little man and his fine clothes and his new bladder. But when evening came it would be too late for him to start crying over what was to happen below in The Bull-Paddock or wish he had stayed with his little nephew and his merry-making bladder instead of going off to chop wood at the woodpile.

## Sweeney's Two Sides

Norrie was the oldest of Smiling Babs' children. From her first weeks' work in Lady Acceptable's kitchen she brought home her few shillings (wrapped inside in a matchbox) and like all good children she dutifully handed it up to Smiling Babs. The kind-hearted girl kept back just a little bit of money for herself and she bought Patches a great big bag of sweets for the courage he had shown on his first day's outing to school and the miserable suffering he'd endured at the hands of his brothers when they baptized him in the river. To Little Cull and Darkie she gave two bags of peggy's-leg sweets with which to turn their teeth from white to blue and then to black. Sweeney also brought home his matchbox from Lord Elegance (with the money safely wrapped inside in it) and, unknown to Fiddler Joe, he gave a small packet of Woodbine fags to Bucko, Golly and Gallant and proved himself every bit as generous-spirited as his older sister. You would never have recognized the cruel boy that had been ill-treating Teddy after coming home from Mass.

## Rambling Jack's Zippity

But whilst such excitement and merriment was going on all around The Open Road there was a bit of bad news not too far away, above in Rambling Jack's cabin. His joy over the killing of his big pig had soon rebounded on him (this very morning) and it was as though the dead pig had been given magical powers to come back and haunt the life out of him from this day forth. Even before Mass had started and when the young larks were still wiping their feathers in the haggart's dock-leaves, he had set out with his noble greyhound (Zippity) in search of a few rabbits for the pot. They were out near Growl River when they suddenly spotted a hare a hundred yards away and across a wide stream and in no great danger from Man or his gun. She was standing stock-still. She was imbibing the freshness of this fine Sunday morning.

Such a distance between a hare and a greyhound would have been too great a challenge for any dog other than Zippity. Rambling Jack leaned forward and he playfully squashed his leathery fingers around Zippity's two ears and an unprintable tenderness sped back and forth between their two sets of eyes. He knelt down beside her and he whispered into her ears. She was already following the line of his eye in the direction of the hare and the two of them were aflame for the hunt and the kill.

He let Zippity off of the leash and away she raced in pursuit of the speeding hare, cutting through the ferns and frightening the young cuirlew-birds in her mad onward rush. What a fire there was in the greyhound's blood as she leaped the stream with a powerful jump from her paws. Nearer and nearer she drew to the terrified hare and Rambling Jack jumped for joy and he clapped his two hands as he saw the mighty stretch of her legs.

At the upper end of the field there was a stone wall and in its middle there was a single rabbit-hole – just big enough for the little hare to squeeze through and make good its escape, if she got half a chance. The hare saw the rabbit-hole and Zippity saw it too. God-in-his-heaven also saw the rabbit-hole and he looked with favour on the little hare and he sent down one of his angels from the clouds. The angel put his arms around the little hare and he directed her paws towards the rabbit-hole – to give her another day of freedom. With her snarling teeth Zippity made a final lunge and hurled her palpitating mass against the stone wall. The hare disappeared through the rabbit-hole and bolted out into the next field's safe haven. It was the last that Zippity ever saw of her.

Oh, poor, poor Zippity! Would any of us ever forget it? As she neared the ditch she couldn't stop her immense surge of speed and she cracked her skull wide open off of the stone wall. So close had she come to killing the little hare that when Rambling Jack ran through the ferns and came up to her, she had the white smoky trails of the fur of what must have been a bewitched hare (he said) still stuck to her front teeth. The race had been too great even for so famous a dog as our legendry Zippity. He looked down at his faithful friend and the sadness of her unnecessary death (at a broken mass and a broken neck) and his heart was fit to burst asunder.

Poor Rambling Jack! A list of regrets now followed: no more would he and Zippity ramble together through yon greenery in The Forest of Lisnagorna: no more would the great dog wrap her warm body around her master's legs to keep his toes warm in the bed each night: No more would she see the little rabbits shaking the dew from their hind legs in the early dawn: no more would she stand at the stream and let the cows drink their fill. He knelt down and he picked up the still-warm body and then he began to howl like a banshee.

With the greyhound on his shoulders, he wobbled homeward and he buried Zippity underneath the holly-bush and then he hid his face underneath his cold bed-sheets and he wished he had never been born. Yesterday the pig had cried miserable tears when he'd heard the approaching wellingtons of his proposed killers. Today it had been the turn of Rambling Jack and he continued to bawl in the bed where nobody could hear or see him or share in his pain. Red Scissors came down quietly and he went on preserving and salting the pig-meat and keeping the second pig fattened up for the market the following Thursday. None of us knew if Rambling Jack would ever again rise out of his bed, so low were his spirits, so broken was his heart.

# *Teddy And His Blissful Bladder*

Whilst so much miserable news was filtering its way down along The Open Road, Teddy was having the fine time of it and heading with his bladder towards the Bull-Paddock and John's Gate. The other children were spread out everywhere across Rookery Rally and there wasn't a soul in sight. Gallant had gone off with his father and the horse-and-cart to bring back a load of turf from Bog Boundless in the hope that nobody would be mean enough to report him to Father Accessible for working on the Sabbath day. Patches and Little Cull were sitting comfortably in the rattletrap inside in the turf-shed and with an armful of roasted crabapples they were also having a fine time of it and were as happy as two larks. Their brother (Bucko) had roasted half-a-dozen spuds for himself in the hot fireside embers and he was sitting on top of the haggart ditch and enjoying his feast and feeling every bit as good as the high and mighty Lord Elegance.

His little sister (Darkie) left her cubby-shop. She couldn't get Teddy's recent humiliation out of her head and she started searching all over the place to see if she could find her little friend. Like the others, she had always been told by Dowager to keep a watchful eye on him and at last she saw him away in the distance. He was sailing his bladder-and-twine in between The Bog Wood and the old oak tree, a spot she knew well. It was where he kept one of his two pretend farms of berries for his sheep, his cattle and horses. It was his private little theatre and it was hidden in leaves and clay. He shared it from time to time with her – and only with her. She could see how extremely careful he was in keeping his bladder as far away as possible from the harmful briars. She heard him shouting: 'Coom on mee bladder! Coom on mee bladder!' He was full of meadow-madness as he tried to dance away from the everlasting shadow of his frivolous bladder. He ran in and out of the rushes and he ran in and out of the ferns and the merry bladder wouldn't let him escape from it. The calves had already tumbled in fear to the far end of the field. They had their heads huddled together underneath the crabtree and were more than bemused by the strange sight of a small boy and his ingenious toy – the pig's bladder.

## The Arrival Of The Serpents

Above in Smiling Babs' yard Sweeney was nursing his sore head and bruised gable-end and remembering his recent tumble from off of Slowcoach's back. Himself and Golly had no wish to approach their ass again and get themselves another sound kick in the head. There were other matters (unpleasant ones) on their mind this very minute. The Devil himself had come calling them, oozing his way into their hearts; there was nothing that would do them now other than the downfall of The Little Englander and his bladder.

Teddy was at last well and truly exhausted. Unaware of Darkie's approach, he lay down in a pool of shadow beneath the oak-tree. He was looking up at the branches stirring to life over his head. He was looking at the sunlight patterns of the late afternoon moving about bewilderingly. It was then that he saw his little friend as she came skipping towards him from John's Gate. She was like a welcome vision to him.

By this time, however, the sharp ears of Sweeney and Golly had heard his encouraging shouts to his bladder and (as though they were carried on a dragon's wings) the two of them came bounding down the road and stole stealthily in over John's Gate and entered The Bull-Paddock. They saw Teddy and they saw their little sister, Darkie. These two little innocents were lying side-by-side with the bladder next to them, in under the shade of the oak-tree.

## The Penkife For Turnips

The solitary bit of bread-and-jam was all that most children had in their book-satchel when they made the three-mile journey each day to the school-house and that's when their penknife always came in handy. For as soon as they passed Turfman's Cross, every child would be on the look-out for the next field of turnips. The eldest child would root up a few suitable turnips with his penknife and then he'd scrape off the dirty skin and he'd share out the juicy pieces and the younger children would wash them in the stream under The School Bridge. Nobody thought it was stealing (not even the farmer) and no children ever mentioned it when they went into the confession box to tell their sins to the priest each month.

Now that Sweeney was working for Lord Elegance and learning how to plough and tend to the garden, it was Golly's turn to carry the penknife to school. And here in The Bull-Paddock this penknife was about to prove a most valuable tool. The two phantoms (Sweeney and Golly) came up behind Teddy. By now he had forgotten the mean way they had treated him in The Thistle Field and he rose to his feet and gave them a cheerful little wave.

## The Brutal Attack

Sweeney pushed him back against the tree. Golly kicked his startled feet out from under him and brought him crashing to the ground. They flung themselves on top of him. He felt his head spinning round and around as though his body was splitting asunder. The angry faces of his tormentors seemed to be breaking into smithereens all about him. 'Hand me the penknife,' snapped Sweeney. Before you could blink an eye or before little Darkie could get a word in to stop her brothers, he cut the twine with the penknife and he snatched the bladder from Teddy's wrist. 'Now it's our turn, mee brave Little Englander, (said the triumphant Golly, waving the bladder in the air) to race over the fields with Rambling Jack's bladder and have ourselves a fine old time of it.'

Sweeney tied the bladder onto Golly's wrist. 'Give it back! Give it back! It's mine! It's mine!' wailed the misfortunate Teddy. But he was like a bird between two cats and was far too frail to prevent what was happening. Darkie saw the uncontrollable trembling in him. She saw how his face had turned the colour of chalk. There was a mighty howl of anger inside in him (like when Red Buckles came to steal the sow) but this anger was too frightened to make its way up and out of his throat. Like Patches in the recent river's baptism there was no-one who could help him other than little Darkie and all she could do was moan: 'Stop! Stop! Don't ye know that God is watching the pair of ye?'

Teddy remembered the way these two had treated him in The Thistle Field and suddenly he knew (for the first time) what it meant to be The Little Englander – what it meant to be the little boy (as Blue-eyed Jack told him) who'd come to Rookery Rally in the big ship and the big train.

Sweeney and Golly would have loved such excitement as that and to their everlasting shame they had turned their anger against him and the fine clothes he was always wearing and they had made him their victim.

Teddy had never had a bad thought against them – at least not until the trickery with the filthy poolie. He had never felt like betraying any of them, not even when Mikey cornered him the previous week and asked him who were the rogues that were robbing his orchard. But at last he found his voice and (imitating the manly words that he had learnt from the visiting card-players) he let rip the vilest of curses on top of their heads: 'May ye shitty pair of feckers rot in hell – may The Devil eat the arses off of ye,' he cried.

Even this angry outburst could do nothing to stop the hard eyes piercing down on him. Like a chicken under the hatchet he struggled to get himself free and get at least one good kick at his enemies. But Golly was lying across his legs and keeping him as firm a prisoner as the pig had been on the cart. There flashed before Teddy's eyes the image of Rambling Jack's poor pig being pinned down with the reins on the cart. Darkie saw the great big tears in her little friend's eyes. They were as big as diamonds and were hanging in clusters down along his cheeks. She was beside herself with grief and she couldn't hold back her tears.

Teddy had been a friend to all of them. He had always been ready to steal a few cuts of bread from Dowager's table. He had always made sure it had plenty of butter and sugar on it when he came up the road to play with them. It was with him that she always shared her precious box of coloured buttons on the flagstones and now he was robbed of his bladder and was lying there like a dead fox on a dung-heap. In the branches overhead the little birds were as dispirited as she was and they peered down at the little man and they fetched their inquisitive eyes from the left to the right above him. Then Darkie remembered the sweets that Norrie had given her and she took them out of her bib-pocket and she threw them at her brothers: 'Ye're good for nothing, that's what ye are – like a pair of wild dogs. Here – take the sweets and go to hell,' she said.

They raised a shout and were about to go off with the bladder and the sweets when Golly noticed Teddy's brown sandals: 'What need has The Little Englander for these leather sandals when none of us ever get to wear such fine things?' said he. They ripped off Teddy's precious sandals. They threw them up into the overhanging branches. Worse might have followed if The Devil had had his way, for Sweeney took one look at Teddy's expensive trousers ('not even the priest has such fine things') and he was tempted to drag them off of him. He gave Golly a nudge and he whispered in his ear: 'While we're chastising The Little Englander, let's pull down his britches – let's show Darkie his private credentials – let's use the penknife to cut off his precious bits and feed them to the cat.' This heinous idea produced a bout of loud guffawing from Golly and he almost choked with malicious laughter. Teddy would have fainted and died on the spot had he heard what they and their whispers were half-planning for him and Jesus himself looked down from the clouds and he wept.

## His Life Had Flown From His Body

With the loss of his bladder and his sandals the little man felt as though his life had gone clean out of his body (like the pig). He couldn't understand the meaning of it. He had known only love's abundance from Dowager and Blue-eyed Jack. He had always been able to bury his head in his grandmother's black apron at the slightest fear (even his fear of the sow and the gander). He had always been able to snuggle up to Blue-eyed Jack in the bed at night, with his tiny feet tucked safely between the big man's legs. But now there was no guardian angel to come to The Bull-Paddock and rescue him and all the woodland fairies and the river fairies seemed to have fled far away from him and they were all much too distraught to stay with him and witness such a dark and terrible attack on him. Where on earth was his beloved grandmother? Where on earth was Blue-eyed Jack?

## Away Flew The Joyful Miscreants

Sweeney and Golly raced away with the bag of sweets and the stolen bladder. They reached Mikey's gate and they turned in towards his hayshed and they tied the bladder in under the roof to the topmost metal stanchion so it wouldn't run away from them. But they had no use for it now. All that they had wanted was to take it away from this foreign child with the fine clothes, from the child who had bravely held out his pan for the pig's blood. But next day when their cruel deeds would be known the length and breadth of The Open Road, nobody would want to have anything to do with the pair of them or their stolen bladder. As far as anyone cared it could stay glued to the hayshed until it withered away with as many wrinkles on it as an old woman's jaw.

From his upstairs bedroom window Mikey spotted Sweeney and Golly. He saw what they were doing with Teddy's bladder. He knew the way the little man had bravely held out his pan and how Blue-eyed Jack had given him the bladder for all his hard work at the killing of Rambling Jack's pig. He was about to empty from the upstairs window the double contents of his piss-pot when a cute little thought – a very good little thought – came into his wily old head. The two rascally children were making their way back from the hayshed. They were passing beneath his window when he emptied the foul contents of his piss-pot down on top of their heads and sent them squealing from his yard. They were covered in filth and soaked to the skin and crying blue murder against him and his race.

They hurried to their sanctuary in the grove. They sat down in misery on the fallen tree where they felt very sorry for themselves. They finally began to calm down and a certain amount of reason and common sense started to creep back into their heads. In spite of themselves they were too ashamed to smoke their stolen fag-butts and they felt they couldn't go home to their mother. Then they hid their heads in their hands and they bowed down low and kept saying to one another, 'What have we done? What on earth have the two of us done?'

## Little Darkie Proves Her Worth

Meanwhile Darkie threw rocks up at the branches until her arm began to ache. She finally retrieved Teddy's sandals and she helped the dazed child put them on. With the corner of her bib she wiped away the tears from his eyes and cheeks. From the scrape of bushes under the oak-tree she took out his treasured berries and with these she tried to drag him up from the deep well of his sadness. She selected some of the better berries and she helped him make ditches for his pretend farm and she made four fields out of the mud for him. She places some satiny leaves inside each of Teddy's fields for his grass and slowly (so very slowly at first) he placed his berries into each of his fields – the horse into one and the asses into another and the cows into another and the sheep into another.

## Blue-Eyed Jack At John's Gate

Blue–eyed Jack had been to the creamery with the fresh milk and had returned to Dowager with the butter and the skimmed milk for his calves. He brought down Moll-the-mare as far as John's Gate and he took the winkers off of her. As usual he whispered into her ear, 'You're the best mare in the whole of Ireland, that's what you are,' and he let her loose to run in through the gate and out onto The Bull-Paddock.

It was then that he saw Darkie. He saw Teddy too. The little man looked up at the speeding hooves of Moll-the-mare as she passed him by and he saw his uncle coming in through John's Gate. Here lay his safety. Here lay his kindness and he ran towards the big man. His heart was nearly bursting in his chest and another river of tears began running down the sides of his nose. Darkie ran after him and she dragged Blue-eyed Jack by the hand towards the oak-tree where he could see that the bladder and the twine were gone. In a volley of words the little girl's story unfolded: about Golly and Sweeney: about the penknife: about the fierce way they had robbed Teddy of the bladder: about the taking of the sandals: about throwing them up into the overhanging branches.

Blue-eyed Jack put his hands to his ears. 'Stop! Stop!" he cried. Then he let out a terrible roar that must have frightened even Jesus above in his heaven. He picked up Teddy and he cradled him in his arms. He could hear the little man's heart thumping inside in his shirt: 'What a fool I have been! What a complete and utter bleddy fool I have been! In God's holy name, why, oh why, wasn't I here when I was needed the most?'

## Rage, Pure Rage

He went marching up the road and he rushed into The Welcoming Room and without so much as a look at his startled mother (and leaving Darkie to inform her of the desperate deeds done to Teddy) he took his ash-plant from behind the half-door, spilling half the bucket of water in his angry haste.

From their hiding-place in Mikey's grove Sweeney and Golly saw him storming up the road. They didn't dare show their faces but ran across The Thistle Field and hid themselves on top of the turf in the turf-shed where they felt safe from his anger and his ash-plant.

If the half-door had been closed Blue-eyed Jack would have kicked it in off of its hinges as he marched in upon the startled Fiddler Joe. The quiet man had never before seen him in such a towering rage. Blue-eyed Jack told him of the wickedness of Sweeney and Golly and how they had defiled his little nephew and how the little child had no means of defending himself against the likes of them: 'Either you whip the arses off of them or I'll do it myself here on this floor for you!' he roared.

Fiddler Joe went to the bedroom and he brought back the razor-strap. He went to the turf-shed where he found the two miscreants, still soaked with the contents of Mikey's piss-pot. He marched them down to the yard-stream and he stood them in the middle of it as though some sort of ceremony was about to take place. It had always been the same in Rookery Rally (the stream and the punishment) when dark deeds needed to be addressed. There and then he laid into them with the relish of his razor-strap and he mercilessly chastised their legs till drops of blood ran down into the water and the two children felt they were within an inch of their lives. At each stroke he cried: 'That'll teach ye! That'll teach ye! That'll knock the devil out of ye!' He threatened then with The Guards' Prison Cell at Abbey Cross. He threatened them with the schoolmaster, Dang-the-skin-of-it. He threatened them with the curses Father Accessible could bring down on their heads, turning them into swine if they ever again raised their hands against Teddy. Their earlier howls of laughter that had echoed off of Mikey's hayshed when Teddy was washing his teeth in Darkie's poolie, were now replaced with howls of anguish ('Oh father, father! please please stop!') as they begged for forgiveness and mercy, until the exhausted Fiddler Joe's shaving-strap finally ceased its work.

# Time, The Great Healer

But even the wounds of childhood are mended in the course of time. A few weeks later the welts on their legs would heal. The hurt inside Teddy would start to mend itself and disappear. The sun would blaze again. It would come in through the windows of The Big Cave Room where the little man slept. The sky would turn cloudless and blue. Peace would slowly return and old friendships would be renewed. Dowager and Smiling Babs would have an earnest and sensible discussion, as women do. Teddy's fine new clothes would be put back tactfully into the suitcase and left there forever. Dowager would go down to Lady Elegance and bring Teddy back a big bowl of jelly and ice cream and be more than careful not to let the other children see what she was doing or start a row and bring a plague on her little man all over again. Teddy would eat it in the secrecy of Dowager's small bedroom and he would lie down beside her. Finally he would poke his nose out the half-door and dawdle around the yard before daring to set foot across the flagstones. He'd walk as far as the haggart and The African Sink outside the cowshed. He'd spend time staring at the cows' piss and dung and the cleaned-out straw that was in it. He'd stare at all that yellow and blue scum floating on its surface and for a while he'd feel as dirty as that. And yet (slowly but surely) he'd begin to feel peace returning to him out here in the haggart where no other child could bother him or ruin the simple thoughts in his head. He'd breathe in the stale odour of The African Sink and love the smell of it. Then he'd shiver out of his dreams and go back into the fireside and spend a while looking into the glowing embers burning in its heart and Blue-eyed Jack would smile across at him, even though his own heart was breaking in two and hurting him like hell.

It took a week for Fiddler Joe to calm down and be his good self once more. The following Sunday, even before the Mass was half-finished, he had a chance to examine his soul whilst he was kneeling on his cap at the back of the church. He came home and he stood outside his half-door. He called his children to him and they came in from the haggart (Sweeney and Golly too, unable to look their father in the eye). They sat in a row on the floor in front of him and crossed their legs and awaited his latest news. He went to the press-cupboard and he took down the bowl of dripping and he brought out his razor-strap from the bedroom. He covered both sides of it with thick lard. Then (as though it were a religious ceremony like giving out holy-communion) he passed it from hand to hand along the row of his children. Then he placed it in the middle of the flames and he watched it burn away in a mighty blaze: 'Ye can all go off and play now,' said he. Not another word was said from that day to this.

## *Forgiveness And Amends*

Sweeney and Golly felt they had finally been forgiven and they were anxious to make amends for their sin. That evening they walked the two miles over to Copperstone Hollow and into Black Sal's farmyard where her greyhound bitch had just delivered four small puppies. The weakest of these was in a box by the fire and Black Sal herself was nursing him with warm milk and a sop of bread. She listened to their sad news about the bladder and she shared in their shame. She handed them the box and the puppy and they carried it the two miles home. For the rest of the evening Fiddler Joe helped them feed it with sops of bread and milk and they made it comfortable with new straw.

Next morning Sweeney did not go back working for Lord Elegance but pleaded a cholic in his belly. Himself and Golly took courage in both their hands and they stepped down the road. With heads bowed low they entered Dowager's Welcoming Room and they placed the box and the newborn puppy on the floor. Teddy's eyes bulged at the sight of it. They asked Blue-eyed Jack if himself and Teddy would go with them to Rambling Jack and put the great hunter out of his misery with the gift of this tiny newborn greyhound. The big man leapt to his feet and he put his arms around the two recalcitrant boys: 'This is what I was praying for all night long. There's good and bad in each of us and God in his heaven sees it all and he knew that the two of ye would turn round a corner and help Rambling Jack get up out of his sick bed.'

Sweeney, Golly, Blue-eyed Jack and Teddy (he was still holding onto his uncle's hand) made a small procession up the hill and the sun turned almost scarlet in its joy. They reached Rambling Jack's yard and the two bigger boys gave Teddy the box and they let him tiptoe into Rambling Jack's Welcoming

Room with it. The hunter was snoring soundly in his bed. Teddy went in the bedroom door and he placed the puppy on the floor and Blue-eyed Jack followed him in with a few fistfuls of hay. Himself and his little man made the puppy comfortable in the hay and they placed some milk and some bran-mash beside him and then they tiptoed out again.

After that, the sun poured its light in through Rambling Jack's bedroom window and he woke up and blinked the sleep out of his eyes. His room was hot and it was bright and it was as though an angel's footsteps had passed across the floor and out through the walls. Was he dreaming? Had an angel really been here? He gazed at the little puppy and his heart began to race all over his body. 'I will call you Lightning,' said he. 'That's what I will call you.' And before the hour was up the whole of Rookery Rally heard him chopping his firewood at the woodpile and soon great balls of smoke were rising up into the sky from his chimney.

Big Tall Paddy brought Teddy a small hurley-stick with two metal hoops on it. He had shaved it with the plane until it was smooth enough to hold and he'd given it a coat or two of varnish. From now on the hurley-stick would walk with the little man whenever he went with Blue-eyed Jack to fetch the cows; he did not take it with him when playing with the other children for fear it would start another war. Mikey brought him up a penny-go-cart and put a few dabs of paint on it – blue and green and red. It had a longer string on it than the bladder's twine and it could never be destroyed by the bushes or the briars. Up and down The Welcoming Room the little man pulled his cart. He took it down the length of the yard and the ducks followed behind him in a line. As with the hurley-stick, he was not allowed to take the penny-go-cart with him when (peace now being restored) he was playing up the road with the other children.

In the meantime Smiling Babs' children would return once more to Mikey's grove. They would sit on the fallen tree and put smoke to the heavens from the fag-butts stolen from Fiddler Joe. Gallant and Bucko would take Teddy to the spring-well and show him the spider-web patterns and they would try to sketch them for him on the back of their fag-packets. In one way or another all the children would coax Teddy out of the final stages of his misery and sadness. They'd bring him the rusty rim of Shy Dennis's disused creamery tank (it was better than Gentility's rusty one) and they'd take him up to Sheep's Cross. From there they'd teach him how to bowl it all the way down to the metal bridge. With all these gifts (the hurley-stick, the penny-go-cart and the bowlee-wheel) childhood happiness would finally win out the day for The Little Englander. The angels would return from on high. They would dance their way back into his heart and into the hearts of Sweeney and Golly. The Devil would depart with his tail between his legs. He'd have to look for new highways and new pastimes. Here in Rookery Rally he had been totally vanquished. He had been utterly diminished and destroyed. Enough said.

TEN

# The Day Of The Swimming

*When Teddy went swimming in Growl River*
*beneath The Mighty Mountain*
*and when Patches saw the underworld.*

It was getting towards the end of September in this year of 1944. As soon as the hay was saved and the oats and barley were thrashed men had time on their hands. To celebrate the hard work they'd been doing they would meet on a bright September Sunday above at Sheep's Cross. It was the same every year as far back as anyone could remember. With a little army of boys following in their wake and each of them with a towel wrapped around his shoulders they'd make their way into the hills and hurry to their favourite resort, the great big Sally-Hole, where they'd be sure to get a few good lung-fuls of clean mountainy air (said Fiddler Joe to himself as he reached for his towel).

The Sally-Hole lay on the hidden curves of Growl River, a river that made its way through Bog Boundless and on to The Mighty Shannon River that was twelve miles away in Limerick. It was on the outskirts of our own known world and it was hidden from the eyes of man and beast alike. You wouldn't see a single soul out there except for one or two remote turf-gatherers like Bill-the-Herd and Joe Solitary. In the eyes of everyone the unreal beauty of this tranquil spot outshone even the bishop's palace across in Clare.

'It's a mile from the start of Obscurity,' said Dowager and it's half-ways to Eternity.'

'Ah, it's you that have the great big rocks of words,' Blue-eyed Jack said, laughing across the firelight at his mother and her usual fanciful way of saying things. Dowager gave him a shake of her head and she stopped poking at the fire: 'The two eagles above on The Mighty Mountain,' said she, 'don't even know where this sally-hole is and it's an awful pity that they haven't got wind of it or they'd come swooping down and snatch away bold boys like Sweeney with his recent bouts of roguery and make a tidy little meal out of him.'

## Holiday Hearts For One And All

This was a day for holiday hearts and light laughter, a day for our men to try their hand at swimming and show off their fine strokes in the water. But there was always a practical purpose to such an outing: it was the one day in the year for them to give their bodies a full washing from head to toe and make ample use of the foamy bars of carbolic soap: it was the one day when they felt they were being baptised all over again and young Patches couldn't help shuddering when he recalled his recent far-from-light-hearted baptism below in the river.

For Teddy it was going to be another day of intense excitement. As soon as he realised where he and Blue-eyed Jack were going, he threw himself out from under the blankets and his heart was as light as a butterfly's wings. It was earlier than usual for him to be hopping around in The Big Cave Room – so early that the cockerel (Rampant) hadn't yet stepped out to salute the yard. Nor had the sunlight filtered its rays in over Dowager's geraniums to turn them from red to pink. Blue-eyed Jack looked down at his nephew and he smiled at him. With a sigh of relief he saw that the little fellow had retrieved most of his former happy smiles and had almost (but not quite) forgotten his recent savage treatment below in The Bull-Paddock. The journey to the sally-hole would do him a power of good; it would remind him of those glorious days when he'd gone off with Dowager to greet Mother Nature and visit Gentility. The child would come face to face with the roaring majesty of Growl River and see it snarling its way passed the foot of The Mighty Mountain. Always the teacher, the big man would point out to him the many scenic wonders on their journey. He'd make sure that he felt the presence of those wilderness spirits who had roamed these banks since time immemorial.

## The Open Road Was Calling To Them

The two-men-of-us hurried through their Blessing prayers and they sprinkled each other with the holywater. Dowager got Teddy his corduroy britches (he'd never again have to wear those rich grey flannel ones) and she helped him into them. She placed two hard-boiled eggs in Blue-eyed Jack's fists and he put them into his pocket. Her two men were ready for the road. She smiled proudly at them and they gave her their last salute. They turned on their heel across the flagstones and the crystal stream and they never looked back.

When they reached Sheep's Cross, they were greeted with: 'How's the Little Englander today?' The crowd was as noisy as The Pig and Cattle Fair Days or the congestion at the creamery gates when the monthly money was being paid to the men for their cream. Sheep's Cross was a good spot to be getting together for this day's great big outing; it was where their parents used to hold their crossroad dances when the farmers came back from the harvest-time mill – where the only music ever heard was Handsome Johnnie's concertina and the button-box of Hammer-the-Smith's father (Philly) and the paper-and-comb polkas played from inside Shy Dennis's ditch by The Shy Scissors Sisters ('Don't ye be looking at us – we're too shy!').

## The Procession Went Out Passed Hammer-The-Smith's

At a goodly pace the men went out passed the side of Hammer-the-Smith's forge. They held their heads high and self-importantly as if they were a crowd of Wran Boys going off to catch the little wren that had betrayed Jesus while he was praying in The Garden of Gethsemane. Up at the head of the procession was Lord-to-God and Simon-not-so-Simple as well as Split-the-Wind. These three (like the rest of us) had their own peculiar gifts, which compared favourably with men long vanished from Rookery Rally. Lord-to-God was a short man and his face was covered in freckles and he was fat and bald-headed. It was rumoured that he had webbed feet on him like a drake. The children couldn't wait to get a glimpse of these feet of his as soon as the good man took off his britches. Simon-not-so-simple was as thin as a rake but it was said that he had a pair of monumental legs on him with calf-muscles as swollen as a pair of mutton chops. This too the children were very anxious to clap their eyes on. As for Split-the-wind, he had what some said was the greatest gift of all. He had just recovered from an operation on his bowels inside in The Roaring Town Hospital and some of the children had already witnessed his new and charming gift. These days he was back to his normal old self and as fit as a fiddle and he found he could emit the most captivating music out of his bum. The old rascal could make squeaky mouse-like noises. He could make long-drawn-out trumpet noises. And all the time he'd be looking around him as though he was wondering where on earth the sound was coming from. He would pause for a few tantalising seconds and keep the children waiting in pure frustration and have them guessing ('Fart for us! Fart for us! Oh please please fart for us!') as to which of his musical notes he was going to make next. Indeed he was better than The Daffy-Duck Circus and before he finished his quaint performance he'd have everyone rolling around on the grass in pure fits of laughter. Finally he'd turn himself into a thinking statue and the expectant children would make themselves quieter than a church mouse. Then he'd put his hand up to his ear as though he was listening for the sound of some faraway train on its way up to Dublin. Then he would let out an enormous volley of thunder from the depths of his bum. 'Byze-oh-byze, that was a good one!' he'd say and the children would tear down the fields in a heap of head-over-heels abandonment. At their earliest opportunity they'd report the news of Split-the-Wind's extraordinary performance to their schoolmaster (Dang-the-skin-of-it) and this be-whiskered gentleman would hide his undignified face behind his blackboard and hold his aching sides in a scarcely-controlled bout of silent laughter.

## Boys At Their Swimming Strokes

Apart from the full washing and the scrubbing with the soap this day was a day for the children's attempts at learning to swim. Only one or two grown-ups could swim even a stroke, for the men in Rookery Rally were a pack of timid little lambs when it came to water and they rarely let a drop of it near their inner bodies. This was also true of the women, hardly any of whom went even into the shallows of nearby River Laughter and only dabbed their wetted fingers to their cheeks when they were hurrying out the door to Mass. Indeed they'd rather be hiding in the haggart or underneath the horse-and-cart than putting their toe into anything as cold and frightening as a river of fresh water.

Today, however, there was no time for the men to show such natural cowardliness of the river and they threw out their chests: 'By the living Lord,' said one to the other, 'we're not one bit afraid of you, Growl River' and they hid their fears from the boys and they told them about the big splashes they were going to make in The Sally-Hole and how they were going to quieten the very heart out of this great big river. 'Let the frightened women busy themselves with their cake-baking and their knitting needles,' they said, 'and let the little girls stay at home and play on the ass-and-car with their coloured buttons and their daisy-chains'. All the children (even Sweeney) believed that they were about to learn at least one or two good strokes of swimming from the men before the day was over.

## They Reached The Wild Moorland

The adventurous bathers quickly reached the flanks of The Hills-of-The-Past and went clambering on towards The Wild Moorland where nothing but black cattle and wild ponies grazed, the grass being too rough for the likes of our own cows. The warm sun was now beaming and splintering its bright rays down on them and the sky was unbelievably blue with but the gentlest of breezes and a few ribbed clouds that were already bound for those faraway places out passed Galway and Mayo. They soon found themselves hemmed in by twisted furze bushes and grasping hawthorn shrubs as the road curved itself on towards the great river and at last narrowed itself down into a ribbon until it finally became a horse-dung laneway.

For a good stretch of the journey Blue-eyed Jack carried Teddy on his shoulders. But as soon as he got the pins and needles in his arms he put him down and he let him ramble on ahead with the rest of the children. The little man had never been so far away from Dowager and his eyes kept darting from left to right and all around him. He could see the cascades of honeysuckle. He could see the foxgloves and blackberry bushes and the wild ponies and black cattle. They were all new both to himself and the other smaller children, who also kept staring around them in awe and wonder. They seemed to be travelling outside of themselves (as if out of their very skins) for they were journeying to the mystical Bog Boundless that encircled their known world of Rookery Rally.

The hearts of the men were by this time full of delight and they were anxious to get to The Sally-Hole as quickly as possible and get their toes into its shallows and then venture out into the deeper water. The children had to run fast to keep up with them and they hadn't time to waste in collecting blueberries and crabapples. Crossing the brow of the last hill, they came to The Stepping Stones where the lane had eroded into no more than a yellow scar and was just an overgrown gully with a few worn-out briars and withered trees trying to grab them and choke off their way.

Blue-eyed Jack was again carrying Teddy on his back and next to the little man was his young friend (Little Cull), sitting royally on the shoulders of his father (Fiddler Joe). The two happy-faced four-year-olds were as excited as calves to be seen perched up so high at the end of this long and momentous journey. They kept turning round to see the disappearing fields and the last of the cattle and ponies. The bigger boys (Sweeney as ever in the lead) couldn't be stopped from running blindly down the final slopes towards the bank of the river: 'Come back, ye little fairy-men, or ye'll get yeerselves drowned,' yelled Red Scissors racing after them. But these boys were full of their own exuberance and they paid not the slightest bit of heed to him but flung their arms out wide as if to greet the majestic roars of this great river.

## Sweeney's Talent Would Shine Forth

And now some astonishing news reached the children. Sweeney, as soon as his legs had healed after his father's thrashing of him with the razor-strap, had spent the last couple of days trying to win back his good name in the eyes of the rest of The Open Road. Every afternoon he hid himself behind the bushes in the haggart and in secret he buried his head in the depths of a bucket of water and tried to pick out with his teeth the three-penny-bit that lay at the bottom of the bucket. And now (he boasted) he could accomplish this feat again and again with the utmost ease. You should have seen the cocky strut of the jaunty fellow! You could never keep his spirits down – that's the way he was. The eyes of the other children (especially Golly and Gallant) were like saucers when they heard this piece of wonderful news (what a great attraction he'd be!) and they couldn't wait to reach The Sally-Hole where their big brother would be the only boy able to dive down beneath the water. They felt like clapping him on the back and even the men were bursting with anticipation to witness Sweeney's fearless skills once they reached the river.

## *The Wild Growl River*

The bigger boys were already at the edge of the river. They looked down into the twinkling waters and they dared each other to touch the surface with their toes. It was achingly cold and it had the hurt of snow in it. The little ones followed along reverently behind them. They marveled at the great river's blustering hisses and its bellowing roars and they saw the purple heather coming down and brushing the river's edge. Behind the heather towered The Mighty Mountain itself, chiseled out by God, and it held sway like a mighty pyramid from ancient Egypt. Beneath it Growl River seemed to be introducing herself to these mere mortals as if to say, 'I'm a match for all of ye put together – come towards me and swim in me if any one of ye dare!'

With the little ones almost glued to their backs, the men crossed carefully over the stepping-stones. The children were sure they had reached Wonderland and were walking into an unforeseen dreamworld. Looking down from the men's high shoulders they saw the bright sunlight reflecting their bodies back up at them from the river's silvery water and its loose white pebbles. The bigger boys had crossed over onto the heather and (though the roars of the river stifled out their voices and you could barely hear their happy shouts) it was a glorious sight to see the way these merry half-men had struggled their way up onto the far bank like a flock of wild deer.

## Spare-Ribs, The Master-Swimmer

The only man, who could swim more than a few strokes, was Spare-Ribs and he was known to have the doggie-paddle off pat. He was reputed to have swum The River Tigris, no less, but then our men were known for their woeful tendency to exaggerate and tell lies for their hire, if they got half a chance. They had made up another story to follow this one and they said that Spare-Ribs had a few extra ribs to spare on both sides of his chest and that this was the reason his mother had given him his peculiar nickname. Up until now none of the children (not even Sweeney) had been given the chance to count these extra ribs of his and they were looking forward to him stripping off his clothes so that their fingers could have a feel of his ribs and count them one by one and bring back another report to Dang-the-skin-of-it – to go alongside the news of Split-the-Wind's farting backside. The tale of Spare-Ribs would be stranger than Split-the-Wind's and even better than their schoolbook story of old Adam and the ribs God had given him. There could be no argument against it: poor old Adam (they felt) would have been beaten hands down by Spare-Ribs when it came to the counting of the ribs, for the earth's first man hadn't a single spare rib on him and he even gave up one of his ribs so that God could put him to sleep and make the first woman (Eve) out of that rib. But not even Sweeney knew the real truth of the matter, which was that Spare-Ribs hadn't a single spare rib to his name and (if anything) he was extremely thin and spare in that department of his body for he was nearly always dying of the hunger and looking for a bite to eat.

## Matt-With-The-Machinery

Everyone knew that the best man at leaping from the top of High Rock into the ten-foot pool was going to be Matt-with-the-Machinery. He was a giant of a man (as tall as an elephant, said the older boys) and the younger children looked forward to seeing him landing down and disappearing under the water with a great big splash. If any man could terrify the life out of this fierce river, it would be Matt. However, it was for another far less salubrious reason (as yet unknown to any of the children) that Matt would prove himself the greatest attraction on this memorable day and even Split-the-Wind would have to take second place to him. The men knew that Matt was a very shy and innocent man. But they also knew that he had between his thighs the most enormous piece of machinery you ever laid your eyes on. On every other day of the year it was kept firmly concealed inside his britches. But today it would be the prime subject for discussion and envy: 'Our ass (The Lightning Whoor) would be proud to call it his own,' said Blue-eyed Jack to Stonemason Tim, who was next to him and still nursing his bruises after his tussle with Rambling Jack's pig. 'Good God-in-heaven,' said Tim, 'a man like Matt has the makings of a pure aristocrat,' and they both laughed and shook their heads.

When Sweeney (the devil that was in him) heard this outrageous piece of news he lewdly clamped a stick between his legs to demonstrate to the other children the size of Matt's machinery and the younger boys laughed nervously. Their expectations for the day had just risen higher than ever: 'Ah-ha!' said Red Scissors, 'the blessings of God this happy day be on Spare-ribs, our mighty swimmer, and on Matt with the great gift between his legs!'

## On Through The Willows

The group had all crossed over and they turned left through the willows, the men's eyes forever glued on the children in case one of them should fall into the rolling current and get himself carried off towards Limerick and out onto The Ocean. There was still a half-mile to walk before they reached The Sally-Hole but it was well worth the trudge for its water came up to a man's chest and even higher in some parts and it was the only spot deep enough to try out a few handy swimming strokes, even if they were made with one leg firmly fixed to the bottom of the pool.

## The Great Big Sally-Hole

They reached the glade with its soft grass around The Sally-Hole. The dappled sunlight poured its way through the leafy fingers of the few tall trees surrounding the pool and the translucent water was as bright as silver. The children's faces gleamed with pure excitement and they let out a unanimous sigh as the fairy breezes began whispering in their ears. No sheep, no bird or wild beast had ever found this place and no bough or twig or leaf had ever fallen into its clear waters. It was no wonder that our men for years back had always chosen this spot. It was full of magic. It was a piece of heaven's self.

The big men speedily undressed down to their skin and they threw their shirts and britches to the four winds. Some of them had pink flesh as soft as meat and others had flesh as white as cream and they all looked so delicately-coloured against the lush background of the green grass. The boys followed their example. Without a stitch on them there was a mischievous look in the eyes of one or two of the growing boys and they began to strut brazenly up and down the grass and to flex their imaginary muscles. What a belt of her yard-brush Smiling Babs would have given a few of her older children, could she have seen them now – and not a trace of modesty about them.

It was different with some of the men. They were giving the odd little nervous cough and grinning sheepishly and taking sly looks at the other men's bodies and peering down at their own curly-haired nakedness. Their memories went far back to those earlier years when they'd go and wash their bodies in River Laughter only to find that some of the more brazen women had taken their stealthy steps down through The Bog Wood to spy on their nakedness in a fit of sweaty lust. Since then they had become the coy little fellows when it came to stripping off their clothes and it was a thing unheard of to be doing this in front of their women even in the secrecy of the marriage bedroom. And even here in The Sally-Hole (where there wasn't a woman to be seen) a good few of them still felt that their very heart and soul were being exposed when they had no clothes to protect themselves with.

The children sat on the grass and they gazed at these new types of men with no shirts or britches on them. They blinked and they marveled at the mass of hair on the men's chests and in under their armpits and around their private credentials and they wondered would they themselves be as hairy as a bunch of old apes one day in the future. They could scarcely hold back their laughter at the sight of Matt as he stepped down to the edge of the river to test its coldness, but he had his hands clasped coyly around his precious piece of machinery and they never got the chance to see it – much to their disappointment.

The rest of the men followed Matt and they tiptoed gingerly through the broken twigs towards the edge of the pool and they timidly dipped their testing toes into the cold water. Then they went back a bit and they took a little run from the bank and then with a tremendous roar they jumped down into the pool, splashing one another to high heavens and pelting fountains of water into each other's eyes with their hands. The boys had never before seen the men so abandoned and excited – except at a hurling-match.

## Those Nervous Little Boys

Sweeney and the rest of the children had stopped strutting around and they stood shivering nervously and sheepishly on the bank. The men were beginning to relax and grow less fearful by the minute. They kept beckoning the boys to come down and join them but they were over-cautious and a bit too frightened to adventure passed the river's edge. To avoid being labeled cowards, however, the older boys sought out their own form of amusement and once again they paraded up and down the grass. They threw out their chests and they bent their knees and they lifted their legs into unusually comical and ungainly gestures. And then (isn't lewdness a fine thing?) they started to compare those more intimate areas of their bodies. Some were more developed than others in what they believed to be their manliness and Sweeney spread his legs and leaned back and he cried out, 'Matt! Matt! Come and have a look at this fine specimen!'

They pretended they were wild animals from out of their storybooks and they swung and cavorted on the nearby branches. Their shouts and antics made Teddy and Little Cull and the other younger ones (like Patches and Bucko) laugh themselves silly at all the fun that was going on. With gaining confidence and at a nod from Sweeney, the bigger boys rushed madly towards the pool and they plunged down into its tumbling waters and they pushed the heads of the startled men headlong down under the surface as though they were trying to drown the very life out of them.

## *Poor Patches And His Worries*

Following the earlier baptism that Sweeney and Golly had given him under
the metal bridge, Patches was in no mood to take off his shirt and britches
and he remained a little way off on his own. Bucko came and took Teddy
and Little Cull by the hands and he led them to the sandy shallows just
below the pool itself. The watchful eyes of Blue-eyed Jack and Fiddler Joe
were constantly on the three of them like a couple of hens with their chicks.
At first the children were like young cats caught out in the rain and their
toes were achingly cold and the white stones were as sharp as needles under
Teddy's unhardened feet. As the water crept up into all the corners of their
goose-pimply skin they shuddered and they screamed but they soon got
used to its smoothness. Tentatively they stepped further and further in from
the side of the river and the water reached their kneecaps and finally they
ventured almost waist-deep towards the centre of the pool and the water
began to feel warm on their bellies and it was the most wonderful time that
Bucko, Little Cull and Teddy could ever remember.

## *What Fine Swimmers!*

The day began to belong to the children, especially the older ones. What
fine swimmers they thought they were! They made their way slowly along
the shallower side of the pool with one leg glued firmly to the bottom of
the pool and the other leg floating aimlessly behind them like a young frog.
Oh, the roguery of these little liars as they tried to impress themselves upon
the men. They thought that nobody could see beneath the surface of the
water to know if they were swimming or not. Scoundrels like Sweeney
thought that they'd fooled even Spare-Ribs into believing they were a new
breed of swimmers with this doggy-paddle display of theirs and they
continued to thrust their arms out in front of their raised chins the way they
saw the great swimmer himself doing. The men smiled and they shook their
heads. 'Isn't nature a wonderful thing?' they mused, for they had used the
very same piece of deceit and chicanery when they were young and they
sighed and applauded the swimming efforts made by the children and they

praised them for the excellent style of their swimming strokes. So intent were the boys on making these sly little hops up and down on their fixed leg that they forgot to count the ribs of Spare-Ribs.

The day ticked along pleasantly like a melody and you'd love to see the twitching bodies of Teddy and his little friends jumping up and down in the shallow stretches. You'd laugh your sides off to see Sweeney and the others running up onto the bank and then tearing back and charging into the water in an attempt to unsettle the men and knock them down all over again. There were enough shouts to frighten the sky and the clouds, as the startled men fell in a pile under the surface of the river and then the heather shook with the curses rained down on the boys from the fallen men (aren't ye the little feckers?) and they were just like boys themselves and as playful as an armful of kittens. The two eagles above on The Mighty Mountain would never get a minute's peace at this rate.

## New Games

Then the men came up with a new game and like a herd of galloping horses they ran their races (full of spray and laughter) upstream against the current. From the barefooted days of their childhood they had feet on them as hard as leather and they put no heed in the sharp stones and they made an almighty racket with their legs. Bucko, Teddy and Little Cull started imitating the men. They plunged and pitched about in the shallower reaches and the men turned around and they laughed at them and then they went back to throwing themselves into the races against the might of the river.

The next hour passed along most pleasantly and the flushed faces of the bathers took away the dazzle from the glittering sun herself and so great was the excitement that one or two boys sat at the edge of the bank and they slyly christened the river with their warm stream of poolie. The men came and joined them and they sat side-by-side and they wallowed in the lapping shallows and their feet tore at the little pebbles like the pig in her sty. Sweeney was anxious to appear good-natured in the eyes of all, but he was still unsure if he had redeemed himself in the eyes of Teddy. Suddenly he knelt down underneath the water. He kept his eyes wide open and he looked back up at Teddy and the rest of them from beneath the surface and they marvelled at the bravery of him. Was Sweeney still a mere boy? Was he turning himself into a fish? Was he now a fairy-man in the eyes of Teddy, to be doing such a peculiar thing as this? Wishing to go one better and having everyone's attention Sweeney took to doing handstands in the middle of the pool and the children now realised that he had been completely bewitched by the spirits of the river. The bewildered Red Scissors was left scratching his head and was the first to speak: 'Did ye ever see the likes of Sweeney? Look at him and he upside-down and his head nowhere to be seen and he wriggling his skinny legs around in the air like a young pig that won't enter the cart on Market Day'. Even Spare-Ribs had to stop and stare in wonder at Sweeney.

## Into The Deep Waters

After their refreshing rest from their river races and the time spent watching Sweeney's grand show, the men made their way to the centre of The Sally-Hole where the water was as high as their chests. The children looked on in awe as these hairy horses bobbed up and down like a load of floating corks. The three little ones would have loved to follow them but Blue-eyed Jack and Fiddler Joe shook their heads and told them to keep away from this dangerous part of the pool in case they got drowned and taken off by the angels. And what would poor Dowager and Smiling Babs do then? On the far bank there was the overhanging ledge (High Rock) and though it was a temptation for Sweeney, Golly and Gallant to climb it, not one of them (not even Sweeney) had the courage to go up and jump out into the ten-foot hole that lay beneath it. The men were totally fearless by now and they climbed onto the rock and they held their noses with one hand and they shyly cupped their other hand between their legs. There was an expectant pause like the frustrating one that Split-the-Wind had made and then with a sudden rush and a roar out of them the men and their crane-legs leaped all together into space and they landed (*Splash!*) in the middle of the pool.

What an unmerciful sight it was to see their heads coming back to the surface a second or two later! The children sighed with relief to see that their men were not dead and the renewed laughter of everyone filled the glades and the men couldn't wait to climb back onto High Rock and start all over again. And now (what every child was waiting for) Matt himself scaled to the rock's highest peak. He turned away his shy body and he walked back a short distance from the rest of the men and he rocked on his front heel for a second or two and prepared to make his long run. Suddenly and with the legs of a speeding greyhound (as once were poor Zippity's), he raced out across High Rock and (clasping his right knee up to his bent chin) he sailed through the air. You'd think he was a German plane flying in from the big war as he sliced through the glassy sheet of water with the splash of a great big hippopotamus. He almost drowned the rest of the swimmers with the towering waves his body made and the children wondered if there'd be a drop of water left in Growl River, were he to go back and do this jump a second time. What a noble baptism he had given them all!

Matt stayed down under the water for what seemed an eternity and the seconds passed by. The children grew frightened and they thought that the poor man had gone and drowned himself and they'd have to bury him like Father Chasible. Patches was seen to be crying wholeheartedly and then ('Ah-ha! mee brave byze!') up came Matt with the roar of a bull. His hair was plastered to his head like black satin and the water was running out of his ears and nose. What with all the excitement of Matt's great leap, Teddy, Cull and Bucko had the misfortune not to have taken even a tiny peek at the famed machinery between Matt's thighs. The giant was no longer his shy self and he chased all the older boys across the pool and he even waded down as far as the little one: 'Ye are not properly baptised yet,' he roared with a wink at Blue-eyed Jack. 'Didn't Jesus throw himself headlong into the depths of the river when his cousin was giving him the holy treatment?' He carried Bucko and Little Cull on his back and he jogged up and down the river with them. Blue-eyed Jack got into the fun of things and did the same with Teddy. You should have heard the shrieks out of these children as their laughter got mixed up with their tears each time Matt threatened to throw them into the deepest part of the pool and submerge them for a new and hilarious christening. It was all in good sport, for this harmless man had the heart of a child and he would never have subjected them to such a cruel atrocity.

## The Challenge

Not to be outshone by Matt's merriment, Spare-Ribs challenged him and the rest of them to see which of them would remain under the water for the longest amount of time. Matt and the other men took up the great swimmer's challenge and Sweeney joined in the fun and they all went down under the water. Once more the seconds ticked by and Teddy and the younger children wondered if the divers would ever come back to earth or had hell swallowed them all forever. In the end it was Spare-Ribs who stayed down the longest and won the laurels of the day. The outing had turned into a pure festival and nobody had ever before had such an outing as this one.

## The Frothy Carbolic Soap

It was time now for the men to bring down the half-dozen bars of carbolic soap and they began pelting the slippery bars across The Sally-Hole, trying to hit one another in the jaw and knock each other down. The women below in Rookery Rally must have heard the fierce curses (feck, feck and feck again) pouring out of them when the soap slipped through their fingers and they had to duck down under the water to catch it before it ran away on them. Once more everyone was steeped in laughter,

The time came for the earnest scrubbing of the children as requested by the women. In the evening when they got home, there'd be a full inspection and, if they weren't as clean as new babies, Smiling Babs' brood would find themselves once more the victims of a sound leathering with her yard-brush. For a while all the laughter stopped as each sad child prepared for the worst. The men marshalled them to the lower end of the pool where the water came gushing out of a shadowy rock and they got down to the serious business of the washing. They paid particular attention to the back of the children's necks and the insides of their ears. They gave their hair a right good lathering, soaping it all over in case of the head lice; for these little nippers were known to be experts at hopping from head to head in Dang-the-skin-of it's school-house.

Getting themselves fiercely scrubbed like this was taking a good bit of the fun out of the children's day and they quickly got tired of the men turning and twisting them about as though they were a few sops of hay. Even the little ones had a bit of pride left in themselves and they took the soap from the men and they began washing themselves under the arms and around the top of their legs. They tended especially to the bits of cow-dung that might still be ingrained behind their knees throughout the year. Finally they held their noses (for by now they were able to do this, like the men) and they ducked their heads down into the pool and they washed off the soapy suds from their bodies. When they came back up with their hair streaming and the water trickling and glistening down their sides, it was indeed as though they had been baptised like their blessed Saviour. They shook themselves the way dogs did when getting out of a river and they clapped each other on the back for being so brave. The men gave them a final look-over and they nodded to one another in satisfaction: every child was as clean as a new priest or nun.

# A Peaceful Lull

There came a lull and a calmness to the day, almost a delirium. The men, who had washed the boys so vigorously with their rough hands, now stood motionless and awkwardly beside them. One or two of the more rascally ones pointed to the sky and they shielded their eyes as though they were earnestly trying to make out the outline of some imaginary eagle or a German airoplane hurrying their way from over The Mighty Mountain. The bigger boys were still little innocents at heart and they strained their own eyes and tried to get a glimpse of this new sighting. Suddenly the men grabbed them by their legs and knocked them crashing into the river. The boys, enraged at the unexpected unfairness of this, shattered the recent peace and quiet ('Go 'way ye pack of basthards!') with their roars of blasphemy. They fired the water into the men's eyes and the men fired the water back at the boys, sweeping the spray at them like a flat stone skimming the pool.

Then Sweeney and the rest stumbled out of the river, glad to get away from the men's clutches and they started running races through the rough ferns to dry themselves. Their feet were so fast that they made the ferns whistle and the breezes scurried along the bank after them and got into their ears and tickled the fur on their bellies. Some of the boys ventured further along the bank to reach the shadier side of the river and they sat on the boulders like wagtails and dangled their feet in the river. Others played higher and higher and they jumped over sticks stretched across the bushes. More played feet off ground and they ran up into the heather and they played hide-and-go-seek amid the peeping shadows. Then they rolled all over the grass and they dried the last of the water off of their bodies.

For the next half-hour they lay sprawled languorously beneath the sun and the reddening afternoon turned their skin a shadowy pink. It was one of the few languid and listless moments in their young lives. It was this one chance in the year to breathe into their lungs this profound silence and they purred inwardly, their hair trailing behind them in the grass. They closed their eyes and fell into a doze, lulled into a mood of serene enchantment by the fairies of this ancient place. And all the while the river and its distant sound (increasingly lively since Matt's mighty splash) traveled majestically onwards towards The Mighty Shannon River.

But such a seemingly endless moment of enrichment couldn't last forever and mad abandonment and caprice came out to play once more and it took a hold of their spirits. The mood of Sweeney and Golly and Gallant turned to lasciviousness and downright lewdness and they grabbed each other from behind and with the lust of young bulls they tried to squeeze the life out of each other's private credentials. And all along the bank you'd hear their delirious shouts ('Sweet suffering saints, aren't ye the dirty little whoors?'). But soon they were worn out and they lay down again and they laughed themselves silly till the tears rolled down their jaws and their sides were sore.

## Patches And Those Deadly River Fairies

Of all the bathers only Patches had refused to remove his shirt and take off his britches. With Bucko, Teddy and Little Cull he wandered dreamily down along the bank. Here the sunny river wound its way around a few small tree roots and tufts of vegetation and there were no sharp rocks to be seen. It was a shallow and seemingly harmless stretch of water and it made a sandy bank where it went into a smooth curve. The children's sharp eyes scanned the riverbed for new coloured stones to add to their collection of drawing stones back home and they bent down in the wet sand and with the palms of their hands they squashed out sandy ditches like they did with the mud and horse-dung at home. In a short while they had made a long ditch almost twenty feet from end to end and then they aimlessly tiptoed into the twinkling water.

Patches was having a great time of it, his toes clenching into the yellow sand and dashing to pieces the tiny crystal wavelets. Bucko added to the fun and made a spider-thin flaggard boat from the nearby rushes and he showed Patches how to sail it into the little wavelets from the creamy sides of the bank and watch it ride off on its journey over the white pebbles. The children made three more boats, one for each of them, and they sailed them out into the water where they slipped away into the current and disappeared down towards the stepping-stones. They were as happy as larks and they watched the brown trout, slippery-quick and smooth and with pale rings on them. The trout hung for a moment on the current and they gobbled up the water midges and then they hurried on, frightened by the presence of the boys. By now Patches had forgotten his earlier fears and he was getting braver by the minute. He rolled up his trousers above his knees and he paddled further in, ahead of the other three.

The afternoon's joy was too good to have lasted for suddenly (would they ever forget it?) Patches' feet slipped out from under him into a huge hole underneath his legs.

WHOOSH!

For a second the poor child disappeared from their view and was clean gone! Poor Patches! He had come out here for a day's recreation and fun (like everybody else) and he had stepped too far out into the middle of the river. The sand had been too soft and had given way underneath his feet. Down, down, down he sank and the water whirled around him and dragged at his body to claim his life if it could. Teddy and Cull and Bucko could see his wide staring eyes. They could see his legs floundering. They could see him up to his neck in the river. His face seemed to be bulging in sheer terror and then his hair was buried beneath the snarling surface of the river and all that could be seen were his two little arms thrashing wildly at the air (like the drowning pup that Slipperslapper had once thrown into River Laughter) and then he disappeared altogether and they could only see the splattering air-bubbles.

'Oh, Patches! Poor Patches! Will we ever see you again? Gone to an early grave before your time was up!' The wilderness fairies had heard the screams of the children and they called to the heavens for help and God in his goodness smiled down from the clouds and he stretched out his hands towards Patches. The children's screams had alarmed the men in the nearby pool, giving them not a second to think or blink. Running faster than the wind, Blue-eyed Jack sped through the air and his powerful arms were suddenly stretching out past the three terrified children as he threw himself into the middle of the river, scraping his feet on the underwater briars in his hurry to get to Patches and rescue him from Death. But Fiddler Joe had already reached the drowning child before he could get there. Patches was his son.

Would their little friend live or would he die? The bathers were all out of their minds with worry as they watched this mighty confrontation between Man and The River. With the strength of wild horses the two men broke the fierce spirit of the river-demons and they scraped up the drowning child into their arms – and a cartload of sand along with him! It was impossible to describe the chattery-teethed Patches and he in the very jaws of his death. The two men carried him out and up onto the bank and they shook him the way you would a rag and they shushed the little boys away and he lay there on the grass, outstretched like a corpse.

The trousers that the once-shy Patches had refused to take off were dragged unceremoniously from him along with his shirt. Fiddler Joe rinsed the sand out of them and he left them on a bush to dry. Bucko, Teddy and Little Cull sat huddled under the trees. Patches' lungs must have been saturated with gallons of water and maybe a gallon of sand and a few fishes too! They tried to laugh a little nervously to one another but it was no use. All three of them were sadder than a dead rabbit and they still believed that Patches was dead and gone from them and that he'd be buried like Father Chasible before the week was out and be covered up with the clay like him below in Abbey Acres.

## It Was A Pure Miracle

Miracles do happen and the saints and angels are often close at hand, for in a few minutes Patches got back a little of his strength. He was crying like a baby and he looked very frail. He was ashamed of not having been able to control the river like the rest of the children had done. He was ashamed at not having been able to avoid getting himself half-drowned. Without any clothes he sat there at the edge of the river and he shivered and he felt more mournful than ever in his short life and he was lost and alone with his thoughts in his own little world. He realised how near to death he had been and he was utterly afraid. He made his poolie silently into the river and at last he began to feel a little better.

The near-tragedy of Patches had taken the joy out of the day and had deprived the swimmers of their recent hilarity. They had no more heart for swimming and bathing. They murmured among themselves and they said what a terrible thing it was to have seen poor Patches almost drowned and to see him looking so wretched and sad in the middle of them.

## *But All Ends Well*

They made up their minds to put the heart back into him. Once more they clambered up the slippery rocks at the far side of the pool and together they jumped down into the deep pool and they sent splashes to the heavens in imitation of Matt.

The next minute Bucko's two eyes were bulging inside in his head and he nudged Patches and Teddy and he pointed up at High Rock: 'Will ye look at Matt!' And then the tear-stained Patches saw Matt looking down at them. The giant lifted up his mighty arms and his chest puffed out like a pig's bladder as he got ready for his final big splash of the day. Like Bucko, Patches' own eyes went spinning around like saucers as at last he beheld the great big size of Matt's famous machinery. To the joy of everyone he found himself laughing out loud and he couldn't wait to get home and tell Smiling Babs of the enormity of Matt's great big machinery.

The day of the swimming had come to an end. The children (including Patches) sat on the bank and they watched the men racing each other through the ferns like a crowd of schoolchildren. They watched the older boys (oh, how they'd like to be men themselves!) challenging the big men to the races and the wrestling bouts. The good–natured men ('We're not too old to trounce ye at the races or the wrestling bouts') were full of the fun of it. Like Lazarus, Patches had finally been restored to life and everything was sunshiny once more. The men were exhausted from all the day's sport and they flopped down on the grass and they lit their pipes and their eyes twinkled inside the smoke. The lovely smell of the tobacco filled the children's mouths and noses as the men spat down into the river. Their talk was as delicious as a ripe apple and for once in their lives the fairies of the river and moorland were outdone and the men and boys had become the new hobgoblins.

At length ('Well, byze, 'tis sad to be leaving the river') they put on their clothes and with the swish of their wellingtons they returned through the long heather to the stepping-stones. Once more the men carried the little ones on their shoulders. It was goodbye to Bog Boundless and The Mighty Mountain, soon to be hidden in clouds. It was goodbye to the pearly waters of Growl River and the lonely Sally-Hole, with the echoes of their laughter and shouts now gone from it. It had been one day in a lifetime and the men, weary as they now were, felt better than getting drunk below in Curl 'n' Stripes' drinking-shop. They tramped up once more and out onto The Bog Road and the fissure of the rocks near Joe Solitary's cosy nest and Tracey's Sandpit. They'd soon be down into The Hills-of-The-Past.

Everyone was ravenous with the hunger and in the hedges the children went hunting for crabapples, unripe sloes, blackberries (never mind the white maggots!) and wild strawberries. Their world was dyed with the redness of evening and the sun in her final moments was preparing herself for twilight. The evening chill was about to come on and the day would soon fade away from them.

'It's been a picture-book of a day,' said Blue-eyed Jack to himself as he looked down fondly at Teddy. There was a peaceful intimacy between them all as they strolled on. A little sadness, however, had crept into them too. They knew they were no longer in the dreams of Fairyland. They had become their own selves once more. Except for the mournful cry of the cuirlew, there was silence. There was stillness. Nobody spoke (just their reveries) and the day was frozen timelessly in their minds like an old brown photograph.

Teddy couldn't wait to get back to Dowager and tell her the tale of the day – how Patches had nearly got himself drowned and had swallowed a dozen fishes and how he himself had seen the two eagles flying around The

Mighty Mountain and their wings as big as houses (the little liar!). Oh, how Dowager ('Ah-ha, mee two fine night-walkers!') would tussle his hair and turn her face away towards the fire to prevent being seen laughing and Teddy would be sure to report on Matt's famous machinery and Dowager ('That'll do, child!') would smile to herself, recalling a memory or two of her girlhood.

From that day onwards the summertime would fade from them all. They knew that, like The Past itself, they would never get this day back again. But they knew they'd be going to Growl River again next year and the following year after that. They knew they'd be going swimming all over again and they would thrash the mighty river with their laughter and their tears. Yes indeed they would! But one thing that none of them knew (not even Blue-eyed Jack and Dowager) was that by this time next year their Little Englander would be gone from them forever.

# ELEVEN

# *Lost*

*When Teddy and Little Cull
went to see The Mighty Mountain.*

It was Springtime in the year of 1945. The school holidays were over and the adventures of Teddy's new friends came to a halt. Five of them were already headed back to the school-house of Dang-the-skin-of-it and those who were even older (Norrie and Sweeney) were back earning a shilling again at the home of Lord Elegance. On the three-mile trek to the school-house the bigger boys marched the little ones reluctantly in front of them, prodding them ever onwards with their ash-plants ('get a move on, ye ashy pets, or else we'll be late') and on the journey they taught them how to recite their singsong Tables.

Teddy and Little Cull were four years old and they were still too young for this long walk to school. They found themselves lonely during the dull mornings. With no-one to play with, they were often left sighing over the lost excitement of summer's adventures in the rivers and the fields. How often had they been left straggling behind Darkie and the older deer-footed boys, especially when it came to climbing the highest trees or robbing the finest orchards. How often had the woodland fairies seen them with their palpitating hearts languishing in frustrated tears after they had given up the chase behind these bigger children! They were not as strong as the mighty Sweeney. They were not even as strong as the half-drowned Patches or Darkie in her cubby-shop. They weren't even strong enough to use the hurley-stick on Rampant the cockerel's head in an effort to kill him for taking a lump out of Red Scissors's neck. They weren't strong enough to frighten the fierce gander and send him and his flock out over the singletree and into the safety of Mikey's grove.

They had a growing sense of aimlessness (almost tedium) and without the magical inspiration of the older children they didn't know what they'd be doing from one day to the next. They looked at the once-noisy hens and these little creatures appeared to be sad like themselves and to have lost their acute interest in the life of the farmyard and the haggart. They looked at the geese and the ducks and these creatures seemed to be singing their shrill songs in a less cheerful manner too. They looked at the crows and these seemed to hover languorously above the rookery in Mikey's grove, not knowing whether to take themselves off to the cornfields or stay becalmed around The Open Road for the rest of the day.

For a while the two children were left scratching their heads and doing a great deal of thinking. Of course not one of the big people could guess what was lying in the back of their little minds. Teddy had seen the excitement of the recent pig-killing at Rambling Jack's shed, where he got himself the bladder that caused all the ructions with Sweeney and Golly. Little Cull (together with Patches) had seen the pig-killing at Simon-not-so-simple's a few weeks before that. They had both been into The Roaring Town and had witnessed the sale of the cattle at The Market Cross on The Fair Day and had been lucky enough to go down to Abbey Cross and watch the noble antics of the sportsmen and the telegraph-pole jugglers at the Daffy-Duck Circus. They had both been to look at the dead body of Father Chasible and attend his grave. But now there was nothing left for them to get excited about, at least not here within the bounds of Rookery Rally.

The thinking and the pondering went on a little while longer. The air in Little Cull's trees brought a few fresh breezes in around the back of the pig-house and sent the leaves trembling at the haggart singletree. Fairy spirits danced the morning away in the ditches and they began to whisper all sorts of nonsense into this little boy's ears. They seemed to be imploring him to look for something new to amuse himself with. 'There's so many hours in the day and so much you could be doing, Little Cull,' they whispered, 'and every day is moving away from you – faster and faster and faster. It's time you were on the move.'

## Teddy's Contemplation

While he was wisely contemplating these poetic thoughts, Teddy was wiping
the sleep from his eyes. Blue-eyed Jack and Dowager had gone down to
The Bull-Paddock to fetch the cows. The little man sloped over to the
window in The Big Cave Room and he saw that the daylight was on its way
in over the red geraniums. Those night-time clouds that had seemed to
increase his recent terrors and fears after the robbery of his bladder and
sandals, had fled at last from his dreams. He turned towards the broken-
glass window at the back of the bedroom, where the moody ass (The
Lightning Whoor) was already braying in at him bad-humouredly. He
spotted a little patch of pigeon blueness above the cowshed. It was coming
across from Corcoran's Well. It was time for him to rise up and go forth
and meet the great big world and give it his greeting once more. He
stretched his steps towards the half-door and he stepped out half-heartedly
into the cold-spirited morning. The sun had grown a little higher in the sky
and the flagstones would soon be sun-bleached. He felt an inexplicable
longing, which he had never felt before and he was much too young to
explain it. He shook himself free of his boredom and he hurried his feet
into the whispering breezes, which were already blowing one or two leaves
down from the tall autumn trees around the yard.

## Little Cull Starts His Day

Meanwhile Little Cull was subjecting himself to Fiddler Joe's rough
washing of his face, neck and hands. He had already said his Blessing prayers
with the help of Smiling Babs. He had leathered into his duck egg, dipping
the spoon of butter into it and circling the salt around in the yellow of it.
He was looking out the half-door at the upturned ass-and-car (his ivory
tower) where he often sat with Darkie and Norrie and examined the
beautiful painted court-cards. In the early morning light The Open Road
beyond the yard-stream seemed to shine silvery and it laughed and
beckoned to him. By now his thoughts were getting clearer: the laurel
bushes at the singletree leading to Mikey's grove (the holly bushes too)

sparkled and seemed to call out to him too: the ivy climbers at the haggart-stick joined in, hoping to welcome him out amongst their natural finery.

He was still unsure of these new impulses calling him to do something unusual. He sat in the clay near the yard-stream at his mother's gateway and with a twig he drew the image of what he believed his future school-house would look like. The only tall buildings he had ever seen were the church in Copperstone Hollow and the creamery at the fork of the Limerick Road. Surely a school-house was as big as either of these? He watched an old beetle rolling a ball of dung across the flagstones, just as in earlier days he had watched the golden-brown caterpillars crossing The Open Road at their dinnertime. If only he could be like his oldest brother Sweeney and find something exciting to do, like catching Timmy's tiger-barred cat and swinging it round and around by its tail and sending it sailing back over The Easy Stile. What great fun that would be!

He could smell Hammer-the-Smith's old tractor spluttering down the lane at Sheep's Cross. What must it be like to sit on a tractor with Hammer-the-Smith, he wondered. A crowd of buzzing flies followed the progress of the beetle and the ball of dung and the ants came out from their home in Darkie's tin mug and they joined in and darted around behind the flies.

A shadow appeared and loitered above him. It was his young friend, The Little Englander. He had left behind him his new white shirt and his grey britches and his brown sandals (all the fine clothes that had caused so much jealousy) and he dipped his bare feet in the waters of the yard-stream. Little Cull had long forgotten Teddy's anger when he had thrown the mug of Darkie's poolie all over him.

There were marked differences between the two of them: Teddy was somewhat on the frail and fragile side: Little Cull was round and sturdy-limbed: His skin was as brown as a berry and Teddy's skin was as pink as Blue-eyed Jack's potatoes: Teddy's hair was flaxen and his eyes were a robin's egg blue: Little Cull's hair was as black as a crow and his eyes were as dark as the laurel berries. And now the cold sunlight glistened on the new arrival's bald-patched curls and his presence was as fresh as a daisy. It banished the gloomy air around the little beetle-watcher and suddenly the sky (still a little grey and black) seemed to be blue and white.

## How Fine A Thing To Have A Visitor

Little Cull took a look at Teddy and Teddy took a look at Little Cull. How fine a thing it was to have a morning visitor! The Little Englander was carrying a purple bellflower that he'd plucked from the ditch of Dowager's garden. He handed it to Little Cull and the two of them walked down The Thistle Field. They slipped down the dyke and they placed it in the jam-jar on Darkie's cubby-house shelf. There was a moment's silence as they weighed up the need for adventures to enliven them. But neither child was sure of himself. They were still just two frail children – that's what they were – looking for the excitement of past days when the whole of Rookery Rally had seemed to heave with the happy faces of the older children.

They could see the gallant sun beginning to cross over Fort Dangerous. It might soon be blinding their eyes and scorching the flagstones. It was time to stop gazing after an old dung beetle or to be twig-drawing an imaginary school-house. It was time to stop musing about what might be done with the tail of Timmy's tiger-barred cat. They decided they'd give themselves up to higher thoughts, which would lift them away from the loneliness of this dull day. There was (and they knew it only too well) another side to life. Like The Sally-Hole, it lay far beyond Rookery Rally. It lay towards the mysterious purple hills, those awe-inspiring hills that rose to The Mighty Mountain and looked down on the glassy sparkle of The Mighty Shannon River. They could feel the call of the spirits telling them to get up on their hind legs and go seek this great big mountain and see what fine fun was to be had up on top of it.

## The Two Little Boys' Plans Take Shape

They would tell not a soul. For the first time in their lives they were listening to this deafening call: the call from another world. Children in bygone times had heard this same call. It would be the greatest adventure since sailors had sailed the seven seas. They remembered how much Sweeney and Norrie had bragged when they came back from The Mighty Mountain after braving the incredible bog-holes of Bog Boundless. That

264

unforgettable night the two ravenous wolves had eaten an entire apple batter and another half a rhubarb batter between them. They told the younger children how they had fought with the fierce unlicensed bulls beyond Growl River and how they had seen the bloodstained doors of Balaraggin, who had once cut his own throat for the love of his departed mother. They told how sailing across the dreamy skies they'd seen the two eagles that had their nest in a hollow cleft near the summit of The Mighty Mountain and could carry off a man and devour him in a single gulp! That's what they said (the little liars) and they had filled the younger children's heads with many unfulfilled dreams.

## But First A Bit Of Knavery

Before they set sail on their mighty adventure Teddy and Little Cull ventured on a bit of childish knavery, which would (they hoped) absolve them from any feelings of guilt they might be having. They collected two big bunches of bright wildflowers from Timmy's ditch and they filled out these fine nosegays with a few green dock-leaves. Little Cull handed his bunch of flowers in over the half-door to Smiling Babs, to add the finishing touches to her bedroom altar. 'What a wonderful child you are, to be thinking so dearly of your mother,' said she. ('What a rascally boy you are, to be planning an escapade into The Hills-of-The-Past,' said his guardian angel). Teddy ran home and he placed a similar bunch on Dowager's bedroom altar before she got herself back from The Bull-Paddock with Blue-eyed Jack. Then he raced up the road to start out on his great big adventure.

## What A Great Big Adventure It Would Be!

What fine tales of their travels the two of them would have to tell when they returned triumphant at the end of this day? Imagine the stunned face of Sweeney (such a big brave boy to have robbed Teddy of his bladder and his dignity) when the two of them returned home and shut his mouth for him with the wonder of their adventures! But they had another inquisitive little thought: just as the big men looked up at the stars and wondered how far away they might stretch, so the two of them wanted to know what were the depths of the mountains and who were the people who lived on these mountains and where did the eagles have their nest and what lay beyond The Valley of The Pig and what lay beyond The Valley of The Cattle and what was on the other side of The Mighty Mountain? Their heads were full of it.

'Why,' said Teddy, 'there must be more and more mountains.' They were old enough to realize that in the end they could go no further than Ireland, for they would come to The Ocean and that was the very end of the whole wide world. Bedad-sez-I was the most famous adventurer to have lived in Rookery Rally. He had known this very thing. They'd been told how he once walked out passed Galway and had his photograph taken in the stormy waves without a stitch of clothes to cover him and how these photos sold in their thousands all over Galway and how he came home and said, 'I'll die in a peaceful bed this blessed night – now that my two eyes have seen The Ocean'.

## The Call Of The Open Road

With yearning hearts they got ready for The Open Road. It stretched ahead of them towards the honey-brown hills. The winds were hushed at the sight of them and tried to give them Nature's first warning. 'Poor innocent children!' it whispered, 'Ye don't know what ye're doing. Take care, little ones! Take very great care!' Then the branches bowed down towards them and gave them a further warning. 'The Open Road is a place of many dangerous twists and turns,' they whispered. Then the little birds followed them out over the flagstones and they began to shriek their loudest chitter-chatter over their heads and they gave them yet one more warning. But the two adventurers paid not a blind bit of heed to any of these warnings: they had made up their minds and nothing was ever going to get in their way. And then the tattered clouds scudded away from the growing sun's heat and began to tell the news to each other – about the two impending adventurers and the great big journey their brave little hearts were contemplating.

'Coom on – blasht it! – let's be attacking these mountains,' said Teddy, imitating the only language he knew, that of the grown-up world. The two of them scampered out across the flagstones and (sadly) didn't give a thought to the worries anyone back home might have had over their whereabouts. They desired nothing else but to see all that Sweeney and Norrie had seen – the mystery of the hills and (above all) The Mighty Mountain – and if good fortune prevailed the haunted shack where Balaraggin had cut his throat and left the blood dripping in streaks down his green door. And if they were to believe Sweeney and Norrie, they would find themselves greeted by the fairies themselves, for the hills and the mountains were the realms of Fairyland. Any fool knew that.

## *Two Brave Boys Step Onwards Towards Sheep's Cross*

They turned their bare feet left and they headed in the direction of Sheep's Cross. It was as though they were two startled donkeys let loose as they galloped on towards Shy Dennis's Shack. They didn't give themselves a minute to look for wild strawberries or blackberries inside the prickly brambles (not that they'd find any at this time of the year). They would shortly get to know the first hills and beyond those hills they would get to know Bog Boundless and Growl River and beyond that they'd reach The Mighty Mountain.

It was getting on into the morning and Fatty-Matty's haycart had already gone chuckling down towards Abbey Cross to bring back a few trams of hay and his bag of sausages and black puddings. The rest of the ass-and-cars and their milk tanks would soon be on their way to the creamery gates in Copperstone Hollow. As yet no-one other than the hens and the sparrows in the turf-shed had seen the two of them stealing away and Dowager and Smiling Babs would only think they had gone off to play in the cubby-shop. They had never before ventured alone on their own as far as Sheep's Cross. But they'd be there soon enough and they would recognize the forge of Hammer-the-Smith where they had previously seen the shoeing of the ass and had admired the heat from his fiery furnace. At this stage there'd still be time to stop and think and to go back home if they wanted to.

They looked back to the right and they waved goodbye to Fort Dangerous and the laughing leprechauns who hammered nails into fairy shoes. Their feet stopped running and they began scuffing the stones in front of them. They were beginning to pant and puff as they rounded the bend. Smiling Babs' farm now lay far behind them. This was the first slope of many. At Missus Fidget's gate they came upon their first difficulty when they met up with her vicious little terrier standing in the middle of the road and ready to make a feast of their legs. They tiptoed passed the sharp-eyed beast, remembering how his rage had once caused him to bite Bucko's backside and draw his blood and give him and his so-called bravery a soaking wet britches. They were not tempted to look back at the dog.

They were at the crossroads, the place where Shy Dennis's dead mother had come back from the grave in her ass-and-car to collect her hat and cardigan to accompany her on her journey to the next world – The Beyond. Once more they tiptoed by and they never gave the shack a single look. The little breezes still scurried frantically after them from bush to bush and the little birds followed them too: 'Go back!' they continued to tweet. 'Go back, go back, ye little wobbledy-headed children,. Go on home!' Ahead of them a grey cloud sailed threateningly like some forlorn ship across the sun, its dark edges reddening as it drew near. By now they should have heeded the many warnings being planted inside their heads but (ah, the incautiousness of little boys) they thought they could roam through the great big world that lay beyond their safe paradise of Rookery Rally!

They had walked a good stretch by now. The sun was still low in the morning sky and they had yet to feel the full force of its noonday heat when there mightn't be a puff of air left for them to breathe. They were at the fork of the road where they had a difficult choice to make. A small bit of panic crept into them. For just a second it told them to run back home. To the left of them was the little donkey-lane, almost covered in briars, and they knew it was no use stepping down that way. The road ahead of them led on towards The Valley of The Hollows and to far-away Tipperary Town in the south. There would be no mountains to climb there. The road to the right (and weren't they the lucky children to have guessed it!) led straight into The Hills-of-The-Past and eventually to Bog Boundless.

# Towards The Valley Of The Pig

They took this road and they marched on to The Valley of the Pig and soon reached the trickling sounds of Red Scissors' spring well. They knelt on the slab and they cupped their hands for the water and they drank avidly. They looked to the left and they looked to the right, in case Warts-the-Journeyman might dash out (Corkscrew also came into Teddy's mind) and put them in his sack and sell them at The Fairy Fair. To comfort themselves they gathered a few old crabapples that were lying around the foot of the scabby trees near the well. They knew they'd be the two hungry savages like Sweeney and Norrie before the day was out. Nearby they heard the hooves and snorts of Sikey's terrifying bull stamping pace for pace along with them – he on the inside of the ditch and they on the outside and only a few feet separating them. They wondered if there might be a gap in the ditch when they came to the end of the road and if this huge bull might rush out and pelt them with his horns so high in the air that they'd sail out over the haysheds and land in the eagles' nest and be eaten alive – even before they had a chance to have their great big adventure?

They went passed the bend and the raging bull was nowhere to be seen, thank God. They were now high enough in the hills to look back at the length of the road behind them and it was as white as an old cattle-bone. In front of them were further hill-slopes and countless trees with their leaves twinkling and shining in the morning sunlight. There was sinister laughter hidden in the depths of those trees and new and wicked spirits were inviting them to come in there and shake hands with Danger. They were in The Valley of The Black Cattle. They heard the squeals of Jack-the-Herd's pig as he was sent flying out from his pigsty so that Jack could clean out the dung from his sty and inspect the pig's shape for the next morning when he'd be killing it. They hoped and prayed they'd be home in time to get the pig's bladder and race across The Bluebutton Field with it. Teddy cursed Sweeney all over again and he felt good about it and he hoped that the rascal would go and drown himself below in River Laughter for stealing his bladder.

They heard rifle shots echoing over Sikey's hayshed and they knew that another young rabbit was bleeding and at death's door. Teddy thought of the suffering of Rambling Jack's big pig and the suffering of this little rabbit. He remembered what the visiting card-players had recently told him (they were always teasing him and getting him to curse and swear) about the sufferings of other children at school and how his own little bum would soon be getting a fine thrashing from Dang-the-skin-of-it's sally-switch for not being able to recite his Poetry and Tables. He believed that this very thing was happening to the bigger boys this very minute and he felt it was a great pity that Sweeney had left school and wasn't getting his backside a fine good thrashing with the master's stick. That would teach him and the other rascals to go stealing Cackles' gooseberries and not share them with smaller children like himself and Little Cull.

## The Field Of The Ghost Hurler

They came to the gate looking out over the field where the mysterious stranger once strolled by on a summer's evening and asked the hurlers could he join in their sport. The young men soon saw his unbelievable wizardry and skill until finally they realized he was no mere mortal man at all but a demon hurler from another kingdom beyond the grave.

At sunrise they ran to the priest's door and he blessed each one of them. He blessed their hurley-sticks and he sent them away with a few buckets of holywater. They arrived home and they blessed themselves all over again and they blessed all belonging to them and then they went across to the hurling field and they sprinkled the bucket of holywater in all four corners of the field. Teddy and Little Cull had heard the tale of this strange ghost-hurler a hundred times whilst sitting round the bedtime fireside. And now they began to shudder and quake – to think that this ghost might still be in the field inside the ditch and ready to waylay them at any moment. Maybe he'd be sitting on the very next gate and smoking his pipe and shaking his sides with laughter at their childish impudence in walking so very far away from their known universe. And their two legs began to devour the road at a most admirable speed.

# *Is Bog Boundless Near Or Very Far?*

The morning was turning to noon and the hill-slopes were rosy with the growing efforts of the sun. They couldn't be too far away from Bog Boundless (they thought) with its carpet of purple heather. They had seen it not only when swimming in The Sally-Hole the day Patches almost got himself drowned, but the time they were bringing home the turf in the horse-and-cart with Blue-eyed Jack and Fiddler Joe. And now they recognized the furze bushes with a buttercup yellowness beginning to show on them. They recognized the ditches, soon to be dripping in the purple, pink and orange of the foxgloves and honeysuckles. The road had turned into a grassy lane and it soon became a mere donkey-track with neither a nest for the crows nor a cartwheel track or an ass's footprint to be seen anywhere. The light seemed misty here and the sun played foxy games of hide-and-go-seek with them – one minute appearing above the rusty remains of a long-forgotten cowshed and the next minute disappearing just as suddenly where the tall bushes intertwined.

They were very tired and had walked the legs off of themselves. They sat on the grass by a gate at the edge of the track. Opposite them was the deserted shack of Old Moonshine. The yard was a mass of thistles and loose weeds. The vacant windows and the half-door seemed sad and lonely whereas years before there had been children's voices gladdening the hearts of all within its walls and across its yard. A stray wildcat peered out at them from its perch on top of a rusty tar-barrel. It looked bemused at the sight of these two strange little visitors but couldn't tell them they'd soon be at Balaraggin's bloodstained doorway.

They got back on their feet and they padded on. The track in front of them changed to sloppy mud and their bare feet and legs took on the colour of pitch-tar and the nettles and thistles grew more and more densely on each side of them. The fairy-folk inside the bushes shook their gloomy heads and a flock of windy birds suddenly flew out over the ditch and scudded off to the safety of their nests in the fields far down below them and frantically indicated that the young adventurers should follow them down home (there was still time) and that nothing but impending darkness lay ahead of them. 'For the love of sweet Jesus on his cross, go back home.

Ye have reached The Land of Mystery and there is no room here for small men like ye.'

Neither Teddy nor Cull wished to admit that they were very much afraid. Trampling through the nettles and slapping their bare feet through the bindweed, they continued along the track until it became no track at all. Was this really the end of the world? The two of them could have cried out their fears if only they were old enough to put them into words: 'Oh, that we had been let follow the older children down The Open Road to school. Oh, to be leap-frogging and playing tag in the school field around the bridge. Oh to be running along the sunny banks of River Laughter among the pine-trees and underneath the blue skies of Rookery Rally.' But instead, all they could hear was the whispering of the fairy-folk penetrating into their frightened hearts and the sinister sounds from Balaraggin's snoring ghost close at hand. If only God would help them now. If only He would forgive them for deceiving Dowager and Smiling Babs and setting off to find the top of The Mighty Mountain and driving these two poor old women out of their minds with worry.

## In Balaraggin's Ghostly Yard

They went into Balaraggin's yard. Was this the yard where his dead mother (like the mother of Shy Dennis) had driven back her ass-and-car with its rattling chains? They half-expected to see her pouncing out on them and attacking them like a cat playing with two small mice. She might put them in her suitcase along with the few possessions that she'd come back to take with her. She might carry them off to The Beyond on her ghostly ass-and-car. But they saw nothing only the greenflies wandering aimlessly about in the sunshine and singing in the light.

They sat among the brambles and briars near the ruined remains of Balaraggin's pig-house. Next to it was his lopsided hayshed with its rusty roof fallen to the ground like a box-player's bellows and it was covered in ivy and dock-leaves big enough to wipe a giant's bum. Around the edge of the yard were the shadows of bony trees and overhanging thorn-bushes, all black and gnarled with old age. The yard was covered in nettles and mallows and straggly dead poppies peeped out between the cracks in the cobblestones. They had never before seen such a place and the silence was eerily motionless and overpowering.

They gazed at Balaraggin's sad-looking cabin, a grey cobwebby ruin just like the hayshed and leaning on its side. Its rafters were open to the heavens and sickly-looking ferns grew out of the thatch and chimney and more of them peered out from the broken windows where once there grew boxes of glistening geraniums. And the ghosts of Balaraggin and his mother were both looking out at the intrusive shadows of the two wanderers standing there in their yard – a yard that had once been full of glossy hens and geese and the shouts of Balaraggin and his mother – a yard that had once been a happy place with their echoing laughter, just like Old Moonshine's yard had once been and all the other yards back home in Rookery Rally were this very day.

As though in a dream the children walked towards the doorway. They had heard of Balaraggin whilst listening to the bigger boys' tales and eating their potato-skins on Smiling Babs' ditch. They knew about his cut-throat razor and his dying screams and the tears rising up inside in him and the unforgettable mournfulness in him after the death of his mother – a dead mother, who had left poor Balaraggin behind her, to stare at the miserable darkness in his fireless black chimney-space. They knew how Balaraggin was seen rambling along the moonlit donkey-tracks, drifting from field to field under the pale stars and slowly losing his mind – gentle and kind one minute, cruel and hurtful the next. Hadn't he chased Old Moonshine with the four-grained fork the time the old villain suggested Balaraggin was trying to take his young wife away from him and carry her into his own bed? And yet at other times (when Old Moonshine was sticking the black knife into one of his pigs) hadn't Balaraggin gone down to that yard and sunk down on his bended knees and prayed for Old Moonshine to spare the poor pig's life – the pig that had never hurt anyone in all its innocent pig's life!

And now the two dreamy children were here and the moment had come and they were at the frightful door itself. They saw the green paint hanging down in long flakes the length of the broken slats. They saw the huge blood-spatters (now turned brown) and they were mesmerized and terrified at the sight. And whilst the older children were saying their poems far off in the school-house, the two of them now were feeling what no book of poems could ever seep into their souls: astonishment and wonder – and it was all too much for two small children to take into their heads. It was as though they had drifted into The Past and were listening to its sad music. Their sunlight had disappeared from their hearts and the darkness and the sorrow for poor dead Balaraggin had taken its place.

All around them stood suggestive shapes (but not the spirits of laughter and dancing) and these spirits peeped out at them from the yard bushes and the withered trees and they haunted them with the dread of meeting Balaraggin's ghost with the razor in his fist and they were frightened that they might hear the ass-and-car and the rattling chains of his mother's ghost coming in across the yard.

They squeezed each other's hand tightly, not knowing whether to proceed or to run back home (if they could ever find the way again) and then they tiptoed in passed the bloodstained door and they found themselves in the most uninviting Welcoming Room in the entire world. The whitewashed walls were yellow and crumbly, not like their own home. Inside the doorway was Balaraggin's woodpile, with the grass growing up through the woodchips. They made their way across the stone-slabbed floor beneath the overhanging webs of giant spiders. On the wall was the Sacred Heart picture that guards all homes but had failed to do the job when it was most needed and on the nail beside the picture was Balaraggin's rosary-beads. There was no sign of his tobacco-pipe and there was no sign of the damnable razor, thank God. On the dresser were his mother's hat and her cane and her big black boots and they could almost hear the click-clack of her ghost walking around in her bedroom.

Older children had boasted of their bravery and had told Teddy and Little Cull how they had deceived their parents and climbed out the window in the dead of night and how they had gone up the hill to Balaraggin's yard and how they had stood there for the silence of eternity in the midnight moonlit yard and how they had looked at the bloodstained door and bravely put their hands down along it. They told of how they had heard the rattling ass-and-car and the chains of Balaraggin's mother and how they had heard her opening her press-cupboard drawers in search of her cardigan: a year later and they might have told them about her long-lost memories of those lovely men (the poachers) who had once played delicious games-of-love with her in the fields and had preceded her on the journey to The Beyond. These big brave boys swore that they had seen her ghostly face after she got drowned in the boghole abroad in Bog Boundless and how it had an unutterable look of sorrow in it as though it was her doom to spend eternity vainly searching for her cardigan and her belongings to take away with her in her ass-and-car.

Mindful of all these stories, Teddy and Little Cull's hearts were chilled by the icy coldness of Balaraggin's Welcoming Room. There wasn't a single friendly angel to give them a little bit of courage – only the witches from their storybooks were here. Was any child ever as lonely as the two of them now were?

## Who Is The Wild Witch Of The West?

Moreover they had heard tell of The Wild Witch of The West and they could now feel her presence all around them and they had no wings on their legs to help them escape if she came swooping down into the yard to seize them and swallow them up. Hadn't many another child been snatched away abroad in Bog Boundless by the cruel spells of The Wild Witch of The West? It was too much for them to bear. Where had all their childish laughter disappeared to? What were these huge tears now streaming down along their jaws?

They stumbled out from The Welcoming Room and they sat in the yard. It was two o'clock (the hottest time of the day) and the sky above them was as hot and livid as a bruised eye and their tears continued to glisten like diamonds and their two sets of tightly-gripped fists had become like glue. If only a kindly ghost would appear like their guardian angels! In a daze they staggered through the gateway and they left behind them the ghosts of Balaraggin's hens and geese and the ghost of Balaraggin when once he was a boy, sitting on his youthful chair in the yard alongside his mother with his concertina resting on his knees. They didn't know what to do next or which way to turn. They were at the end of the world, they were sure of it.

## Lost! Lost! Lost!

Lost – that's what they were. Lost in the heart of the hills. Lost in one of the most forgotten places on earth with not even the song of a blackbird to raise their spirits. They were ravenous with the hunger and they were far from their warm fireside and their manly little spirits were finally knocked arseways out of their bodies and they sat themselves down to cry and to die there and then. How foolish they had been to go off adventuring! Nobody would ever find them and they were so very young to be dying like this. What was it like to be dead like Father Chasible below in his grave and lying in his box and like Rambling Jack's pig in the barrel? It must be a terrible thing. There'd be no more Fiddler Joe. There'd be no more Blue-eyed Jack. There'd be no more Dowager or Smiling Babs to chide their little backsides with the leg of the chair or the lid of the sweet-gallon. There'd be no more Sweeney, Golly, Gallant or Norrie. They would never get the chance to stand on top of The Mighty Mountain. They would never see the two eagles. They even feared that these very same eagles were looking down at them and laughing at the pair of them from above on their nest and thinking how these small men had the damnedest cheek and impudence to believe they could come and visit them on top of The Mighty Mountain.

They closed their eyes and they waited for the eagles to swoop down and fly away with them like they did with the newborn lambs and carry them out over The Ocean. And at last they knew that the other children were a pack of filthy liars and that not a one of them had ever been as far as this and they believed they had reached Fairyland itself where the fairy-folk of their storybooks spent their days beneath the thumb of The Wild Witch of the West. They could almost feel her hovering above them with her broomstick and her army of banshees and boodeemen waiting on her every beck and call.

## The Witch Herself!

But life is never quite the same as a storybook and at this very moment (the lowest moment in their young lives) The Wild Witch of The West was out taking the air for herself in the nearby fields of Lisnagorna. She was gathering twigs and furze bushes for her fire. Her legendary fierceness was nothing more than a sly old myth spread abroad by the big people to prevent little ones wandering too far from their yard and their half-door. Indeed the poor old woman lived all by herself and was to be pitied rather than feared.

But there was a time (long ago) when she had been the loveliest young girl and had danced the shoes off of her feet at every crossroads-dance in the hills and her beauty had spellbound the minds and hearts of many young men, including the youthful Balaraggin. And then the day came when The Land of The Silver Dollar had sent her the call and she crossed the seas like many before her. And then the time came for her mother to die and pass on to The Beyond and leave her father behind at the fire, alone and crippled with pains in his knees and an ache in his heart. She – who was later to earn the name of The Wild Witch of The West because of her extraordinary powers of curing the sick from their various ailments – came back to comfort the old man. With gusto she took to farming their land, as good as any man. She'd carry out bundles of hay on her shoulders to feed her cattle in winter's harshness. She'd follow behind her speeding plough and horses in the late springtime. She'd tram the hay and with her rake she'd trim the reek in the haggart at harvest time. She'd bawl after her lost cow or goat and she'd chastise her jinnet when he got himself trapped in the briars.

That was all many years ago. And now she was far too old to go work the land and all the hardships of her past life were a thousand miles from her, thank God. With the death of her beloved father she was mistress of all the land she surveyed and had all that she wanted from life – her few simple strolls through the quietness of the silent hills, her cottage with the one solitary rose bush blooming its redness in summertime and her yard which she kept as clean as the driven snow. The land she sold to The Forestry. To keep her company in the long hours of the night she had her beautiful parrot that she'd brought home from The Daffy-Duck Circus with its tail-feathers as long and golden as any cock-pheasant and she had given it the charming name of Gold-shit.

And now she heard the sobbing tears of Teddy and Little Cull and she stood stock-still in her tracks as though she had heard a goose just caught by a fox. She let fall her bundle of twigs and in her long black skirts she hurried to the crying children, jumping out over the ditches. In the eyes of the two horrified adventurers, when they suddenly saw her landing in a great big blur and towering above them, it seemed as though this little old woman with her sharp-hatchet face and her bewitching eyes had stepped straight out through the walls of the Universe. This was the day of their doom. They were face-to-face with The Wild Witch of The West!  The fireside stories of the witch's black cauldron and the boiling water and the little children eaten alive – these stories had all come home to roost and the two of them wrapped their arms around each other in an unimaginable terror that no words could describe and they prepared to meet their death.

'Lambkins! Lambkins! Lambkins!' sighed the old woman and her voice was as welcome as a shower of the summer's rain. One minute they were about to meet their death and the next minute they found thremselves in the presence of their guardian angel. Her melodious voice had the tone of a choir of angels singing in their ears and their tears took flight from them and their hearts took on a renewed courage. If they were ever to get home alive again, there would be no need to boast how they saw buckets of Balaraggin's blood spattered around the middle of his yard. There'd be no need to boast of the barrels of his blood they had seen inside his half-door. Instead they'd have the tale of all tales to tell – how their lives were spared by no less a vision than The Wild Witch of The West herself! This was no ordinary witch from the pages of a storybook, who had come to put them in her pot and boil them and gobble them up. This old lady had tears in her eyes. This old lady had a tender love welling up inside her as she spoke to them: 'What have the good saints in Heaven brought me this fine spring day? God-sakes, what a holy fright ye lost souls gave me!'

She reached out her healing hands towards them and she stroked away the tears from their cheeks. The two little boys threw themselves into her arms and she wrapped them in her apron-skirts. Her seaweed coils of sympathetic hair fell down around their faces and (recalling the inexplicable fears she had felt during her own childhood) she almost devoured them with her hot breath.

## To The Rescue She Came

With her skirts rustling, she took the entranced children by the hand. She guided their weary footsteps down the lane and out over the stile to the haggart. They crossed the stream and came into her yard. Her cabin was as clean and fresh as a new pin and was surrounded by apple trees – enough to be eating for the rest of their life. The children entered her Welcoming Room where a bit of coloured matting covered the cobblestoned floor.

They remained huddled together near the half-door, still unsure of what might happen next and they were ready to bolt and make good their escape at the very first sign of danger. The Wild Witch of The West lit her oil-lamp and her two candles in the candlestick holders. With the lid of her sweet-gallon she blew up a blaze underneath her furze bushes and she threw bits of candles into the flames and it blazed up cheerfully and soon warmed their hearts and souls.

The old woman beckoned them to shove in from the half-door and sit by the blaze of her fireside and her cheerfulness banished the last traces of their fear. With a dishcloth she wiped the black mud from their legs and the tearstains from their red eyes. She soon had the kettle singing on the crane and she poured them out a mug of warm tea each. She gave them slices of her currant-cake and they pounced on it as though they hadn't eaten for a week. She gave them mountains of bread and jam and then she wiped their sticky fingers and faces, using the dishcloth once more. No king or queen could have been treated with such cordiality.

## *Gold-shit*

The surprise of all surprises came when down from the chimney flew not some ancient cobwebby ghost but the squawking parrot, Gold-shit. He had been sleeping on a long blackened stick that stretched across the upper hob, halfway across the chimney. In the brightness of the firelight Teddy and Little Cull could clearly see his beautiful colours and how he got his name and how his beauty contrasted with the withered features of The Wild Witch of The West. And then a strange whispering conversation (like a long drawn-out litany in some foreign tongue) took place between the parrot and The Wild Witch of The West and for the next few minutes Teddy and Little Cull might as well have been back in Balaraggin's yard or above on the moon.

Gold-shit (thanks to the old woman's coaxing) was no longer afraid of the children and he now sat himself on a lower perch at the side of the fire. He edged from one end of the stick to the other to make himself more and more comfortable and warm his feathers. He began to sway slowly and his dreamy eyes began to close and at last he fell sound asleep. His dignified dreamland was soon shattered when he overbalanced and fell down from his perch, landing with a scream straight into the middle of the fire.

Such a commotion filled The Welcoming Room that it could surely be heard below in Rookery Rally as Gold-shit staggered out of the hot ashes like some drunken old man with his feathers scorched for the hundredth time. The Wild Witch of The West suddenly got herself into what seemed a venomous rage and (losing her gentle voice) she shouted her indignation across the firelight and she swiped at her dazed parrot with her dish-cloth: 'God-sakes, will ye look at Gold-shit, that shitty little article – he's at it again!' Then the hearty old lady (with the tears of laughter in her merry old eyes) chased him good-naturedly around The Welcoming Room as though she would beat the living daylights out of him with her tongs. 'He'll get himself burnt to a cinder,' said she and she laughed till the tears ran down her jaw. Gold-shit could hardly have escaped from the old woman for he was trapped at the half-door where he looked very foolish and dazed.

This was a merry little game that was played out a number of times between the parrot and the old woman in the course of the next half-hour. The children had never seen anything like it before. They had seen little thrushes caught in winter cages in the yard for them to look at before being set free to fly off again. But the sight of the magnificent Gold-shit sitting on a black stick under the hob above the blazing fire and then falling asleep and then tumbling off his perch and landing in the hot ashes and then struggling with the blazing sods of turf in the fire and The Wild Witch of The West chasing him round the floor – this was something that would stay with them for many days to come.

Sensing the ever-present danger of Gold-shit falling into her skillet of sweet-smelling cabbage, The Wild Witch of The West continued to chide her pet. 'Is this what I reared you for?' Finally she picked him up in her arms (all the time fondling and stroking him) and she marched him off to his cage in her bedroom. She put a towel around the cage and he became quiet for the rest of the evening. She took her lid from off the burner and waved it at her two young guests and she shook her head and sighed. 'That bleddy ould eejit, Gold-shit, what a nuisance of a bird he is these days!' Then she looked down into the depths of the burner. 'I have often been tempted to put him in the pot and boil him with the spuds and cabbages.' Like all the grown-ups she was a terrible liar, for both Teddy and Little Cull could see how dearly she loved the companionship of her beautiful Gold-shit and how afraid she was of ever losing him in the flames of her fire. They could see that by falling asleep and all the time falling off of his stick, Gold-shit was very old and had very poor balance and they felt he was as many years on this earth as the old woman herself and might well be as old as Judy Rag – one hundred and five.

## But The Fear Lingers On

In spite of the layers of currant-cake and the bread and the jam and in spite of the comical antics of Gold-shit, the children had become aware of the sun's glow beginning to fall down the sky and an increasing darkness creeping its way in through the half-door from the overcast trees of the haggart. Fairy voices in the yard were whispering to them to hurry on home before the late afternoon turned itself into evening. The Wild Witch of The West sensed the growing uneasiness in their empty eyes. It was usual (she knew) for children to spend the day running around the secret haunts of Rookery Rally, but it was never heard tell of for any child (especially these little ones and they being so young) to be caught roaming around the world in the dark. Why hadn't she thought of it before? Poor tortured Dowager and Smiling Babs would be out of their minds with worry. They'd be waiting at the half-door with their eyes grainy from looking out for these small ramblers and wondering if they had got trapped in a boghole or caught in the briars inside in Fort Dangerous. The two little children would be missing their home and their own fireside and they'd want nothing more than to find their way back to Rookery Rally. Would Dowager and Smiling Babs this very minute be combing the haggart and the dykes and The Thistle Field in search of them? Would Fiddler Joe and Blue-eyed Jack be running in panic along the banks of River Laughter in a demented search for them?

She went to her half-door. The tops of the hill-slopes were shot through with the last of the red sunset. The pine-trees were painted with the sun's very last rays and her own dusky yard was about to be hidden in the inky clouds of night-time. She put on her coat and her old bonnet against the chill of the evening dew. She took Teddy and Little Cull by the

THE EARLY MORNING LIGHT

hand and she hurried off with them into the orchard. She climbed up into the trees and the two boys caught the cooking and eating apples that she twisted and threw down to them. With their pockets full of apples they were as excited as ever they'd been and even more delighted when the good creature said she'd walk back with them to Rookery Rally.

## Night Clouds And Time To Go Home

The Wild Witch of The West threw a sup of water onto her fire so that the place wouldn't catch fire when she was gone and that Gold-shit wouldn't get burnt to death. She closed her front door and she put the key in the geranium box and the three of them (the wind filling their chests and their feet scarcely touching the ground) set off for The Hills-of-The-Past and home. Not another soul was abroad. It was just the three of them and their echoing feet thumping down the lanes and onto the roads. The little explorers were more than glad of the old woman's company as she knew all the lanes and roads like the back of her hand. When darkness arrived she'd have the eyes of a fox to lead them down to Sheep's Cross and out on The Open Road.

The watery moon had finally risen from its hiding-place behind the pine-trees and the children went skipping their way ahead of the old woman and she could hardly keep up with them since the wings had returned to their feet. They could see the blue-lit gaslights of The Roaring Town sparkling merrily in the darkness of the valley below. Behind them the piled-up hills and Bog Boundless had faded into misty blueness. The ghosts of fresh fairy-folk whispered encouragingly to them and a trace of merriment (even though they were sick with tiredness) warmed their hearts.

Oh, to be going home! Oh, to be no longer lost! What tales there would be to tell! What great big lies there would be to tell! Tales of Balaraggin's ghost, who had stared out at them from his window and how they heard the rattling chains and the ass-and-car and how Balaraggin and his mother were seen having their tea in the haggart and how the two ghosts took the scrub-brush and wiped away the spatters of blood from off of the green door. The lies would go on trotting out of their mouths for the next week-and-a-half!

They ran down the last of The Open Road. Dowager and Smiling Babs (and Fiddler Joe and Blue-eyed Jack too) had already worn away their knees from saying decades of the rosary on their beads. They had prayed to Saint Anthony (the patron saint of finding what seemed lost) and heaven and the saints had listened to their prayers. With their ears forever cocked, they at last heard the bare feet of Teddy and Little Cull staggering in across the flagstones.

## The Sheer Joy And Relief

'Ye little fairymen – what on earth kept ye – where on earth have ye been till this hour of the night?' The two women (their faces red with pleasure, their eyes full of happy tears and their arms outstretched) ran across the yard to meet the mighty ramblers. Dowager wrapped her locks of hair around her little man and Smiling Babs lifted Little Cull to the very sky. They were like two old hens that had found their lost chicks.

The Wild Witch of The West (the children's saviour from the mountains) came puffing and panting in the gate and (for what seemed an age to the boys) herself and Dowager and Smiling Babs whispered excitedly and incoherently at the gate. The children knew that the conversation was far above their heads but could see the agitated frown-lines crossing the faces of Dowager and Smiling Babs and their fingers twisting and fidgeting continuously. Then (what none of us had ever seen before, for physical affection had never ever been demonstrated one to another among the big people) Smiling Babs and Dowager grasped The Wild Witch of The West in their arms and they hugged her half to death. The old woman was startled and confused by all the hugs and she wiped a little bit of wind out of the corner of her salty eyes. She had saved the lives of these two little wobbledy-heads. Without her timely rescue and the currant-cake and the bread and jam and the distractions of Gold-shit they might well have found themselves dead or carried off by the two savage eagles.

Turning to the downcast children, Dowager and Smiling Babs explained in words of crystal clearness the terrible dangers that could have killed the pair of them – the unseen fairy creatures and the wild unlicensed bulls and the two great big eagles. The shamefaced little adventurers (having been at first more than joyful to be home) were almost as unhappy now as when they'd been thinking of the boiling cauldron supposedly bubbling in the cabin of The Wild Witch of The West. And they vowed with all their hearts that they'd never go off roaming again.

Smiling Babs invited the mountainy woman to take a cut of her soda-cake and have a mouthful of tea. Refusing this gesture politely, The Wild Witch of The West placed her hands on the shoulders of Teddy and Cull. She gave them a last fond look from her loving eyes, to be remembered for evermore as it flew from her eye and into theirs. Prodded by Dowager and Smiling Babs, they shook her hand in gratitude, knowing that what had started out as a childish adventure had almost turned into a terrible disaster.

## And Then – The Witch Vanished

Then (almost abruptly) the little old woman's black figure turned roundabout and like a lively puff of chimney smoke she swooped away out the half-door and was gone! Her black skirts rustling again, she headed back towards her Land of Mystery and not once did she look back. The last the children ever saw of her was at the shoulder of The Open Road near Shy Dennis's Shack where she got sucked away into The Hills-of-The-Past. They could hear the echo of her boots behind her as the last twilight melted into night and the day finally closed into cloister-quietness. This old saviour of the day would be tired and weary and (sad to say) she'd be feeling as lonesome as a lost lamb before she reached her front door and Gold-shit.

## A Little Celebration Is Called For

Inside in The Welcoming Room of Smiling Babs, the plates were laid out and there was a fresh smell of the melting juices of cabbage, boiled spuds and turnips. Teddy and Little Cull licked their lips in anticipation. In spite of their feasting at the table of The Wild Witch of The West, they were so ravenous that they could have eaten a bag of horse nails, their appetite having been stimulated by the cold air which fills the mountains, but more so by their unadulterated fear throughout the day. They emptied the plates and they washed the food down with two or three mugs of milk, followed by further mugfuls of spring-water. There was a moment or two of silence in which they realized what they had done. To have caused such worry and anxiety to Dowager and Smiling Babs and the two big men and not to have let anyone know or sought anyone's permission before setting out on their foolish quest — this had been their first great sin and Father Accessible would have to be told all about it (said Dowager) in his confession box a year or two from now.

# The End Of A Risky Day's Rambling

It was the end of a memorable day. Dowager took Teddy out into Smiling Babs' yard. She waved a hurried goodbye to her neighbour. Smiling Babs and Fiddler Joe closed the half-door and the big door behind it, sending away the darkness. The lamp and the candles were lit and the rosary-beads were taken out for the prayers. Dowager almost had to carry Teddy the short distance down the road. She filled her warming-jar with hot water from the kettle and (something she had never done before) she placed it not inside her own blankets but in the sheets of Teddy's bed. He crept gratefully into his nest and for once he forgot to say his prayers at his bedside. He was soon in a mountainous sleep.

Thanking God for this day's miracle, Blue-eyed Jack went out to ease himself before retiring for the night. He listened again to the gentle sighing of the winds through the pine-trees in the haggart and he watched the clouds climbing all over the moon. Inside in The Welcoming Room the night had given way to the dancing firelight and the warmth of safety and comfort had returned.

Behind The Hills-of-The-Past and even further beyond still (in the heart of her untouched wilderness) The Wild Witch of The West was struggling onwards the last few strides. She entered her yard and she looked up at the millions of stars across the black heavens, so very far away. They seemed to be winking down at her, acknowledging the noble way she had saved the lives of two small souls. Wearily she opened her door with the key. The rescuer of young lambkins was back in the peaceful quiet of her comfortable little nest. She was back with Gold-shit, the droopy companion she could always depend on. She lit the yellow oil-lamp and it threw a petal of cheerful light around her Welcoming Room.  Later she merged herself down into her small bed beneath her five blankets. 'God is good!  God is great!' she sighed and soon she melted into the black pool of a blissful sleep, her forefinger resting on her motionless lip.

## Such Brave Little Boys!

In the long-winded days that followed, the entire population of Rookery Rally was full of the news of how two small boys met The Wild Witch of The West. The older boys (especially Gallant and Golly and Sweeney, none of whom had ever traveled out so far, except in their imagination!) were fit to burst with rage, so great was their envy. And God had evened things up nice and neatly between Teddy and Sweeney and the robbing of the little man's dignity and his bladder had become just a piece of ancient history. Nothing could ever again compare with the bravery of this daring adventure into the Land of The Unknown and the realms of The Wild Witch of The West. Not since Adam and Eve had there been so great an expedition. And to think that Teddy and Little Cull had come back alive to tell the tale of it!

For the rest of the week their exaggeration and downright lies ran away with themselves as they told every blessed soul (in a language that stuttered in fits and starts) how they had almost reached Galway and The Gates of Heaven and The Ocean itself – and even The Mighty Mountain and even the splatters of blood on Balaraggin's green door had to take second place to all their tales.

For many more days to come two small boys were seen parading up and down The Open Road, their chests sticking out like a pair of proud little turkeycocks. But, in Balaraggin's yard, if you had been up there and found yourself looking in through the bars of the gate, it was a far different story: for just inside the gate you would see two little streams of yellow poolie, where Teddy and Little Cull (our two frightened little wanderers) had severely wet both their britches.

# TWELVE

# Teddy And The Mountainy Men

*When Teddy joined The Mountainy Men*
*on The Day of The tar-barrels in Cackles' yard.*

It was Summertime in the year of 1945. We all knew that there was the laughter of the hyena but it could only be found elsewhere in foreign climes far away from Rookery Rally. As for ourselves, we had the laughter of the hen after she had laid an egg amongst the nettles and dock-leaves in the haggart, where we'd have the devil's own job finding herself and her egg. You'd think it was the very first egg that she had ever laid, the laughter that she came out with. But better than that we also had Cackles and her very name will tell you what a peal of laughter she had inside her blouse. 'It's louder than The Angelus Bell in Copperstone Hollow,' said Dowager and 'Cackles can make a cat laugh,' said Blue-eyed Jack. This left Teddy wondering what it was like to see a cat laughing. There was something new for him to learn every day. 'She's like a hundred hens laying their eggs at one and the same time abroad in the hayshed – that's why she cackles so much,' said Dowager and that was supposed to be the end of the matter. Teddy, however, knew that this bit about the hundred hens was just another of his grandmother's damned lies – like her tall tale about The Wild Witch of The West and The King of The Leprechauns.

## Cackles And Johnnie-Tackle-The-Ass

Cackles was nearer to fifty than forty years of age. Her husband was Johnnie-tackle-the-ass and he was the centre of her good nature and devotion. He was seventy years old and he was forever tackling up his ass and going off in the direction of The Bog Wood for yet another cartload of ferns. That's how he came to get his name. Dowager (who was always nosey and forever peeping out the front window on tiptoes to see who was passing by) would watch him speeding down The Open Road and she would say to herself, 'Johnnie, go and tackle the ass and bring a load of ferns.' These words turned into a regular singsong expression of hers that Teddy heard day in and day out. She might want Blue-eyed Jack to do some out-of-the-way job for her: 'Jack, avic, go and tackle the ass and bring a load of ferns.' Of course she didn't mean him to head off down to The Bog Wood (like Cackle's good man) and bring her back a load of ferns; Blue-eyed Jack knew that she wanted him to roll up his sleeves like Johnnie did and go out the pig-house gap where there was a pile of timber waiting for him to chop into logs and bring in for the fire.

## Little Sing-Me-A-Song

Between Johnnie and Cackles (miracle of miracles, now that he was seventy) they managed to produce one of the loveliest children known to us here in Rookery Rally and the name of this child was Sing-me-a-song. She had dimples on her cheeks, although we all had these. But then she had dimples on her wrists and she even had them on her elbows and on her knees. So some of us thought that Dimples might have been a far better name for this little girl.

The years went by all too quickly and Sing-me-a-song was growing up just as lovely as Nature intended her to be. Again and again the old pair did their best during their tumbles in the four-poster bed to give her a little brother to play with. But they were far too old for this sort of thing. Wasn't it high time for Father Accessible to come and tell them to give up trying? Even the biblical Sarah had produced only the one child as late as this in her lifetime. But a year or two later, to the astonishment of us all (not least to Cackles herself) she had another birth. Without the visitation of the nurse (Black Bess) she gave birth to a pair of premature twins, crossing and uncrossing her legs on The Welcoming Room floor whilst Smiling Babs did the best she could for her. But (oh and alas) they were dead as soon as they arrived and Cackles was out of her head with grief and she didn't know what to do. She quickly buried them (the way you would a dog or an ass) abroad in the haggart behind the potato-pit. Then she tearfully covered them along with a big heap of laurel bushes so that the rats wouldn't get at them. Then she went back to the bedroom and lay down on the bed and she cried and cried and she stayed there for the rest of the week, leaving Johnnie-tackle-the-ass alone and sad and scratching his head. We wondered if she'd ever take up laughing again.

Although the twins were gone before they'd had a chance to give her a few little smiles, there came a growing compensation for herself and Johnnie whenever they looked across the firelight at their lovely little daughter. Even before she hit the road for Dang-the-skin-of-it's school-house Sing-me-a-song turned out to be the sweetest of singers in our midst and her songs made her the life and soul of The Open Road. In the course of time Cackles and Johnnie put aside the cause of their grief and they started to realize (thank God) where their true happiness lay. The famous laughter of Cackles was once more restored to her and it filled our valleys and hills whenever she listened to Sing-me-a-song singing. The little girl would clear her throat with a mug of spring-water from the bucket behind the door. Then she would trot out: 'No-one to welcome me home', a song that made us all weep with its sentimental journey of an old man coming back from The Land of The Silver Dollar. She'd follow this up with: 'Why are you loitering here, pretty maiden?' or 'Dim in the twilight I wandered alone'. We could stay listening to her for half-the-day as though we had nothing better to do with ourselves. How on earth did a little child like her keep stored in her head all the big words that were in these songs? 'God must have given her a dozen brains,' said Blue-eyed Jack to Teddy and the little boy wondered was there a child anywhere on earth who had so many brains floating around inside in their head.

# Her Gift Of The Double Whistle

She had already developed a gap between her two front teeth and such a gap was said to be the birthright of anyone in Rookery Rally hoping to live beyond a hundred years of age. But the gap in Sing-me-a-song's teeth had another consequence for it gave her the gift of the double-whistle (like the one you'd make by whistling on a piece of card) and it was as though two people were whistling inside in her mouth. For hours on end (and with Dowager cursing him for not coming in to his tea) Teddy sat on his heels and he listened to this strange whistling of hers. You'd pay good money down at the Daffy-Duck Circus to go and listen to it. So instead of himself and Little Cull (fresh back from their adventures with The Wild Witch of The West) going off paddling in River Laughter and bringing back coloured stones to draw with – instead of them following the bigger children down over the wire-fence and half-kicking to death Mikeys's two pet dogs in his yard – they now preferred sitting in the ashes of Cackles' fire and listening to Sing-me-a-song at her whistling. As important as the two small adventurers were in the eyes of us all, it was admitted that Cackles' daughter and her melodious gifts beat the two of them hands down. She held Rookery Rally in the palm of her hand.

There were times when Teddy and his friends (but mainly the older girls) would follow Sing-me-a Song down into Mikey's grove. They didn't give her a moment's peace and they kept her sitting on the fallen tree and pestering her to open her mouth and roll her tongue so that they could find the reason for her mysterious whistle. Wasn't that what children in Rookery Rally had always done whenever they found a dead thrush? They opened its beak to see how on earth so small a creature could come out with its wondrous music. Sing-me-a-song (the good-natured child that she was) patiently opened her mouth and she twisted her tongue so that they could see the source of her split-whistle. No matter how they leaned down towards the inside of her throat or tried to twist their own lips and place their tongue at the back of their teeth to copy this double-whistle, they never got the hang of its unique mystery – until finally they saw that it was the gap between her two front teeth that was the cause of it and they gave up trying to copy her and went off home dejectedly.

For a day or two, they had other things to occupy their minds. Golly brought home a dead crane and he asked Gallant to cut its belly open with the carving knife. After all the snipping was done, the children and Teddy saw several small fishes wrapped up inside in its guts. They were just as puzzled as they had been with the thrush's small beak and all the beautiful notes of music that it had once sang. The question set for them now was: how could a crane have held so many fishes inside in its belly? They were beaten again and they had no answer. This brought them back to the same question: how on earth could Sing-me-a-song's teeth have taught her the double whistle and what was so special about the gap? They were one and all enthralled.

## But She Has No Boots To Put On

Every child in Rookery Rally went bare-footed. Even when they had to have boots on their feet for the school-house, they slung them round their necks until they were within a yard of the school. Only then (because they had to) did they deign to put them on. They were far happier to be in their bare feet where they could run around like a pack of hares. But that didn't stop them from frowning about the fact that Sing-me-a-song had no boots to wear. She was a year older than Little Cull and Teddy and she'd be going to school in a year's time and she needed to get into the habit of covering her feet with boots. They got it into their heads that they should try and get her a pair and they paraded the length and breadth of The Open Road until at last they found one old boot for her. It was a shade too big for a five-year-old child, being the leftover of a passing tinker-woman. They spent the whole of the summertime searching for a comrade for that old boot until in the end Sweeney found an ancient wellington in the dyke at Red Scissors' well-hole. He cut it down to size with his father's penknife and then, together with the boot which they had stuffed full of moss, it made a fair enough pair of boots for our little heroine to put on.

Teddy wanted to help and he asked Dowager for the blacking-tin that she kept in the bottom of the press cupboard, the green tin with the lovely face of the black racehorse on its lid. Then he gave it to Sweeney. The big lad (a friend once more with Teddy after the sad time of stealing the bladder from him) gave the wellington and the boot a good rinse in the yard-stream. He dried them out on the ditch and he gave them a polishing that would have befitted a racehorse. The children (making sure that the little singer was nowhere to be seen) gathered round and wondered at the new boot and wellington that lay shining like the sun. They marched Sing-me-a-song down to Mikey's well-hole and with a degree of ceremony and ritual they handed her their gift. It was their reward for her being the finest singer and whistler they were ever likely to listen to.

# Dinny The Yankee Boy

Cackles missed little Sing-me-a-song when she started off with the other children on the daily three-mile trek across the fields to Dang-the-skin-of-it's school-house. But the good woman's loneliness didn't last long, for who should come running home amongst us in a great big flurry – back home again from The Land of The Silver Dollar – but Dinny-the-Yankee-Boy. He was Cackles' favourite nephew and he had come back to keep her company. 'But only for a short while,' he warned her. He had a lot of serious business on his mind (he said) and he had to go marching off again in a few weeks time. Cackles was duly impressed.

From the moment he arrived he was full of business around Cackles' yard. All the while he kept looking back over his shoulder as though he were expecting to see a mad bull leaping out over the ditch and tossing him up into the air. The children were left wondering why he had come here and why he'd be leaving us just as quickly. Those who had previously gone out to The Land of The Silver Dollar had seldom (if ever) come back. It was the same as though they had gone off to the moon or had been lost for good in a boghole or were lying below in the graveyard. And if indeed any of them ever did make the return trip, it was only their sentimental dreams that had forced them to come back in their very old age – with a small Yankee pension in their pockets and a hatful of dollars (if they were lucky). Their return proved to be no happy-ever-after tale for (would you believe it?) none of these old prodigals could settle down when they came home to The Old Sod. The friends of their youth were resting in an early grave – thanks to all the rheumatic pains that our damp climate had given them –

or else they'd been sent down (a good few of them) to The House for The Nervous Disorders to have their bad nerves looked at and these never returned home either and a few more of them had been shipped off to The County Home amidst the hypocritical tears of their children. Enough said.

Dinny's return was a bit different. It took only half-a-dozen pints of Curl 'n' Stripes' stout (the 'black doctor') to be poured down his neck for him to give us the news that we all wanted to hear – why he'd hot-footed it back to Rookery Rally from across the seas. It was then that he took on an almost god-like stature amongst the children. He said he was a man on the run ('ah, the poor fellow,' said Dowager) from a bunch of Yankee hoodlums – from men who would like to have tasted his blood after he had embezzled them out of a few crates of their finest whiskey. When the rest of the drinkers heard this astonishing tale below in the drinking-shop, you should have seen the way they slapped The Yankee-Boy on his shoulders. 'Fair play to you, Dinny!' they shouted, 'if only you had thought to bring us back a few crates of the hot stuff for ourselves!' And Curl 'n' Stripes' drinking-shop rang with laughter.

Dinny had always been a prime boy, but he was in the direst danger now. What was he to do? Where was he to go? He couldn't go back across The Ocean. He knew that the gangsters would give him a right royal welcome and (he said) a bullet up his arse. In the meantime all the children were left scratching their heads at the sight of him. They had never seen a young man like The Yankee-Boy. The Bishop and his high hat was one thing, with the red robes that he wore at their Confirmation. But Dinny was an entirely better sight to be gaping their eyes on: a man on the run and a mad pack of gangsters from The Land of The Silver Dollar soon to come steaming over The Ocean and making pig's meat out of him. Maybe the entire population of Rookery Rally would have to go to war and get out their old pitchforks for the protection of their lovely Yankee-Boy.

The days rolled into weeks and all the children grew more and more in awe of Dinny. It gradually came out that he had stolen a good deal more than the crates of whiskey: he had stolen a suitcase full of the gangsters' dollars. It was for that reason that he could ape the great showman when he stepped down from the train in The Roaring Town. The children (even Sweeney) compared their own few raggity bits of clothes with his silk suit and his garish tie and his sparkling brown brogues, not to mention the new moustache sprouting from under his nostrils. They were damned if they too wouldn't get themselves off to The Land of The Silver Dollar one of these fine days and get themselves a rich set of togs like his.

To see him step out into The Bluebutton-Field was the wonder of wonders as he carelessly threw off his expensive coat. The children made a grab for it and spent ages feeling the lovely silkiness of it, in the hope of finding a few dollars dropping of their own accord out of the pockets. The Yankee-Boy took off his rich shoes and his herringbone socks and he challenged all the children to a running race. It was easy for him to be challenging the likes of these poor scholars. You should have seen the get-up of him – he had muscles all over his chest and shoulders and more of them coming out from his two ears and he towered a foot above Sweeney, who was the tallest of the children. They all lowered their eyes shyly and admitted defeat.

'Coom on (blasht it!), ye little whoors!' laughed The Yankee-Boy. 'I'll lay ye down ten of these crinkly dollars that none of ye will be left in the field once I have finished with ye and I'll give each of ye a ten-yard start in a dash to the withered tree.' Before anyone had a chance to clear their throats, the speed of him had taken him almost as far as Curl 'n' Stripes drinking-shop door and to the astonished eyes of all the children there wasn't even a puff out of him – he hadn't even broken sweat! After this performance he led them out into the haggart, casually leaping out over the five-barred gate as he ran on ahead of them. It couldn't be denied – The Yankee-Boy had established himself in the annals of Rookery Rally for all time.

## Dinny Comes To A Wise Decision

Cackles brought in her armful of washed sheets from the bushes for a final airing round the fire. As she waddled in and out from the half-door, her nephew stood looking across the yard. He was thinking. He was thinking awfully hard. And then he shook his head. The savage rains (as with Smiling Babs the previous year) had flooded Cackles' stream as never before and by now it was half-ways up her yard. It would soon reach her half-door and she would be trapped on the flagstones around the front of her cabin for days on end and she wouldn't be able to set foot across the stream and go get her sausages and black puddings to feed Dinny.

Cackles was thinking of the previous plight of Smiling Babs and how the good woman's new tar-barrels had been laid side-by-side, to make a tunnel for the waters from the hills. She was dreading the next few days for, unlike Smiling Babs, she had no tar-barrels of her own with which to tunnel the waters of her stream. She was resigned to her sad fate and there was no way she could stop the stream coming in the door and onto her Welcoming Floor and all over the settlebed.

Herself and Johnnie-tackle-the-ass started twiddling their rosary-beads in great earnest. They felt heartily ashamed of themselves. They remembered the Great Flood ten years ago when it had emptied the contents of their cabin and sent them gaily floating down the swirling waters to be swept away in River Laughter. There was every chance it was going to happen all over again. 'How the hell would any of ye expect Cackles to get across the swollen stream and get down to the shop?' quizzed Blue-eyed Jack, 'unless we can teach her to swim across the stream and get herself out onto the road!' But by now even Teddy knew that nobody except Spare-Ribs could swim even a stroke, not even Matt-with-the-machinery.

Dinny had the answer to the problem. 'What need have we for the silver beauties of the stream's galloping waters and the heavenly music that she brings with her?' said he (he had become almost as poetical as Dowager since learning the fine big words across the seas). When Cackles heard Dinny's words she blessed him a thousand times over and she said he was a pure saviour sent to her from God in heaven.

## There's A Job To Be Done

The very next morning Dinny tackled up Johnnie's ass (Raggity) – this time not to go and get a load of ferns for them. Sweeney borrowed Dowager's ass-and-car together with The Lightning Whoor and the two ass-and-cars headed off together to The Roaring Town. They arrived at the Railway Station and they told Neddy-the-Stationmaster they needed eight empty tar-barrels. These he gladly helped them to load up onto their carts as they were lying around useless and forever tripping him up. Dinny and Sweeney balanced these old tar-barrels (four apiece) onto The Yankee-Boy's and Sweeney's ass-and-car. Neddy wondered if Dinny was going to form a new musical band with the tar-barrels and might he be performing at The Show-Fair next year.

Armed with their prized load, Cackles' two brave heroes hurried back towards Rookery Rally in a tidy little procession – the two important-looking asses and the rattling sound of their tar-barrels in the ass-and-cars behind them. Numbers of staring children followed behind them as far as The Sheep Field and they wondered who on earth in Rookery Rally would want so many useless old tar-barrels.

# The Arrival Of The Mountainy Men

The next day brought in the sunshine. In Cackles' haggart a crowd of men came together and rolled up their sleeves. They had brought with them forks and shovels and spades. They had sledgehammers, sickles and scythes. They had wheelbarrows and several bags of cement from The Quarries. They had buckets and they had hosepipes for the transportation of the stream's water. There was Hammer-the-Smith and there was Jack-the-Herd and there was Jim-the-Jinnet and there were even one or two of the High-and-Dry men and The Lackadaysicals down from over the hills. They leaned on their implements and they studied the stream from the safe distance of the haggart where they had placed the tar-barrels in a neat little row along by the hay-reek. Behind them stood Blue-eyed Jack with Teddy, the little fellow keeping an eye on all the preparations and proceedings. He was with his friend (Little Cull) and he remained standing between Blue-eyed Jack's legs. They were both full of excitement. They had never seen so many tar-barrels before and they wondered what sort of contraption the men were going to make with them and might they be putting wheels on these barrels and turning them into a train or a tractor – they weren't sure.

Cackles brought out a handful of rosary-beads that she had collected from the nearby women. She handed them out amongst the men to pray for the success of the tar-barrels. They bowed their heads solemnly and they began mumbling the responses to the rosary, saying the second part of The Hail Mary after The Yankee-Boy and Cackles. Finally all the children understood it: they were going to make a big tunnel through which Cackles' stream could be carried along and tipped into a great big waterfall below in the dyke before rushing on into Mikey's grove.

You wouldn't believe the way the men set about the work. The children had never witnessed such a sight before: the warding-off of the waters with a makeshift dam from Timmy's ditch: the stream raging itself down along The Open Road and into the ditch instead of into Cackles' Welcoming Room: the new trenches that the men's picks and shovels were making faster than a hen that had made up her mind to lay an egg: the meticulous measuring of the straight line for the tar-barrels: the bucket-loads of fresh cement. In the end there was no sight left of a single tar-barrel because all of them were buried beneath the cement. And then the sods of grass were piled high on top of the cement. The work was completed with the speed of light, the men all the while laughing and telling yarns and swearing good-naturedly and cursing one another's mothers and forefathers for giving birth to the likes of one another. And then they all traipsed back to the haggart, feeling a pious need to celebrate the birth of the tunneled stream. They dug their fists down into the buckets of stout and liberally consumed several mugs of the black stuff. There'd be a second need for a few more decades of the holy rosary in the evening when the women would ask God to help them in their everlasting war against the damned drink and the amounts of it that their men were always downing into their bellies if given half a chance. The whole day was as good as a circus and nobody would ever forget it.

## *Children's Sports In The Nettle Field*

It wasn't over yet. The afternoon suddenly came upon them. It was the turn of the children to show the men what they themselves were made of and to celebrate the baptism of the tar-barrels in their own childish ways. The men sat and looked on at them and they lowered the galluses of their britches and let their bellies (well full of the drinking medicine) hang out over their trousers like a sow's paunch. They waved their hands authoritatively and they gave out instructions for the start of the children's races in Cackles' Nettle-Field. They ordered the boys and girls to set up the twigs and long sticks for the start and finish of the races. They took off their own socks and they tied them around the children's ankles and taught them the three-legged race. Then there were the wheelbarrow races and the hop-step-and-a-jump and finally there was the pelting of the heavy rock, to see which of them could put it hopping off of Mikey's hayshed and damage his eardrums some fifty feet down the field.

In the meantime the little ones were lining the banks of the stream near Mikey's dyke, waiting for the arrival of the new waterfall. When they saw it coming out of the tar-barrels in a great big gush they jumped up and down and gave a tremendous cheer. The speed of the stream was immense. It was time for the men to gather armfuls of flaggards. With these they made their studious flaggard-boats and they passed them around amongst the children. They assembled the little contestants half-ways down the field where the bend gave the stream a chance to drop their new flotilla of ships into it. The race could now begin.

'Ready! Steady! Go!' yelled The Yankee-Boy.

The children let slip their boats and the bigger boys raced hell-for-leather down the field to see could they beat the flaggard boats sailing speedily down the stream. Each of them vied to be the first one to reach the wire-fence at the end of the field. The men and the children were all in their Heaven!

## The Hide-And-Go-Seek

Yet still the day of the tar-barrels hadn't ended. The last of the fun was the hide-and-go-seek. This was the best time of the day when the children (after relishing all the memories of what they had been seeing and doing) looked out over the haggart-stick and pined over the last of the reddening sun beyond Corcoran's Well. They could hear the little birds achingly calling to one another (telling their news of the day) as they settled themselves down in the trees for their roost and they could hear the faraway yelping of the vixen and the frightened responses of Gret's flock of turkeys as they scurried up into the pine-trees behind her hayshed. Everyone (old and young alike) now scattered themselves everywhere, looking for good places in which to hide from their seeker. One or two climbed on top of the haystack or on top of the turf and logs in Johnnie's two barns (the one for the ass and the horse and the other for the four calves) or they hid themselves in the upturned rattletrap.

Then came the best part of hide-and-go-seek: the absolute silence, as though the world was standing on its head or had come to an end: not even a single giggle out of anyone: a frozen moment in time. Would the seeker discover them in their remote hiding-place and would they be caught and made a fool of before they could reach the safety of the home-tree? The waiting in their lair and the listening for the approaching footfall was sheer agony and they nearly wet themselves with excitement.

The men (the women would never be caught acting so childishly as their men, the big simpletons) and the young girls and boys were each spinning their own fairy-tale webs through the charms of this new evening. But the men and one or two of the older boys had other things on their minds, the rascals. They made several playful attempts at lifting the older girls' dresses and to catch a glimpse ('they're lavender!') of the colour of their knickers. The squeals of the girls ('Go 'way – ye pack of basthards!') was mixed up with their own unladylike brazenness, for they were just as mischievous and lascivious as the men. Some of the younger boys got in on the act ('aren't ye the dirty little whoors!') and copied the men and made a grab at the skirts of some of the young women, who were at least ten years older than themselves. Jack-the-Herd pinned the beautiful Nora down behind the haystack near the hen-house and he wouldn't let her go until she offered him a big wet kiss. With her eyes closed and her mouth quivering, she was only too ready for the forfeit but (the devils that these men are!) he tiptoed away and he left her standing there like a pure eejit with her puckered set of lips and her expectant set of flickering eyelids. He ran down the haggart followed by her angry curses ('Ye whoor-of-all-whoors!') and his two sides hurt him from his sudden fit of laughter.

## Those Sad-Faced Fairies

But those solemn and sad-faced fairies that hide themselves in the trees and the streams and the ditches are never satisfied with a crowd of merrymakers and they were lurking close by. Gallant had been hiding a long way away from the rest of the children down behind the blackcurrant bushes. He was not alone. With him was the shy and breathless Noolah, Madge-the-Child's youngest daughter. The clumsy poet that he was, Gallant was trying to whisper into her ear (oh, the cheek of him! – had he no shame in him?) how much pain he'd been suffering of late from all the love he had for her. Noolah's eyes were starting to glow and she felt as high as the elm trees at home, for she had never heard such words of love spoken to her before.

The magic of the day, however, was punctured suddenly by Gallant's tragic screams and the leprechauns in Fort Dangerous must have hopped out over the ditch to see who had been killed. For as soon as this dreamy young lover and his dewy-eyed temptress thought they might be discovered in their hiding-place, they ran like hares in a bid to reach safety and escape the outstretched hands of the seeker (Hammer-the-Smith). Gallant had almost reached the home-tree when he tripped over Jack-the-Herd's discarded shovel and landed in the heap of briars that Johnnie had placed against the back ditch to keep out Timmy's cattle. When his screams were heard the games had to be stopped there and then as one and all came to stare at the damaged youth. The innocent face of poor Gallant was a river of blood. It reminded everybody of the sad face of Jesus and his crown of thorns. Indeed Gallant had the selfsame sad look of Jesus about him except that when the pain was inflicted on poor Jesus he had held on to his usual dignified composure and didn't shatter the ears of Jerusalem with his screams.

## *To The Rescue!*

Johnnie-tackle-the-ass had been sitting on his stool at the half-door and smoking his well-earned pipe and had not taken part in the evening's amusements. What would a man of seventy years of age want chasing after a bunch of young women and lifting up their skirts to see what was underneath them? Since the death of his little twins himself and the knickers had bidden each other a fond farewell (he'd have you know). When he heard Gallant's roars he found the energy of his past youth. He leaped up from the stool and like a rabbit after the gun is fired he ran behind the ditch where the briars were. He reached into their depths and caught Gallant by his two heels. He dragged him through the air for fifty feet down to the waterfall and he shook him the way you would a dead fish. The rivers of blood began to disappear from Gallant's face as Johnnie dried his wounds with bunches of dock-leaves. And then the good man called for the laurel leaves and he rubbed the juice of them onto Gallant's face. This (his grandfather had once told him) was the best of all cures for staunching the blood. He brought out the goose's quill and the bottle of iodine; he knew that before the first star rose over Rookery Rally's sky, Gallant's face would be as good as a new one.

Blue-eyed Jack took Teddy home, well-satisfied with the day's proceedings and making sure to thank God in their night prayers for the gift of the new tar-barrels that were tunneling Cackle's new stream away from her yard and for the healing hands of Johnnie-tackle-the-ass. When Rookery Rally's children closed their eyes for the night they knew that they had found themselves a new doctor, one that would compare very well with Doctor Glasses himself. In the days that followed (whenever they got an unhealthy cut or a thorn too deeply embedded in the soles of their feet) they would shout, 'Go fetch the doctor!' Everybody made a beeline for Johnnie-tackle-the-ass's yard, for they knew that he was the new doctor and they needed his laurel pastes and his quills and his iodine. Doctor Glasses wasn't going to make a shilling out of them for months to come. Indeed Johnnie-tackle-the-ass had become almost as sacred as the-bonesetter (Fingers Jack) who dealt with any breaks to the arms and legs of the men. And Cackles smiled with pride to think that Rookery Rally had found a master doctor in its midst in the shape of her own sound man and she all but canonized him.

## Cackles And Her Thoughts

When the shovels and the spades and men were gone away and when life had returned to normal, Cackles continued to be a subject for the road's attention. She laughed on her way to the creamery and she laughed on her way to Mass. She laughed when she was out in Bog Boundless and she laughed when she was pelting the spuds into the ass-and-car above in the wind on Smiling Babs' Heights. She laughed when she saw that Gallant's face was made new again and she laughed and put her hand to her chest when she realized she was the proud owner of a new tar-barreled stream. From time to time whenever she noticed a few passersby she would call them in the gate and she'd put her ear to the ground and she'd listen for the echoing sound of the water running through the tar-barrels. And they'd catch her laughing all over again when she led them into her haggart and hopped out over the ditch and inspected the new waterfall as it hissed out into Mikey's dyke below her. 'God is good! God is great!' she'd say.

## The Yankee Boy Has A Serious Thought

The time had come for The Yankee-Boy (the tar-barrel engineer) to pack his suitcase and take to the high road. He made the wise decision not to take the ship back to The Land of The Silver Dollar; it was too hot a place for so young a soul as himself and he was too young to go meet his death. With the announcement from Herald-the-Post that the great big war with the Germans was soon to be over and that these warriors had been well and truly chastised and put back in their box, The Yankee-Boy wrote a few lines to his brother (Jimbo) in The Land of John Bull. He had enough money still stashed in his hip-pocket to take Cackles and Johnnie-tackle-the-ass with him and he wanted to show them the fame and the beauties of that great big city, in spite of the fact that half of it had been blown to bits by the German bombs.

Johnnie-tackle-the-ass would hear none of it. 'I'm too old for this sort of thing,' he sighed and he waved The Yankee-Boy aside. Indeed he was terrified of the speed and the roars of the trains. He had heard dramatic reports of the sea's mighty waves and their pitching and tossing from shore to shore and the mere thought of it made him sick in his stomach (he had always had a weakness in that bit of him, he said).

## London Calling

The Yankee-Boy and Cackles took the holywater and they set out on their great big adventure. With a hop and a skip and a jump they reached London in less than a day-and a half and found themselves well-suited to the many glories that were to be seen in that great big place. With the dollars of the Yankee-Boy itchy to escape from his fist they had themselves a merry old time of it and Cackles began to feel that she had landed on the moon. She got herself up into the dome of The Great Cathedral itself and she walked around its Whispering Gallery and she toured around the statue of The Great Sailor in a place she called 'Travel-car Square'.

## The Glorious Return

After two long weeks she returned in a triumph that the bespectacled pope would have thought fitting only for himself. Before her return, however, the poor woman had been forced to say farewell to her Yankee-Boy and leave him behind in a greasy lodging-house in the dirty backstreets of London. She now held several audiences in her Welcoming Room and (isn't invention a fine thing?) she told her astonished listeners of her wonderful trip to The King's Palace. It was then that the lying tongues of the old gossips gave themselves a right good airing. They reported that Cackles had been to see The King and his lovely Queen and that The King had taken a real shine to Cackles and that he was more than pleased when she told him of the stream and the tar-barrels. The Queen laughed politely when she heard of Sing-me-a-song and her double-whistle. The King said he would write to the little whistler and invite her over for tea and a slice of his soda-cake. All this news was better than a circus, the way these old gossips went at it and spread it around. Did you ever hear of such lying hounds? The heathens that we breed here in Rookery Rally!

## A Tired Old Lady

Now that she was back amongst us, Cackles was seen to be a different woman from the one that had set sail with The Yankee-Boy. She hadn't become as proud as you might have thought or grown too grand in her ways so as not to talk to the rest of us. It was something else: she had lost most of her gaiety: her renowned laughter was seldom if ever heard. Hadn't Johnnie-tackle-the-ass desperately warned her not to be making a fool of herself and taking on such an arduous journey? Cackles had listened to none of his pleas. She knew better than him – as always. Now she knew how wrong she had been – the excitement of the trip had all been too much for her and she felt a strange foreboding rising up inside in her chest. She told no-one. She was a week short of sixty and she had laughed her way throughout her life, more than anyone else had ever laughed. But just as some of our women work themselves to the bone (even to the point of death) so it now was with Cackles: she had worn herself to a thread.

## Cackles And The Children

There was one more trick left in her. When the fuss of her first few days back home had died down, she summoned the children from up and down The Open Road into her yard and she showered them with presents that she'd bought them with The Yankee-Boy's dollars. The rusty bowlee-wheels and the box of coloured buttons and the sock-balls (and even the pig's bladder) could all go and bury themselves in the river!

In the following weeks, she spent hours on end telling the children her stories of the great big city. She herself was beginning to believe the tales spread about her. She told them how she had seen The King and his lovely Queen a number of times. It was then, perhaps, that one or two of the children (including Teddy) began to think that she had openly visited The King inside in his palace. Her tales grew and grew until the children believed that Cackles was sick and tired of having to go and take tea with the sad-faced King.

## And Then Came The Crash

A month to the day after her return, Cackles was abroad in her yard. She was watching the antics of Sing-me-a-song as the child was attempting to do cartwheels amongst the dock-leaves. The children heard a little cough and then they heard an almighty crash. Cackles had given them her last burst of laughter and she fell back down in her yard and she lay there like a stone, close beside the invisible stream that continued to flow underneath her feet. Sing-me-a-song ran to her mother and she gazed down into her glazed eyes. With her heart racing, the little girl leaned over the dear soul. 'Mother, mother, mother! Oh, dearest mother of mine, can you hear me?'

The old eyes blinked. The old hands reached out towards the child and the child felt the last squeeze of her mother. Then (what sort of heavenly angel must have taken hold of Sing-me-a-song's soul?) the little girl began to whistle. She whistled a tune that not even she had ever heard tell of before. Teddy and the other children stopped to listen and they jumped down from where they were swinging on the haggart gate. They came out through the gateway and the stream that had since disappeared. They saw the poor misfortunate Cackles stretched out on the broad of her back on the ground and they saw Sing-me-a-song and they heard the whistling-music pouring out over the face of her mother. The saints and the angels had come down from Heaven. They had entered the body of Sing-me-a-song and they had caused her to soothe away these last few moments of her mother's life. The children knew in their hearts that all the ghosts of their ancestors were standing nearby and were watching the sadness in the yard. They were giving Sing-me-a-song the strength and encouragement not to let her salty tears escape and overflow from her childish eyes, but to continue pouring out her unearthly whistling.

Johnnie-tackle-the-ass came in from the barn. He walked slowly down the yard in a daze. He knelt down beside the dying Cackles. The whistling ended. For the last time, Cackles closed her eyes and she and the heavenly music went off together out through the gap, out through The Hills-of-The-Past, The Valley of The Pig and Bog Boundless and she headed for the clouds and the heavenly sky.

Sing-me-a song took her dazed father down to the new waterfall where it continued to lash out into the dyke. She held him by the hands and she stood him alongside her in the very centre of the waterfall as it cascaded all over them. They were both soaked to the skin. The sins of her father and herself (although the child knew not what they were, so innocent was she and so guileless was he) were being cleansed forever and the crowd that gathered felt that the sins of us all were being washed away as they peered down over the wall.

The old man and the little child went up the dyke on the other side by the spring-well. They came into Dowager's yard. They came into The Welcoming Room. In their soaked skins, they stood there, not knowing what to tell her. At last Johnnie-tackle-the-ass spoke up: Cackles is dead,' he said.

'May the Lord have mercy on her soul,' sighed Dowager. She put some sticks on the fire. By now the neighbours had followed into the yard, looking in over her half-door and everyone's heart was as soft as a bog. Dowager poured out the last of the goose-soup and she ladled it into the shivering Sing-me-a-song and her father. She spoke not a word. For once in her life she didn't know what to say and her tongue was as thick as a cow's tail.

It wasn't as though Cackles was an old woman. Dowager could give her at least a ten years' start in the race towards old age. Nor had any of us seen the good woman giving a single day on the bed with any form of sickness. Twisting the dishcloth in her hands, Dowager's heart raced out of her body, full of the joys of their lifelong friendship. It was Cackles with her kettles of boiling water and her hot towels that had helped deliver most of Dowager's fifteen children (apart from the one or two born in haste abroad in the fields or by the well-hole when she was caught out suddenly). It was Cackles that rushed down the road with her candles and lamp and seemed to float through the air in her haste to get to The Welcoming Room. It was Cackles' delicate and persuasive fingers that were needed as Dowager tossed and turned on the bed. It was into Cackles' pair of eyes that the little babies first peered. And when each child landed on the blanket you should have seen the look of pure joy in Cackles as the happy tears rolled down her cheeks. And now she was gone, leaving behind her Johnny-tackle-the-ass to walk up-and-down The Open Road for the short remainder of his life with his perplexed and disillusioned thoughts and no more wish to tackle his ass and go collect a load of ferns. We knew that in her home in The Beyond Cackles was merely waiting for the day (it would soon arrive) when the good man would come and join her in the happiest of all possible reunions. Farewell to you, Cackles. Would we ever see your likes again?

# THIRTEEN

# Teddy And The English Visitor

*When a dark angel came
calling him from out over the sea*

It was August in the year of 1945. By now the purple-headed thistles (the bluebuttons, which gave Dowager's first field its name of The Bluebutton-Field) had all but gone, shedding their final snowy show. It was the season for the hips and haws and crabapples, ripe food for the thrushes and the shy rats. It was the start of autumn's preparations for the harsh winter ahead and (if one must speak plainly) it was going to be a harsh wintertime indeed for this little fellow, Teddy. He had spent his first five glorious years living the life of a royal prince, following in the footsteps of Dowager and Blue-eyed Jack from day to day. But sadly when the war with the Germans was coming to its inevitable conclusion, a hole was about to be torn in the lives of The Old Pair and eventually in the heartbroken child himself. It would be a pitiful and lasting separation, spiriting Teddy away from his pastoral joys and the only life and parenting he had ever known, returning him to the nightmare of a nakedly impoverished bombed-out city and to Little Nell and Shy Patsy, his true (but unknown) parents.

## Herald-The-Post Brings The News

We all knew Herald-the-Post, the man with the green-buttoned charcoal coat and the huge brown leather belt. He was the man whose face was pock-

307

marked like a cabbage-strainer and with radishes for cheeks and a slight lisp to his frothy lips. Unexpectedly one morning (it was just after cockcrow) Dowager found herself jumping to attention on hearing the noise of his rattling bike and the ringing of his loosely-secured bell. The postman raced in across the flagstones, frightening the contemplative ducks as they gazed at their reflections in the yard-stream – so much so that they jumped into the stream and went gliding off backwards towards the rusty blue kettle at the little waterfall. The chickens scurried off behind the ass-and-car and the bewildered cockerel (Rampant) flew up onto the hawthorn tree behind the horse-and-cart. A dust-cloud followed Herald as he swung his bike around the yard and threw it against the whitewashed wall, dislodging one or two slabs of the thick whitewash where his saddle came to rest.

Teddy was already at the half-door to see who was coming to meet them at this unearthly hour of the day. Herald ('How is The Little Englander this morning?') followed him in through the half-door and he dipped his hand into the holywater font and he blessed himself. 'God bless the work and God save all here!' said he and he removed his cap reverentially in the direction of Dowager and Blue-eyed Jack. He looked down at the inquisitive Teddy and he found himself suddenly unsettled by the intensity of the little boy's staring eyes. He didn't know how he was going to break the news to Dowager and Blue-eyed Jack that the war was over at last. It would mean that their little man would be going back to the parents who had sent him here shortly after his birth – to the parents who were unable to cross the treacherous sea themselves throughout this cruel war – to the parents that Dowager spoke of as Nell and Patsy and not as the child's own mother and father (not that Teddy would've had a notion what the word 'parents' meant anyway).

Herald slouched over towards the firelight and he sat down on the rickety three-legged stool. Teddy continued to follow him with those big eyes of his. Like all small boys with nothing else on his mind he absorbed all that was in front of him. Herald had a handy way of dangling his open-peaked cap on the edge of his outstretched knee. Its cardboard innards were the green-and-yellow colour of fresh horse-dung. He tap-tapped the Woodbine fag on his fag-box and he lit it expertly from the blazing fire and then he put back the wire tongs next to the soot on the hob.

Dowager wiped the baking-flour from her hands onto her apron and she ran to welcome her visitor. She was always glad to see Herald for he was the man (more than anybody else) with the most up-to-date news for her. In her eyes he was as refreshing as a sermon from the lips of Father Accessible and he could spend half-the-morning giving her a list of information as long as her arm to pass on to the rest of The Open Road. This morning (she hoped) he might be bringing her some warm news about her seventh son (Soldier Tom) who had settled in England and was fighting for his life on the sands of Africa. Maybe Herald had come to tell her that her son was alive and not yet killed. Oh, how many holy novenas had she made! Oh, how many rosaries had she offered up to Our Blessed Lady!

She had a few cuts of currant-cake hidden next to the icing sugar inside the lid of the rusty piano (Old Harpy) for she knew how much Herald cherished the way she baked it. All Teddy could do (the currant-cake was not for him) was watch open-mouthed as the visitor cheerfully swilled each slice down his throat with a mug of Dowager's weak wartime tea and watch the crumbs spitting from his mouth when the good man tried to speak. Blue-eyed Jack and Dowager were resting their elbows on their knees and leaning forwards with their heads almost inside Herald's mouth so as to hear the big news he was going to give them about the war.

For the past fortnight Rookery Rally and especially Curl 'n' Stripes' drinking-shop had been overwhelmed with hearsay and gossip about the fierce fighting that was coming to an end all over the map. Herald was holding the newspaper in his hand and he threw it down on the floor in front of Dowager. 'The war is finally over,' said he as he fished out a letter from his jacket and handed it to Dowager. She tore it open immediately. In it she read the wonderful news that Soldier Tom was coming out of the war, alive and kicking and with not a scratch on him. She was too old to go dancing a jig-step around the room with Blue-eyed Jack, but her heart almost missed a beat.

## Dowager Has A Dreadful Thought

A second later, however, she had a dreadful little thought to herself; it was the one that she'd been trying for ages to push to the back of her mind and bury altogether. She gave Herald a withered look he wouldn't forget in a long while: 'Yes, this cruel war is over, thank God,' said she. 'But (and she had a very hard job getting the next few words out of her mouth) the war inside in my own heart is just about to begin.' She pointed her finger at Teddy, who was innocently wondering what her words could possibly mean and why she was pointing her finger at him like that and looking so awfully sad and miserable. 'Myself and my little man,' she mumbled and her eyes filled up with big tears. 'My little man and Blue-eyed Jack,' and she threw a tormented look across at the big man who had to turn away from her. As though he hadn't quite believed Herald's latest news, Blue-eyed Jack scratched his head and looked sheepishly into the fire.

'What a terrible thing wars are,' he sighed. A puzzled look came into his sad eyes and at that moment he looked a lot older than he was. There was nothing else to be said and Herald quickly reached for his cap and escaped out the door with the meekest of goodbyes. Dowager reached for her sewing materials on the nail beside the Saint Brigid's cross. The few times in the past that she'd ever had reason to be sad she would made herself busy in this way so as to hide her tears and this was going to be her saddest hour of all. Blue-eyed Jack knew of the pain and the heartache that was going on inside his mother. She couldn't hide it from him for they were as close as two sides of a sheet. She started to concentrate on her sewing and she kept rolling her tongue around silently in her toothless old jaw. Unable to prevent herself, she stabbed her fingers with the pincushion needle as she fumbled amongst her button-box for her thimble and a suitable reel of thread. It was no use. She couldn't concentrate. The light-heartedness, which had brought back a pink glow of youth to her cheeks during these last five years with her little man (everyone talked about it), had suddenly departed from her and she became deeply aware of her big age. Indeed she felt she was growing older by the minute. She threw down the box on the table and she hobbled off into her little bedroom. Blue-eyed Jack didn't know what to do. He tidied up the scissors and the sewing materials and he put them away. He heard his mother foraging for the sweets in her drawer (the humbug ones) to fish a few out for her grandson. She hadn't the heart to tell the child the terrible news and she started blowing her nose repeatedly. She knew that events as alarmingly sad as this one was wouldn't be kept secret or hidden from the child for too long; someone was bound to tell him what the next step was going to be for him.

# *There Had Been Five Good Years*

She'd had five years of unhurried bliss (she was thinking). These were good years here in Rookery Rally and Ireland when she and the rest of the country were forever blessing themselves and thanking God ten times a day that they had never got a lick of the awful killings – that they had escaped the flames from the German bombers which had left poor England in ruins. She grew into her thoughts and she cast her mind back: at a time when there were millions of children starving to death elsewhere, how fortunate was this little man of hers! It was he that had the spud and the cabbage, the rabbit and the fish and the fat meat from the pig in the barrel. It was he that had the woodlands and the hills and the rivers for his playground and the hunting and the fishing and the bringing home of the turf from Bog Boundless alongside Blue-eyed Jack. It was he that had the endless ass-and-car journeys all over the countryside, be it to Hammer-the-Smith's forge or The Copperstone Hollow creamery or Father Accessible's church in the mountains.

But just as there had to be a beginning to this terrible war, there also had to be an end to it – an end to her life with The Little Englander. She wondered what Blue-eyed Jack was thinking right now and she went to her little box-room and she crawled into her bed and slid further down under the sheets and rolled the blankets up around her head. For the first time ever she was well and truly beaten by events. In the days to come it'd be just the two of them (herself and Blue-eyed Jack, The Old Pair) left sitting on their own and looking vacantly across the firelight at one another. In a week or two Little Nell and Shy Patsy (she knew) would demand their rights and the little man would have to go back across the sea.

What had it all come down to? In the end this child had been nothing but a loan (not a gift) to herself and Blue-eyed Jack – nothing more than a bag of sugar to be given back one fine day when the time came. Five years had been and gone and how on earth (tell me this, she said to herself) was a small child like Teddy going to cope with it all – how was he expected to sail back to a set of parents who were as unknown to him as the man in the moon? How would she and Blue-eyed Jack ever be the same two people again? In all but name they were the child's parents and had grown as close to him as the feathers round a chick? Little Nell and Shy Patsy might as well be demanding back their own souls – might as well be snatching away their very hearts from out of their bodies – so much had five years taught them to love and cherish this little fellow. And inside in her little bedroom Dowager went on and on thinking these bitter thoughts to herself – went on and on wiping away her silent tears with the edge of the sheet.

## The Innocence Of A Child

Oh for the innocence of a child! Teddy had no warning whatsoever of the pains that were about to come to him. One bright day was the same as any other bright day as he nestled contentedly under his warm blankets in his lat-board bed with the straw bags underneath him. And after Dowager said the Blessing Prayers with him and washed his hands and face for him in the grey pan and went over his counting and his few poems and songs, he was as free as the Bog Wood pigeons in this little hideaway world of his. And during the next few days, as his grandmother watched him and his stick running like fury through the hens and the ducks, she couldn't take her eyes off of him. It was as though she was seeing him for the very last time. One day soon he'd be taking his little brown suitcase: he'd be heading for that strange steam-train up to Dublin and out over the sea – to a land where a blackened city would pour new and strange insecurities into him and replace forever the simplicities of farmyard chickens and meadows-flowers, rabbits and river fishes and the laughter of red-faced Mountainy Men. That's what she kept thinking to herself. There was no end to her sorrow.

## Blue-Eyed Jack And His Miserable Thoughts

Blue-eyed Jack was abroad in the haggart. He was walking around in circles near the potato-pit where himself and Teddy had stored the Arran-banner and Kerr's pink spuds. The spuds were deep down in the darkness underneath a load of straw to keep the rats out. Like the spuds (he thought) Teddy would soon be gone from sight and stored away from the light of the Tipperary sun. He'd be buried deep in some dark place, deep in some godforsaken hole-of-a-basement in the depths of a bombed-out street in the city that he and his mother always referred to as The City of Pandemonium. That's what he was thinking to himself and the cows would be lucky if one of them got milked this day, so engrossed was he in his hour of sadness. Like his mother he had to busy himself and he wanted to be on his own. He covered his shoulders with the potato-sack against the rain and he trudged down The Open Road to John's Gate and The Bull-Paddock to meet his seven cows. He was soon swallowed up inside the grey misty veils of the cold slanting rain. A few stray jackdaws and mischievous carrion crows hopped and rustled from tree to tree and a family of young rabbits disturbed the morning mushrooms as they skittered back to the safety of The Bog Wood. In a huddle underneath the crab-trees the sleepy cows stood facing him, avoiding the sandpapery cuts of the wind and the rain.

## *Dowager And Her Miserable Thoughts*

Teddy was in his usual dreamland and sitting with his box of coloured buttons on the upturned ass-and-car. Dowager peeped out from her blankets and she looked out her back window where she saw the light rain falling. In the smoky chimney behind her in her Welcoming Room she heard the winds moaning and screeching. She was angry with God and had one or two harsh words to say to him. But (as usual) she began sibilating her prayers and asking him to protect herself and her two men this day and always. A little while later she sneaked out from her bedroom door and she gazed out across the half-door at her yard and the yard-stream and Teddy with his buttons. She looked away from him. Behind the pig-house (in Timmy's Lane) she saw the first of the leaves turning to a waxy yellow. Soon the winds of September would rattle off of the pig-house roof and they would send the leaves gusting all over the yard. Soon the hen-house roof would be crimson with haw-berries and the yard-stream would be fuller than ever, gurgling brazenly on its way towards River Laughter. Later in the day the children would return from school and would race at the piles of leaves that she'd heaped up and they'd crackle them playfully under their feet.

Suddenly she heard Smiling Babs' children (was it eight o'clock already?) tapping their bare feet down The Open Road towards her flagstones. They were always out at this unearthly hour of the day when her cockerel (Rampant) and the hens and ducks were not yet out the hen-house door. Golly prodded the little ones onwards with the ash-plant. They had their boots slung over their shoulders and tied with string. Fiddler-Joe had warned them to save their boot-leather till they came to the school door. 'Quick march!' shouted Golly. 'Lift up your knees and put a spur into it! Left-right – left-right – up and at them!' His back was as straight as a mule and his face was covered with sweat from the marshalling he was doing and the warmth of his echoing voice outweighed the weeping grey skies above him. He knew that Dowager and her natural inquisitiveness would be looking out over her geraniums on the windowsill and admiring the strut of their marching feet.

'Us boys! Us girls!' sang the four children, 'take a look at us – we are the darting fine scholars of the road!' Before they reached the school yard they'd be singing another song in praise of their kindly master (Dang-the-skin-of-it) whose predecessor (Big Screech) was known to have had the strength of a blacksmith in both her fists and to have knocked far more sense out of her pupils skulls than into them. Dowager rested her elbows on the half-door as the little group went by and she gave them a half-hearted wave. They were like fluffy goslings (she thought) – all in a straight line. The misty rain had already washed their feet and ankles and she gave a little sigh as they disappeared from sight (they'd soon be crossing the metal bridge over River Laughter). Once again she was interrupted by a flurry of thoughts about Teddy: he'd not be taking the same trip with these young scholars: he'd not be learning how to write his name and do his sums on his slate alongside them. She turned away from the last faint echoes of their voices and she went in through the half-door, cursing Life and all that it had finally brought her.

# Back In A Gloomy London Basement

Now that the war was over, Little Nell and Shy Patsy were anxious to welcome back the child they had once let go from them. Teddy's mother put her skills with the pen-and-ink to the test and she sent Dowager one or two short and discreet reminders ('It'll soon be time for Teddy to come back home'). Home? Where was the child's home? Surely his home was inside the embracing folds of Dowager's black skirts and up on the broad shoulders of Blue-eyed Jack? His home was in the heart of these timeless hill-slopes. It had always been his home, as far back as his childish mind could remember. Herald-the-Post was quick to deliver each of Little Nell's little notes to Dowager and he was twice as quick to make his retreat from the yard. He guessed what Teddy's mother had written inside each envelope. Dowager (for once in her life) was lost for words and she didn't know how to reply; so she didn't write back. Little Nell threw caution to the winds and she spread her pen and ink rapidly across the pages and posted a series of urgent impassioned letters. Thick and fast they came and they kept poor Herald permanently up on the saddle of his bike. There was no more polite ceremony in the flow of Little Nell's words. Their insistency hit The Old Pair like a lump of gelignite: Dowager and Blue-eyed Jack were asked to make haste and give back the little boy they had tended and nurtured like a young plant in a beautiful garden.

## *Sadness Gets A Complete Hold*

'It's too late now… it's much too late,' cried Dowager.

'We have reared him as our own. Whole and entire, we have loved him as if he were our firstborn son,' cried Blue-eyed Jack.

'We have given him the heart out of our bodies,' the two of them kept whispering to one another across the evening fire.

## *A Futile Plea For Intercession*

The battle had started. Dowager took the ass-and-car and (in lofty language that she never knew she possessed) she made a desperate effort to bend the ear of Father Accessible after Mass. She then went and gave a few heavy raps of her ash-plant on the oak panels of Doctor Glasses' door. She begged these two wise men to put their educated thinking-caps on and put pen to paper and appeal for a stay of sentence – if only for another year when Teddy's schooling would be starting. After that she went racing off to the school-house door. She inveigled the respected voice of Dang-the-skin-of-it to add weight to their cause. And all the time herself and her red eyes spent the evenings with her candle, writing ceaseless letters up at the front table and finally accosting even the ears of the foreign consul in his ivory tower above in Dublin. These skirmishes left a small breathing space for the three souls to remain wrapped together. That was all it was – a little bit of space and a little bit of time for them.

## Those Old Gossips, The Weeping Mollys

Life could sometimes drag on a bit for one or two women with nothing else to do but fold their arms at the well-hole and give their tongues a good airing. This was a great moment for them to start their sad whisperings. They shook their heads lugubriously and their tongues spread their words abroad on cruel wings from one day to the next: 'For-the-love-of-God, wouldn't anyone pity the likes of Little Nell and the fight she now has on her hands – just to get back what is rightfully hers – the return of her own child?'

## The London Plot Is Laid Out

In the meantime Little Nell and Shy Patsy were seated round the table in their damp basement and doing their own bit of whispering and planning what next they might be doing. Across from them sat Polish 'n' Shine (Little Nell's younger sister). She had thrown herself on Little Nell's protection from Dowager's promised pitchfork to her backside after she had mysteriously brought forth a baby boy (Paddy) – a son she'd been tearfully forced to hand over to the nuns, never to set eyes on again. Nobody could say that Polish 'n' Shine hadn't had her own load of grief to bear.

## Polish 'n' Shine

It was a strange name for her to have been saddled with. Out of all Dowager's seven daughters it was she that had a pure mania (Dowager had called it a disease) for keeping everything clean and spotless. Since her childhood she had been fastidiousness itself: dusting here, there and everywhere: washing here, there and everywhere – even removing the dirt from the floor of The Welcoming Room when there wasn't a single bit of dirt to be seen. 'Why,' laughed Blue-eyed Jack as he stopped one day to inspect his young sister's work, 'isn't it time for you to go polish and put a shine on the pigs and the ass and the gander and the drakes?' Dowager had to shake her head. It was true for him and the name of Polish 'n' Shine stuck to her from that day onwards.

Polish 'n' Shine listened attentively to the sorrows of Little Nell. She saw plainly how Shy Patsy too was almost at his wit's end (though the shy man was always loathe to unveil his innermost feelings). It was time for them to decide whether it was safe to cross the sea and fetch back Teddy. The stormy Irish Sea would be just the beginning of their worries: would Dowager simply hand Teddy over to them like a wet rag? This they very much doubted. They'd have to come up with a plan, a way of enticing the innocent child away from The Old Pair and bring him safely back across the sea.

'This is where you'll come into your own,' said the persuasive voice of Little Nell to her sister. It was Polish 'n' Shine's one and only chance to put a polish and shine on her own sad and tarnished image and redeem herself of her sin in the eyes of her sister and Shy Patsy. Like one or two other country girls she had found herself in the coddling arms of one fine fellow and then another fine fellow each of whom had the gift of fine words, each of whom admired her comely features. She had known those hidden joys (it was only once or twice, she said) that come between youthful thighbone and thighbone inside the ditch where she'd avoided the searching lamp of the lascivious priest (Father Loveless) hunting young lovers after Judy Rag's Platform Dance. But with an unexpected child growing in her belly she had been forced to trundle her suitcase and a purse with a brown ten-shilling note in it to the train-station and get the cattle-boat across to England. Father Chasible had been alive at the time. He had made it clear that, if she didn't get herself out across the high sea, he'd blast her from the altar steps. You'd think she was a leper! What choice had she? Staying at home would mean facing the wrathful hands of himself and that pompous old guard (Tommy Hee-haw) and the savagery of the nuns in Kilhooley's Laundry, who would have grabbed her by the throat and dragged her inside their gates and persecuted her for the rest of her days. That's the way it always was, she knew.

## Dowager And The Parish Priest

It had been a very sad time for Dowager. She had become nothing short of a laughing-stock among the old gossips at the well-hole. She saddled up her ass-and-car once more and she leathered her ash-plant into the back of her sulky old ass (The Lightning Whoor). She accosted the alarmed Father Chasible in his own sanctuary: 'I'll give you and your equals some of my medicine, my good man, the way you've been broadcasting my daughter's name all over the place!' She stamped her boots around his room. She waved her ash-plant in the air. She threatened to report him to Bishop High-Hat in his fine palace in Ennis if he didn't restore her daughter's good name and character. Not many women were as brave as Dowager in fighting for her daughter's self-respect against the powers of the priest, but in times like this her heart was as fierce as the gander watching over the nest. She knew in her heart of hearts, however, that it was no use firing her angry bolts at Father Chasible like this. Her daughter and the baby was a pure scandal and she'd have liked nothing better than to drive her pitchfork up into Polish 'n' Shine's 'shitty little arse' (that's what she said, as she raced back home with her terrified ass).

## Polish 'n' Shine Sails Out Over The Sea

After crossing the sea to England – it was shortly before the war started – Polish 'n' Shine found herself without a man to support herself and her baby. That year (1938) wasn't even half over when with mournful eyes she succumbed to the entreaties of the Sisters of Mercy who came knocking at her door and begging her to give up her baby (and he not yet a year old) and to let them carry him back to the orphanage with them. When they reached the doors of the convent they almost sucked the tiny child out of her frail and tearful arms and it broke her heart to see the way they trundled him up the orphanage steps. With his cries and his outstretched arms the little fellow gazed back at her – a gaze on him like Jesus-from-the-cross looking down at his sad mother and that sting-of-all-stings would remain in Polish 'n' Shine's heart forever and ever.

Back home in Rookery Rally the gossiping went on: 'Another child born in lust outside the church's Sacrament of Holy Wedlock (tut-tut-tut!),' said the old cronies (this time, outside the church door). 'Another chain in the fence to keep the bread and milk flowing into the holy nun's coffers,' said Little Nell and Shy Patsy bitterly – and they knew more than most.

But now (yes, now) Polish 'n' Shine was going to stretch out her arms to Teddy, albeit misguidedly. She would show him the warmth that was always in her and she'd bring back to England this little boy (almost the same age as her orphaned Paddy) and she'd deliver him to a city and parents who would teach him a new way of living in his new country. She'd board the train to Wales and she'd bravely catch the midnight cattle-boat to Ireland in the face of the last German rearguard attacks on the sea. She'd use all the wiles and guiles that herself and Little Nell and Shy Patsy had mustered after plotting and scheming at the table in their gloomy basement.

In the years of her childhood it had been Polish 'n' Shine (alone amongst her brothers and sisters) who had dared to get up on the bridge above River Laughter with its slippery moss, ferns and ivy. It was she alone who had dared to walk the twenty-foot length and the four-inch width of the rail that loomed thirty feet above the purling waters. Witness the hush amongst the rest of the children as she balanced her way along the length of the bridge. Even the crows were silent. Would this be the day that Polish 'n' Shine (the daredevil that she'd always been) got herself killed? She had always made it look as though she would fall headlong into the river (especially when she was the last few feet from the pier) but she'd make a balletic little leap towards the pier and land on her tippy-toes to a bout of triumphal applause. Now, however, she was bent on a far more serious balancing-act as she headed across the sea to tempt back Teddy to his parents. She didn't know what to expect. She hadn't set eyes on this little boy since the day she delivered him (a small fluffy package) five years earlier into Dowager's doting arms. This was going to be a difficult and roguish task for a woman like her – a woman who had sinned before God and Holy Mother Church and was in the direst need of redemption. There was no way round it: it was time for her to step forward and perform her solemn duty: it was time for her to win back her previous good name in the eyes of Little Nell, who had been her sole champion when everybody else stood against her: it was time for Teddy to give up his five-year merrymaking and come back to his parents: it was time (though she put this thought completely out of her head) to drag him cruelly away from his happy and blissful life with Dowager and Blue-eyed Jack.

## The Steam Train Trundles In

With a screech and a roar the Dublin train came into the station. It was followed by a great big hiss of steam. During the last half-hour of the journey Polish 'n' Shine had been feverish with a series of mixed feelings. The many stations that she had passed had reminded her of her previous shamefaced journey in the opposite direction the day Father Chasible had banished her unceremoniously from her home. Seeing these same stations again, she was worried sick about what Dowager would say to her and she offered God a few sincere decades of her rosary as the train drew nearer and nearer to The Roaring Town. This day (she felt) was going to be a lot worse than when she stood precariously on top of the metal bridge. She reached for her big suitcase and her hatbox and the other small and empty suitcase that she'd brought for Teddy to take back with him. She prepared herself to face the worst.

## The Guilt Of Little Nell

At that same moment Little Nell and Shy Patsy (almost five hundred miles away) were saying their own decades of the rosary, sensing that there'd be an unholy war between Polish 'n' Shine and Dowager. Teddy's mother felt ashamed for not having had the courage to go back herself to fetch her child and she was glad not to be standing in her sister's shoes this very minute. Had she taken this journey, she would never have been able to look Dowager in the eye since she too had left Tipperary in some disgrace some years back, having had the downright nerve to go off and elope with Shy Patsy and not wait for her mother's blessing. It was a thing no girl in her right mind had ever done before. And had she now been the one that was stepping down from the train she feared she'd be getting the proverbial pitchfork into her hind-quarters for having left home so abruptly (and so thanklessly, as Dowager would have told her).

## Blue-Eyed Jack Goes Into Town

Knowing that Polish 'n' Shine would arrive at noon, Blue-eyed Jack washed himself in the yard-stream (a task he usually reserved only for attending Mass) and he tackled up Moll-the-mare. He held out his palm and gratefully received the eight coppers from his mother – for the toast and the drink when he'd meet Polish 'n' Shine and take her up to The Widda-widda-woman's drinking-shop in Jinnet Street. He was bent on giving his sister a proper greeting and a cheerful welcome home that said all was forgiven. It was going to be no easy task for him as he half-guessed the reason for her visit – to try and take away his little fosterling. With a heart full of mixed emotions he drove into the town and he prepared to meet his young sister and show her when the time came just how happy Teddy was to be living here with Dowager and himself.

He saw Polish 'n' Shine stepping down from the train amid the belching steam and smoke. She was dressed in a stylish red coat with a brooch on it and she was wearing a black hat cocked sideways on her head and she had a new set of high-heeled shoes that must have been crippling the feet off of her. With her painted lips and her powdered cheeks she made a few tentative steps towards him and (acquainted as she was with the new ways of London) she coyly offered him her cheek so that he could plant a big wet kiss on it. Blue-eyed Jack had always been a good-natured fellow with a childish softness near the surface of his heart but he avoided this new and uneasy way of greeting her and he shook her warmly by the hand. Kisses in Rookery Rally were slobbery old things and the death-dealing tubercolosis was rife everywhere and even newborn babies were never picked up to be kissed but were put down on the floor to play with their rattle. Besides, there had always been an awkward shyness in this sort of wet-lipped tomfoolery and no-one had ever seen a man kissing even his own mother – such being the reserved withdrawal and respectful courtesy of us all. Nevertheless, his handshake was firm and it was true and Polish 'n' Shine breathed a sigh of relief, feeling that she had been forgiven for her past sin.

The big man and his smiling blue eyes lifted her cases and her hatbox in between the horse-and-cart's cripplers and he tied them with the secure rope. The two of them hopped up on the lace of the cart and they headed for the archway that led to the ostler's yard behind The Widda-widda-woman's drinking-shop.

## Mick The Drooth

The ostler (Mick-the-Drooth) welcomed them warmly and rubbed his greedy hands together. 'Here comes Polish 'n' Shine and a hatful of her old foreign money,' said he to himself. He knew that there'd be a copper or two in his fist a minute from now. He untackled Moll-the-mare and he gave her a good sop of hay. He stowed the chains and tackling in the loft and he made a grab at the coppers that Polish 'n' Shine handed him. They'd be down inside his belly before you could blink an eye, in the shape of two good pints of creamy stout. The same fellow (it was said) could drink The Mighty Shannon River bone-dry, such was his savage taste for stout whenever he got his hands on a glass of it. Blue-eyed Jack felt a little bit sad to be looking at him. The drinking-shop was rightfully Mick-the-Drooth's inheritance since he was the eldest son. Everybody knew the fact that his younger brother (Red Smiler) had been handed poor Mick's birthright by his dying father because that young scamp was crafty enough never to have let a drop of stout past his lips, the rascal.

## In The Snug Bar

Blue-eyed Jack and his sister headed into the Ladies' Snug-Bar and soon the big man was wiping the froth of the stout from his parched lips with the corner of his coat and his sister was cocking her little finger daintily (in the English way) over her glass of port. All was nice and proper and the ruby port was putting a sparkle on her cheeks. She described in glowing terms the actions of the war back in London. Like the rest of us she was well equipped to throw in a bit of the dramatics here and there and Blue-eyed Jack felt sure that she was telling him nothing but a pack of downright lies.

'On more than one occasion I was damn near bombed out of my shoes,' said she without the blink of an eye. 'And believe you me, Jack, it's a miracle I wasn't removed from the face of the earth with the German bombs and the hot flames hurling down like rain every blessed night of the week – they were as big as bread-vans'. She never stopped to catch a breath, but went rattling on like a steam-engine and the glass of port seemed to give her tongue a fine old oiling. 'And once,' said she, 'they missed me by no more than an inch and that's the God's own truth' and she indicated the distance with her dainty thumb and her forefinger.

To calm her nerves she searched into her purse and she bought another glass of port for herself and a glass of stout for her big brother. And then her tongue raced on again with tales of the torn-off remnants of roofs and the heaps of bricks and the glass and the plaster and the twisted wires and the dead cables and the lolling drainpipes and the air full of the hot dust and smoke: 'I had to fight my way out of the rubble with my torn fingers and my bare nails,' she sighed. 'And it makes my skin crawl to tell you of the shattered windows each morning and the armchairs and beds strewn along the streets and the sight of the latest bombsites at the corner of our road and the crushed people's arms and legs – and their heads everywhere – dead, dead, dead, all over the place.'

To such an extent did she embellish her tales of this terrible war (the second glass of port still only halfway down) that Blue-eyed Jack soon had a smirk on his lips, thinking his young sister was as good as a missioner's sermon and a match for Dowager when it came to telling her great big lies. He placed his hand on her knees: 'Sister, dear sister of mine, will you for god-sake go easy on me and hold back your tongue before you totally destroy me with these terrible tales of yours and how you narrowly escaped Sergeant Death's clutches.' And then he ruined everything completely by saying, 'I could get a few more cunning lies out of you if I could only put my hands round your throat and squeeze them out of you!' Had he been over in London, however, to witness the savage scenes on the midnight streets, he'd have known that his sister's so-called lies were but half a step away from the truth – it had indeed been a most vicious war. For a moment the two of them were silent and then they both started to laugh at each other and to relax in one another's company. Polish 'n' Shine felt good to be back with her warm-hearted brother (the third glass of port helped things along nicely) and they headed out to Moll-the-mare and were soon driving towards the purple mountains – and the dreadful task she knew she'd have to engage herself in, that of enticing back to England her little nephew, Teddy.

## The Scary Reunion

Moll-the-mare brought the cart trundling into the yard and over the stream where Dowager and Polish 'n' Shine greeted one another warmly enough at the flagstones and then there was another sigh of relief from the lady-in-the-rich-clothes as she stood in front of Teddy's staring eyes. As soon as Polish 'n' Shine had seated herself by the fire, Dowager (to stop herself from crying) began her busy chores. From an already-clean yard she started brushing away those imaginary bits of dung left over by her fowl and her sow. You'd think she was Polish 'n' Shine herself, the way she went at it. She scattered anything that got in her way: the chickens and the ducks, the geese and the sow – even the fierce gander and Smiling Babs' cat (Hen-chaser). The rage in her chest was against this daughter of hers – coming back here (and another filthy curse wasn't far from Dowager's lips) to snatch away her little man from underneath her nose, if she got half the chance. But her anger was also soft around the edges for she could never forget the way Father Chasible ('that miserable old cur,' she called him) had forced Polish 'n' Shine to go abroad – as if a good many more young women hadn't married in haste with a child in their bellies. And the sorrow that she felt almost drowned out her rage against Polish 'n' Shine when she remembered the way her daughter had been forced to give up her own little son to The Sister of Mercy – like she herself might now have to give up her beloved Teddy.

## True To Her Name

Polish 'n' Shine was true to her name. The very next morning she was up before the cockerel (Rampant) and as busy as a bird on the nest. She took down the two large goose-wings from amongst the horse's tackling next to the hob. She took the little goose-quills for tending to the delicate corners of each room. So much leeway had she to make up in recompense to her mother that she now outdid even her own high standards in the way she went spit-and-polishing. It was as though she was waving a magic wand and The Welcoming Room became a glorious sight and it shone like a new pin so that Blue-eyed Jack and his dirty wellingtons were almost afraid to come in through the half-door.

Abroad in the yard she scrubbed the two creamery tanks near her mother's garden till they shone like the sweet gallons below in Curl 'n' Stripes' shop-window. She swept all around The African Sink where Blue-eyed Jack's fishing-maggots were sleeping and waiting for the next fishing trip and she heaped up the dung from the pig-house, the hen-house and the cowshed into three great big pyramids. Was there ever a woman in the whole of Ireland so worthy of the name Polish 'n' Shine?

## Just Another Sunny Day

In the meantime the daylight was dribbling in through the shutters of The Big Cave Room and glowing around the razor-strap on the nail and the carmine geraniums in the window-box were shivering in the early morning light. Once more the big man and his blue eyes came in the bedroom door to awaken the child that had been wrapped against his warm belly during the past night and every other night that he and Teddy could ever remember. As he always did, he now stamped his wellington boots past the bee-strewn laurels in the empty chimney-hole, pretending to be a fighting soldier on the march against The Tans. The bespectacled pope in the picture looked down as always. Teddy curled himself up under the five blankets and he listened to yet another sound – Dowager waddling in with her clickety-clackety boots. She had a spoonful of butter-and-sugar for him – as always: 'It's twenty-minutes-to-sixty (the 'sixty' being his usual wake-up call) and butter-and-sugar for Teddy,' she caroled. Blue-eyed Jack stretched out his hands towards the child's golden curls and the bald patches and with a loving fatherliness he rubbed his beardy jaws against Teddy's smooth rosy cheeks. There was a whimper of joy from the child and he leaped out from the nest and he ran over to Dowager's black apron-folds.

There came a third sound – Polish 'n' Shine sauntering into the Big Cave Room. She pretended not to notice the loving playfulness of the three happy souls. She had other things on her mind. With Little Nell she had rehearsed her story with as much care and attention as an actress. The two of them had called their little piece of inventiveness 'The Song of The Swing-Swong' and today would be the day to test it out. She had been awake half the night rehearsing the words of her speech inside in her head:

'There'll be no hunting the rabbits today, Teddy'.

'There'll be no ploughing or tramming of the hay today, Teddy'.

'There'll be no going to Growl River's Sally-hole for the big swim today, Teddy'.

'We're off to see The Swing-Swong.'

But enough for now – there was time later on to put all these plans of hers into action: she'd wait till she got half-a-chance. Teddy rushed out in his shirt to The Welcoming Room and he sat by the blazing fire. The Old Pair went out the half-door. They'd soon be busy at the milking. There wasn't a soul listening. Polish 'n' Shine counted her blessings. She realized that this was as good a time as any for her to perform her dark and dirty deed.

## 'Come With Me Over The Fields, Teddy'

'Would you like to come over the fields with me, Teddy? I can tell you all about the new Swing-Swong?' she whispered in his ear. The Swing-Swong? What on earth was a Swing-Swong? This was a new one on Teddy. Was it some kind of new adventure? Was it some kind of new animal? Was it some kind of new bush or flower? The inquisitive child was anxious to know more.

Dowager, however, had gone out only to fetch in a bundle of logs before going on to the cowshed to help her son with the milking. She was outside the half-door and was just about to come in with her bundle when she stopped. She drew back a step or two and from the pig-house gap she listened to this proposed tale of mystery about a so-called Swing-Swong. She couldn't put her finger on why she was worried but she had the strangest feeling that mischief was afoot inside in her own Welcoming Room – that the serpent from Eden was creeping into her garden and planning some kind of a raid on her own little man. She searched deep in her mind. She tried to find what miserable badness might be lurking in the heart of her daughter but all she could see was a lifeless hole inside in her own old heart and she went back out the pig-house gap to relay her feelings to Blue-eyed Jack.

Polish 'n' Shine took Teddy by the hand. They skipped out the half-door. They went over the haggart singletree, she in her new wellingtons and he in his bare feet as always. The child followed the new woman along the wheel-ruts to The Bluebutton Field in much the same way as the springtime goslings had once tumbled helplessly after their mother. This was a strange little fellow (thought Polish 'n' Shine as she looked down at Teddy) – him and his comical long-striding steps and the straw in his mouth and the occasional spit at a fly in the cow-dung. In the past few years he had developed his own amusing charms, which all the hill-folk had grown to love in him (their Little Englander). It could be seen everywhere – whether he was striding up-and-down The Open Road or taking his gallon to the well for water – whether he was visiting the pig-killing yards or catching the goose with Blue-eyed Jack so that Dowager could take her knife and saw into the blood-vessels in its neck – whether he was racing away from Gret's fierce sow with Gret's shrill laughter ringing in his ears behind him.

The two of them crossed The Deer Field. They left Timmy's Field and its ragwort weeds on their left and they reached the gap with the stick across it. They followed towards the gate with the potato-sack across it to keep the geese from wandering too close to the fox in the Bog Wood. They passed by Corcoran's Well and the fields of rabbits (there'll be no hand-clapping today – to see their scattering white tails as once you did, Teddy). They arrived at The Seventh Field, where the child's mother (Little Nell) had been born those many years ago when Dowager crawled hurriedly out over the ditch to save herself from embarrassment.

# *The Tall Tale*

It was time for The Tale of The Swing-Swong. Polish 'n' Shine sat down on the rusty handle of the nearby plough and a humming-tune dribbled casually from her heart to her head and from her head to her lips. The two of them were silent for a little while as they gazed out at the twin peaks of The Two Goats Hill where the older children were busily chanting their Tables and reciting their patriotic poems for Dang-the-skin-of-it in the school-house.

The woman and the child looked back behind them at The Forest of Lisnagorna, underneath which lay the snug little cabin of Gentility amidst the pine-trees. It was time for Polish 'n' Shine (where was her wretched heart?) to start painting this little boy his new picture – a picture of purest illusion – the most exciting story he would ever hear.

She strolled over to the harrow that was lying in the nettles. She stroked its pink-painted wooden struts and its thick teeth and its long chains. She gazed at the stout swingle-tree beam across it – the same swingle-tree that during ploughing-time had been thrown across the chests of Moll-the-mare and Fandango, shortly before he died from the ragwort poisoning. Teddy followed the new woman's eyes to the harrow – the same harrow that made it so difficult for little birds to get at the seeds – the same harrow that brought joy to the corn when it covered the seeds in their darkness here in The Seventh Field. And then Polish 'n' Shine nodded towards the harrow and the swingle-tree:

'That's a mighty fine harrow you have there, Teddy,' said the weasel in her.

''Tis,' said the child, absentmindedly.

'And look at the fine long chains you have on it,' said the weasel in her. (Was the child listening?)

'And look at the fine swingle-tree across the chains' added the weasel in her. (What strange news was this new woman going to bring him, thought Teddy)

'There are swings across the sea in England,' said the same weasel in her, 'and they are bigger and prettier by far than this miserable little swingle-tree and its chain we have here in front of us.'

She gave a little pause. The pause had been planned and was needed so as to let this great bit of news sink its way slowly but surely into Teddy's young head. And then (the little actress that she was) she threw her arms out as wide as she could: 'The swings in England hang so high in the sky,' said she – and her eyes gave an unbelievable squint upwards as though she was trying hard to find words suitable enough to describe the beauty of these new-fangled swings – as though her eyes and ears couldn't believe the sheer magic of what she was now telling Teddy.

'And they are fixed in the sky on a pair of golden chains,' said she.

'And they can reach into the very clouds in the heavens where God has his own home.'

'And a child can come up into the sky and sit on them'.

'And he can make himself a Swing-Swong out of them and he can swing backwards and forwards, backwards and forwards – all day long, if he wants to,' said she.

She suddenly caught her breath as though she had finished her list. For by now she had said most of what she had come all this way to say.

Of all the wonders on earth what a mighty great machine this swingle-tree was! Never before had there been such an amazing contraption as this in Teddy's few years on earth – a Swing-Swong to sit your gable-end on – and with golden chains on it – and it hanging down from the sky for children across the sea in England to swing like himself, backwards and forwards, backwards and forwards on it. It was beyond all his previous understanding and if ever his jaws fell open wide, it was at this precise moment in his life.

Polish 'n' Shine gripped the plough-handle tightly. She knew that in these few seconds (when the Universe seemed to be standing still around the two of them and there was nobody else in the whole wide world to see or hear the roguery in her) her tale would either sink into oblivion – or it would swim successfully for the child's anxious parents back in England. It was the hook and the maggot. It was the line and the poor fish. But she couldn't be sure.

The afternoon sped merrily along. Polish 'n' Shine was beginning to grow in confidence and her tongue was beginning to run away with itself: "Think of it, Teddy – you… flying through the fairy clouds across the sun – sitting on a giant swingle-tree and scattering the crows in the clouds – clouds like those clouds you see sailing across the hay-fields and over the eagle's nest in Bog Boundless – and you yourself gazing down below from your mighty swingle-tree – gazing at all the curling rivers and the shady woodlands – gazing at all the cattle and horses – gazing at all the sheep and farmyard fowls.'

# A Child And His Astonishment

Teddy's eyes grew wider and wider by the minute. The dreamlike vision began to knit itself together inside in his little brain as he kept pondering and pondering, the way children will do. This new woman and her fine ways and her fine talk had worked herself up into a great head of steam: 'Think of it, Teddy – you… swing-swinging-swinging and sway-swaying-swaying on a Swing-Swong cradle – soaring this way and then that way – one minute landing below in The Great City with myself and Nell and Patsy (who were as foreign to him as a Chinaman) and the next minute landing back home with Dowager and Blue-eyed Jack in the farmyard.

Had she gone too far with her bag of lies, the way she had done with Blue-eyed Jack inside in the town? Teddy gave her a curious look of doubt. 'But, what holds these golden chains up in the sky?' he asked. His mind was already starting to doubt the certainties of his newfound happiness on his new Swing-Swong.

'In God's holy name, you poor unschooled child,' said Polish 'n' Shine, mocking him with the severity of her voice, 'why, the angel Gabriel himself has always had that job – holding up the chains in his fists, even though nobody can see him in his home above the clouds.'

Teddy was silent for a long while and full of precious thoughts: To sit on a swingle-tree and make a Swing-Swong of it, holding onto its heavenly chains – to travel back and forth and the angel Gabriel looking on. Could anything in Rookery Rally ever compare with the likes of this unbelievable contraption? No, there was nothing here to take its place – not even Blue-eyed Jack sitting Teddy on the horse's empty cart and swinging him back and forth the length of the laughing yard till the wheels nearly fell off of the cart and Dowager begged him to stop – not even the big man catching him by his arm and leg and swinging him round and round till he wet his britches before pelting him into the middle of the dung-heap and running off down the haggart and laughing himself to death. This new woman had put her words together with the skills of a solicitor and a bank-manager all rolled into one and not even Dang-the-skin-of-it could have done a better job of it.

# A Child And His Excitement

Teddy had a tendency to get easily excited – whether it was the killing of a pig in Rambling Jack's yard or being carried home on Blue-eyed Jack's back with his manly little hunter's stick of rabbits from the hills around The Valley of The Black Cattle. And now he was completely enthralled by the tale which the weasel-like tongue of Polish 'n' Shine had spun for him about the heavenly Swing-Swong and the adventures he could have on it. He imagined a strange land beyond Bog Boundless – beyond The Mighty Shannon River – beyond the seas – fixed somewhere else at the other end of the world. With one swoosh of his Swing-Swong he would find himself with these new people (Little Nell and Shy Patsy) and the next moment he would come down to earth and stride in the yard and be back with his beloved Dowager and Blue-eyed Jack. What could be more wonderful than flying like a bird through the clouds and looking down at the mountains and the lakes below him – the rest of Rookery Rally looking up at the sight of The Little Englander? What would Sweeney have to say about *that*? What was a pig's miserable old bladder now in the eyes of a small man when he'd be floating above the very earth?

He went bounding off in front of Polish 'n' Shine. He ran breathlessly and stumblingly through the gap, tripping over the goslings' wheel-ruts. He burst in through the haggart and across the yard and in past the startled hens in their mid-morning doze. What palpitating excitement filled his little heart! Ireland and Rookery Rally could go bury themselves in the river. He couldn't wait to tell Dowager and Blue-eyed Jack that he was going to take a magical ride on a heavenly Swing-Swong. His laughter followed him in the half-door and into the folds of Dowager's apron.

'Dowager! Dowager,' he stuttered.

'Slow down, child!'

'I am going away. I am going to The Great City across the sea. I am going to ride on the heavenly Swing-Swong.'

You may as well have hit Dowager in the forehead with a sledgehammer as she struggled to take in this sudden heartbreaking news from Teddy's happy face. How had Polish 'n' Shine (the little shitty-arse) wormed her way into the heart of the innocent child? What in God's holy name was this heavenly Swing-Swong'? Dowager stroked the golden curls that lay in her lap.

'The feckin little schemer! Oh, this basthard-of-a-woman!' cried Blue-eyed Jack fiercely.

## The Big Man Saw Through It All

In a flash he saw it all: the plans the three schemers had been making over in England about a heavenly feckin Swing-Swong with golden feckin chains amid the feckin clouds – all designed for the waylaying of a child's innocence. He looked across at his mother and their two hearts were pierced to the core and the tears began rolling down Dowager's withered jaw before she could stop them. To the worried child (who had never seen her tears before now) she said, 'I have a cinder in my eyes, Teddy,' and she went waddling off into her bedroom, looking for her hankie among the mothballs. That night (when he was fast asleep) she would take the scissors and she would cut a few locks of his golden curls and she would place them in the picture taken of him at The Easy Stile and she would keep them forever and ever. Not since the untimely death of her sixth child (Deelyah) from the bone-marrow disease had she felt such a painful load of sadness. In the secrecy of her bedroom she started bawling unashamedly like the cow she saw lying helplessly in a drain in Timmy's field last year. Who could bear it?

Teddy was standing beside the bucket of water on its stool. Even he could sense The Old Pair's heartache. 'You must not be crying over me, Dowager. I can reach back down to both of you from the Swing-Swong. I can be back in these same green fields as fast as lightning.' The poor little innocent thought it so easy to return to the folds of her apron and the warm waistcoat of Blue-eyed Jack – he thought that he'd be merely exchanging one bit of sky for another whenever he had a wish to do so?

## Guilt And Anger Now Hold Sway

In the meantime Polish 'n' Shine had stood abroad in the yard – almost too afraid to darken The Welcoming Room. She armed herself with the yard-brush and she went out to The African Sink where she began sweeping away the slurry from the edge of the cowshed dung-heap. Blue-eyed Jack couldn't stand it any longer. He went out to the woodpile and he began fiercely chopping the logs into quarters. It was a wonder he didn't put the axe through his foot, so angry was he. He piled the logs up high and then he trudged back through the pig-house gap. He tiptoed into his mother's room. He whispered a son's warmth silently into her ear. He tenderly dried her tears with her handkerchief and he stroked her jackdaw hair with his big rough hands. She was looking at Teddy's new brown suitcase. He quickly stowed it away under her bed.

He returned to Polish 'n' Shine, who by now had sloped in and was sitting somewhat remorsefully at the side of the fire. He looked at the picture of The Last Supper on the wall beside the press (the one of Jesus looking across the table at Judas) and he approached his sister. 'Sister, dear sister of mine – how can I ever again call you my sister? How could you possibly have told such wicked lies to an innocent child like Teddy?' Polish 'n' Shine was already feeling the same as Judas for misleading the little boy with her preposterous tale. She could see it would be impossible for her mother and brother ever to forgive her act of treachery. An unwelcome silence filled The Welcoming Room. With a disdainful backward look Blue-eyed Jack threw himself up towards the half-door. He stopped there for a moment and he directed his gaze at Jesus and Judas in the picture and (quoting Jesus) he pointed his finger at his sister and said: 'Do what you have to do – only do it soon and do it quick – do it tomorrow, if you can.'

He headed off down the haggart. He was a big man and he was a strong man. Yet he now felt as weak as a newborn child. He had the very same ache just below his heart as once he felt when looking down at his dead father (Handsome Johnnie) on the settle-bed with a face on him as yellow as an old pear and the rest of the family bowing their heads and praying on their rosary-beads for the safe-keeping of his soul. There'd be no more rambles early each morning with Teddy slapping his little feet along beside him as they went off rallying in the cows. There'd be no more straddling their legs across the well-hole and rinsing out his own buckets and Teddy's small sweet-gallon for the water. There'd be no more pelting maggots at Teddy when he was digging out the juiciest ones for a day's fishing down at The Big Hole. There'd be no more future joy of squirting the cow's milk into the child's unsuspecting face as he came into the cowshed to watch himself and Dowager filling up the daily buckets of warm milk from each of the cows. There'd be no more filling his little arms with the logs for the fire. He couldn't even begin to fathom how he'd go on living without the child.

## How Much He Had Loved This Little Boy!

Much as he would have loved it he had never had the choice of having a child of his own once his sweetheart (Lilia) had set sail for the end of the map the day after his father died. She knew that her handsome Jack had no choice anymore but to stay and look after his beloved mother – and she a widow with over a dozen children and no man to help her. Little Teddy had given the big man this one and only chance of acting the part of a father and he had grabbed it in both his big hands. And now this happiness was to be wrenched away forever from him – savagely, he felt. He sat himself down behind the reek of hay, next to the spider's web that he had shown Teddy of late, and he bawled his two eyes out like a cow about to lose its calf.

# FOURTEEN

# Teddy Said Goodbye To The Old Pair

*When Teddy went away for good
and lost his dreamy childhood.*

It was September in the year of 1945. Dowager had countless memories to keep Teddy in her heart. His childish laughter had rung out morning, noon and night and there was his comical avoidance of child-talk and his steadfast imitation of old-man-talk: 'Jack, avic, put down that old pipe or you'll sicken your stomach with it!' He had also developed a fine taste for cursing and swearing ('Even if Corkscrew was shitting gold you'd not catch me in the same field as him') taught to him by Red Scissors (the rascal) at the evening card-playing sessions and followed by a bout of uproarious laughter from the other red-faced men that shook the walls. Half-angrily Dowager would threaten the child with her wire tongs for using such fierce language. But there had been no rest from it: next morning saw Hammer-the-Smith stopping at the flagstones and getting down from his horse to teach Teddy his own filthy version of the 'Green Bushes Song' with the words 'piss' and 'shite' in every second line of the verses. Once again Dowager would run for the yard-brush ('Are you trying to drag my little man down with you into the arms of the Devil?') so as to brain Hammer-the-Smith's impudent skull for him and the yard would re-echo with the bold man's laughter. But the child's aptitude for learning had brought him a number of blessings as well: for he speedily picked up from Dowager a whole litany of long prayers such as The 'I Believe in God' and The 'Hail Holy Queen' and he could count well passed a hundred and would soon be at a thousand – thanks to Dowager's daily coaching of him after he'd eaten his egg and had time on his hands. On these occasions Blue-eyed Jack couldn't help noticing the way Teddy gazed in wonder into his grandmother's kind old eyes in the hope of her approval.

## Dowager Tries Hard To Forget

Enough of these bygone thoughts. Dowager shook herself out of bed and she tried to cast her present sadness out of her mind. She knew what she had to do: she had cows to milk: she had bread to make: she had butter to churn in the silver sweet-gallon: she had a goose to catch and hold between her knees and kill for Teddy to take on the journey, sawing at its neck till the little blood vessels burst and sent it drowsily into the next world: she had the same goose's feathers to pluck for Pretty Nora: she had the hidden eggs to collect in the nettles behind the reek: she had apple and rhubarb batters to make in the burner. She would make herself as busy as hell and she'd do her damnedest to forget this little man of hers and she would put him out of her mind and get rid of the pain inside in her heart. But no matter how she tried, it was no use. 'When your heart has been stolen from you and put into a black sack, it's a devil's own job to get it back,' she said and she went on trying to wash the day's spuds in the light of the half-doorway.

Every evening she sat on her chair outside the half-door, having found it difficult to catch her breath by the side of the fire. She couldn't grasp the fact that her little man was going away and leaving her next Tuesday. Having finished with the day's spuds, she even took to washing the next day's spuds and she scrubbed and cleaned them till her fingers bled. To the eager ducks she threw the small snails and slugs from her sack of cabbages and all the while ('may the walls of hell fall down on this daughter of mine') she went on cursing Polish 'n' Shine from off the face of the earth. But the little scapegrace was nowhere to be seen: she spent most of her day in bed and hid her guilty face from the rest of the world.

## *Matt-Saddle-Up*

Matt Saddle-up would be here next week to take Teddy off in his spanking new pony-and-trap and catch the train from Limerick. In former days at Judy Rag's Platform Dance Polish 'n' Shine had been an old-established flame of his and in her present shame over treacherously misleading Teddy with all this Swing-Swong nonsense, she had asked Matt to do her one last favour: give the little child a ride in his beautiful pony-and-trap and help to distract him from the sadness he'd surely feel when the time came for him to leave The Old Pair. She knew what sadness was like the day the nuns had snatched away her newborn son. She knew it would come roaring into Teddy as soon as he reached the station and heard the hissing of the train. She was no fool and already she saw the signs of doubt in the child's eyes. Was it finally dawning on him that he might be leaving Dowager and Blue-eyed Jack forever? Was there really such a wonderful machine as a Swing-Swong in the sky? Was it really held up in the clouds by the invisible hands of the Angel Gabriel? And what if it was all a pack of damned lies?

## *And What Of The Other Children?*

Smiling Babs' children were sitting on the fallen tree in Mikey's grove and they were making clouds of smoke-rings with their fag-butts. 'Teddy, avic, of course there is a Swing-Swong,' said Sweeney in a fit of jealousy, 'but it lies only in the back of your silly little head.' And the rest of the children took a fit of laughing, which was almost as bad as the time they made him wash his teeth with Darkie's poolie. Then they ran across the wire-fence and into Mikey's hayshed and they left behind them the echoing whoops of their sinister laughter. Never before had any of them heard tell of such a stupendous miracle as a bleddy old Swing-Swong and from then on they started to scorn The Little Englander.

## Blue-Eyed Jack Has Only Cold Comfort

Like Dowager, Blue-eyed Jack began to get busier than ever: he brought his mother fresh tomatoes from Missy Lipstick's shop in town: he spent an afternoon gathering blackberries for her from the lane behind Shy Dennis's shack: he brought her wild strawberries too. Each morning he brought her in her tea and her egg in the bedroom even before she started saying her rosary. But his attempts to cheer her up (no matter how hard he tried) were to little avail. Her face seemed to have grown haggard overnight and her hankies were wet through with the tears from her tired old eyes ('I've a cold in my head') and from constantly blowing her red nose.

She spent the lonely nights looking out the window at the faraway moon and going on with her introspective thinking. Yes – she had had her own God-given children (all fifteen of them) and what had it all been for? They brought her joy and happiness when they came back from abroad to see her. Then they left her again. And the pain and the anguish would rise in her when they went off on their separate journeys for she always thought she might never see them again, she being older and older by the day and closer and closer to her death every time they came and went. When they were going away she'd wave her hankie at them from behind the geraniums, hoping they couldn't see in through the window and catch her shedding her tears. Yes – those many children of hers: some of them had been brought into the world in a sudden burst of pain whilst she was thinning and weeding the turnips with her hoe and struggling in over the ditch and twisting herself down like the mare and dropping a child into the soft damp moss of the ditch to be welcomed by the horse-bee. Yes – those many children of hers: all too quickly they were scattered around the world – all except her eldest son (Blue-eyed Jack). He would always be here. He would never leave her. And now Teddy too was going off in a mad rush to the cattle-boat and crossing out over The Irish Sea – and she went on thinking these thoughts to herself throughout each night. But only the moon was listening to her.

She sat on the edge of the bed and then she went and looked out the broken window. Next Tuesday Teddy would be taken from her for good. It was also a Tuesday (back in November 1928) when she lost her Handsome

Johnnie, the very sunshine of her life. With his death went his bagful of laughter and smiles and his concertina and his songs. On that Tuesday his liver had finally burst on him and taken him away from The Roaring Town Hospital and back into the skies and The Beyond. She recalled how he had risen up in his bed amid a crowd of sick people and they all gathering round the rails of his bed as he gave them his last heartfelt rendering of 'The bird in the gilded cage'. This coming Tuesday she'd be getting herself another kind of death when she'd see this little parcel-of-a-child dispatched from her along with the wrapped-up goose for Little Nell. All that would be missing was a label ('this is a sad and fragile little boy and he needs to be handled with the greatest of care') to be put on Teddy – a stamp on his belly and another one on his backside. Then she trudged back into bed and she tried to get a little bit of sleep before the dawn came up.

## A Lonely Man Indeed

Blue-eyed Jack was up even before the early morning light came shining in over the geraniums. The sun would slowly begin to touch the ditch across in Mikey's grove. The tips of the Lisnagorna pine-trees were already changing colour and the light was faintly throwing a grey sheet across the yard-stream and banishing the haze from the dim fabric of Dowager's little garden. The big man was in a faraway dream. The impending dark shadow of the separation had begun to put an immense gulf between himself and the rest of the world. He went trudging off down the yard. He stood at the singletree-stick that led from the haggart to The Bluebutton Field, the stick where he and Teddy stopped yesterday to beat the forehead of the strongest calf as it tried to bury its head in the milk-buckets of the weaker calves. He gazed out across The Bluebutton-Field. He saw the hare amongst the thistles, its nose twitching in the first of the sunlight and its feet drenched in the new grassy dew as its ears were caressed by the daylight breezes. Was it a good sign? Was it a bad sign? He climbed over the stick and he inspected the droppings left by the retreating hare. Were they brown or were they black? If so, what was he to read from this about the future fortune of his little man when he came to live in that far-off city across the Irish Sea? Would it be good? Would it be bad?

Soon enough the sun replaced the darkness and Blue-eyed Jack returned to The Welcoming Room. He took the two buckets down to the well for the water. The sun's gold-and-copper light broke through the slivers in the treetops around Mikey's grove and the blue and the pink of the morning's sky was reflected in the well. He could feel the presence of past children and their ghosts all around him in the silence over the water. He listened for their whisperings and their sympathetic breathing. His mind was befuddled by the mystery of Teddy going away and never returning to him. He hadn't (God forgive him) bothered saying a single prayer this morning. There wasn't a prayer or a drop of holywater that could change what was happening no more than he and his two buckets could stop the sun from rising and falling this day. If only he could persuade God and his mighty powers to come down and take all his pain away. With this stone inside in his chest he hurried from the wellhole and he carried the two buckets carefully out across the ditch.

## Here Comes Glowering Tuesday

Before you could breathe and even quicker than a jig-step the following Tuesday was upon the yard. Get up from underneath your five blankets, Teddy, and wipe the sleep from your eyes. From time to time Dowager peeped into The Big Cave Room to see if her little man was awake. Teddy wondered why it was that during the last few days The Old Pair had been whispering quietly at the fireside before waking him up and why they were letting Polish 'n' Shine stay on sleeping (if she could ever again get another wink of sleep) in The Visitors' Room. Get up, I say. Get up. Can't you hear Dowager vigorously polishing your new sandals – the ones Little Nell sent you – the ones you never wore since the day you were robbed of your bladder? The sky-blue suit (another gift from your mother) is being ironed and made ready for you – the suit that was also cast aside since the day you were robbed of your bladder.

Blue-eyed Jack had the grey enamel pan ready. The water was just right – not too hot and not too cold. It was the same pan that had been used for collecting the pig's blood at the killing of the pig. Shudder to think of a killing this very day. Teddy was now fully awake. His heart was beating quickly and the blood was coursing through him with a confused excitement he had never felt before. He was going off to a foreign land five hundred miles away. Could Sweeney and the rest have ever believed this would be happening to the likes of him? Blue-eyed Jack blessed the child with the holywater and he gently washed his pink cheeks with the rough flannel. The soapy water got into Teddy's eyes and all of a sudden the tears welled up inside in his eyeballs, about to burst open and run down his cheeks. He finally knew (he couldn't put it into words) that he was going away for good and that (Swing-Swong or no Swing-Swong) he would not be coming back. Whatever was going to happen to him this day had at last begun to trickle vaguely into his childish head. He couldn't miss noticing the veiled air of gloom and bitter dissatisfaction all around The Welcoming Room and he held himself rigid (except for a sudden trembling) as Blue-eyed Jack dried him. The big man whispered into his ears (the way he whispered into the mare's ears when throwing the reins over her neck down in the Bull-Paddock): 'Never fear, Teddy – one day you'll come back – I'll see that you'll come back if it's the last thing I do on this earth.'

## Teddy At Last Knows The Truth

The little man now understood (thanks to Polish 'n' Shine and her eager tongue) that he had come to these hill-slopes from somewhere else a very long time ago: had come from far beyond The Irish Sea (wherever that might be). An inexplicable feeling had been growing in him from the moment he left The Seventh Field and the harrow. He had wandered aimlessly amongst the hens, ducks and geese (and without his stick) in his little kingdom around the yard and the haggart. At times he'd feel the eyes of The Old Pair on him from the silent half-door, almost as though they were inspecting him as once they'd looked in over the pig-house door to inspect the fattening pig before its killing and death. At other times he'd catch them peeping out at him from inside the windowpane. What he didn't know and couldn't know was that they were cursing Heaven and Earth for what was happening to them and their little man – a child that would soon become merely another impersonal lost soul walking among strangers amidst the debris of broken-down buildings in that great big city they called Pandemonium.

The previous Monday had seen Dowager out in the yard, washing her sheets with the usual helping of the Rickett's blue. The rest of her washing was hanging delicately on the bushes in the haggart and the clouds were chasing themselves away elsewhere and the sun was up high and blinding her from the yellow sky. Teddy (as always) was standing close to her, the smile not yet wiped away from his jaw as he tried to put cheerfulness back into her. They came back across the haggart-stick, she holding his hand and (as always) guiding him safely over it. They sat on the front of the upturned ass-and-car. The old woman was far too busy to be idling away the time of day in this way. She had a dozen jobs to be doing this very minute. Surely Teddy had far better things to be doing instead of sitting idly here with her on the ass-and-car? Had he no time for playing with his berry farm in under the hawthorn tree? Had he no time for watching the brown-and-ginger furry caterpillars circling the oak tree at the yard-stream – the tree where Blue-eyed Jack had done the upside-down trick for him from the overhanging branch? Had he no sock-ball to be rolling down the back of the house-thatch? Had he no bowlee-wheel to be rolling down The Open Road to the metal bridge? But even then she knew there was something nagging at his mind and she had to get the last few words out of him and be done with it for once and for all. 'Teddy,' she ventured, 'you know you'll be heading off to Little Nell and Shy Patsy across the sea.' She always referred to the two of them as Little Nell and Shy Patsy for she hadn't the heart yet to give up her ownership of this child that had been hers in all but name these last five years.

'Yes, Dowager,' said Teddy, 'I know I'll be going away from you. Polish 'n' Shine told me about the beautiful sights I'll be seeing in that great big city when I get there.' He was careful not to mention the Swing-Swong, for even then (thanks to Sweeney) he was beginning to believe that it was all a cruel hoax and a pack of damned lies.

'Well, my little man,' said his grandmother and she held his hand even tighter than usual, 'are you looking forward to the trip?' She used the word 'trip' as though Teddy was going off on a jaunt to Bog Boundless or Lord Elegance's Bog Wood or to The Daffy-Duck Circus or was tearing off with the other children to paddle in River Laughter rather than being swept away contemptuously from her forever.

Suddenly Teddy came to life and he burst out with a long list of questions that had been troubling him. What was a train like? Was there much steam and smoke coming out of it? Had it many wheels? How fast would it travel? Would it be faster than Jack-the-Herd's jinnet that fled away and broke the cart? How big was the boat? Was it bigger than Noah's boat in the shiny storybook that she read to him from the box under the hob tapestry?' Thick and fast came all his excited questions and he kept pulling at her apron to tell him the answers. He was wearing her ears off with his damned questions, the little fairy-man, thought Dowager to herself in mock irritation.

'Oh,' she sighed and smoothed her apron (trying to satisfy his excitement and hide her own aching sadness), 'you'll see tremendous wonders – more than any child in Rookery Rally has ever seen before.' She knew it wasn't true. In her mind's eye she could clearly see a dangerous spider's web – a complex spider's web that would trap her little man in its gloomy city thralldom and banish from his mind and his very soul the many natural beauties of the countryside that had grown up in him under the careful nurturing of herself and Blue-eyed Jack.

'And when I have seen all these things,' said her grandson excitedly, 'I will come back home and I will stay with you and Blue-eyed Jack forever.' Even though he was a child, the little boy was anxious to let Dowager know that she was not going to lose him or his heart. He remembered that Blue-eyed Jack had told him the day before, 'You'll be back, I'll see to that, my little man, even if Heaven and Earth should fall away.'

Dowager's eyed filled up with tears and she had to make a sudden burst away from the ass-and-car and head towards the half-door with her wobbly boots as though she was bent on searching for something mightily important inside in The Welcoming Room. Teddy followed her in the half-door. He saw her busily mashing up the spuds and the meal in the skillet pot. The hens and the ducks (their heads pitifully on one side, the rogues) were almost on top of her and waiting to be fed. You'd think they never got a bite to eat. They knew what was coming and they couldn't wait to follow her back down to the galavanize sheeting behind the ass-and-car. The old woman and her little man got busy with the mashing of the spuds and the stirring of the meal and neither of them spoke. They couldn't think of anything else to say.

## Blue-Eyed Jack Tries Hard To Forget

Meanwhile Blue-eyed Jack was sitting on his chair at the side of the pig-house. He was whittling away at his sticks, making them six inches in length and pointing them at the base. He had his pinchers and his wire beside him, making snares for the rabbits from The Bog Wood. There'd be one or two of them for the pot and there'd be a few more to sell at Curl 'n' Stripes' shop if he reached them in the snares before the carrion crows made bits of them. He was snorting angry phlegm from his throat and spitting it out at the horse-bees in the pig-house dung. Like Dowager and Teddy, he had nothing more to say. He was sadder than a tree away from water to be losing the companionship of his little man forever.

## Time To Get Ready, Time For Tears

It was time to get ready for the journey. The sandals and the white socks were put on Teddy's feet and the buckles were tied and the blue suit was on him. He looked spick and span, like a new man and as fresh and important as Doctor Glasses himself. Polish 'n' Shine had risen from her nest and was fussing around busily. She had put on her navy suit and she had fixed her brooch in the collar. She had plenty of powder and paint on her face and inside the coat she had a white blouse with a huge frilly collar and she had put on her black patent shoes with the high heels that made her walk awkwardly. She looked every bit as smart as Lady Acceptable. And yet Teddy was afraid to look up at her and neither could she look down and into his eyes. The fear was growing inside in Teddy's chest, holding him fast like those little birds that Blue-eyed Jack once trapped in the winter-yard cage for him to look at and he went out to the ash-pit to make his poolie. The black crows were strangely silent, listening to the water trickling from underneath his trouser-leg and the hens stood unsurely on one leg before marching off down Timmy's Lane. They stayed there, watching him and their eyes were cocked to the side looking for something to happen.

What was happening? The sow inside in the pig-house gave a few disdainful grunts as if to say, 'A fine friend you have proved yourself to be –

to be leaving us here on our own and jaunting off to new heights on your silly old Swing-Swong across the sea!' Oh, how Teddy would miss them all – the fowl and the sow – even the gander! He climbed over the singletree into the haggart and in under the hawthorn tree to say goodbye to his berry farm. He tiptoed over to Mikey's grove and walked around where the grass was struggling to grow in the mud, careful not to dirty his sandals. This was his secret world where he and the other children spent much of their days. By now his friends were all up at the school-house of Dang-the-skin-of-it – all except Little Cull, who had once got lost with him in the land of The Wild Witch of The West. But Little Cull was still in bed and he was fast asleep.

It was peaceful and quiet in the grove. There were no bigger boys here to sit on the fallen fir-tree and puff their fag-butts and send the smoke out through their ears and noses. The Yankee-Boy wasn't here to hurl the shammy ball out over the tops of the pine-trees with his new hurley-stick. Teddy walked towards the lower end of the grove and the well-hole. He walked through the ferns, avoiding the stinging nettles and the blackberry briars. He saw several spiders' webs spun into the dew of this new day. He saw the crabapple tree, fully laden. He'd never again be carrying in the crabs to roast in the hot ashes. The other children would have them all to themselves. There was so much beauty to be leaving behind him and his childish fear was hammering like Hammer-the-Smith's anvil inside in his ears. He had seen hens killed and he had seen geese and ducks killed and he had seen rabbits killed and pigs killed and he had always felt the wonder of their deaths. He was feeling those same feelings now and he couldn't for the life of him fathom the meaning of it. He was simply a child – a timid child with none of his previous bravado – as timid as the white calf the time it was first carried out in Blue-eyed Jack's arms to stand abroad in the immensity of the Bluebutton Field. He stood there silently. He was alone for the first time in his life and he had nobody to turn to or tell what was inside in his child's head.

He returned to The Welcoming Room where his little suitcase lay forlornly in the centre of the room. Everyone tried to avoid looking at it. There was little in it: a few holy picture-books, a rosary to pray on, his blue canister that once caught him the little silver fish down in Mikey's grove to bring home to his grandmother ('Dowager! Dowager! See the fine fish I have *'brang'* you'). Wrapped in paper in his case was the crafted mug with its inlaid purple and green flowers – the one that Lady Acceptable had brought up to him as his going-away present. 'Teddy, dear child, I have no doubt you will be heard tell of in years to come when you're a big man,' she promised.

Today there was no anger. There was no sympathy. There was no voice at all from Dowager or Blue-eyed Jack or Polish 'n' Shine. All he heard was the ticking of the clock on the press-cupboard. All he saw was the sad face of Jesus in the Sacred-Heart picture looking down at him with outstretched hands. He went and sat down by Dowager's knee and he rested his head on her apron as of yore. Absentmindedly, she patted his curls. The smoke from the fire spiraled up out the chimney and it frightened the little birds in the thatch. Smoke traveling far away, like himself soon. The furry soot at the back of the hob seemed to be shivering and shaking as though afraid of the blaze. Shivering like himself this very moment. The twigs in the fire were turning from red to grey and silver and powder. Splintering into pieces, like himself and giving a last glow before dying away and the pots and the pans seemed blacker than before on the crane over the fire.

Blue-eyed Jack went and filled himself a mug of water from the bucket on the stool near the axe. He looked across the hearth at his mother. They were always as one. They'd be closer still in the coming days. They would warm each other's hearts with their countless memories of Teddy. 'Do you remember how he ran away from Gret's sow and wet his britches, the brave little fellow that he always was?' Laughter would then follow. 'Do you remember how he went in under the hooves of Moll-the-mare and tried to shoe her with the hammer and nails and damned near killed himself?' Yes, there'd be several more bouts of laughter in the coming days, laughter mingled with their tears.

## The Loneliness Of Polish 'n' Shine

Polish 'n' Shine sat isolated beside her hatbox and her big suitcase and she tried to comfort herself. She was still thinking of her own heartache the time she had been forced to surrender her little son to those cruel nuns. 'Bad cess to them all! If I had just held tough a bit longer, my little boy would still be here with me,' she thought. And she cast an envious eye at Teddy with something akin to hatred ('Nell and Shy Patsy have their own child, almost the same age as my own lovely Paddy.') and she couldn't get rid of these bitter feelings every time she looked at Teddy. She was almost glad (and it was The Devil sneaking back into her) that another soul, if only a little boy, was feeling some of the pain that she and her little son had felt – the pain of their separation, the pain that would be forever burning in her soul.

## *The Waiting, The Damned Waiting*

*Tick-tock! Tick-tock!* went the blasted clock. Blue-eyed Jack couldn't stand it – all this waiting. All this damned waiting. Here on the floor of The Welcoming Room. Looking at the cases. It would break your heart. If only he could get it all over with! Matt Saddle-up would soon be here to take away the child but not the memory of the laughter and the smiles that remained in every cobwebby corner of this cabin – nor the echoes of the wind-up evening gramophone with the records in the bacon-box and the evening card-players coming in out of the snow and the rabbiters with their bikes full of rabbits.

Dowager went off rummaging, looking for nothing in particular. She was dressed and ready for the road and so was Blue-eyed Jack. She had her blue-basket hat with the long pin in it and she had the dove-grey stockings and her long coat and brooch, buttoned and ribboned across the insides. It was just as if she was taking a trip to see Gentility across the fields. Blue-eyed Jack was in his Sunday suit with his father's cap on his head and he had greased down his hair with the soapy water. He had already showered Teddy and Dowager with the holywater from the font and he'd do the same for Matt Saddle-up and his pony.

Teddy thought he could hear the clip-cloppity sound of Matt's pony coming up from John's Gate. He ran out into the yard. Then he came back in the half-door. 'Now didn't I tell you!' he said. Dowager had her ears pinned back like an ass and she suddenly leaped to her feet. She too could hear the clumping hooves of Matt Saddle-up's pony-and-trap coming up slower and slower as they faced the hill.

## The Nervous Fussing And Fretting

The fuss and the fret of the departure had arrived. Blue-eyed Jack carried the cases and Polish 'n' Shine's hatbox under his arm and he led the little party out into the yard. He drew Teddy over to the creamery tank and he placed a foxy ten-shilling note (a pure fortune and it wrapped in brown paper) into the child's pocket, the only money that he had been able to save or borrow since realizing that the child would be going away.

What a sight now entered the yard! It was the ever-agreeable Matt Saddle-up and his ceremonious pony-and-trap and he was wearing his green jacket with the bit of gold braiding on it. The trap's blue-and-yellow wheels were sparkling like a new penny and the trap itself had shiny black lacquer on its sides. Matt gave Polish 'n' Shine a merry little wink (the crafty devil) and something like a glad eye as he remembered the good times they had had of old above at Judy's dance. He shook hands with Dowager and Blue-eyed Jack and he doffed his hat. In a land where all men wore the cap, he alone (barring one or two old men in The Hills-of-the-Past) was a man for the hat. He was all business and he piled the cases in under the seats. He lifted Teddy up first and he wrapped the tartan rug around his legs, the morning being breezy. Blue-eyed Jack turned Matt around to face him and he showered him with the holywater and he walked solemnly round the pony-and-trap and he gave another dose to the wheels of the trap and onto the nose of the pony.

Dowager sat up beside Teddy. She wrapped her own heather rug around herself and she pressed her fingers into his. Blue-eyed Jack put the key in under the geranium box, having locked the green door of the house. From his high perch Teddy looked down at the yard. The croaking hens were huddled meditatively in under the ass-and-car. The ducks were bunched in a heap near the stream's rusty blue kettle and the crows in the tall nests seemed afraid to bespatter the flagstones with their whitewashed dung. What had any of these creatures to do with a child's departure?

# *Teddy Must Leave It All Behind Him*

The pony shuddered its bridle and tackling so as to shake off the morning flies. A flick of Matt's whip ('coom oop!') against the pony's leathery back and she edged her way round in a backwards circle to face the yard-stream. Then the pony-and-trap echoed out across the flagstones and trundled out of the yard and onto The Open Road. Half-heartedly Teddy said goodbye to the house and the farm animals. There would be no turning back.

They rattled on down the road and the bushes seemed to turn away from him. Blue-eyed Jack was near the pony-and-trap's door. Buried thoughts of his own childhood now rose up inside him. He had been Teddy's age once (just turned five) and sent away to Dublin for the operation on his neck and the mastoids in his ear. The Roaring Town Hospital was too small a place for such an operation and no matter how many sweets and lozenges followed him up the road to that great big city, he had been as lonesome as a lost lamb, missing his mother (Dowager) and her then young husband (Handsome Johnnie).

With moist and salty eyes Teddy looked back over the ditch at the cows and their calves in the Bluebutton Field. He was casting them off like a snake did its skin. He was leaving behind him the only life he had ever known. Inside his pocket he clutched the ten-shilling note and in the other pocket he clutched the bit of straw that Dowager had given him from the thatch. 'This will always remind you of us.'

The doleful little procession sifted its way down towards Mikey's stile and the well-hole. 'Why can't this whoor-of-a-pony go faster?' said Blue-eyed Jack and he gripped the handrail tightly. It was like the funeral procession of Father Chasible all over again. You could almost hear the lament of the tolling church bells as the pony-and-trap plunged its way towards the tree-sheltered valley of Abbey Cross and the graveyard where the priest lay buried. The pony trudged up the other side at Harrington's meadow and the shortcut to the school-house. What were the older children doing now? They were running and laughing towards the school-house bridge across the river? If they knew what was happening today, would they be longing to take the high road with their Little Englander to the faraway city paved with gold? There wasn't one of them here to say goodbye to him.

Never again would he dance with them across The Bluebutton Field and wade with them through River Laughter and climb with them the withered tree (The Easy Tree) and steal with them the apples from Mikey's orchard.

There were no big men (not even Red Buckles) to say their goodbyes to him. What were they doing on this cold morning? They were smoking their fag-butts outside the creamery gate and jokingly telling their yarns and their lying tales ('I have taught my ass not to eat grass anymore but to gobble up the wife's flowers'). Would they be missing him now? Gret and her famous sow was nowhere to be seen. Her gander (Howler) was asleep in the middle of the road and he hardly bothered to move out of the way of the pony. He didn't miss Teddy one little bit. Wasn't there anyone to sing of the daring exploits and doughty deeds of The Little Englander? Was there no soul at Abbey Cross to doff their caps to him respectfully? Was there no soul to wave the odd handkerchief in their fists? There was just the monotonous song of the wheels, taking him ever onwards towards the bombed-out city across the waters.

The pony took The Roaring Town Road with the ferns high on the ditch. Blue-eyed Jack and Dowager ducked their heads to avoid the briars that were trying to hold Teddy back. The lumpy mountains were by now far behind them and the Norman castle and the sharp pencil line of the church's spire appeared in the distance above The Sheep Field. Blue-eyed Jack was trying gamely to whistle but his whistle was a dead one and it made no noise.

The pony-and-trap passed Saddleback House, where the thatch sagged alarmingly in the shape of a horse's saddle. It passed the blue pump at Yawn – immortalized by Bazeen's farewell after the great dance in his honour. With his pockets full of luck-pennies and his barrel full of going-away gifts (and after the crowds and their waving hankies and their salty-tears had said their farewells to him) the brave man headed off for The Land of The Silver Dollar. His comrades in the hills wondered would they ever see his likes again. To their astonishment he came back that very same evening. He had got seasick in Yawn when he was scarcely three miles from his yard and the laughter echoed round Rookery Rally for months on end.

The pony took them past The Sinky Pool where Handsome Johnnie (out of his mind with drink after The Roaring Town Fair) once saw the black lion and threw himself in over the ditch in mortal terror. She took them passed The Quarry-hole where Sammy-the-twin and his floating bag of sausages had stumbled into the green waters of the forty-foot Green Pool, never to get back out again. She took them passed the stone wall where the three Coo-Coolin brothers trapped I'll-Daze-ye and threatened to beat him to a pulp. But ('The good Lord came to my rescue in the shape of a mighty big rock') he reached behind him and grasped a big rock and belted it into their astonished faces and made them squeal like pigs and they bid him a hasty goodbye.

## *They Enter The Roaring Town*

The little procession now entered the town. The pony stuck resolutely to her task and turned to the right. She went passed the neatly-clipped hedges and the house railings in Abbey Street. She was glistening with sweat, like a quivering bird with the heat. From the houses a blue haze of smoke rose up duskily as the townswomen tended to their fires and their cooking. The smell of horses' shit was everywhere. Crowds of townies paraded up and down, cocksure of themselves as always and they glanced disinterestedly at the noble procession of Matt Saddle-up's spanking pony-and-trap. It was as though the three lonely souls were nothing more than three old flies on the white road.

Freshly back from driving the dray-cart up to the station, Mick-the-Drooth (the ostler) stood outside The Widda-widda-woman's drinking-shop. He peered round the corner at Blue-eyed Jack. He started begging as usual with his hands held out for the two customary coppers and he had a neck on him as long as a hungry crane's. 'Let's go in and grease our throats with a mouthful of stout,' he said and he winked at the big man. As a thank-you for the coppers he engaged himself in a bit of whimsicality as he looked across Jinnet Street and in through the window of the bewhiskered Slattery's John, the owner of a small haberdashery shop. 'That filthy little fecker,' said he, 'is so bleddy mean that he sleeps with his mother to save filling a hot bed-jar for her with water from the fire.' Matt Saddle-up laughed at this crude jest and he drove the pony on into the cobbled yard. Mick-the-Drooth untackled the pony and led her to the stable stalls. He tied her to the iron-ringed fetter and he filled her trough with hay from the loft.

# The Widda-Widda-Woman's Drinking Shop

At the beer pumps loomed Pretty Rosie, the red-lipped wife of Mick-the-Drooth's brother, that scamp-of-a-teetotaller (Red Smiler). She was the most beautiful woman in the entire town. She quickly pumped Blue-eyed Jack's glass of stout from the fancy-coloured pumps and she gave him a smile that would soften the Devil's heart. She was looking at Teddy from behind the counter and her chest was as huge as Red Scissors' and her two breasts (the men noticed) were jiggling around like two young ferrets in a sack. On the barrel, warming his bum at the fire, sat a tall stranger. He was leaning on a white cane with a gold-tipped handle. 'Why, it's The Renegade, that long drink-a-water!' cried Blue-eyed Jack and he shook the stranger's hand repeatedly and he called for a glass of stout.

# The Renegade Himself

The Renegade had a drawling twang to his voice. He was returning home this very day after ten years in The Land of The Silver Dollar and with several adventures to his name in that land of plenty. He wore a white suit and a wide-brimmed beaver hat. He had a month's growth of beard on his jaws and his face was as red as a radish. He had a smile on him as good as a slice of cake.

You could see the jealous eyes of the other drinkers in the dark corner of the shop. They looked downright ugly and dowdy beside him. Furthermore there wasn't a man in all Ireland who had a white suit to put on. In our land where men never saw a silver shilling unless at the sale of their pig or their cow, the white suit might not be the right suit to bring The Renegade a cheerful welcome-home, it being a step too high-and-mighty to behold. Humourist that he was, he had put it on just to plague the hell out of the town's old cronies, who were already whispering and sniggering to one another behind their hands. A man with a white suit and a gold-tipped cane and silver coins in his fist and a golden watch and chain was something to be proud of, each of them had to admit. But (like all the townies) they had already heard the report – it had spread through the town

– how The Renegade had been sent packing back across the sea as a result of his long association with gangsters and hoodlums in The Land of The Silver Dollar. The drinkers were like a bunch of church-gate ladies and they began prodding each other and nodding their heads in satisfaction and smiling into their smug little glasses of stout.

The Renegade was the subject of many a fanciful previous tale. He had trounced The Rale MacCoy at pitching-the-shot the week after that great man's return from the ancestral Olympics. Whilst that great athlete was abroad and contesting the world's best pitchers, The Renegade stole the two big weights that held open Biddy Lumpity's barn doors. He carried them the long five miles home beneath his waistcoat in the noonday heat. Inside in his mother's haggart he gave a solid month shotpitching with these tremendous weights so as to be ready for the Abbey Cross Sports.

The great day came. Everybody went to watch the The Rale MacCoy. The Renegade (and a few pints of stout warming his belly) took himself down to the sports-field. He was already considered well past his athletic best. It was said he'd sell his mother's boots for a glass of whiskey and at weddings and wakes he was known to come armed with two straws and a gallon-jar of stout and suck at it for an hour or two in a corner by the fire. And although a great pitcher in his youth, he wasn't fit to lace the shoes of the famed Rale MacCoy (said all the men) and he wasn't even let into the competition.

The shotpitching came on. The Renegade watched the Rale MacCoy pitching his shot to the loud hosannahs of the crowd. He watched him walking off with the gold medal in front of the priests and everyone of note. When the excitement had died down The Renegade strolled across the field. He casually picked up The Rale MacCoy's weight and then just as casually he threw it four full feet out passed the astonished Olympian. 'You know what you can do with your gold medal – you can stick it up your mother's arse!' said The Renegade good-humouredly. His throw was a supreme feat of strength that was talked of for years thereafter. The Rale MacCoy laughed as loud as anyone on Abbey Cross's sports-field and he handed The Renegade his gold medal and he shook him warmly by the hand. 'I'd rather have a pint of stout,' said The Renegade and the deal was made between the two of them inside in Merrymouth's drinking-shop (pint for pint) for long into the evening and it was finished with yet another bout of hand-shaking and laughter.

And now The Renegade took off his hat and he rested his foot on the barrel. Without warning he burst into 'The Big Rock Candy Mountains' and his voice was as sweet as a thrush. He gave his verses those lilting little pauses (the dips and the rises in strength) that enchanted the ears and eyes off of Teddy. To distract the child from his present sadness ('So this is they day you are going away and I am returning home') he started teaching him the chorus of his song – a small present (he thought) to be giving to a downcast little boy. Dowager had to admire this returning exile though she thought him much older and wiser than the young man she once knew and with a lifetime's experiences now to show for himself.

Although Polish 'n' Shine had been a mere shadow of herself early on, she began to get into good humour, remembering all the doughty deeds of The Renegade. The little party was about to leave the shop when the great man handed Teddy ('Here, little whippersnapper, have some snow') a fistful of shiny money from his trouser-pockets. Dowager had never seen so much money. She gave The Renegade her best queenly curtsy and Blue-eyed Jack almost shook the arm off of him, whispering his earnest gratitude into his ear. The other miserable set of drinkers had nothing to say for themselves.

## They Trudge Down Jinnet Street

The sad party trudged down Jinnet Street, with Blue-eyed Jack breathing in deeply and sucking in his breath as it came out. Once more the sunshine had gone out of them. They headed in towards the dusky entrance of the arching vaults of The Roaring Town Station. One or two tramps (bedraggled and unwashed) lurked mournfully around the station-shed and Dowager had to sigh. In their long khaki overcoats they were the last forgotten remnants from the First World War. The porter (Neddy) was at the gateway of the station. With his peaked cap cocked back on his poll he was wiping the sweat from his brow and busily wheeling his trolley ('Mind yer backs!') up and down the platform. Teddy had never seen so busy a fellow – him and his buttoned green waistcoat.

# The Platform Crowds And Then The Train

The platform was a strange and mysterious place for the little man. None of the passengers for the Dublin train were laughing or smiling. There were a dozen black-draped nuns standing there sheepishly. Each one was sadly holding onto their mother's elbow. They were leaving Tipperary to go to England and teach The Faith to the next generation of Irish children (as Teddy himself would now be). They were weeping silently. Blue-eyed Jack felt his chest collapsing, like a toy with its spring broken down. Dowager's lower lip was trembling and quavering and there was no help for it. She turned away towards the ticket office and began to wipe away the tears that were running down her face.

The train should be here by now. What's keeping it? Look at all the people with their eyes peering up the dolorous platform and praying that a wonder might happen (thought Blue-eyed Jack). He was hoping the blasted train would break down and they'd all be tucked up in bed that evening back in Rookery Rally. Teddy opened his mouth as though about to speak. But tears (the language of a child's eyes) closed his mouth for him. Polish 'n' Shine was blowing her nose and the prick of shame had risen inside in her for being the one who was taking Teddy back to Little Nell and Shy Patsy.

What else could she have done – what on earth could she possibly have done? There was darkness inside them all and it wanted to scream out to the hills around them. Then came the sound of the sombre train and its rattling rhythm as the tan-and-chocolate-coloured carriages came pounding along the silver tracks and into the station. The shudder came with it, followed by the steam's hiss and the station was sucked into an envelope of smoke. Nothing like this had ever entered into the little boy's head before. And then he saw the fervid activity of the guard and his flag flying a greeting to one and all as though he had come among them from the mountains of the moon.

Neddy and his trolley was again garrulously roaring ('mind yer backs! mind yer backs!) as he and his shiny silver buttons wheeled the cases sinuously and expertly in and out through the crowd. With his carriage-door keys he began to lock everybody into the train's compartments like a bunch of sheep. 'All aboard! All aboard! Come along now!' roared the Limerick guard from the other end of the platform and he held his silver whistle in his hand. 'We have to reach Dublin before nightfall.'

Blue-eyed Jack had his hand on the carriage door-handle. He looked at the child and the child looked at him. Dowager stood silently in the darkness behind the shoulders of Blue-eyed Jack, peering at Teddy. Unspoken speeches flew between them, each knowing the words that could not be spoken and fearing that they'd never meet again. Teddy clung desperately to the big man's hand and the big man held Teddy's fingers gently in his.

'God keep you, Teddy,' he at last whispered and he turned away, not daring to betray his tear-stained face or smeary eyes to his little friend. His voice seemed to float huskily towards Teddy as he whispered the final choked goodbye up into the child's face and wiped away the two fat tears running silently down the furrows beside Teddy's nose. 'You know. You know. Only you know how much we love you – how much we will miss you.'

Matt Saddle-up handed in the two cases and the hatbox to Polish 'n' Shine. She (now utterly bemused by this scene of unbounded love) smiled bravely from the steps of the carriage and her eyes were full of bloated tears and her lips were twisted in sadness. And again she asked herself – what could she have done? What on earth could she possibly have done?

## Where Had Happiness Fled To?

The doors clapped shut. The separation seemed so unreal and so heavy. Old hearts broken are bad enough, but a young heart… ah, dear me! Polish 'n' Shine steered Teddy from the door. She found a seat to settle him in near the window. Teddy looked at Dowager and Blue-eyed Jack and they looked back at him and they lifted their hands in a half-hearted wan gesture at being robbed of this child. There was a look that seeped through them like fire, never to be forgotten by Teddy. 'You will come back, you will come back'. There was a moment of lingering and then the train whistle howled and Teddy heard the last strident farewell whistle from the guard. Suddenly he could hear the harsh sounds of the grinding and banging of the couplings and the sharp piercing crash of the escaping asthmatic steam and the oily clank and the rumble.

*Puff-puff-puff!* The carriages swayed and rocked over the noisy points and the train trundled slowly underneath the station railway bridge. There were fat gusts of steam and smoke as the long gloomy platform disappeared from view and then the train gathered speed and fled, mingling with the horizon and leaving behind the two silent old witnesses. The shock that once they had felt so many years ago when the Tans' bullets were flying around them now came back to haunt Blue-eyed Jack and Dowager all over again. They felt the same feelings of fear and foreboding as the departing train's thunderous volley of sound filled their ears – the shock of the angry wheels on the great big metal beast that was speeding Teddy away forever from Tipperary and themselves. They stood there like a couple of old fools and they watched the light of their life departing from them – forever. Their legs were unable to run down the track after the train and turn it back.

## It's Time For The Old Pair To Go Off Home

Matt Saddle-up stood silently beside The Old Pair. He knew pain only too well, having lost his mother a year back with the dreadful tubercolosis. That sort of pain (he knew) would now continue to fill the man and the woman and the child. He crossed himself ('Ah me!') and he put out a comforting hand toward Dowager as he led her to the pony-and-trap at the gate.

## The Silence And The Awkward Train Journey

Polish 'n' Shine put the two cases up on the rack. She couldn't look her little nephew in the eye. From her handbag she fished out the bag of humbug sweets and she sat down fussily beside the quietly-weeping child, the sweets resting in her lap and gently she rustled them into Teddy's hands. She felt the same mournful sadness of the morning she gave up little Paddy to the nuns at the orphanage gate. Why on earth had she come back to Dowager on this saddest of all trips? Why had she let Little Nell bamboozle her into bringing back this little fellow in such a misleading and wicked way? Little Paddy was lying far-off in some god-forsaken nunnery – far away from herself and her wretched bag of sweets. Why, oh why, had she let her own little boy go from her? Why, oh why, hadn't she found the heart and determination to go after him and retrieve him (instead of this little nephew of hers) and bring him back to her? She'd never forgive herself.

Teddy looked away from her. He gazed out at the dizzying flash of the track. What speed the train was making – rushing into the unknown future! You'd think it would run off the rails and smash itself to bits. Forget the ass-and-car or the horse-and-cart. Forget even a shining bike. Was the likes of a train ever seen before? The spire of The Roaring Town church and the tower of The Norman Castle petered away. Listen to the disjointed rhythm of train and the track. *Rumpity-tum. Rumpity-tum!* They seemed to speak their own goodbyes. Arched bridges (like the dark underside tin of a great big hen-house roof) were followed by whitewashed cottages and rusty haysheds. The red misty cattle stood behind huddles of holly bushes and scabby trees in the corner of the fields, hiding themselves away. Teddy saw children swimming happily in The Roaring Town River with not a care in the world in them. He had one last glimpse of The Mighty Mountain growing smaller and smaller in the distance. It was soon replaced by the high-pitched sibilance of windy telegraph wires around which the crows whirled and then wheeled away back behind the train. If only he could join them! The child's eyes couldn't take it all in. Opposite him in the corner of the compartment sat a big red-faced priest and he gently tapping his pipe with tobacco. Then anger (the bad seed was being sown) came into the little boy and it conquered his sorrow and he felt as wounded as a cat in a trap.

## The Sad Arrival At The Flagstones

Back on The Roaring Town Station platform the ticket-office shutters were closed up and Neddy hurried off home to tend to his cabbage-garden. Matt closed the pony-and-trap's door behind Dowager and Blue-eyed Jack as they stumbled up onto their seats. Matt saw just a little old lady and a little old man now as Dowager's tongue started rolling around in her jaw, dead in her mouth. And again she murmured, 'Blasht it! I have a cold in my eyes!' Blue-eyed Jack kept sniffing and from deep down inside in him a wave was pressing against his heart and he thought he'd get sick. He held his mother's hand in his own – to put the life back into her body where he knew the darkness was threatening to take hold.

The pony smelt the fresh air beckoning them back to Rookery Rally and their home in the hills. She clip-clopped her feet eagerly out from The Roaring Town, eating up the road and leaving it in smithereens behind her. Like the clouds of last summer or the dew of any morning, The Old Pair would have to forget the child taken from them. Tomorrow would bring in the same sun and the same moon, wouldn't it? They must pull themselves together. They must get over the hump of sorrow on their backs and the ache in their hearts. The same seven cows would be waiting every day at John's Gate to be milked. Perhaps (like the snails and the gooseberries) they had loved this child too much. In a time of war when other children were being maimed or scarred by the cruel deaths of their fathers killed on the battlefields the two of them had lorded the little man with their entire affection and had given him a love that was unique and binding. Why wouldn't they? After all, he had been spared The German Blitz in his cradle. They were dumbfounded now – never having realized that it was all an illusion, a happy dream that would one day have had to come to an end.

The pony-and-trap came in over the yard-stream and circled the cobbled yard. 'Ye're back! Ye're back,' cackled the hens. But where was Teddy? Thanking Matt Saddle-up for his many kindnesses to them this day, The Old Pair showered him with the holywater once more and they sent him on his way. Dowager took the key from under the geranium box and she unbarred the door. The house was silent. There was no ringing laughter. They came in, almost apologetically, and they sat down in the purple darkness of the twilight. Not bothering to light a fire, Blue-eyed Jack fumbled about in the cluttered darkness and he struck a match and lit both candles. Dowager lit the wick of the oil lamp and turned up the screw and their two shadows stretched out loomingly into all four corners of the Welcoming Room. 'He'll be at King's Island Station by now,' said Dowager. And a little while later she remarked, 'He'll be on the ship by now'.

Blue-eyed Jack got up and walked to the half-door. He looked out at the fading daylight in the yard and he listened to the evening birds chirruping in the fuschia bush by the pig-house. He closed both doors and he came back and lent forward in his chair. His head in his big hands ('What have we done? What have we all done?'). He stared abstractedly into nothing.

# Teddy Arrives At King's Island And Dublin's Big City

In the meantime the train carrying Teddy had reached King's Island Station and its ugly intersecting railway lines and its mysterious stationery boxcars. In the dirty fog the cherry-red sun was going down. This was Dublin! How often had Blue-eyed Jack tossed the rosy-cheeked Teddy high up to the rafters, roaring 'Can you see The Big City? Can you see Dublin?' How often had Teddy sent a hot river of his poolie down Blue-eyed Jack's back, the little devil, in his fit of joy! Polish 'n' Shine and Teddy and a porter passed by the black horse-cabs that stood in ranks on the cobbles where the metal shoes of the horses rang impatiently. Important-looking hackney drivers jogged and jollied the horses in and out of King's Island Station. Soon afterwards they boarded a second train and it whisked them away to the sea and The Black Harbour. Below the carriage-wheels Teddy could see the shoreline and the colonies of greedy seagulls, gathered like a shower of wild geese, floating on top of the sea like little twigs. He looked out at a flat stretch of tide-marked sand and the little birds paddling and marching across The City Bay and the sea winds whistling through their feathers. He saw little riverlets gasping over the rocks on their way to The Irish Sea. He saw one or two distant little specks of children. They were collecting cockles and mussels to sell.

The train halted at the harbour and the child and his aunt hurried down to the dull and dolorous shore and the false benediction of The Black Harbour's church bell. It was getting nearer to dusk now and there were one or two small boats out in the harbour, fluttering like bobbing corks against the wavelets and there were already one or two winking lights around the harbour. Teddy looked down into the seaweed bristling against the wooden dock. Its new smell filled his nostrils. The big bass notes of the ship's savage hooter and the black sooty smoke from its red funnel filled the air all around him as he held tightly onto Polish 'n' Shine's hand.

Behind them were several little houses in rows, looking cheerful and bright inside and children were laughing and playing inside the windows. They were washing and praying and getting ready for bed but the cold air gripped Teddy instead. There was no warm bed for this child! There were no warm legs of Blue-eyed Jack ('put your doggies in the nest') for him to put his own legs through. On the quayside stood a crowd of well-wishers, who had walked out to a point where they could see into the belly of the ship and wave their hankies and give a last goodbye to loved ones on the ship's deck. From the ship's gunwale several faces clutched at their hats and gathered in groups to wave back at them across the dismal bit of water. 'Oh, Dowager, if only I could fly like the seagulls!' thought Teddy in his child-talk. So empty was his unwanted heart. The ship's engine roared mightily and there was a little river of hot poolie at Teddy's feet. It had not been there since the days of his babyhood.

## The Great Big Ship Sets Sale

The ghostly veil of the ship pulled off into the twilight. It gradually lessened and lessened until it became a misty dot and was out of the harbour and onto the limitless sea. Wet and cold and embarrassed Teddy stood in his piss-puddle and Polish 'n' Shine dried him with the towel from her hat-box. 'What came over you, Teddy?' He couldn't tell her of his fears – that he was gone forever from his home in Tipperary.

The crowds on deck looked back at City Bay and their homeland, The Old Dart as emigrants called her. Then they turned away and they looked forward across the sea. Teddy's fingers were white from clutching the cold rail and his hair blew back into his face in the cajoling wind. The mouse-grey harbour behind the V-curved streak of the ship's foamy wake merged with the greyness of the Eastern Mountains and the charcoal of the promontories and the sky and the necklace of harbour lights appeared strongly behind the ship.

In an hour or two, they'd see the studded lights of England's own necklace of lights in Holy Island and the winking searchlight of the Welsh lighthouse. Already the evening stars were coming out one by one to greet the emigrants and the phantom moon reflected herself shiningly all along the sea. In less time than the child would have wished the cables of the ship screeched and the ship dashed against the deep waters of this new harbour. A new crowd of seagulls garrulously greeted those adventurous seagulls that had sailed along with the ship on its journey across The Irish Sea. Aching with tiredness, all the passengers trudged down the gangplank. They were like a crowd of grey rats. They were in this new country, shuffling into a silent black harbour at night-time. It was blacker than the Big Cave Room, which had often filled Teddy's dreams with ominous spirits and the Boodeeman. He held on to Polish 'n' Shine's hand tighter than ever, submissively.

Where were his friends now? Where was Blue-eyed Jack? Where was Dowager? Snug under their warm fat blankets. Those ancient joys (the sun on the laurels, on the ivy) were gone too. It was just the shivering harbour all around him and yet another train to catch, this time bound for the great big city of London. Teddy and his aunt and countless more passengers boarded the train for the south where many an Irishman of old had brought his extravagant hopes with him. Six long hours lay in store for Teddy and Polish 'n' Shine – hours of speed and heat and (hopefully) sleep. Ahead of them was an expanse of track through the brown hills of Wales and soon the little man was asleep like a little dormouse and Polish 'n' Shine gazed haplessly down on him.

## The Train's Mad Dash To London

After the long halt at Crew the train and its monotonous wheels sped headlong again – towards London. The woman and the child slept heavily. The backs of their legs were roasting from the burning heat of the grills under their seats. And while they slept, the Angel Gabriel came down from his heavenly hold upon the Swing-Swong chains and he looked haplessly upon the scene. In dreamland Teddy addressed him.

'I was here for the cutting of the hay?'

'You were,' replied Gabriel.

'I was here for the drying and turning of the rows?'

'You were.'

'I was here for the tramming and the suganning of the hay against the Kerry winds?'

'You were.'

'And for the making of the reek?'

'You were'.

'And then I was gone.'

The angel Gabriel tiptoed sadly out the carriage doorway and flew away out the window.

# 'We're Here! – The Towering City Of London And A New World'

Little shroud, awake from your slumbers. Come see morning's grey and haunting light in this laughter-less sooty city and its bombed-out rubble strewn all over the place. It was a Wednesday morning in the world's biggest city on earth. Teddy was suddenly standing there among the mailbags, unready for his homecoming back to his parents. Later that morning he would find himself in the Paddington basement puzzling over several new mysteries. There would be the flushed lavatory in place of the dock-leaves with which he had previously wiped himself clean abroad at the ditch. There would be the electric light bulbs lighting up when he was asked to scratch the wall and watch the light coming on in a bottle. He had always known only the candles and the oil lamp. There would be the water gushing out from the taps. There'd be no more running to the well-hole and gazing down at his reflection in the depths of the water.

As soon as Teddy and Polish 'n' Shine landed through the door of the basement, Little Nell and her undoubted enthusiasm did her level best to show her son all these new wonders. But her hilarity and her merry eyes and her pretty face were achingly unwelcomed by this new in-between child (neither Dowager's or Little Nell's child from now on) and his wet-eyed fury, though utterly daunted, was plain to see. The sad sight pierced his mother to her heart's core, knowing that she was unable to comfort him in his agonizing ache to return to the old haunts of Rookery Rally and the warmth and security of The Old Pair and the only love he had ever known. And this image of him – standing at the window and looking out into emptiness – would fill the poor woman's dreams and wear away her rosary-beads for years to come. One day (please God) – yes, one day – the sun would again shine its early-morning light. One day (please God) the good days would return as when once herself and Shy Patsy had lit the platform dance-floor with their heel-and-toe jig-steps at Judy Rag's meadow and the sights and the memories of this wretched war would become nothing else but a long lost memory.

And then there was the embarrassed silence of Shy Patsy, not knowing what on earth to do – whether to stay or run for the door and the bomb-shelter across the street outside Missus Bickering's door – and he still reading his *Daily News,* instead of getting up on his damned hind legs to give this little son of his a big hug. The shy man wished that this scene would vanish away completely from his eyes. It was as if the little fellow was a stranger, an unwanted nuisance-of-a-child, an object like dirt on a shoe that had landed in freshly from a house around the corner.

## And Then Came The Next Unimaginable Day

Next morning Little Nell and Shy Patsy walked with Teddy all around the bombed-out streets and what was left of the huge buildings – more walls than he had ever seen before. The remaining sidewalls of these once proud buildings stood all around the little man, so tall that they surely reached the sky. He had to hold up his chin to see the tops of them. Around by the shops he saw the streets strewn with bomb-craters. Some were twenty feet deep and children were playing in them and looking for gasmasks. He heard the noisy racket everywhere as the cars and new red buses went thundering by at a tremendous speed, filling his eardrums. He looked at the strange people rushing into shops and coming out again with their two shopping bags clutched protectively in their arms. It seemed as though the whole world was in a terrible turmoil. There was no slow clip-clop of ass-and-car here! There were no free-flowing streams and rivers. There were no green fields or woodland or Bog Boundless. It was a baffling new world, uninhabited by his loved ones, Dowager and Blue-eyed Jack. Where were the flowers? Where were the hens and the geese? These were the contrasting questions inside in his child's head and he could utter no words to the strange man and woman who were now holding him, a captive, by the hand. In front of the puzzled Little Nell and Shy Patsy stood this pale image of a once-laughing child – a fugitive little mite, the soul of him still left behind in Rookery Rally, on Tipperary's purple hills. And from this moment onwards Teddy's childhood freedom (they have got rid of me!') was swallowed up and it came to a sudden end.

# *The Night Before That*

On the night before this the million stars and the white moon had shone down across Dowager's yard and the Rookery Rally hill-slopes.

'He was here for the cutting of the corn?' said Blue-eyed Jack, addressing his mother, Dowager.

'He was.'

'He was here for the stooking and the sheaving of the corn?'

'He was.'

'He was here for the making of the stack and the bagging-up behind the thrashing machine?'

'He was.

'And then he was gone.'

Blue-eyed Jack took the enamel mug of water and he raked out the last few squinting cinders into a ring. He threw the mug of water onto the ashes and the fire was quenched. Then he lit the two candles in the candleholders. He filled his mother's stone jar with hot water so that he might wrap it around her feet in the bed. 'Ma'am, it's over... it's over now.'

Dowager nodded slowly. They both knew that a child was gone forever. Blue-eyed Jack led his mother to her bedroom and he tucked her into her bed with the hot jar. Then he snuffed out both candles and he blew out the lamp under the hob tapestry so as to end the withering of this wretched day. He went into The Big Cave Room and he slipped out of his trousers and, as always, he went into his damp bed in his shirt. For once in his life, he had forgotten to kneel down on the damp sacking and say his night-prayers. He felt cold and he felt lonely. He had no child to press into his warm belly anymore.

Dowager lay silently in her bed and she looked up at the tri-cornered box on the wall. For many an hour she would listen for the sound of Teddy's voice. Oh, what she would give to hear his cries and his laughter, his prayers and his cursing and counting, his whispery echo. Through the broken windowpane she gazed out at the ass (The Lightning Whoor) in the haggart. It was a long silent gaze, at eternity. Perhaps the child will come back. Perhaps they'll write to me to say I can keep him after all (she thought). Perhaps they'll decide it was all a bad mistake to take him from his natural home like this.

A black cloud fell across the moonlight, forebodingly, and she knew she was only dreaming. Once the water is spilt from the bucket there is no gathering it up again and she pulled the bedclothes up over her ears and she turned her burning face to the wall. It was late and in the middle of the night. The moon was looking in the windows of the thatched cabin. Time stood still and all creation seemed as old as the bog-land itself. Like a dead leaf fallen down from a tree a child from the fields of Tipperary had gone away from the little farm in Rookery Rally as though flown into the airs of eternity. The cattle stood in a huddle under the crevices of the crab tree and they gazed at the beauty of the white clouds under the lofty stars, those heavenly wonders sailing imperiously off beyond Corcoran's Well and The Danes' Hill. The baggy-bearded goats beyond the school-house were chewing the night-time bushes on the Two Goats Hill. Then a new dawn came up and the early-morning light returned from beyond the mountains above the church in Copperstone Hollow and the moon finally went to sleep in the west, out beyond Galway and Mayo. Enough said.

*Farewell – it's time to be going, it's time to pass on.*

*Dowager with her little evacuee*

*Blue-eyed Jack at the daily woodpile*

*For Grannie and Jack,*
*who carved out the pathways*
*of my early Irish childhood.*

*Dowager with her little evacuee at The Easy Stile*

*Ploughing-time in the Seventh Field*

*Teddy with the ass*

## Author's Note:

I have attempted to create a realistic storybook portrait of a child's life, living in a small hilly region of Ireland prior to the middle of the twentieth century. Any likeness to present-day individuals is to be taken as coincidental and appropriate only to the overall progression and continuity in the book. If there are any inaccuracies of historical fact or errors of judgment in relation to rural matters, these are entirely my own fault and all other people remain blameless.